Tunisia

David Willett

Tunisia

1st edition

Published by
Lonely Planet Publications
Head Office: PO Box 617, Hawthorn, Vic 3122, Australia
Branches: 150 Linden Street, Oakland, CA 94607, USA
                10a Spring Place, London NW5 3BH, UK
                71 bis rue du Cardinal Lemoine, 75005 Paris, France

Printed by
Colorcraft Ltd, Hong Kong

Photographs by

Glenn Beanland	Bethune Carmichael	Jon Davison
Hugh Finlay	Frances Linzee Gordon	ONTT
Peter Ptschelinzew	Damien Simonis	David Willett

Front cover: A front door to be proud of – the characteristic studded nail pattern and blue paint of a door in Sidi Bou Saïd, near Tunis. (Paul Trummer, The Image Bank)

Published
July 1998

National Library of Australia Cataloguing in Publication Data

Willett, David.
Tunisia.

1st ed.
Includes index.
ISBN 0 86442 512 0.

1. Tunisia - Guidebooks. I. Title.

916.110452

David Willett

David is a freelance journalist based near Bellingen on the mid-north coast of New South Wales, Australia. He grew up in Hampshire, England, and wound up in Australia in 1980 after stints working on newspapers in Iran (1975-78) and Bahrain. He spent two years working as a sub-editor on the Melbourne *Sun* before trading in a steady job for a warmer climate. Between jobs, David has travelled extensively in Europe, the Middle East and Asia.

From David

My thanks go first to my partner, Rowan, and our son, Tom, for their patience and understanding during this project – and for holding the fort at home during my numerous trips to Tunisia. Thanks also to my friends Kamel and Lamia Grar, Chokri ben Nessir and Henda Salhi for their hospitality; and to Kamel ben Brahim from the Tunisian National Tourist Office in Tunis for his help in gathering information.

Last but not least, I'd like to thank editor Isabelle Young and the team at Lonely Planet for their constant support and enthusiasm.

This Book

This book grew out of the Tunisia chapter in Lonely Planet's *North Africa* guide, first published in 1995. David Willett updated the original Tunisia chapter and researched and wrote this guide.

From the Publisher

This first edition of *Tunisia* was edited by Isabelle Young and proofed by Emma Miller, Joyce Connolly, Kristin Odijk and Michelle Glynn. The mapping was done by Glenn van der Knijff and Tony Fankhauser, assisted by Andrew Smith and Anna Judd. Tony was responsible for the layout of the book and many of the illustrations. Additional illustrations were drawn by Trudi Canavan, Verity Campbell, David Andrew and Greg Herriman; Paul Piaia was responsible for the climate charts. David Kemp and Adam Mc-Crow produced the fantastic cover. Thanks

to Bethune Carmichael for taking some stunning photos for the book.

Richard Plunkett produced some additional boxed stories at short notice; Ann Jousiffe wrote the boxed text on murex; and Jamila Keppie shared her engaging insights on Tunisian women in the boxed text 'Poor Thing'. David Andrew produced yet another great section on bird-watching, and Frances Linzee Gordon was responsible for the core text of the Islamic Architecture section. Thanks to the Tunisian National Tourist Office in London for help with research.

A very special thanks goes to Roger Sheen of Maison de Tunisie in Melbourne for his useful insights into Tunisia, his enthusiastic help with research, the boxed text on modern painting and – best of all – for allowing us to photograph exhibits from his Aladdin's cave of a shop.

Cathy Lanigan, Michelle Glynn, Katrina Browning and Geoff Stringer provided invaluable advice and support throughout this book's prolonged gestation and eventual birth. Finally, special thanks is due to David Willett who battled many obstacles, not least a cow in the road, to reach the end, with sanity, enthusiasm and humour intact.

Warning & Request

Things change – prices go up, schedules change, good places go bad and bad places go bankrupt – nothing stays the same. So, if you find things better or worse, recently opened or long since closed, please tell us and help make the next edition even more accurate and useful.

We value all of the feedback we receive from travellers. Julie Young coordinates an enthusiastic team who read and acknowledge every letter, fax, postcard and email, and ensure that every morsel of information finds its way to the appropriate authors, editors and publishers. Everyone who writes to us will find their name in the next edition of this guide and will also receive a free subscription to our quarterly newsletter, *Planet Talk*. The very best contributions will be rewarded with a free Lonely Planet guide.

Excerpts from your correspondence may appear in new editions of this guide; in our newsletter, *Planet Talk*; or in updates on our web site – so please let us know if you don't want your letter published or your name acknowledged.

Contents

Map Legend

ROUTES

├─┼─┼─┼─┼─●─┼─┼ .... Train Route, with Station
‒ ‒ ‒ ‒ ‒ ‒ ‒ ‒ ‒ .... Ferry
.... Path through Park
· · · · · · · · · · · · · · · · · · .... Walking Tour
‒ ‒ ‒ ‒ ‒ ‒ ‒ ‒ ‒ .... Walking Track

Regional Maps

═══════════ .... Freeway
───────────── .... Highway
───────────── .... Primary Road
═════════════ .... Unsealed Road
───────────── .... Minor Road

City Maps

═══════════ .... Highway
─ ─ ─ ─ ─ ─ ─ ─ ─ ─ .... Unsealed Highway
───────────── .... Primary Road
─ ─ ─ ─ ─ ─ ─ ─ ─ .... Unsealed Road
═══════════ .... Street
═ ═ ═ ═ ═ ═ ═ ═ ═ ═ .... Unsealed Street
───────────── .... Lane

AREA FEATURES

.... City Park, National Park
.... Building
.... Pedestrian Mall, Plaza
.... Market
+ + + + + + ... Cemetery
× × × × × × .... Non-Christian Cemetery
.... Built-Up Area
.... Ancient or City Wall

BOUNDARIES

.... International Boundary
.... Disputed Boundary
.... Provincial Boundary

HYDROGRAPHIC FEATURES

.... River, Creek
.... Intermittent River or Creek
.... Lake, Intermittent Lake
.... Salt Lake

SYMBOLS

✪ **CAPITAL**	...... National Capital	✈	.... Airport	☻	... Islamic Monument
◉ **Capital**	...... Regional Capital	∴	. Archaeological Site	🏮	.... Lighthouse
● **City**	.... City	❸	.... Bank	👤	.... Monument
● Town	.... Town	🏖	.... Beach	⬡	.... Mosque
● Village	.... Village	🚲	.... Bicycle Hire	▲	.... Mountain
		⚲	...... Bird Sanctuary	🏛	.... Museum
■	.... Place to Stay	⊞ 🏛	... Cathedral, Church	🌴 🌴	.... Palmeraie
⚑	.... Camping Ground	⌒	.... Cave, Grotto	⛽	.... Petrol Station
⛺	.... Caravan Park	◉	.... Embassy	○	..... Place of Interest
▼	.... Place to Eat	⛩	.... Fort	★	.... Police Station
⛉	.... Pub or Bar	✿	.... Garden	✉	.... Post Office
⚱	.... Café	ⓗ	.... Hammam	☎	.... Telephone
		⊕	.... Hospital	▣	.... Tomb
		❶	.... Information	◒	.... Transport

Note: not all symbols displayed above appear in this book

Introduction

Tunisia has a list of attractions that would do justice to a country many times its size – superb beaches, spectacular desert scenery and a wealth of historical sites dating back 2500 years to the days when the ancient city of Carthage dominated the entire Western Mediterranean.

Beaches are the country's major drawcard and the cornerstone of its well-developed tourism industry. The coastal resorts of Hammamet, Monastir and Jerba have long been favourite destinations for holiday-makers seeking to escape the grey skies of Northern Europe for a week or two of guaranteed sunshine. They are the places to go if you want to spend your days lazing on the beach and your nights wining, dining and dancing.

For many travellers, though, the major attraction is the opportunity to explore the world's greatest desert, the Sahara, which

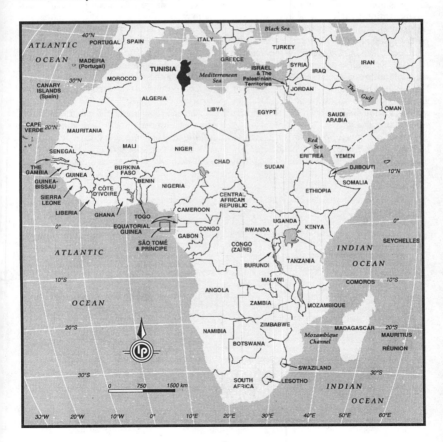

9

covers the southern tip of Tunisia. Tourism has boomed here in recent years but, for the more enterprising individual, there is still plenty of scope to get right off the beaten track. There's no better way to get a feel for desert life than to go on a camel trek, which can be easily organised from the village of Zaafrane, near Douz.

The regions on the fringe of the Sahara are every bit as remarkable as the desert itself: the spectacular hill-top Berber villages of the Ksour district around Tataouine, the troglodyte village of Matmata, the glimmering salt flats of the Chott el-Jerid and the beautiful old oasis towns of Nefta and Tozeur.

Tourism remains very low-key along the north coast, although it is one of the prettiest parts of the country. The contrast with the arid south couldn't be greater – the densely forested Kroumirie Mountains overlook a narrow, fertile coastal plain. There are some fine beaches around the small resort town of Tabarka, and the hill town of 'Ain Draham makes a good base for walks through the surrounding forests.

Tunisia's colourful past has left it rich in historical sites. Little remains of ancient Carthage, which is now surrounded by the plush northern suburbs of the capital, Tunis, but elsewhere there are some magnificent Roman ruins. The colosseum at El-Jem rates among the finest Roman monuments in Africa, and the ruins of Bulla Regia and Dougga follow close behind. The Bardo Museum in Tunis houses a fantastic collection of Roman mosaics – one of the best in the world.

Tunisia's Islamic heritage has produced architecture that is every bit as impressive, including the mighty ramparts that surround the ancient medina cities of Sfax and Sousse, and the medina of Tunis, which is a treasure trove of Islamic architecture dating back more than 1000 years.

Tunisia is an easy place to get around. Distances are short, and public transport is cheap, fast and efficient. You'll find a good choice of accommodation in all the major towns, whether you're looking for a clean budget room or for the latest in star-studded luxury.

Tunisia is also a safe place to travel. Street crime is almost unheard of and political stability has become a feature of the country, which has had just one change of government in the 42 years since independence.

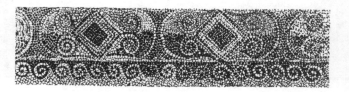

Facts about the Country

HISTORY

Tunisia may well be the smallest nation in North Africa, but its strategic position has ensured it an eventful history. The Phoenicians, Romans, Vandals, Byzantines, Arabs, Ottomans and French have all come and gone in this part of the world. The name that looms largest in Tunisian history is Carthage, arch enemy of Rome in the 2nd and 3rd centuries BC. Now a well-heeled northern suburb of Tunis, Carthage was once a Phoenician trading post that emerged to dominate the Western Mediterranean in the 6th century BC. Modern Tunisia is virtually identical to the area controlled by the ancient city state 2500 years ago, with the exception of the Saharan south.

Prehistory

The earliest humans to set foot in Tunisia were probably a group of *Homo erectus* who stumbled upon the place a few hundred thousand years ago as they joined a general migration north-west across the Sahara from East Africa. In those days, the Sahara enjoyed a very different climate to today, with regular rainfall. The massive swathe of desert that now isolates the fertile north coast of Africa from the rest of the continent is believed to have been covered in forest, scrub and savanna grasses, much like the plains of Kenya and Tanzania today.

The earliest hard evidence of human activity in Tunisia dates back about 200,000 years, which is the age archaeologists have put on primitive stone tools discovered near the southern oasis town of Kebili. Migration from the south became less and less viable as the Sahara began to dry out at the end of the last Ice Age. The regular rains that watered the region are thought to have finally ceased in around 6000 BC.

By this time, people had begun to arrive from other directions. The most significant new arrivals were people of the Capsian culture, who lived in southern Tunisia from about 8000 to 4500 BC. Named after finds uncovered near the city of Gafsa (ancient Capsa), the Capsian people were of proto-Mediterranean stock and had travelled across North Africa from the near east. The finely sculpted stone and bone implements found near Gafsa point to a relatively sophisticated society. Settlement of the north followed a different pattern, with waves of migration from Southern Europe between 6000 and 2500 BC.

It is from these Neolithic peoples that the Berbers (the indigenous people of North Africa, including Tunisia) are thought to be descended. Allowing for regional variations and the lack of hard evidence, they appear to have been predominantly nomadic pastoralists. By the time the Phoenicians arrived in 1100 BC, these local tribes were well established.

Carthaginian Dominance

The Phoenicians were drawn to the Tunisian coast in search of staging posts along the trade route between their mother city of Tyre (in modern Lebanon) and Spain. The first of these staging posts was established at Utica, about 35km north of Tunis, in 1100 BC. By the end of the 9th century BC, this lone outpost had expanded into a chain of ports that stretched right along the North African coast. The most important ports were Hadrumètum (Sousse), Hippo Diarrhytus (Bizerte) and, of course, Carthage.

Carthage remained relatively unimportant until Phoenicia was overrun by the Assyrians in the 7th century BC. Carthage then quickly established itself as the leader of the western Phoenician world, first by alliance and then by subjugation. By the early 5th century BC, it had become the main power in the Western Mediterranean. It controlled a stretch of the North African coast from Tripolitania (western Libya) to the Atlantic and had established colonies in Gaul, Sardinia, Spain and Sicily.

Time Line

BC

c8000-4500 Capsian people, early hunter-gatherers, living in southern Tunisia around Gafsa

c6000-2500 Migration of people from Southern Europe, ancestors of the Berbers, to northern Tunisia

1100 Phoenicians found Utica

814 According to legend, Carthage founded by Phoenician queen, Elissa Didon

310 Greeks, led by Agathocles, invade North Africa

263-241 First Punic War between Rome and Carthage

241-238 Truceless War between Carthage and its mercenaries

218 Hannibal crosses the Alps; start of the Second Punic War

202 Hannibal defeated by Roman general, Scipio, at the Battle of Zama

149-146 Third Punic War ends in destruction of Carthage; Tunisia becomes part of the Roman province of Africa Proconsularis

112-105 Numidian rebellion led by Jugurtha

44 Carthage refounded by Emperor Augustus as a Roman city

AD

439 Vandals capture Carthage

533 Byzantines under General Belisarius defeat Vandals; start of 150 years of Byzantine rule

570 Birth of Prophet Mohammed in Mecca

647 Arabs defeat Prefect Gregory at Sbeitla

670 Arab leader Uqba bin Nafi al-Fihri founds Kairouan

701 Berbers, under leadership of Al-Kahina, defeated by Arabs at El-Jem

797 Ibrahim Ibn al-Aghlab becomes governor of Arab province of Ifriqiyya and establishes Aghlabite dynasty

909 Fatimids, led by Obeid Allah (El-Mahdi), defeat Aghlabites

921 Fatimids found Mahdia

1049-1159 Hilalian invasions from Egypt

1160 Almohads from Morocco capture Mahdia

1229 First Hafsid caliph

1270 Crusaders land at Carthage

1332 Historian Ibn Khaldoun born in Tunis

1534 Muslim corsair, Khair ed-Din Barbarossa, captures Tunis

1574 Sinan Pasha claims Tunis for the Turks; Tunisia becomes an Ottoman province

1591 Deys seize power from the pasha

1631 Hamuda Bey assumes power from the deys; establishes Muradite bey dynasty

1705 Hussein ben Ali founds Husseinite dynasty

1846 Abolition of slavery

1869 International commission takes control of Tunisia's finances

1878 Ottoman Empire divided up at Congress of Berlin; France claims Tunisia

1881 French invade Tunisia

1883 Convention of La Marsa signed; Tunisia becomes a French protectorate

1934 Habib Bourguiba founds Neo-Destour Party

1938 Demonstrators killed by French troops in Tunis; Bourguiba arrested and removed to France

1942-3 WWII Tunisian campaign

1955 Bourguiba allowed to return

1956 Tunisia granted independence, with Bourguiba as prime minister

1957 Bourguiba declares Tunisia a republic and becomes its first president

1960 Opposition to reform by religious leaders culminates in fighting in Kairouan

1981 First multi-party elections held; National Front (Bourguiba's party) wins all seats

1984 Withdrawal of bread subsidy sparks riots; subsidy is reinstated and opposition leaders are freed

1987 Bourguiba declared incompetent to rule and replaced by Prime Minister Zine el-Abidine ben Ali

1991 Gulf War; Tunisia supports the USA-led alliance

1994 Ben Ali elected to third term as president

1995 Tunisia signs an Association Agreement with the European Union, leading to free trade in 12 years

Carthage itself rapidly grew into the metropolis of the Phoenician world, recording a population of about half a million at its peak. While it grew rich through its domination of trade in the region, Carthage also developed the hinterland, particularly the fertile Cap Bon Peninsula and the Medjerda Valley.

This regional primacy led Carthage into inevitable conflict with the other great powers of the Mediterranean, first Greece and then Rome. Sicily, just 80km north-east of Carthage, was the main bone of contention. Carthage fought numerous wars with the Greeks over the island and suffered its share of setbacks along the way, notably in

310 BC when Greek raiders led by Agathocles landed in North Africa, starting a trail of destruction which lasted for three years. When the Carthaginians finally took control of the island in the middle of the 3rd century BC, they found themselves squaring off against an expansionist Rome that had just completed the conquest of southern Italy.

The scene was set for the first of the so-called Punic Wars that were to preoccupy the two powers for the next 100 years. Rome launched the first war in 263 with a campaign to win control of Sicily. In spite of a couple of early Roman successes on land, the supremacy of Carthage's navy resulted in a stalemate that dragged on for the next 20 years. An attempt by the Romans to carry the battle to Carthage resulted in the defeat and capture of the Roman general Regulus.

Rome finally got the break it wanted when its fledgling navy destroyed the Carthaginian fleet off Trapani (eastern Sicily) in 242. Navyless and close to broke, Carthage was forced to accept Roman terms and abandon Sicily, followed by Sardinia and Corsica in 238. Trouble at home grew as unpaid mercenaries revolted, sparking a bitter three year conflict that became known as the Truceless War because of the mercenaries refusal to accept peace overtures. The savagery of the war later inspired Gustave Flaubert's over-the-top novel *Salammbô*.

Carthage then turned its attention to consolidating its position in Africa, and established itself in the former Phoenician settlements of southern Spain under the leadership of Hamilcar. It wasn't long before Carthage felt strong enough to take on the Romans again. In 218, Hamilcar's son Hannibal set off from Spain at the head of an army of 80,000 troops backed by 300 war elephants. He crossed the Alps into Italy and inflicted crushing defeats at Lake Trasimene (217) and Cannae (216) in what came to be known as the Second Punic War. Rome seemed powerless and only after Hannibal had been stranded in southern Italy for some seven years waiting for reinforcements were the Romans able to forget about the threat of being overrun.

The Carthaginian general, Hannibal, who in 218 BC led his army across the Alps to threaten Rome's supremacy.

The Roman general Scipio retook Spain and landed in Africa at Utica in 204. Carthage was teetering; Hannibal was recalled from Italy in 203 in an attempt to halt the Romans but was resoundingly beaten at Zama (near Siliana) in 202. Carthage capitulated and paid an enormous price, giving up its fleet and all its overseas territories. Hannibal fled to Asia Minor, where he eventually committed suicide to avoid capture by the Romans in 182.

Carthage wasn't finished though, and over the next 50 years it steadily re-established itself as a commercial centre in spite of losing much of its former territory to the Numidian king Massinissa (see the following section, The Romans), whose cavalry had fought alongside Scipio at Zama. The city's continued revival began to create increasing unease in Rome, where there were many who thought that Carthage remained a threat as long as it existed. Whipped up by men like Cato the Elder, an eminent statesman and writer who became well known for his vehement opposition to Carthage, Rome launched the Third Punic War with the intention of settling the issue once and for all. In 149 BC, the Roman army again landed in Utica and laid siege to Carthage for three years. When it finally fell in 146, the Romans showed no mercy. The city was utterly destroyed, the people sold into slavery and the site symbolically sprinkled with salt and damned forever.

Overall, the Carthaginians were great traders and merchants but they were ruthless rulers who managed to alienate the indigenous Berber peoples around them. It is often claimed that the Berbers learnt advanced agricultural methods from the Carthaginians but many were simply forced into the desert and mountain hinterland. It is unlikely that many mourned Carthage's demise.

The Romans

Carthage's territory became the Roman province of Africa, Africa Proconsularis. At first Rome showed little interest in its new acquisition. The Empire was expanding fast and Africa was fairly low on the priority list.

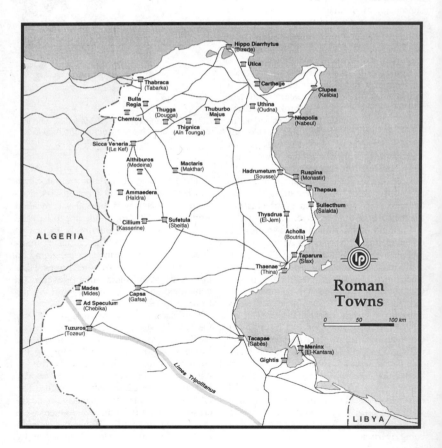

It was happy to leave most of the country to the Numidians. Under Massinissa, the Numidians had established a kingdom that stretched from western Algeria to Libya. Its major towns included Sicca Veneria (Le Kef), Thugga (Dougga) and Vaga (Beja). On Massinissa's death in 148 BC, Rome attempted to cut the kingdom down to size by dividing it up between his three sons. The tactic worked well until the kingdom was reunited by Massinissa's grandson Jugurtha, who then incurred the wrath of Rome by massacring a Roman company sent to Cirta Regia (present day Constantine in Algeria), sparking a war that lasted from 112 to 105 BC. Jugurtha was eventually betrayed by his father-in-law, King Bocchus I of Mauretania, and captured.

Rome was prepared to give the Numidians another chance, splitting the kingdom into a western half centred on Cirta Regia and an eastern half based at Zama, near Siliana. The last of the Zama kings, Juba I, backed the wrong side in the Roman civil war (based on the power struggle between Julius Caesar and Pompey) and was trounced by Julius Caesar at the Battle of Thapsus in 46 BC, along with the remnants of Pompey's army.

The battle left Rome firmly in control of its African outpost and it was time for settlement to begin in earnest. The emperor Augustus refounded Carthage as a Roman city in 44 BC and it became the capital of the expanded colony of Africa Proconsularis.

Agriculture was all important. By the 1st century AD, the wheat-growing plains of the Medjerda Valley and the Tell Plateau were supplying more than 60% of the Roman Empire's grain requirements. The great cities built by the Romans on these plains are now among Tunisia's principal tourist attractions. Africa also supplied the majority of the wild animals used in amphitheatre shows, as well as gold, olive oil, slaves, ivory, ostrich plumes and *garum* (a fish-paste delicacy).

The Romans were also the first people to recognise the attractions of the Tunisian coastline, establishing a string of coastal colonies for army veterans that assisted the spread of urbanisation and Roman ways.

Berber communities also prospered and some Berbers were granted Roman citizenship. It was these wealthy citizens who donated the monumental public buildings that graced the Roman cities of the region. Africa even provided an emperor, Septimius Severus, a Libyan from Leptis Magna who took power in 193 AD and died in Yorkshire, of all places.

The Vandals & the Byzantines

By the beginning of the 5th century AD, Roman power was in terminal decline and the Vandal king Gaeseric (or Genseric), who had been busy marauding in southern Spain, decided that Rome's North African colonies were there for the taking. He set off across the Straits of Gibraltar in 429, bringing the entire Vandal people (about 80,000 men, women and children) with him. Within 10 years, the Vandals had fought their way across to Carthage, which they made the capital of a short-lived empire that also controlled most of the islands of the Western Mediterranean.

The Vandals appear to have lived up to their reputation. They did little more than help themselves to what they found. They built no great monuments and left virtually no trace of their rule. The Vandals confiscated large amounts of property and their exploitative policies accelerated North Africa's economic decline. The Berbers became increasingly rebellious and, as the Vandals recoiled, small local kingdoms sprang up.

The Byzantine emperor Justinian, based in Constantinople (modern Istanbul), had in the meantime revived the eastern half of the Roman Empire and had similar plans for the lost western territories. His general Belisarius defeated the Vandals in 533, ushering in 150 years of increasingly ineffective Byzantine rule. Like the Vandals before them, the Byzantines found themselves living in a state of constant siege, with Berber chiefs controlling the bulk of the country. They built with their customary zeal, however, and many of Tunisia's Roman sites feature later Byzantine modifications, in particular, churches and forts.

The Coming of Islam

No-one could have guessed that the emergence of an obscure new religion in the distant peninsula of Arabia in the early 7th century AD was about to completely change the face of North Africa. Islam's green banner was flying over Egypt by 640 (see also Religion later in this chapter), and soon after Tripoli was in Muslim hands too.

In 646, with the Arab armies on his doorstep, the Prefect Gregory added a farcical footnote to the Byzantine era by declaring himself the ruler of an independent state based at Sufetula (modern Sbeitla). It lasted less than a year before the Arabs attacked Sufetula and Gregory was defeated and killed. The Arabs withdrew with their spoils, allowing the Byzantines to hold on to their possessions in the north for a while longer.

It was not until Uqba bin Nafi al-Fihri began his campaign of conquest that the full military force of Islam was brought to bear on North Africa. For three years from 669 he swept across the top of the continent, stopping on the way to establish Qayrawan (Kairouan), Islam's first great city in the Maghreb. With his army of Arab cavalry and Islamised Berber infantry from Libya, he is said to have marched until he reached the Atlantic.

The Berbers adopted the religion of the invaders readily enough but not Arab rule, and in 683 the Arabs were forced to abandon North Africa after Uqba was defeated and killed by a combined Berber-Byzantine army at the Battle of Tahuda, near Biskra in modern Algeria. The victors were led by the Berber chieftain, Qusayla, who then established his own Islamic kingdom based at Kairouan.

The Arab withdrawal was only temporary. They retook Kairouan in 689 and dislodged the Byzantines from Carthage in 698, but continued to encounter spirited resistance from Berbers who had rallied behind the legendary princess Al-Kahina (see the boxed text below). She defeated the Arabs at Tébessa (Algeria) in 696, but was eventually cornered and killed after a legendary last stand at El-Jem in 701.

North Africa, with Kairouan as its capital, became a province of the fast-expanding

---

A Berber Boadicea

In Tunisia's otherwise male-dominated history, two female names stand out: Elissa Didon (see the boxed text 'Elissa the Wanderer' on page 137), founder of Carthage who was immortalised in Virgil's *Aeneid*, and the Berber princess Al-Kahina, who led the last, futile resistance to the Arab invasion at the end of the 7th century AD. As befits such a heroine, facts are few and varied but legends abound.

Al-Kahina was the widow of the leader of the Jerawa people in the Aures mountain region. 'Al-Kahina' means 'Prophetess' or 'Priestess' and she is said to have been able to predict the future. Rallying the Berbers around her, in 695 AD she succeeded in throwing the Arabs out, driving them back to Egypt. For three years she ruled the area of central Tunisia known as Byzacenus.

In 698 the Arabs, under the command of Hassan ibn Numan, returned and retook Carthage. Once again, Al-Kahina prepared to face them. This time, however, friction between Al-Kahina's nomadic followers and the sedentary farmers, as well as the understandable unpopularity of her scorched earth policy (landowners were ordered to burn their crops and houses), meant there was mass defection to Hassan. The scorched earth policy is said to be responsible for the barrenness of the country around El-Jem today.

Prepared to fight to the death, Al-Kahina ordered her three sons to convert to Islam, before rallying her forces around her and retreating to the colisseum at El-Jem. A long and bloody battle ensued, and the damage to the colisseum seen today is said to date from this time. This Berber Boadicea is said to have stood on top of the colisseum, brandishing a still-quivering fish at her enemies below; proof, it is said, that the underground passages of the colisseum led to the sea.

As with all good stories, there are two endings to choose from: she either met her end on the ramparts of the colisseum or she was pursued by Hassan through the Jerid and finally took refuge in the Aures Mountains, where she died at the age of 127, still fighting Arab forces!

Isabelle Young

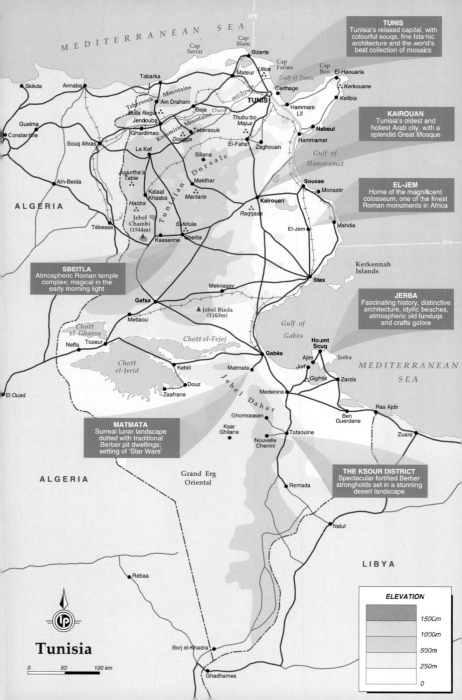

MEDITERRANEAN SEA

TUNIS
Tunisia's relaxed capital, with colourful souqs, fine Islamic architecture and the world's best collection of mosaics

KAIROUAN
Tunisia's oldest and holiest Arab city, with a splendid Great Mosque

EL-JEM
Home of the magnificent colosseum, one of the finest Roman monuments in Africa

SBEITLA
Atmospheric Roman temple complex; magical in the early morning light

JERBA
Fascinating history, distinctive architecture, idyllic beaches, atmospheric old funduqs and crafts galore

MATMATA
Surreal lunar landscape dotted with traditional Berber pit dwellings; setting of 'Star Wars'

THE KSOUR DISTRICT
Spectacular fortified Berber strongholds set in a stunning desert landscape

Skikda · Annaba · Tabarka · Cap Serrat · Cap Blanc · Bizerte · Cap Farina · Cap Bon · El-Haouaria

Mateur · Utica · Gulf of Tunis · Carthage · Kerkouane · Kelibia

Guelma · Constantine · Kroumirie Mountains · Ain Draham · Beja · Oued Medjerda · TUNIS · Hammam Lif · Nabeul · Hammamet

Bulla Regia · Jendouba · Ghardimao · Tebersouk · Thuburbo Majus · El-Fahs · Zaghouan

Souq Ahras · Le Kef · Dougga · Siliana · Gulf of Hammamet

Aïn-Beïda · Jugurtha's Table · Makthar · Sousse · Monastir

ALGERIA

Haïdra · Kalaat Khasba · Mactaris · Kairouan · Raqqada · El-Jem · Mahdia

Tébessa · Jebel Chambi (1544m) · Kasserine · Sbeitla · Sufetula

Kerkennah Islands

Gafsa · Meknassy · Sfax

Metlaou · Jebel Biada (1163m)

Chott el-Gharsa · Chott el-Fejej · Gulf of Gabès

Nefta · Tozeur · Houmt Souq · Jerba

Kebili · Matmata · Gabès · Ajim · Jorf · Gightis · Zarzis · MEDITERRANEAN SEA

El Oued · Douz · Zaafrane · Medenine · Ras Ajdir

Ghomrassen · Ben Guerdane · Zuara

Ksar Ghilane · Tataouine · Nouvelle Chenini

ALGERIA · Grand Erg Oriental · Remada · Nalut

Rebaa · **LIBYA**

Borj el-Khadra · Ghadhames

Tunisia

0   50   100 km

ELEVATION

1500m
1000m
500m
250m
0

FRANCES LINZEE GORDON

DAMIEN SIMONIS

DAMIEN SIMONIS

DAMIEN SIMONIS

FRANCES LINZEE GORDON

DAMIEN SIMONIS

The varied faces of Tunisia bear witness to the many invaders, including Phoenicians, Romans, Vandals, Byzantines, Normans, Arabs, Spaniards, Turks and French, who have influenced the nation's history over the centuries.

Islamic empire controlled by the Umayyad caliphs, based in Damascus. Under the command of Musa bin Nusayr, the Arab armies now turned their attentions to the conquest of Spain (711-19). In 732, Musa advanced as far as Poitiers in France before being turned back.

Meanwhile, the tyrannical behaviour of Arab troops stationed in North Africa had pushed the Berbers to the brink of yet another rebellion. The Berbers were inspired by the teachings of Kharijites, a puritanical Islamic sect whose egalitarian beliefs contrasted sharply with the arrogant and worldly ways of the Umayyad elite. A local uprising in Morocco in 740 quickly spread across North Africa. Although it was suppressed in 743, regional problems continued to flare.

By the time the caliphate shifted to the Abbasids in Baghdad in 761, North Africa and Spain had effectively broken away from the eastern part of the empire. Morocco became the stronghold of the Idrissids, who had fled Abbasid persecution in Baghdad and established their own kingdom in northern Morocco, and most of Algeria was ruled by the Kharijite Rustamids from Tahart.

Abbasid attempts to win back the remaining third of North Africa floundered until the appointment of Ibrahim Ibn al-Aghlab as governor of Ifriqiyya (Tunisia and parts of Libya) in 797. Operating from Kairouan, he soon secured control of an area covering western Algeria, Tunisia and the Libyan province of Tripolitania. He was rewarded for his efforts by being made hereditary emir and was the founder of the successful Aghlabite dynasty that ruled until the arrival of the Fatimids in 909. The Great Mosque in Kairouan and the *ribats* (monastic forts) at Sousse and Monastir were all built during the Aghlabite period.

The Fatimids

The Fatimids were a group of Berber Shiites (see Religion later in this chapter) from the Kabylie region of central Algeria on a mission from god – to depose the Abbasid caliphate and declare their leader, Obeid Allah, as the new caliph. Obeid was known to his followers as El-Madhi (The Saviour).

Through alliances with disaffected Berber tribes, the Fatimids quickly conquered North Africa. The Aghlabites were defeated in 909, and a year later Obeid Allah was declared as the true caliph at Raqqada, south of Kairouan. Anticipating reprisals, the Fatimids built a new capital, Mahdia, on a small, easily defended headland on the coast and set about plotting the capture of Egypt. Their plans almost came unstuck in the face of a Kharijite revolt in 944 led by Abu Yazid, who captured Kairouan and laid siege to Mahdia before being driven off by Berber tribesmen led by Ziri ibn Manad. When the Fatimid caliph Amir al-Muizz defeated the Egyptians and moved the capital to Cairo in 969, the Zirids were rewarded by being left in charge of the Maghreb.

They held the reins capably enough for a while, but with the Fatimids off the scene pressure began to mount for a return to religious orthodoxy. In 1045, the Zirids caved in and officially returned to the Sunni mainstream in open defiance of the Fatimids. The reply from Cairo was devastating: the Beni Hilal and Beni Sulaim tribes of upper Egypt were encouraged to invade the Maghreb, and over the following century North Africa was slowly reduced to ruins.

The Normans, led by Roger II of Sicily, took advantage of the chaos to occupy a number of towns along the Tunisian coast, including Mahdia and Sfax.

Berber Empires

The power vacuum was eventually filled by the Almohads, who came to power in Morocco at the beginning of the 12th century. They completed their conquest of North Africa with the capture of Mahdia in 1160, but the empire grew too fast and soon began to crumble under its own weight. As it caved in, the Maghreb split into three parts: Ifriqiyya came under the Hafsids; Algeria under the Banu Abd al-Wad; and Morocco under the Merenids. Although borders have changed and rulers have come and gone, this division remains more or less intact today.

The Hafsids managed to hang on until the middle of the 16th century, when they found themselves caught in the middle of the rivalry between Spain and the Ottoman Empire that followed the Christian reconquest of Spain.

The Ottoman Turks

The Spanish had early successes, capturing a number of ports along the North African coast, including Algiers. Their opponents in the early days were Muslim corsairs, or pirates, who were drawn to the fight by religious conviction as well as the profit motive. The most famous of these corsairs were the Barbarossa brothers, Aruj and Khair ed-Din, sons of a Turk from the Greek island of Lesbos, who had established themselves on the island of Jerba. Aruj captured Algiers from the Spanish but was killed when they retook the city in 1518. Khair ed-Din turned to the Turks for help, who jumped at the chance. He was given the title of *beylerbey* (governor) and supplied with troops. In 1529 he managed to boot the Spaniards out of Algiers once again and five years later was in control of Tunis as well.

Tunis was to change hands four more times in the next 45 years before Sinan Pasha finally claimed it for the Turks in 1574, forcing the last of the Hafsids into exile. Tunis became a *sanjak* (province) of the Ottoman Empire. It was ruled by a pasha, whose authority was backed by a force of 4000 janissaries. These troops were divided into units led by *deys*, who were the Ottoman army's equivalent of sergeants. The deys were in turn commanded by *obasdashis* (lieutenants), *bulukbashis* (captains) and an *agha* (chief), who made up the *diwan* or assembly.

This model Ottoman province didn't last long. In 1591, the deys staged a coup, massacring their senior officers and taking control of the military. They took the process a stage further in 1598 when Othman Dey seized power, downgrading the pasha to a figurehead. The dey ruled Tunis, Kairouan and the major coastal towns, but control of the interior was put in the hands of a provincial governor, called the *bey*. The bey was given his own army with which to tame the Berber tribes, defend borders and – most importantly – collect taxes.

So successful were the beys that their power soon surpassed that of the deys, leading to the accession of the Muradite beys. After a period of great prosperity under Hamuda Bey (1631-59), the Muradites slowly self-destructed in the course of 40 years of internecine warfare. The line came to a violent end in 1702 when Ibraham Sherif, commander of the bey's cavalry, seized power. The last Muradite ruler, Murad III, was captured and executed along with all of his family. Ibrahim Sherif survived until 1705, when he was captured by an army sent by the dey of Algiers to attack Tunis.

He was succeeded as bey by Hussein ben Ali, the son of a Turkish janissary from Crete who had followed Ibrahim Sherif's career path as commander of the beylical cavalry. He turned back the Algerians and founded the Husseinite line of beys, who survived until Tunisia became a republic in 1957.

The French Protectorate

Ottoman power was in serious decline by the beginning of the 19th century. France was the new power in the Western Mediterranean, and the beys in Tunis came under increasing pressure to fall into line with European ways. Privateering was outlawed in 1816, slavery was abolished in 1846 and a constitution (*destour*) – the first in the Arab world – was proclaimed in 1861.

These western reforms, however, exacted a heavy toll on the country's limited finances, necessitating heavy borrowing in the form of high-interest loans from European banks. Proposed higher taxes led to internal revolt, and by 1869 the country was in such a shambles financially that control of its finances was handed over to an international commission.

A final attempt to hold off European control was made by the short-lived ministry led by the reformer Khaireddin (1873-7), but he was forced from office and his plans were scuttled. At the Congress of Berlin in 1878, the major European powers divided up the southern Mediterranean region, and the only challenge to French dominance in Tunisia came from the Italians.

In 1881, in order to consolidate their position, the French sent 30,000 troops into Tunisia on the pretext of countering border raids by Tunisian tribesmen into French-occupied Algeria. They quickly occupied Le Kef and Tunis, and the bey was forced to sign the Treaty of Kassar Saïd. The treaty acknowledged the sovereignty of the bey, but effectively put power in the hands of a French resident-general.

The French took the arrangement a step further in 1883 with the signing of the Convention of La Marsa, which established co-sovereignty and parallel justice systems. Under this arrangement, Europeans were judged under French law and locals under a modified form of Islamic law. The protectorate prospered under French rule, although most of the benefits went to the European population.

The French went about the business of land acquisition more discreetly than in neighbouring Algeria, where land was sequestered on a massive scale. In Tunisia, the French managed to get their hands on the best of the fertile land without confiscating property from individuals; they simply took over the large tracts of the Cap Bon Peninsula and the Medjerda Valley that had previously been controlled by the bey or used by nomads for grazing their animals. The citrus groves of Cap Bon are a legacy of this time, as are the vineyards that provide the bulk of the country's wine grapes.

The south was too arid for agriculture and was left largely alone – until the beginning of the 20th century when it was discovered that the hills west of Gafsa were made of phosphate. The massive mining operation begun by the French remains an important export earner for modern Tunisia.

In 1920 the first nationalist political party, the Destour Party (named after the short-lived constitution of 1861), was formed. The Party's demands for democratic government, though supported by the bey, were ignored by the French, and the nationalist movement lost its way for some years.

In 1934 a young, charismatic Sorbonne-educated Tunisian lawyer, Habib Bourguiba, led a breakaway movement from the Destour Party. He founded the Neo-Destour Party, which soon replaced the old guard of the Destour. Support for the party soon spread. On 9 April 1938, dozens of people were reported killed when the French turned their guns on demonstrators in Tunis. The party was banned, and Bourguiba was arrested and removed to France.

Wartime Tunisia

With the fall of France during WWII, the Neo-Destour leaders, who had been imprisoned there, were handed over to the Italians by the occupying Germans. Although they were well treated in Rome, they refused to support Italy.

In 1942 the Germans landed in Tunis in the hope that they could turn back the Allied advances from east and west: the Americans were on the way from Algeria and the British forces, led by Field Marshal Montgomery, were driving back Rommel's Afrika Korps in Egypt and Libya. The campaign in Tunisia raged for six months and the Allies lost more than 15,000 men before they captured Bizerte on 7 May 1943.

In the same year, the Neo-Destour leaders were finally allowed to return to Tunisia, where a government with Neo-Destour sympathies was formed by Moncef Bey.

Towards Independence

When the French resumed control after the war, they were as uncompromising as ever: the bey was deposed and Bourguiba was forced to flee to Cairo to avoid capture. In the next few years he organised a propaganda campaign aimed at bringing Tunisia's position into the international limelight. He was extremely successful in this, and by 1951 the French were ready to make concessions. A nationalist government was set up and Bourguiba was allowed to return. No sooner had this been accomplished than the French had a change of mind – Bourguiba was exiled and most of the ministers were arrested. Violence followed, and the country was soon in a state of total disarray.

In July 1954, with few alternatives left, the French president finally announced plans for negotiations for Tunisian autonomy. In June 1955 an agreement was reached, and Bourguiba returned to Tunis to a hero's welcome. The agreement reached was restrictive in the fields of foreign policy and finance, and was condemned by Salah ben Youssef, former secretary of the Neo-Destour. He attempted to lead an armed insurrection, but without popular support he was soon forced to flee the country.

Tunisia was formally granted independence on 20 March 1956, with Bourguiba as prime minister. In the course of the following year, the last bey was deposed, the country became a republic and Bourguiba was declared Tunisia's first president.

Independent Tunisia

Bourguiba was quick to introduce sweeping political and social changes, looking to westernisation as the way to modernise. His ideals were socialist and secular, and he regarded Islam as a force that was holding the country back.

He set about reducing the role of religion in society by removing religious leaders from their traditional areas of influence, such as education and the law. Probably the most significant step was the abolition of religious schools. This deprived religious leaders of their grass-roots educational role in shaping society. The religious school at the Zitouna Mosque in Tunis, a centre of Islamic learning, suffered the indignity of being incorporated into the western-style University of Tunis.

The *shari'a* (Qur'anic law) courts were also abolished, and more than 60,000 hectares of land that had financed mosques and religious institutions were confiscated.

Bourguiba also introduced major changes to the role of women in society. His 1956 Personal Status Code banned polygamy and ended the practice of divorce by renunciation. He called the veil an 'odious rag' and

Habib Bourguiba, the first president of independent Tunisia, and father of the nation.

banned it from schools as part of an intensive campaign to end the wearing of a garment he regarded as demeaning. (See also the section on Women in Tunisia under Society & Conduct later in this chapter.)

However, when Bourguiba began urging workers to ignore the Ramadan fast in 1960 he met serious opposition from religious leaders. He regarded the dawn-to-dusk fast as economically damaging because of its effect on productivity. He mounted an ingenious argument against the fast, declaring that Tunisians were exempted because they were waging a *jihad* (holy war) against poverty – and that the Prophet Mohammed himself had excused warriors engaged in a jihad from fasting so that they could be at full strength to tackle the enemy.

Not surprisingly, religious leaders didn't swallow the argument. Trouble broke out in Kairouan following the removal of a senior religious figure who had denounced the government, and the fighting took 24 hours to subdue.

Opposition

Despite his autocratic style and frequent prolonged absences through ill health, Bourguiba managed to keep the bulk of the population on his side, and in 1974 the National Assembly made him president for life.

The 1970s were significant, however, for the gradual emergence of an Islamic opposition in the form of the Islamic Association, led by popular preacher Rashid Ghannouchi. Disillusionment with Bourguiba and his Parti Socialiste Destourien (PSD) – as the Neo-Destour Party became known in 1964 – increased dramatically following the use of the military to crush a general strike called by the UGTT (Tunisia's first trade union federation) in January 1978.

After promising more political freedoms, the government persuaded Bourguiba to call the first multi-party elections in 1981. The Islamic Association became the Islamic Tendency Movement (MTI), which advocated a return to Islamic values. Bourguiba, who didn't have much time for opposition of any sort, was certainly not prepared to tolerate an Islamic party and refused to license the MTI.

The elections were a total letdown for the new opposition parties. The National Front (an alliance formed between the PSD and the UGTT) took all 136 seats on offer, drawing cries of foul play.

After the elections, Bourguiba cracked down hard on the MTI. Ghannouchi and its other leaders were jailed and remained so until 1984, when riots were sparked by the withdrawal of a bread subsidy. The rioting lasted six days and stopped only when Bourguiba resumed the subsidy. The riots were notable for the shouting of slogans such as 'God is Great' and 'Down with America', and eventually the MTI leaders were freed to ease tensions.

Bourguiba's Final Years

As the 1980s progressed, Bourguiba was seen to be more and more out of touch both with the people at home and with Tunisia's position in the Arab world. An example of his erratic behaviour was his sudden decision in 1986 to sack Prime Minister Mohammed Mzali, just weeks after naming Mzali as his successor. Mzali's replacement, Rachid Sfar, lasted only a year before making way for the tough minister for the interior and former army general, Zine el-Abidine ben Ali, who eventually orchestrated the ousting of the ageing Bourguiba.

As minister for the interior, Ben Ali had presided over yet another crackdown on the Islamic opposition, which had produced more than 1000 arrests. In September 1987, 90 of those held, including Ghannouchi, were put on trial on charges ranging from planting bombs to conspiring to overthrow the regime. The bombings were a curious affair. Twelve tourists were injured in blasts at hotels in Sousse and Monastir, and responsibility was claimed by the pro-Iranian Islamic Jihad organisation. The government, however, held the MTI to blame, even though most of those charged had been in jail at the time.

The trial produced seven death sentences, while Ghannouchi was given hard labour for life. Bourguiba demanded the death sentence for all the accused and was furious at the outcome, insisting on retrials and that Ghannouchi and 15 others be executed by 16 November 1987.

It was against this backdrop that Ben Ali made his move. The arrest of Ghannouchi had sparked street battles, and there were fears that executions could lead to a popular uprising. On 7 November 1987, a group of doctors assembled by Ben Ali were asked to examine the 83-year-old president, who, predictably, was declared unfit to carry out his duties. It seems that, despite a heart condition, his physical health was not too bad for a man of his age; it was his mental health that was causing the concern.

Bourguiba was held for some time in detention in his palace in Carthage before being shunted off to 'retirement' in another palace outside Monastir, where he remains today.

Bourguiba's greatest achievements were the fostering of a strong national identity and the development of a standard of living which puts Tunisia at the top of the pile in the developing world.

President Ben Ali

Ben Ali moved quickly to appease the Islamic opposition. He headed off on a heavily publicised pilgrimage to Mecca to establish his own credentials as a good Muslim, and ordered that the Ramadan fast be observed. He also promised a multi-party political system, although he baulked at legalising the MTI – which by now had changed its name to Hizb al-Nahda (Renaissance Party).

Political prisoners were released, the State Security Court was abolished and police powers of detention were limited. Political exiles were invited to return, and many decided that it was safe to do so.

However, the general elections held in April 1989 didn't exactly reflect a new liberalism. Ben Ali's Rassemblement Constitutionel Democratique (RCD), as the PSD had become, won all the seats amid charges of vote rigging. In the presidential elections, Ben Ali was re-elected with 99.27% of the vote.

Hizb al-Nahda was not allowed to contest the poll, but many of its candidates stood as independents. Estimates of their share of the vote varied from 13% up to 40% in some urban areas.

This result, coupled with the successes of the Islamic Salvation Front (FIS) in municipal elections in Algeria, prompted Ben Ali to rule out official recognition of the Hizb al-Nahda.

However, no major move was made against the party until after the 1991 Gulf War. Tunisia officially supported the USA-led alliance, but popular sentiment was very much behind Iraq's Saddam Hussein. In May 1991, the government announced that it had uncovered a Hizb al-Nahda plot to establish an Islamic state by force. A sizeable number of those arrested were members of the military.

Opposition Today

The rules were changed for the elections of March 1994 to ensure the presence of a few opposition members in the National Assembly. The RCD claimed an overwhelming 97.7% of the vote and 144 seats, while the

Mouvement des Democratiques Socialistes (MDS) were awarded 10 seats for their 1%, making them the official opposition. Another nine seats were distributed around the five other legal parties participating. Ben Ali retained the presidency unopposed.

The Ben Ali government's main concern continues to be the Islamic opposition, especially in light of the situation next door in Algeria.

There is no suggestion, however, that the government is anything other than in complete control. Politics is not a popular (or advisable) topic of conversation, but many Tunisians express what appears to be a genuine admiration for Ben Ali's leadership.

Foreign Policy

Much of the esteem in which Ben Ali is held stems from Tunisia's high standing in the Arab world. The country has developed a reputation for stability in a volatile region. Tunisia was home to the Arab League for most of the 1980s, but it returned to Cairo in the late 1980s as Egypt re-entered the Arab fold after years on the outside for having made peace with Israel in 1979.

The Palestine Liberation Organisation (PLO) was based at Hammam Plage, just south of Tunis, after it was forced out of Lebanon by the Israelis in the early 1980s. The headquarters were badly damaged by an Israeli bombing raid in 1985 in retaliation for the killing of three Israelis in Cyprus. In mid-1994, Yasser Arafat and the PLO returned to the Israeli-controlled occupied territories to set up a local autonomous government.

Tunisia has also been an important opening to the outside world for Libya since an international air embargo was imposed over Libya's alleged involvement in the Lockerbie jumbo-jet bombing.

Relations with France have been generally good since independence, despite a few major hiccups in the late 1950s and early 1960s. In 1958, France bombed the Tunisian border village of Sakiet Sidi Youssef, claiming that Algerian rebels had crossed into Tunisian territory and that France had the right to pursue them. The Tunisians demanded that France evacuate the military base at Bizerte which it had retained after independence. Tunisian troops opened fire on the French, prompting a bloody retaliation in which more than 1000 Tunisians died. The French finally withdrew in 1963.

Another incident flared in 1964, when Tunisia suddenly nationalised land owned by foreigners. France responded by cutting off all aid, a situation that was not remedied until 1966.

Under Ben Ali's leadership, Tunisia's foreign policy has become steadily more pro-western. The Americans are the major supplier of equipment to the Tunisian army and Tunisia officially supported the USA-led western alliance during the Gulf War.

GEOGRAPHY

Tunisia occupies the northernmost point of the African continent, right at the centre of the north coast. Sicily is the closest European landfall, just 80km to the north-east across the Straits of Sicily. Tunisia borders Algeria to the west and Libya to the south-east. The ragged and irregular 1400km Mediterranean coastline forms the eastern and northern boundaries.

With an area of 164,000 sq km, Tunisia is by far the smallest country in North Africa. Tunisia measures 750km from north to south but only 150km from east to west. Put into perspective, it's a fraction larger than England and Wales combined, or about the same size as Washington state in the USA or Victoria in Australia.

Topographically, the country divides fairly neatly into the mountainous northern one-third and the flat southern two-thirds.

The main mountain range is the Tunisian Dorsale, which represents the eastern extension of Algeria's Saharan Atlas and the High Atlas mountains of Morocco. The Dorsale runs north-east from Tébessa, just across the Algerian border, to Zaghouan, just south of Tunis. It includes the highest mountain in the country, Jebel Chambi (1544m), west of Kasserine. After Zaghouan, the mountains taper off to form the Cap Bon Peninsula.

The majority of the country's viable arable land lies north of this line – the region referred to in history books as the granary of ancient Rome. It covers the high plains of the Tell Plateau and the fertile valley of the Oued Medjerda. The Medjerda, which rises near Souq Ahras in eastern Algeria, is the country's only permanent river. Its waters are used for irrigation and the generation of hydroelectricity. To the north of the Medjerda are the Kroumirie Mountains, stretching along most of the north coast from the Algerian border. This range gives way to a narrow coastal plain.

Directly south of the Dorsale is a treeless plain, 200m to 400m high, which drops down to a series of chotts (salt lakes) before giving way completely to desert in the south. Abundant artesian water makes cultivation possible in places and from these green oases come some of the finest dates in the world.

The sand sea (erg) which completely covers the southern tip of Tunisia is the eastern extremity of the Grand Erg Oriental (Great Eastern Erg), which covers a large area of Algeria.

CLIMATE

Northern Tunisia has a typical Mediterranean climate, with hot, dry summers and mild, wet winters. The mountains of the north-west occasionally get snow. The further south you go, the hotter and drier it gets. Annual rainfall ranges from 1000mm in the north down to 150mm in the south, although some Saharan areas go for years without rain. (For more information, see the climate charts over the page.)

ECOLOGY & ENVIRONMENT

Water, or the shortage thereof, is the country's major environmental issue. The further south you go, the more pressing the issue becomes. Problems are looming in the oasis towns of the Saharan fringe, where the huge water requirements of the tourist industry have depleted artesian water levels and dried up springs. Hotels everywhere have signs urging tourists to *économisez sur l'eau* (save water). You can help by turning the tap off

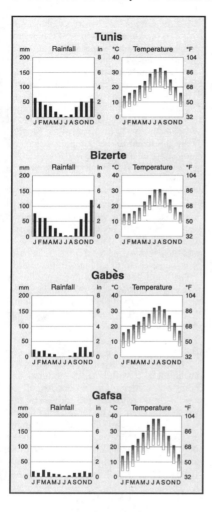

Tunis

Bizerte

Gabès

Gafsa

clean as you'll find city streets anywhere, but unfortunately the same cannot be said of the countryside, where many people have yet to come to terms with the fact that most 20th century packaging is not biodegradable. Discarded cans and plastic junk spoil many a beautiful setting.

GOVERNMENT & POLITICS

The 1959 constitution of the Republic of Tunisia gives legislative power to the chamber of deputies, which consists of 144 members elected directly by universal suffrage to a five year term.

The president, who is elected separately, has executive power and is the head of both the state and the government. The constitution states that the president must be a Muslim and can serve for no more than three consecutive terms; however, the first president of independent Tunisia, Habib Bourguiba, was elected president for life in 1974 before being ousted in 1987.

The current president, Ben Ali, is now in the middle of his third term. Elections are due in 1999. Ben Ali is the dominant political figure – his smiling face features on posters everywhere. The only other figure who gets a mention occasionally is Prime Minister Hamed Karoui, who was appointed by the president.

ECONOMY

The mixed Tunisian economy, in which both the public and the private sectors participate, relies heavily on tourism and on remittances from nationals working abroad, primarily in France and Italy, and also, up until the Gulf Crisis, in the Gulf states.

Petrol and petroleum products account for about 25% of exports, but Tunisia's lack of refining capacity means that most of the country's heavy petroleum needs have to be met with imports. Other important exports include textiles and leather (30%), fertilisers and chemicals, with the main destinations being France, the USA, Italy and Germany. Imports consist chiefly of food, raw materials and capital goods.

continued on page 33

while you brush your teeth and having showers instead of baths.

Soil erosion is a serious problem in the Tell, where 2500 years of deforestation and overgrazing have taken a heavy toll. The country loses an estimated 23,000 hectares of arable land to erosion every year.

The streets of Tunisia's major cities are as

Flora & Fauna
of Tunisia

Title page: Camels grazing in the arid regions of the south. (Photograph by Jon Davison)

The strawberry tree is covered in striking, fragrant white flowers in autumn. Despite its name, the fruit is disappointingly tasteless.

FLORA

Rainfall dictates what grows where. The Kroumirie Mountains of the north-west receive the lion's share of the country's rainfall and are densely forested. These forests mainly consist of the handsome evergreen holm oak and the cork oak. Another common species is the strawberry tree, so-called for the striking reddish fruit that ripen in November/December. The fruit are edible, if somewhat tasteless, and you'll see small boys offering punnets of them for sale at the roadside. As striking as the fruit are the dense panicles of fragrant, white, urn-shaped flowers that cover the tree in autumn.

The plains of the Tell were once covered in forests of Aleppo pine, but only small pockets remain. The largest remaining stand is between Siliana and Makthar. Further south, the *Acacia raddiana* forest of Bou Hedma National Park, east of Gafsa, is the last remnant of the old pre-Saharan savanna.

The semi-arid Sahel region in the east-central part of the country is dominated by the olive tree, cultivated on a large scale since before Roman times. Passing through the area by road or rail, the rows upon rows of olive trees seem to stretch forever. If you fly between Jerba and Tunis in daylight, you get an even better idea of the enormous area under olive cultivation. Another feature of this area is *Opuntia tomentosa*, better known as the prickly pear. This cactus species can grow to a height of 7m and is used as a hedging plant as well as for its fruit.

The treeless plains of the south support large areas of esparto grass, which is gathered for use in the production of high-quality paper. It is also woven into bags, hats and a range of tourist paraphernalia.

Further south, the vegetation gives way altogether to desert, and, apart from the occasional oasis, there is barely a bush or blade of grass to be seen. One curiosity of this area is a plant called the Jericho rose. It rolls around the desert, carried by the wind, with its branches curled up in a tight ball that encloses its seeds. It opens only on contact with moisture. In the oases, towering date palms provide shelter for a surprising variety of fruit trees, which in turn provide protection for vegetable crops.

FAUNA

Tunisia was once home to an exotic range of wildlife that included elephants and big cats such as lions and cheetahs. The war elephants employed by Hannibal were North African forest elephants, smaller cousins of the modern African elephants. They disappeared along with the trees when the Carthaginians and the Romans began clearing the forests of the interior to grow wheat.

Christians thrown to the lions at the Colosseum in Rome had every chance of being eaten by a Tunisian specimen. Thousands of big cats were shipped off to provide entertainment for the citizens of Rome. Lions survived in limited numbers until the middle of the 19th century, when the last was

The fennec, with its huge, radar-like ears, was once common in southern Tunisia but is now an endangered species.

shot near Haidra. Lynx still survive in the forests of the north-east, but reports of leopard sightings sound a bit fanciful.

French hunters also shot their fair share of species to the brink of extinction. These include Barbary deer and a couple of species of gazelle, all now recovering under government protection. Two antelope species, the addax and the oryx, were wiped out in Tunisia, but have now been reintroduced to Bou Hedma National Park. The addax sports a set of impressive spiral horns. Other species that are being reintroduced at Bou Hedma are ostriches and maned mouflon (a wild sheep).

The only large mammal that exists in large numbers is the wild boar, but this shy animal is seldom seen. Sightings of mongooses, porcupines and genets (a spectacular arboreal, cat-like carnivore) are even rarer. All live in the forests of the north. Jackals are more widely distributed and striped hyenas are found in the south.

The desert regions are home to camels. There are no wild camels – all the animals you see in the desert, even in what appears to be the middle of nowhere, are owned by somebody.

The wild animals of the south include gerbils, foxes, hares and the cute, squirrel-like suslik. The fennec, a nocturnal desert fox with enormous, radar-like ears, was once quite common but is now extremely rare in the wild.

There's more chance of spotting some of the region's reptiles, including the desert varanid (lizard) – a smaller member of the family that includes Australia's goanna and Indonesia's Komodo dragon.

Tunisia's version of the Australian goanna – the desert varanid.

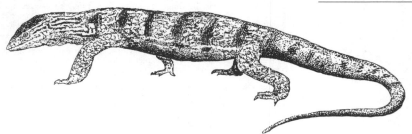

The south has lots of snakes, including horned vipers, and also scorpions. The presence of these creatures means that you should wear solid shoes when walking in rocky areas.

David Willett

BIRDS

Owing to its proximity to Western Europe, its mild climate and importance as a stopover for migratory birds, Tunisia has much to offer the bird-watcher. More than 200 species have been recorded and, with habitats ranging from estuaries to mountains and true desert, some spectacular, unusual and colourful birds can be seen. These include migrating storks, hawks and eagles in spring and autumn; colourful bee-eaters and rollers; and a host of wading birds and waterfowl. There are no endemic species to draw the hard-core birder; rather, Tunisia is a place to enjoy a good variety of birds in a mild climate within a comfortable distance of towns and other attractions. Dedicated bird-watchers seek out rarities such as Audouin's gull, and local specialities include Levaillant's woodpecker and Moussier's redstart.

Although the number of resident species is comparatively small, bird numbers swell when the migrants return. As they head north in spring they must cross the formidable barrier of the Sahara, and on their southward journey in autumn they run the gauntlet of hunters' guns in Sicily and Malta as they cross the Mediterranean. Either way, landfall in Tunisia provides a welcome respite for exhausted and hungry birds. The migration in spring and autumn is the best time to see birds of prey, when there may be vast flocks of a single species, such as honey buzzard, or mixed groups including other large species such as storks.

Where to See Birds in Tunisia

Many birds are wide-ranging, but the vast majority have feeding, breeding or other biological requirements which restrict them to a habitat or group of habitats. For example, ducks are adapted to feed in water and are rarely found far from it. Of course, creatures as mobile as birds are not totally hemmed in by their preferred environment (in fact, the habitat of some, such as swallows, could perhaps best be described as 'air'), but travellers will probably notice a change in the variety of birds to be seen as they move from place to place. Unfortunately, only a few national parks can be visited at present (see National Parks later in this section), but birds can be seen almost anywhere, especially during the migration season.

Only common, unusual or spectacular species are included in this guide; for more extensive coverage of Tunisian birds, readers are urged to refer to one of the guides mentioned later in this section.

The black kite, a scavenging bird of prey, can often be seen flying over the outskirts of towns in Tunisia.

Towns & Villages Since these will be the first stop for nearly all visitors, it is worth mentioning a few birds that could be seen in the urban environment. Some are familiar denizens of human settlements the world over: the house sparrow and its cousin the Spanish sparrow, which may be seen on the outskirts of settlements, where starlings and crows are also found. Orchards and gardens can support a surprising number of small birds, including the chiffchaff, and willow and Bonelli's warblers. The common bulbul is most often recognised by its loud, melodious call. The colourful European bee-eater sallies forth from perches after flying insects, particularly, as its name suggests, bees and wasps. The roller is another colourful member of this family. The black kite is a scavenging bird of prey that commonly cruises over the outskirts of towns.

Although not related to each other, the swallows and swifts are superficially similar and can be seen just about anywhere, flying after insects. Both groups have long wings and streamlined bodies adapted to lives in the air; both fly with grace and agility after insect prey; and both are usually dark in colouration. However, swallows can perch on twigs, fences or even the ground, while swifts have weak legs and rarely land except at the nest. Two species of swifts – common and pallid – may often be seen darting about; swallows and house martins often nest under eaves.

The sight of a mass of flamingos on Lake Ichkeul is one of the bird highlights of Tunisia.

Ichkeul National Park This 12,600 hectare reserve is recognised by UNESCO as a Biosphere Reserve. It protects a permanent body of water, plus associated marshes and streams, and is easily accessible from Tunis and the northern resorts. Lake Ichkeul is a haven for water birds of all types, while the surrounding shores are carpeted in a dazzling display of wild flowers during spring. See also the boxed text 'Ichkeul National Park' in the Northern Tunisia chapter.

Different groups of birds use the lake in different ways: some hunt along the shoreline or probe the soft mud at the water's edge; others stride on long legs into deeper water to seek prey. The brightly coloured kingfisher is a living jewel that dives for prey, and warblers, finches and rails skulk in dense vegetation. This habitat provides some of the best opportunities to view birds for beginner and expert alike.

Ichkeul's shores are thronged with stilts, sandpipers and stints. Aptly named wagtails strut about; and grey herons and little egrets stalk the shallows for fish and frogs. In spring, thousands of 'passage migrants' arrive from south of the Sahara, stopping briefly to replenish their energy before flying on to fan out across Europe.

The resident species are joined by migrants, such as squacco herons, white storks and cattle egrets. Skulking in the reed beds, the bittern, a well camouflaged relative of the heron, is more often heard than seen, and Cetti's, great reed and moustached warblers make a riot of sound as they proclaim their territories. The purple gallinule pokes among the vegetation on long, splayed toes; its bright blue plumage and red bill make it virtually unmistakable, especially when the sun picks out its beautiful colours.

The greater flamingo is a large and graceful – if bizarre – bird that often concentrates in large flocks in shallow lakes. Although flamingos are nomadic and may not always be present in large numbers, one of the bird highlights of Tunisia is the sight of a mass of pink birds sifting for food through the shimmering water.

As summer wanes and autumn draws on, the summer 'shift' of migrants disperses south again to be replaced by birds escaping the northern winter. Chief among these are the waterfowl (ducks and geese) – for sheer numbers of these, Lake Ichkeul has few rivals in the region. Up to 100,000 waterfowl are sustained by the lake, which at this time of year is replenished by winter rains. Among the flocks observers should see good numbers of ducks, such as wigeon, teal, gadwall, pintail and, further out, pochard. As many as 15,000 greylag geese have been reported over-wintering at Ichkeul. Other waterfowl specialities include white-headed duck and marbled teal, and coots may be present in great numbers.

You may be lucky enough to spot the handsome Audouin's gull around Tunisia's coast.

Ocean & Seashore The narrow strip where land meets sea – sandy beach or rocky platform – is one of the most dynamic habitats on earth. Inhabitants of this environment are adapted to being inundated twice daily by the sea and battered by the elements in between. Many of the creatures that have adapted to this lifestyle – such as crustaceans and shellfish – make tasty morsels for both humans and birds. In Tunisia this habitat varies between the rugged, rocky coast of the north and the shallow, sandy Gulf of Gabès.

Rocky headlands such as Cap Blanc make good vantage points from which to view birds at sea, particularly when onshore winds drive them close to land. Among them are the beautiful gannet, which feeds by plunging from a great height after fish, and the graceful Cory's and Yelkouan shearwaters (considered by some to be a race of the manx shearwater), which can pass by the Tunisian coast in great flocks. Cap Bon is another good site; it's also a good location from which to observe migrating birds of prey soar overhead in spring.

Tidal flats along the Gulf of Gabès attract shorebirds known as 'waders'. With a few exceptions, waders are found near fresh and saline waterways, feeding along the shores on small creatures or probing intertidal mud for worms. Many keen bird-watchers relish the identification challenge waders can present during migration.

Gulls and terns are close relatives of the waders, although they look very different. Several species of gulls and terns inhabit the Tunisian coasts: slender-billed and Audouin's gulls, and Caspian terns are three handsome species eagerly sought by bird-watchers. Uninhabited coastal islands, such as La Galite, Zembra and Zembretta, support the main breeding colonies of gulls and other sea-going birds. Most colonies are protected by the military and access is currently not allowed.

Grassland Natural grasslands have largely been modified by grazing and agriculture, but seed-eating birds in particular can adapt quite well to this environment. Grassland specialists include various species of larks, pipits and finches; some spectacular 'game' birds such as bustards; and birds of prey.

The various species of hawks, eagles, vultures and falcons are collectively known as raptors, and together they number about 25 species in Tunisia. All birds of prey have sharply hooked bills and talons for tearing flesh. Some have specialised hunting techniques: harriers hunt by gliding low over fields and dropping onto prey; the falcons prey mainly on other birds and are celebrated for their speed; and kites and vultures are scavengers of carcases.

Although larks are not the most spectacular group of birds, they are biologically significant to the grasslands they inhabit. Their identification can pose some challenges, but a few species are readily seen in Tunisia. The

The distinctive crested hoopoe, with its striking plumage, is related to the kingfisher and is best looked for in spring.

crested lark is commonly seen on the side of the road, and other species include Dupont's, shore, Thekla, thick-billed and hoopoe larks. The hoopoe lark bears some resemblance to the hoopoe but it is not related.

Forest Although not much lowland forest remains, quite extensive forests of pine and cork oaks still cover the mountains in northern Tunisia. Surviving lowland forests include mixed cork-oak woodlands, and feature warblers, woodpeckers, birds of prey and the bizarre, crested hoopoe, whose distinct salmon-pink plumage is offset by bold black and white markings. The woodlands near 'Ain Draham, in the north-west, are reported to be a productive bird-watching area.

Other woodland and forest birds include the attractive russet, black and white Moussier's redstart; the nightingale, famed for its song; the great grey shrike, which is a voracious predator of small animals; and, among the raptors, the red kite. In more mountainous terrain, look for birds of prey, the lovely blue rock thrush, black wheatear and rock bunting.

Desert Much of Tunisia is desert or subdesert – a stark and dramatic landscape of rocky plains and outcrops, sand dunes and sparsely vegetated steppe. The number and variety of life forms are diminished in this harsh environment, but this habitat supports a few interesting birds. Bird-watchers should head south for the Chott el-Jerid and the oases on the edge of the Sahara to seek out some of the following.

The lanky stone curlew is a large wader with weird wailing cries; it feeds on spiders and insects at night, and relies on its camouflaged plumage to remain cryptic during the day. The Barbary partridge is an attractively marked game bird of desert steppes. It typically shelters in *oueds* (seasonal rivers) but can sometimes be seen in agricultural land or scrubby habitat.

The swift-flying sandgrouse are nomadic birds adapted to feed on seeds in the arid steppes and grasslands. Although they can be quite common, they are superbly camouflaged and can appear to vanish among the rubble of oueds. Two species, the pin-tailed and black-bellied sandgrouse (the latter in more montane areas), may be seen flying in to waterholes in the evening. The Houbara bustard is a graceful game bird often sought out by hunters as well as birders; the lanner, a large falcon, is one species used in the ancient art of falconry to bring down Houbara. Other desert birds of prey include the long-legged buzzard and Egyptian vulture.

Oases are a haven for wildlife of all types and bird-watching can be a treat around oueds, gardens and plantations. Trumpeter finches may be seen feeding around the droppings of tethered camels, and desert sparrows replace the familiar house sparrow on the outskirts of towns. Migrating flocks of birds can literally drop out of the sky into a welcoming patch of greenery for a few hours' rest. Laughing doves are familiar and approachable, with a distinctive call. Wheatears are boldly marked birds of arid regions that are easier to spot than larks; females can be difficult to identify, and desert, mourning, red-rumped, black and white-crowned black wheatears could keep bird-watchers on their toes.

Some Tips for Watching Birds

A pair of binoculars will reveal subtleties of form and plumage not usually detected by the naked eye. Be warned – once you've seen the shimmering colours of a glossy ibis or the brash tones of a bee-eater through binoculars you may get hooked! Binoculars will also considerably aid identification and help you nut out the subtle – and vexing – differences between the warblers, for example. Basic models can be purchased quite cheaply from duty-free outlets.

If you get serious about bird-watching you may want to invest in better quality optics: brands such as Leica and Zeiss, although expensive, should last a lifetime and offer unrivalled quality. Both brands come in handy, pocket sized models. You may also want to consider getting a spotting scope and several manufacturers (such as Kowa, Swarovski and Leica) make excellent

The forests of Northern Tunisia are home to the attractive russet, black and white Moussier's redstart.

The fertile oases in southern Tunisia's otherwise barren landscape are a haven for wildlife of all types, including several interesting species of birds.

JON DAVISON

examples. With a magnification usually at least twice that of binoculars, they can give stunning views. The drawback is their size (they must be mounted on a tripod for best results); on the other hand, a camera can be attached to some models and a scope then doubles as a telephoto lens.

Listed below are some tips to help you get the most out of bird-watching in Tunisia:

- Try to get an early start because birds are generally active during the cooler hours of the day. This is particularly so in arid regions and during hot weather.
- Approach birds slowly and avoid sudden movements or loud talk. Try to dress in drab clothing so as not to stand out. Many species are quite approachable and will allow opportunities for observation and photography. Birds are not usually too concerned about people in a vehicle and stunning views can often be obtained from the roadside.
- Water birds and waders respond to tidal movements and are usually best seen on a falling tide as they search for food.
- Always ask permission before birding on private property.
- Do not disturb birds unnecessarily and never handle eggs or young birds in a nest. Adults will readily desert a nest that has been visited, leaving their young to perish.
- Remember that weather and wind can adversely affect viewing conditions and you should not expect to see every bird mentioned in this section at first attempt.

Books on Tunisian Birds

The best guides to European birds also cover Tunisia. The popularity of bird-watching has inspired a number of excellent illustrated titles to suit all budgets and levels of interest. *Birds of the Middle East and North Africa*, by Hollom, Porter, Christensen & Willis, is the definitive guide to the region. *Birds of Europe with North Africa and the Middle East,* by Lars Jonsson, is superbly illustrated and covers all species likely to be found in Tunisia. The *Collins Pocket Guide to Birds of Britain & Europe with North Africa & the Middle East,* by Heinzel, Fitter & Parslow, is an excellent little book and fits into a large pocket.

David Andrew

NATIONAL PARKS

The government has attempted to do something to protect the country's disappearing environmental heritage by declaring a number of national parks, each protecting a surviving remnant of a typical ecosystem. There were six at the time of writing and a further three are planned.

Unfortunately the parks are not particularly user-friendly. Most are very hard to get to, and a couple double as military areas – which rules out any possibility of a visit. The only park with facilities for visitors is Ichkeul, 30km south-west of Bizerte, which protects Lake Ichkeul and adjoining Jebel Ichkeul. See the Northern Tunisia chapter for more information on the park.

Bou Hedma National Park, 85km east of Gafsa near the small town of Meknassy, has great potential but no attempt has yet been made to exploit it. The park protects some 16,000 hectares of acacia forest, representing the last pocket of the extensive savanna forest that once covered the region. The park is being used to reintroduce a number of species previously extinct in Tunisia, including addax, maned mouflon, oryx and ostrich.

The other national parks are listed below:

Boukornine National Park
Just 18km south of Tunis at Hammam Lif, Boukornine is a tiny park of 1900 hectares surrounding Jebel Boukornine (576m). The park is home to wild boars, jackals, porcupines – and the military.

Chambi National Park
Located 15km west of Kasserine, the park protects 6700 hectares of forest surrounding Tunisia's highest mountain, Jebel Chambi (1544m). Most of the forest is Aleppo pine, but the moister eastern flank of Jebel Chambi supports a pocket of cork oak and juniper. Animals include mountain gazelles and striped hyenas.

Feija National Park
Near the Algerian border 20km north-west of Ghardimao, this park covers 2600 hectares of oak forest. Animals include Barbary deer, wild boars and jackals.

Zembra-Zembretta National Park
The islands of Zembra and Zembretta lie in the Bay of Tunis about 15km west of Cap Bon. The military are the only people who get to see what's there. The official list includes three types of algae!

David Willett

continued from page 24

The agricultural sector has become smaller in the last 20 years and now provides work for less than a quarter of the workforce; almost 40% of food has to be imported. Despite the fact that large areas of the south of the country are desert, almost 50% of the land is cultivated. The main crops are wheat, barley, maize, sorghum, dates, olives and oranges.

Major industries are the processing of agricultural produce and minerals, including olive oil, textiles, foodstuffs, cement, steel and phosphate. The importance of Tunisia's mining industry is reflected in the fact that Tunisia is the world's sixth-largest producer of phosphate.

Once a socialist economy, Tunisia is now slowly privatising many state-owned industries. Tax and employment laws have been changed to favour the private sector and the country is being marketed abroad as an investment opportunity. The transition has not been easy, however. Unemployment is widespread and the situation is exacerbated by the fact that most manufacturing is small scale and most businesses employ no more than five people. In 1995, Tunisia signed an association agreement with the European Union (EU), ushering in a new era of trade relations with Europe. Under the terms of the agreement, all customs tariffs will be dropped over a 12 year period, leading eventually to full free trade between the EU and Tunisia. The government hopes that this will open new markets for Tunisian goods and encourage the inflow of investment capital, although in the short term it is likely to have a negative impact on the economy.

Socioeconomic Conditions

Unemployment, currently around 13%, is the main social issue, as it seems to be almost everywhere in the world. As a visitor, one of the first questions you will be asked is what the unemployment rate is in your country, closely followed by a question about the chances of finding a job.

While the social security system provides old age and disability pensions, and compensation for sickness and injury, the unemployed get nothing. They survive thanks to the closeness of the family network; often one working adult has to support four or five other adult family members.

In spite of this, living standards are generally good and are considered high by developing-world standards. Per capita GDP is around US$4250.

Health care is also free, and low-income earners are eligible for extra benefits such as free milk for newborn babies and free school lunches. Although there are still shortages of trained personnel and modern facilities, general health conditions have improved dramatically in the last 20 years. The government claims it has 96% coverage for its immunisation program, which is the most comprehensive in the developing world.

POPULATION & PEOPLE

The population of Tunisia is just over nine million, according to recent estimates. The vast majority (98%) are Arab-Berber, with Europeans and Jews making up the remaining 2%.

The country has a fairly high population growth rate of about 2.5%. Almost half the population is under the age of 15, which places a great strain on social services. Another problem is the population distribution, which varies from over 2000 per sq km in Tunis to less than 10 per sq km in the south.

The Berbers were the original inhabitants of the area, but waves of immigration over the centuries have brought Phoenicians, Jews, Romans, Vandals and Arabs. There was a major influx of Spanish Muslims in the 17th century. The Ottoman Turks have also added their bit to the great ethnic mix.

EDUCATION

Education is free and, thanks to the high government spending (typically 25% of total expenditure), there has been a rapid increase in the number of schools since independence. Literacy is fairly high at 66.7% (78.6% for males; 54.6% for females).

ARTS

Literature

There are countless streets in Tunisian towns named after Tunisia's national poet, Abu el-Kacem el-Chabbi, whose poem *Will to Live* is taught to every schoolchild.

Few Tunisian writers have been translated into English. One who has and whose work is available internationally is Mustapha Tlili, whose novel *Lion Mountain* tells the story of the disasters wrought upon a remote village by progress and tourism. You won't find it in bookshops in Tunisia.

Acclaimed author Albert Memmi qualifies as Tunisian by birth, but he lives in Paris and writes in French about the identity crisis faced by North African Jews like himself. His books include the *Pillar of Salt* and *Jews and Arabs. Sleepless Nights* by Ali Duaji is a collection of short stories and sketches about life in and around Tunis during the first half of the 20th century. It's available only in Tunisia.

Architecture

There is a huge range of architectural styles to be seen in Tunisia, from Punic and Roman ruins to the red-tiled 'Alpine' houses of 'Ain Draham (see the Northern Tunisia chapter for more details), the Islamic architecture of the Arab medinas and the Berber structures of the south.

In spite of the wealth and power of the Carthaginian Empire, the Romans did such a good job of eliminating all trace of their arch rivals that nothing over knee-high remains. The two main places to see Punic ruins are at Carthage (see the Around Tunis section of the Tunis chapter for more details) and at Kerkouane (see the Cap Bon Peninsula chapter), where the ruins are better preserved.

Modern Art in Tunisia

Introduced by the French, painting is a well established contemporary art medium in Tunisia. It ranges from the highly geometric forms of Hédi Turki through intricate free-flowing Arabic calligraphy, such as the work of artist Nja Mahdaoui, to traditional western styles that aim to encapsulate the essence of Tunisian daily life and culture, including scenes of cafes, hammams and music and dance performances. The work of Yahia Turki and Ammar Farhat, in particular, falls into this last category.

Under the French, the ambient lifestyle of Tunisia attracted European artists who, entranced by the North African light and architecture, depicted their interpretations of orientalism. Perhaps most famously, Tunisia was a source of inspiration to the Swiss expressionist, Paul Klee, who first visited Tunisia in 1914.

A Tunisian Salon, heavily dependent on colonial styles and set up by European painters, was established in 1894 in Tunis. In the 1940s, a collection of professional and amateur artists broke away from the Salon to establish the more nationalist École de Tunis. It welcomed Tunisian members and was responsible for popularising Tunisian life as a subject matter for painting. Early members of this school include Yahia Turki who is widely considered to be the father of Tunisian painting. Other well known names (within Tunisia, at any rate) include Ammar Farhat, Jellal Ben Abdallah, Zoubeir Turki, Hédi Turki and Abdelaziz Gorgi. Sérès Productions does a series of publications, available from art bookshops in Tunisia, on the life and works of the most prominent members. If you can't afford to buy a print, you could just settle for a postage stamp – these depict the work of some of the more celebrated national artists.

Modern art galleries in Tunisia are mainly confined to Tunis and its wealthy suburbs, especially the traditional artist's haven of Sidi Bou Saïd. The inside back page of the English-language weekly *Tunisia News* has a list of exhibitions. Galerie Alif, behind the French Embassy in Tunis, is a gem. It has a vast collection of art books, including ones they publish themselves. They usually have an an art exhibition – photography, painting, prints and installations – in the basement that changes every couple of months. Espace Diwan 9, in the Tunis medina at 9 Rue Sidi ben Arous, also has a good collection of art books focusing on Tunisia and the Maghreb.

Other places in Tunis that may be worth checking out include Galerie Yahia on Ave Mohammed V, Galerie Artémis at 30 Rue 7232, El-Menzah IX, Galerie des Art at Centre Jamil, El-Menzah VI, and Galerie Gorgi at 23 Rue Jugurtha, Le Belvédère.

Roger Sheen

There are a number of impressive Roman sites in Tunisia, including Bulla Regia, Dougga, El-Jem and Thuburbo Majus. Bulla Regia is famous for the underground villas built by the Romans in a bid to escape the heat – following the example set by the Berbers in the south. The colosseum at El-Jem is the most dramatic of the many fine Roman buildings in Tunisia. Tunisia is also famous for its mosaics; the Bardo Museum in Tunis houses the best of the mosaics from around the country.

The best examples of traditional Berber architecture are the troglodyte houses of the Matmata region, made famous by being the setting of the movie *Star Wars*. The *ksour* (fortified Berber strongholds) around Tataouine are no less interesting. These arched structures were originally built to store grain but were expanded and fortified after the Arab invasion in the 7th century AD. Usually strategically placed, they occupy some spectacular hill-top sites. The mud houses of the mountain oases west of Gafsa are also fascinating places to explore. Tozeur and Nefta are famous for their traditional brickwork, in which protruding bricks are used to create intricate geometric patterns. See the Southern Tunisia chapter for more details.

The architecture on Jerba is very distinctive. The traditional dwellings are called *menzels*, and resemble small, whitewashed fortresses with four square turrets and windowless walls. The roof consists of a series of arches and small cupolas. These defensive features reflect Jerba's history of frequent invasions and were designed to protect against both attack and heat.

Islamic architecture comes in many styles. The early Islamic dynasties were great builders – it was their responsibility to transform towns to suit the Islamic model. The great mosques of Kairouan, Sfax, Sousse and Tunis were all built by the Aghlabites in the 9th century, together with the *ribats* (monastic forts) at Monastir and Sousse.

Styles became steadily more ornate over the years. The Andalusians arrived from Spain with their round minarets, while the Turks brought octagonal minarets and beautiful faïence tilework. See the illustrated Islamic Architecture in Tunisia section at the end of this chapter.

The French, too, have left their mark. There are some extravagant neo-classical façades in the French-built suburbs of Sfax and Tunis.

Film

Tunisia has a busy film industry, but few locally produced films make it beyond the Arab world. The best known director is Ali Laâbidi, whose films *Halfouine* and *The Silence of the Palace* have both won critical acclaim in Europe. Look out for his latest film, *Redeyef 54*.

Tunis plays host to the biennial Carthage International Film Festival (October, odd-numbered years). See also the boxed text 'Starring Tunisia' in the Facts for the Visitor chapter.

Music

Malouf, which means 'normal', is the name given to the form of traditional Arab-style music that has become a national institution in Tunisia. Introduced into Tunisia in the 15th century by Andalusian refugees, this distinctive Hispano-Arabic style of music rapidly became so popular that it replaced the existing forms of Arab-Muslim music. It consists of instrumental pieces, which serve as preludes and breaks, and vocal works performed in a set sequence, called a *nouba*. Traditionally, malouf was performed by small ensembles using a *rbab* (a kind of two-stringed violin), *oud* (lute) and *da-buka* (drum, usually made of terracotta with a goatskin cover on one side), with a solo vocalist. Today, ensembles are more likely to be made up of large instrumental and choral groups, playing a mixture of western and traditional Arabic musical instruments. The repetitive melodies and lack of tonal variation can be a challenge for western listeners.

Malouf was adopted by the Sufi religious brotherhoods to play at their ceremonies (see also the boxed text 'Sufism' under Religion later in this chapter). It gradually declined in *continued on page 38*

Mosaics

An astonishing number of floor mosaics has been discovered in Tunisia and it's likely that many more remain undiscovered. Reasons for this abundance of mosaics include the wealth of Africa Proconsularis in the 2nd and 3rd centuries AD (based on trade in wheat and olive oil), the availability of coloured stones, including marble, and influences from the Romans in Italy via Sicily and the eastern Mediterranean. In addition, Tunisia's warm, dry climate has meant that the mosaics have generally been well preserved.

Mosaic is an ancient technique which flourished from the 4th century BC to the 14th century AD and was particularly popular during the time of the Roman Empire. The mosaics found in Tunisia date mainly from the 2nd to 6th centuries AD, although a simple early type of floor mosaic, *opus siginum* (cement with a sprinkling of marble fragments), has been found in Punic houses, leading to the suggestion that mosaic art originated in Carthage in the 4th and 3rd centuries BC. It's more generally accepted, however, that mosaics were introduced to Tunisia from Sicily, which was at the edge of the Carthaginian Empire.

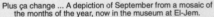

Plus ça change ... A depiction of September from a mosaic of the months of the year, now in the museum at El-Jem.

The early mosaics, dating from the 1st and 2nd centuries AD, show evidence of Italian and Alexandrian influence, but by the middle of the 2nd century, distinct schools of mosaicists were established and working in Tunisia, mostly in the El-Jem/Sousse region. By the end of the 2nd century most cities of any size in Tunisia had a local workshop, and from this time on mosaics were a standard form of floor decoration and possibly also of wall decoration, although few wall mosaics have survived. Tunisian mosaics from the 3rd century onwards show a distinctive African style, characterised by larger dramatic compositions with vigorous colour and realistic subjects such as amphitheatre games, hunting and scenes of life on the African estates. They appear to have been primarily decorative in function, unlike elsewhere in the Roman Empire where they were used for a variety of purposes, including shop signs and advertising.

Most of the mosaics to be seen in Tunisia are the type known as *opus tessellatum*, in which patterns are formed out of little squares or pieces of stone called tesserae (from the Latin, meaning cubes or dice). The technique involved laying out a setting bed of mortar in which the tesserae were placed.

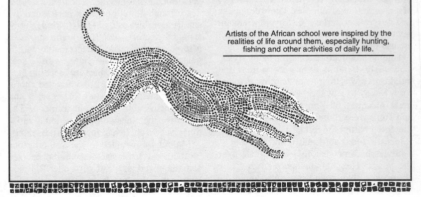

Artists of the African school were inspired by the realities of life around them, especially hunting, fishing and other activities of daily life.

The decorative frameworks around the pictures are often as stunning as the pictures themselves.

Underpaintings discovered in floor and wall mosaics indicate that preparatory sketches served as a guide for the placement and colour of the tesserae. Not much is known about the artisans who produced the mosaics, although a few have signed their names on their work.

The majority of the mosaics found in Tunisia come from private houses; the second major source is public baths. The houses were usually the property of wealthy merchants and landowners. The mosaics were distributed throughout the houses, with the most elaborate mosaics being found in the main reception rooms, to impress visitors and clients. A certain amount of 'keeping up with the Joneses' was presumably responsible for the extraordinary quality and quantity of mosaics found in these houses.

The themes depicted reflect the preoccupations and interests of the commissioning house owners and include banquets, amphitheatre games, mythology, the sea and daily life on the great estates. In Tunisian mosaics, the depiction of time (eg personifications of the seasons) is a common theme, denoting the harmony and permanence of the universe. Good examples include the Seasons and the Months mosaic in the El-Jem Museum and the La Chebba mosaic in the Bardo Museum in Tunis. Dionysus, the god of fruitfulness and wine, who had the gift of being able to free the spirit of worries, was another very popular subject. At El-Jem more than 20 mosaics depicting Dionysian themes have been found, including the Triumph of Dionysus (now at the Bardo Museum). Another common theme was the sea, with the emphasis being on its inexhaustible riches, seen especially on mosaics from the Sousse region. The fishing scenes mosaic at the Sousse Museum shows four boats floating on a sea filled with fish and shellfish. Mosaics with sea themes are also found in houses further inland, perhaps reflecting both the house owners' love of the Mediterranean and the contribution shipping made to their wealth.

The mosaics that depict life on the great African estates in the 3rd and 4th centuries AD are among the most impressive in Tunisia and are distinctively African. They are both narrative and descriptive and portray the life of the rich landowners who commissioned the works. The Lord Julius mosaic at the Bardo Museum, shows one such landowner, with his wife, in four scenes corresponding to the four seasons.

In the 4th to 6th centuries, mosaics were influenced by early Christian beliefs and themes such as the mosaic of Daniel in the Lion's Den in the Bardo Museum. They were commissioned for the pavements of basilicas and tombs, such as those found at Tabarka. The tomb mosaics depict either a conventional image of the deceased in an attitude of prayer or just an epitaph. By the 7th century, with the Arab invasion, mosaic art fell into a decline, although mosaic pavements have been discovered in the ruins of the Aghlabite palaces at Raqqada, perhaps dating from the 9th century, and 10th century Arab mosaics have been found at Mahdia.

Isabelle Young

Marine themes were very popular in Tunisian mosaics.

continued from page 35
popularity as it was superseded by a new light style of music introduced from Egypt in the mid 1920s. Malouf underwent a revival in the 1930s when Baron Erlangen, a musicologist living in the Tunis suburb of Sidi Bou Saïd, set up the Rachidia ensemble. The Baron's six volumes on the history and rules of malouf are testament to his passionate involvement with the art form. Although purists might argue with the authenticity of the ensemble, the Rachidia became the official centre for malouf music and is where most of Tunisia's leading musicians trained.

After independence, malouf was adopted as a symbol of national identity. Since then, with the dissolution of the Sufi brother-hoods, it has become institutionalised to a great extent, with the government offering courses in malouf at the National Conservatory of Music in Tunis and an annual cycle of festivals and competitions culminating in the International Festival of Malouf in Testour. It has also become an established form of tourist entertainment.

Stars of the malouf scene include the El-Azifet ensemble (a rarity in this part of the world – an exclusively female orchestra) and the oud player Anouar Brahem. Tourist restaurants often put on live performances of traditional music; the Restaurant M'Rabet in the Tunis medina is a good place to try – see the Tunis chapter for more details.

For something a bit different, the colosseum at El-Jem makes a spectacular setting for the El-Jem International Symphonic Music Festival, held every July.

SOCIETY & CONDUCT
Women in Tunisia

Thanks largely to the efforts of their secular, socialist former president, Habib Bourguiba, conditions for women in Tunisia are better than just about anywhere in the Islamic world – to western eyes, at least. Bourguiba, whose first wife was French, was a staunch supporter of women's rights, and they were one of the first issues on the agenda after independence. His 1956 Personal Status Code banned polygamy and ended divorce

by renunciation. It also placed restrictions on the tradition of arranged marriages, setting a minimum marriage age of 17 for girls and giving them the right to refuse a proposed marriage.

Bourguiba was outspoken in his criticism of the *hijab* (the veil worn by Muslim women), which he regarded as demeaning. He called it an 'odious rag', and banned it from schools as part of a campaign to phase it out. He didn't quite succeed, although it is now very unusual to find a women under 30 wearing one. You may see some interesting mother/daughter combinations wandering around, with mother wearing a hijab and daughter wearing the latest western fashions.

The Tunisian government is fond of trumpeting its record on women's issues, which helps to deflect criticism of its treatment of political opposition. It likes to point out that life expectancy for women has increased from 58 to 70 years since 1985; that girls now have equal access to educational opportunities; and that women now make up 21% of the workforce.

The government is less keen to discuss the social impact of these reforms, the most serious of which is an extremely high divorce rate. No statistics are available, but the government acknowledged the extent of the problem in 1992 by setting up a special fund guaranteeing alimony payments for divorced women and their children. Men, it seems, are having trouble coming to terms with the expectations of modern Tunisian women. While not advocating a return to the pre-Bourguiba days, many men complain that the pendulum has now swung too far the other way.

Cafes

Cafes are an integral part of Tunisian life. They are much more than a place to stop for a coffee. It is here that the menfolk gather in the evening to smoke their *chichas* (water pipes), exchange gossip and play cards. It has been estimated that 60% of the male population smoke the traditional chicha. Cafes provide the chicha free, charging only for a plug of tobacco.

The main card games are rummy and *quarante*, a game with no western equivalent that is played with such speed and enthusiasm that it's impossible to figure out the rules. Watching the animated participants is entertainment enough.

Hammams

See the Activities section of the Facts for the Visitor chapter for information on hammams (public bathhouses).

Dos & Don'ts

Despite Tunisia's liberal reputation, it is a Muslim country and most people are conservative about dress. Although dress codes vary quite widely from the chic resorts and cities to the conservative countryside, you can save yourself trouble and embarrassment by erring on the side of modesty in what you wear.

Women, in particular, are well advised to keep shoulders and upper arms covered and to opt for long skirts or trousers. Stricter Muslims consider an excessive display of flesh, whether in a man or a woman, offensive. Women disregarding such considerations risk not only arousing the ire of the genuinely offended but also the unwanted interest of the lecherous. Men wearing shorts (away from the coast at any rate) are considered to be in their underwear and can occasionally arouse indignation too. A little common sense goes a long way. You can get away with a lot more on the beaches of Hammamet and Sousse than in the villages of the interior.

Public displays of affection are frowned upon in most parts of the region.

RELIGION

Islam is the state religion in Tunisia. While there has been a definite resurgence of religious adherence, particularly among the young and unemployed, Tunisia remains a fairly liberal society. There is a small Jewish community, living mainly in Tunis and on the island of Jerba (see the boxed text 'The Jews of Jerba' in the Jerba section of the Southern Tunisia chapter), as well as about 20,000 Roman Catholics.

Islam

The first slivers of dawn light are flickering on the horizon, and the deep quiet of a city asleep is pierced by the cries of the muezzin exhorting the faithful to the first of the day's prayers:

> Allahu akbar, Allahu akbar
> Ashhadu an la Ilah ila Allah
> Ashhadu an Mohammed rasul Allah
> Haya ala as-sala
> Haya ala as-sala

Of all the sounds that assault the ears of the first-time visitor to Tunisia, it is possibly the call to prayer that leaves the most indelible impression. Five times a day, Muslims are called, if not actually to enter a mosque to pray, at least to take the time to do so where they are. The midday prayers on Friday, when the sheikh of the mosque delivers his weekly sermon, or *khutba*, are considered the most important. The mosque also serves as a kind of community centre, and often you'll find groups of children or adults receiving lessons (usually in the Qur'an or Muslim holy book), people in quiet prayer and others simply sheltering in the tranquil peace of the mosque.

Islam shares its roots with the great monotheistic faiths that sprang from the harsh land of the Middle East – Judaism and Christianity – but it is considerably younger than these religions. The holy book of Islam is the Qur'an. Its pages carry many references to the earlier prophets of both the older religions – Adam, Abraham, Noah, Moses and others are recognised as prophets – but there the similarities begin to end. Jesus is seen merely as another in a long line of prophets that ends definitively with the Prophet Mohammed.

What makes Mohammed different from the rest is that the Qur'an, unlike either the Torah of the Jews or the Christian Gospels, is the word of God, directly communicated to Mohammed in a series of revelations. For

Muslims, Islam can only be the apogee of the monotheistic faiths from which it derives so much. Muslims traditionally attribute a place of great respect to Christians and Jews as *ahl al-kitab*, the people of the book. However, the more strident will claim Christianity was a new and improved version of the teachings of the Torah, and that Islam was the next logical step and therefore superior. Don't be surprised if you occasionally run into someone wanting you to convert!

Mohammed, born into one of the trading families of the Arabian city of Mecca (in present-day Saudi Arabia) in 570 AD, began to receive revelations in 610, and after a time started imparting the content of Allah's message to the Meccans. Its essence was a call to submit to God's will (*islam* means submission), but not all Meccans were impressed.

Mohammed gathered quite a following in his campaign against Meccan idolaters, but the powerful families of the city became so hostile that he felt forced to flee to Medina in 622. Mohammed's flight from Mecca, or *hijra* (migration), marks the beginning of the Muslim calendar. In Medina he continued to preach, while increasing his power base. Soon he and his supporters began to clash with the Meccans, led by powerful elements of the Quraysh tribe, possibly over trade routes.

By 632, Mohammed had revisited Mecca and many of the tribes in the surrounding area had sworn allegiance to him and the new faith. Mecca became the symbolic centre of the faith, containing as it did the Ka'aba, which housed the black stone supposedly given to Ibrahim (Abraham) by the Angel Gabriel. Mohammed determined that Muslims should face Mecca when praying outside the city.

On his death in 632, the Arabs exploded into the Syrian desert, quickly conquering the areas which make up modern Syria, Iraq, Lebanon, Israel and Palestine. This was accomplished under Mohammed's successors, the caliphs (or Companions of Mohammed), of whom there were four. They in turn were succeeded by the Umayyad dynasty (661-750) in Damascus, followed by the Abbasid line (749-1258) in the newly built city of Baghdad.

Islam quickly spread west, first taking in Egypt and then fanning out across North Africa. By the end of the 7th century, the Muslims had reached the Atlantic and thought themselves sufficiently in control of the Gezirat al-Maghreb (Island of the West, or North Africa beyond Egypt) to consider marching on Spain in 710.

Five Pillars of Islam Islam is now the religion of almost all the inhabitants of the Maghreb. In order to live out a devout life, Muslims are expected at least to carry out the five pillars of Islam:

shahada – this is the profession of faith, Islam's basic tenet: 'There is no god but Allah, and Mohammed is the Prophet of Allah' (*Allahu akbar, Ashhadu an la Ilah ila Allah, Ashhadu an Mohammed rasul Allah ...*). It is a phrase commonly heard, as part of the call to prayer and at many other events, such as births and deaths. The first part has virtually become an exclamation good for any time of life or situation. People can often be heard muttering it to themselves, as if seeking a little strength to get through the trials of the day.

sala – sometimes written 'salat', this is the obligation of prayer, ideally five times a day, when muezzins call the faithful to pray. Although Muslims can pray anywhere, it is considered more laudable to do so together in a mosque (masjid or *jami'*). The important midday prayers on Friday (the loose equivalent of Sunday Mass for Catholics) are usually held in the jami', which is the main district mosque.

zakat – the giving of alms to the poor was from the start an essential part of the social teaching of Islam, and was later developed in some parts of the Muslim world into various forms of tax to redistribute funds to the needy. The moral obligation towards one's poorer neighbours continues to be emphasised at a personal level, and there are often exhortations to give posted up outside mosques.

sawm – Ramadan, the ninth month of the Muslim calendar, commemorates the revelation of the Qur'an to Mohammed. In a demonstration of the Muslims' renewal of faith, they are asked not to let *anything* pass their lips from dawn to dusk and to refrain from sex every day of the month. For more information on the month of fasting, see Islamic Holidays later in this section.

hajj – the pinnacle of a devout Muslim's life is the pilgrimage to the holy sites in and around Mecca. Ideally, the pilgrim should go to Mecca in the last month of the year, Zuul Hijja, to join Muslims from all over the world in the pilgrimage and the subsequent feast. The returned pilgrim can be addressed as 'hajji' and, in simpler villages at least, it is still quite common to see the word 'al-hajj' and simple scenes painted on the walls of houses showing that their inhabitants have made the pilgrimage. For more details see Islamic Holidays later in this section.

Sunnis & Shiites The power struggle between Ali, Mohammed's son-in-law and the last of the four caliphs, and the emerging Umayyad dynasty in Damascus caused a great schism at the heart of the new religion. The succession to the caliphate had been marked by considerable intrigue and bloodshed. Ali, the father of Mohammed's male heirs, lost the struggle, and the Umayyad leader was recognised as the legitimate successor to the caliphate.

Those who favoured the Umayyad caliph became known as Sunnis. The majority of Muslims are Sunnis, considered to be the orthodox mainstream of Islam. The Shiites, on the other hand, recognise only the successors of Ali.

The Sunnis have divided into four schools of religious thought, each lending varying degrees of importance to different aspects of doctrine. In Tunisia, where the population is almost entirely Sunni, it is the Malekite school that predominates. The Malekites, along with the Hanafite school, are somewhat less rigid in their application and interpretation of the Qur'an than the other schools.

This liberal trend had already emerged by the 15th century, when *qadis* (community judges) are recorded as having applied shari'a (Qur'anic law) in accordance with local custom rather than to the letter.

Saints & Mysticism From an early point in the life of Islam, certain practitioners sought to move closer to God through individual effort and spiritual devotion, rather than simply living by God's laws. These people

Sufism
The mystical Islamic sect of Sufism was formed by ascetics who wished to achieve a mystical communion with God through spiritual development rather than the study of the Qur'an. This brought them into conflict with the religious orthodoxy, but because they were prepared to make concessions to local rites and superstitions, they were able to attract large numbers of people who had not embraced Islam. The Sufis also believed in the miraculous powers of saints, and saints' tombs became places of worship. A particular aspect of Berber Sufism in North Africa is maraboutism – the worship of a holy man endowed with magical powers.

Literally hundreds of different Sufi orders sprang up throughout the Islamic world. The differences between them lay largely in the rituals they performed and how far they deviated from the Qur'an. They were regarded with a good deal of suspicion, which was exacerbated by some of their peculiar devotional practices such as eating glass and walking on coals (which they did in order to come closer to God).

The Sufis held positions of power in Tunisia, particularly in rural areas, following the breakdown of Almohad rule in the 13th century. ■

came to be known as Sufis (from *suf* meaning wool and referring to the simple cord they tended to wear as a belt), and various orders emerged throughout the lands where Islam held sway.

Orthodox Muslims have always regarded such manifestations with suspicion, particularly as the orders tend to gather in the name of a holy man (or *wali*, a term which has come to be loosely translated as 'saint', although saints in the Christian sense play no role in Islam). Public gatherings take many forms, from the dances of the whirling dervishes to more ecstatic and extreme demonstrations of self-mutilation (participants may, for instance, push skewers into their cheeks, apparently without feeling any pain).

The orders generally gather at the mosque or tomb of their saint and follow a particular *tariqa* (path), or way of worshipping. Various orders have acquired permanence over the

FRANCES LINZEE GORDON

A location to die for – the mosque below the hill-top village of Chenini.

centuries, and 'membership' can run through generations of the same families, tracing their lineage back to the original saint or spiritual master and through him to the Prophet (the veracity of such links is of secondary importance).

For orthodox Muslims, veneration of the saint is tantamount to worship of an idol, although Sufis would not see it that way. The wali is a 'friend' (the more literal meaning of the word) of God and so an intermediary, and all marabouts (or holy men) are regarded in a similar fashion. The great *moussems* or pilgrimages to the tombs of such saints are as much a celebration of the triumph of the spirit as an act of worship of a particular saint.

Islamic Customs When a baby is born, the first words uttered to it are the call to prayer. A week later this is followed by a ceremony in which the baby's head is shaved and an animal is sacrificed.

The major event of a boy's childhood is circumcision, which normally takes place sometime between the ages of seven and 12.

Marriage ceremonies are colourful and noisy affairs which usually take place in summer. One custom is for all the males to get in their cars and drive around the streets in a convoy making as much noise as possible. The vows are made some time prior to the ceremony, which usually takes place in the home of the bride or groom. The partying goes on until the early hours of the morning, often until sunrise.

The death ceremony is simple: a burial service is held at the mosque and the body is then buried with the feet facing Mecca.

When Muslims pray, they must follow certain rituals. First they must wash their hands, arms, feet, head and neck in running water before praying; all mosques have an area set aside for this purpose. If they are not in a mosque and there is no water available, clean sand suffices; and where there is no sand, they must just go through the motions of washing.

Then they must face Mecca (all mosques are oriented so that the mihrab, or prayer niche, faces the right direction) and follow a set pattern of gestures – photos of rows of Muslims kneeling in the direction of Mecca with their heads touching the ground are legion. You regularly see Muslims praying by the side of the road as well as in mosques. In everyday life, Muslims are prohibited from drinking alcohol and eating pork (considered unclean).

Islamic Holidays The principal religious holidays in Muslim countries are tied to the lunar Hijra calendar. The word *hijra* refers to the flight of the Prophet Mohammed from Mecca to Medina in 622 AD, which marks the first year of the calendar (the year 622 AD is the year 1 AH). The calendar is about 11 days shorter than the Gregorian (western) calendar, meaning that in western terms the holidays fall at different times each year. See under Public Holidays in the Facts for the Visitor chapter for a table of dates of Islamic holidays.

Ras as-Sana This means New Year's day, and is celebrated on the first day of the Hijra calendar year, 1 Moharram.

Achoura This is a day of public mourning observed by Shiites on 10 Moharram. It commemorates the assassination of Hussain ibn Ali, grandson of the Prophet Mohammed and pretender to the caliphate, which led to the schism between Sunnis and Shiites.

Mawlid an-Nabi This is a lesser feast celebrating the birth of the Prophet Mohammed on 12 Rabi' al-Awal. For a long time it was not celebrated at all in the Islamic world. In the Maghreb this is generally known as Mouloud.

Ramadan & 'Eid al-Fitr Most Muslims, albeit not all with equal rigour, take part in the fasting that characterises the month of Ramadan, a time when the faithful are called upon as a community to renew their relationship with God. Ramadan is the month in which the Qur'an was first revealed. From dawn until dusk, a Muslim is expected to refrain from eating, drinking, smoking and sex. This can be a difficult discipline, and only people in good health are asked to participate. Those engaged in exacting physical work or travelling are considered exempt. In a sense, every evening during Ramadan is a celebration. *Iftar* or *ftur*, the breaking of the day's fast, is a time of animated activity, when the people of the local community come together not only to eat and drink but also to pray.

Non-Muslims are not expected to participate, even if more pious Muslims suggest you do. Restaurants and cafes that are open during the day may be harder to come by, and at any rate you should try to avoid openly flouting the fast – there's nothing worse for the strung-out and hungry smoker than seeing non-Muslims cheerfully wandering about, cigarettes in hand and munching away.

The end of Ramadan, or more accurately the first days of the following month of Shawwal, mark the 'Eid al-Fitr, the Feast of

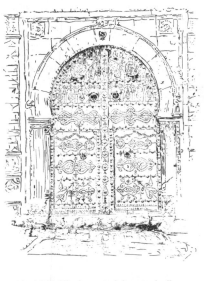

An intricately decorated door, typically Tunisian, from a 19th century engraving.

the Breaking of the Fast (also known as the 'Eid as-Sagheer, the Small Feast), which generally lasts for four or five days, during which time just about everything grinds to a halt. This is not a good time to travel, but can be a great experience if you are invited to share in some of the festivities with a family. It is a very family-oriented feast, much as Christmas is to Christians.

Hajj & 'Eid al-Adha The fifth pillar of Islam, a sacred duty of all who can afford it, is to make the pilgrimage to Mecca – the hajj. It can be done at any time, but at least once should be accomplished in Zuul Hijja, the 12th month of the Muslim year. At this time, thousands of Muslims from all over the world converge on Islam's most holy city.

The high point is the visit to the Ka'aba, the construction housing the stone of Ibrahim in the centre of the *haram*, the sacred area into which non-Muslims are forbidden to enter. The faithful, dressed only in a white robe, circle the Ka'aba seven times and kiss the black stone. This is one of a series of acts of devotion carried out by pilgrims.

The hajj culminates in the ritual slaughter of a lamb (in commemoration of Ibrahim's sacrifice) at Mina. This marks the end of the pilgrimage and the beginning of the *'Eid al-Adha*, or Feast of the Sacrifice (aka the Grand Feast, or *'Eid al-Kabeer)*. Throughout the Muslim world the act of sacrifice is repeated, and the streets of towns and cities seem to run with the blood of slaughtered sheep. The holiday runs from 10 to 13 Zuul-Hijja.

Islamic Architecture
in Tunisia

Title page: Interior of the 7th century Great Mosque at Kairouan. (Photograph by Damien Simonis)

Above: The minbar is the place from where the sermon is delivered.

Above: Minaret of the Zitouna Mosque in Tunis, from a 19th century engraving.

History

From the 7th century onwards, Tunisia – like the rest of North Africa, the Middle East, northern India and Spain – came under the control of Islam. The resulting impact on the country's culture was enormous and Tunisia's architecture, like many of its arts, was heavily influenced by Islamic styles.

With the course of time, however, Tunisia developed its own style. The country's particular climate, history, social structure and natural resources all played their part in this, as did its situation on the major trade routes which brought it into contact with other foreign influences. The angular, austere style of early Aghlabite mosques, for example, is in stark contrast to both the opulent buildings of the Ottoman Turks and the decorative, Persian-influenced structures found in Iraq.

Nevertheless, much of the philosophy and the basic principles behind Islamic construction remained the same throughout the Arab world, including Tunisia.

Religious Architecture

Mosques The mosque or *masjid* (also known as *jami'*) embodies the Islamic faith and represents one of its predominant architectural features. The building was developed in the very early days of the religion and takes its form from the simple, private houses where believers would customarily gather for worship.

The prototype for all designs is said to be the house belonging to the Prophet Mohammed in Medina. The original setting was an enclosed, oblong courtyard with huts (housing Mohammed's wives) along one side wall and a rough portico, or *zulla*, providing shade at one end for the poorer worshippers.

This plan can be seen in almost all mosques. The courtyard has become the *sahn*, the portico the arcaded *riwaqs* and the houses the *haram* or prayer hall. Divided into a series of aisles which segregate the sexes, the prayer hall can reach immense proportions in the larger mosques. Running down the centre is a broad aisle which leads to the *mihrab*, the vaulted niche in the *qibla*. Built to face Mecca, this wall indicates the direction of prayer.

It is also the site of the *minbar*, a kind of pulpit raised above a narrow staircase. As a rule, only the main community mosque, or jamaa, contains a minbar. In grander mosques, the minbar is often ornately and beautifully decorated. They are less commonly found in the smaller local mosques.

On Friday, the minbar is the place from where the *khutba* (weekly sermon) is delivered to the congregation. Islam does not recognise priests as such, but the closest equivalent is the *imam*, a learned man schooled in Islam and Islamic law. Often he doubles as the mosque's *muezzin*, who calls the faithful to prayer five times a day.

Before entering the haram and participating in the communal worship, Muslims must perform a ritual washing at the mosque's fountain or basin. This is placed in the middle of the courtyard and is usually carved from marble; in the older mosques, it's often worn from centuries of use.

Beyond its obvious religious function, the mosque also serves as a kind of community centre, school, and point of social contact. You'll often see groups of children or adults sitting cross-legged on reed mats in quiet discussion or studying the Qur'an. Others choose to shelter here or pause for thought in the cool, peaceful tranquillity that the mosque invariably provides.

The most important mosque in Tunisia is the Mosque of Sidi Oqba (Great Mosque) in Kairouan, founded at the end of the 7th century. Rebuilt by the Aghlabites in the 9th century, its typically austere exterior is in marked contrast to the elaborate interior decoration, developed over many centuries. Unfortunately, as with other mosques that are open to tourists, non-Muslims are not allowed beyond the courtyard.

Minarets The minaret (from the word *menara*, meaning lighthouse) is the tower at one corner of the mosque. Usually (based on the design of Syrian towers) it consists of a square base leading to more slender cylindrical or

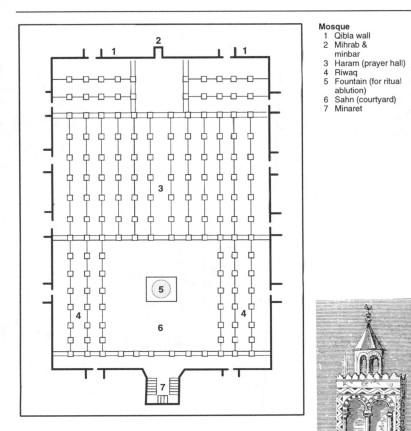

Mosque
1 Qibla wall
2 Mihrab & minbar
3 Haram (prayer hall)
4 Riwaq
5 Fountain (for ritual ablution)
6 Sahn (courtyard)
7 Minaret

octagonal stages. Most minarets have internal staircases for the muezzins to climb; the advent of the microphone saves them the effort now.

In the Maghreb (Tunisia, Algeria and Morocco) and Spain, however, the dominant style of minaret is square-based all the way to the top. This is the most prominent characteristic of what is often referred to as Andalusian religious architecture. The comparison between such minarets and the bell-towers of many Spanish churches is revealing.

Medersas Originating in 10th century Persia, medersas served as residential colleges where theology and Muslim law were taught. Some also functioned as early universities. They comprise an open-air courtyard, with an ablution fountain in the centre and a main prayer hall at the far end, surrounded by an upper gallery of student cells. The medersas are remarkable not so much for their architecture, but for their incredibly elaborate decoration, which includes detailed carving, zellij tile work, Kufic script and muqarna stuccowork. There are some good examples of medersas in the Tunis medina, including the three near the Zitouna Mosque on Souq des Libraires. The Medersa of the Palm Tree still serves as a Qur'anic school

Minarets usually have internal staircases, which the muezzins used to have to climb to call the faithful to prayer.

and is closed to the public, but the Medersa Bachia and Medersa Slimania can both be visited.

The master craftsmen who designed them liked to challenge visitors to find a single square inch free of artwork.

Medersa
1 Main Entrance
2 Shops
3 Porticos
4 Courtyard
5 Fountain
6 Lecture Rooms
7 Student Cells
8 Prayer Hall
9 Mihrab & Minbar
10 Mosque
11 Qur'anic School
12 Minaret
13 Toilet

Zaouias Other religious buildings in Tunisia, in complete contrast to the medersa, include the very simple *zaouia*. Dotted throughout the towns, villages and countryside of Tunisia, these whitewashed, earth-walled huts mark the tombs of *marabouts*, Muslim holy men. The word 'marabout' is also used to refer to the tomb; zaouias are an expanded version of a marabout, with a prayer hall and, sometimes, lodging for visitors.

Widespread as they are, the zaouias play a very important role in the lives of the local communities. They serve not just as sites for pilgrimages (for those in search of *baraka*, a blessing), but also as weekly markets and charitable and community centres. Once a year, a *moussem* is held in honour of the marabout, and is the occasion of often very exuberant festivals. (See also the boxed text 'Sufism' under Religion in the Facts about the Country chapter.)

Whitewashed domes of marabouts dot the Tunisian landscape.

Mausoleums The mausoleums are similar to the zaouias, but on a much grander scale. Although Islam forbids the building of elaborate tombs, mausoleums erected in the memory of great rulers became, after mosques and palaces, the most important structures in Islam.

For a powerful leader, a building constructed after his death was as important as one built during his life: they symbolised above all his great power. Although Tunisia has nothing in the same league as India's extraordinary Mughal

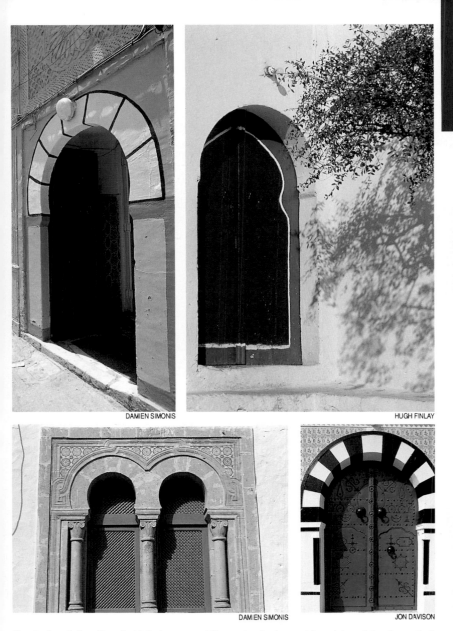

DAMIEN SIMONIS

HUGH FINLAY

DAMIEN SIMONIS

JON DAVISON

Symbolic of the threshold between public and private worlds, elaborately decorated doorways are a feature of many Tunisian houses.

Doors, such as this one in the Tunis medina, are usually made of solid wood, decorated with metal studs. They are set within characteristic keyhole-shaped stone frames, which are sometimes painted black and white. The small metal grilles are the only opening in what is meant to be a barrier between family life within the home and the public world.

tomb, the Taj Mahal, several tombs are nevertheless very much worth a visit. Unusually, they are open to non-Muslims. Among them is the Tourbet el-Bey in Tunis, built during the reign of Ali Pasha II (1758-82) to house the tombs of the Husseinite beys.

Military Architecture

Islamic military architecture is characterised by three major features: walls, gates and citadels (*kasbahs*).

Initially, such fortifications were only erected in frontier towns. From the late 9th and 10th centuries, right up until the advent of artillery rendered them useless, vast fortified walls, mighty towers, and elaborate gates became a crucial feature of almost every city and town.

Walls & Towers Vast city ramparts are a feature of many towns and cities in Tunisia. Undistinguished architecturally, they are impressive more for their size. The most impressive city walls are those surrounding the ancient medinas of Sfax and Sousse, built by the Aghlabites in the 9th century AD.

Typically, they were constructed of rock set in clay, and served as barracks, granaries, and arsenals. Other features of the walls include crenellations, walkways and machicolations.

Gates The Islamic gate, or *bab*, was designed above all to impress. It was a symbol of power, security and riches, as well as a fortified entrance to the city. For historians, gates are also a very useful indication of the building techniques and

DAMIEN SIMONIS

Built to impress and daunt – the formidable walls of Sousse medina.

materials of the time. Mahdia's formidable Skifa el-Kahla is a good example of a gate that was designed to daunt rather than welcome.

In general, two crenellated, stone-block towers flank the central bay in which the gate is set. The arch itself most frequently takes the horseshoe form and encloses or is enclosed by multifoil curves. The gates are usually highly decorated with friezes, using geometric, flower and foliage or shell motifs.

Citadels The citadel or kasbah, as it's commonly known in the western Islamic world, was usually constructed at the same time as the city walls and gates. From the 9th century, almost any town of any significance had one.

Usually the kasbah was built astride the city's walls, or positioned in a commanding corner. Its location was designed above all to dominate both practically and symbolically the city it overlooked. There are some fine examples of kasbahs in Tunisia, including those at Bizerte, Monastir and Sousse, but none of them can rival the magnificent setting of the kasbah that towers over the ancient fortress city of Le Kef.

Domestic Architecture

The Tunisian town house has remained largely unaltered for five millennia. Known as the *dar* or interior courtyard house, it is typical of the Islamic dwellings of the Middle East and Mediterranean.

DAMIEN SIMONIS

Black and white arched doorways, such as this one at the Jamia al-Medina Mosque in Bizerte, are a distinctive feature in Tunisian medinas.

The principal feature is a central courtyard, around which are grouped suites of rooms in a symmetrical pattern. In the wealthier houses, service areas are often tacked on to one side, and these in turn might have their own courtyard as necessity and means dictate.

The interior courtyard serves a very important function as a modifier of the climate in hot, dry regions. With very few exterior windows, the courtyards function as a kind of 'light well' into which the light penetrates during the day, and an 'air well', into which the cool, dense air of evening sinks at night.

One of the great advantages of this set-up is that it permits outdoor activities, with protection from the wind, dust and sun. The system also allows natural ventilation. Because the house is surrounded by tall walls, the sun's rays cannot reach the courtyard until later in the afternoon. When they do reach the courtyard, and heated air rises, convection currents set up a flow of air that ventilates the house and keeps it cool.

While rooms in European houses are usually allotted a specific function, the rooms in Muslim houses are more multipurpose. Rooms can be used interchangeably for eating, relaxing and sleeping.

The function of interiors can also change with the time of day. In summer, the hottest part of the day is spent in the cool of the courtyard, and at night, the roof terrace can be used as a sleeping area.

Again, reflecting the Islamic architectural concern with the interior space of a building, decoration is reserved for the internal elements such as the courtyard, and not, as is the European style, the external elements. The street façade is usually just a plain wall, and the only opening is the entrance door. Any other openings are small, grilled and above the line of vision of passers-by. This reflects the strict demarcation of public and private life in Islamic society.

Sometimes the doors of houses can be elaborately decorated, marking the symbolic importance of the house entrance – the vulnerable threshold between private and public worlds. Auspicious symbols, designs and colours are often used, such as the stylised design of the hand of Fatima, seen so commonly in the medinas (old city quarters) of Tunisia.

The importance of privacy is also extended into the interior of the house. The word for women, *harim,* is related to the word *haram* (harem), 'sacred area', which, far removed from its western connotations, denotes the family living quarters.

Courtyard House
1 Entrance (placed to obscure view into courtyard)
2 Men's reception room
3 Courtyard & gardens
4 Living & sleeping area (harem)
5 Service & storage area
6 Stable
7 Formal salon
8 Kitchen
9 Toilet
10 Well
11 Fountain/pool

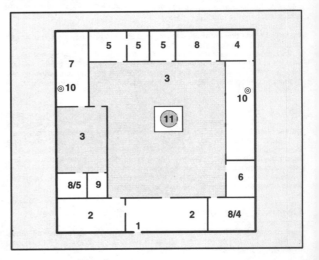

The harem, or domestic area of the house, is primarily the women's domain. The husband usually has his own room just outside this area. In the interiors of some houses, *mashrabiyya*, or perforated wooden screens, are sometimes erected in front of a harem which opens onto the reception room. This allows women to observe men's gatherings and festivities without being observed themselves.

Forming an essential part of the wealthier town houses are the interior gardens. These can be elaborately paved with ceramic tiles, and richly planted. Paths, often raised above ground level, divide the flower beds. Usually the centre of the garden is dominated by a fountain or pool – even the poorer houses may contain some focal point such as a tree, shrub or ornamental object. This design again is closely connected to the climate: the evaporation of water and the presence of plants both raise the humidity and keep the air cool.

The garden also has a strongly symbolic and recreational function too. To the Muslim, the beauty of creation and of the garden is held to be a reflection of God. Within the dusty wilderness of the city, and hidden behind a small door, lies a sudden paradise of vegetation and tranquillity.

Medinas, like this one at Kairouan, are great places for just sitting and watching the world go by.

DAMIEN SIMONIS

Urban Architecture

Unlike European urban centres, Islamic villages, towns and cities rarely conform to any geometric symmetry of town planning. More commonly, cities are divided into town quarters.

This ancient system is found throughout the Islamic world, and is thought to have originated in 8th century Baghdad. Again, in contrast to western towns, quarters are not divided by social status; instead, the communal mosque, hammam, fountain, oven and school, are shared by all residents, rich and poor.

Despite their chaotic appearance, the old Islamic towns (medinas) are carefully adapted to the rigours of the climate. Like the domestic house, the deep, narrow streets of the medina keep the sun's rays from the centre during the day, and draw in the cool, dense evening air during the night.

The massing of multistoreyed structures sharing walls also reduces the total surface area exposed to the sun. Traditional building materials such as earth, stone and wood absorb water, which then evaporates from their surfaces and cools the surrounding air.

Souqs The *souq* or bazaar, along with the mosque and possibly the hammam, make up the quintessential elements of a Muslim town. The souq is also the commercial backbone of the city.

At first sight, it appears a hotchpotch of houses randomly erected wherever the tiniest space allows. In reality, a very particular order governs the layout of the souq. This pattern is amazingly constant, and can be found all over the Islamic world, from the Maghreb to India.

The standard plan consists of a network of streets covered with vaults, domes or awnings. The streets are lit by openings in the central bays which allow light to penetrate, but keep the interior cool and well ventilated. The design owes much in its form to the classical Greek precedent with the agora and its surrounding buildings, and colonnaded market place.

The congregational mosque provides the focal point of the souq, and around it the shops are grouped in a strict hierarchy. First come the vendors of candles, incense and other objects used in the rites of worship. Next to them are the booksellers, long venerated by Muslim cultures, and the vendors of small leather goods. These are followed by the clothing and textile stalls, long the domain of the richest and most powerful merchants.

The hierarchy then descends through furnishings, domestic goods and utensils, until, with the most ordinary wares, the walls and gates of the city are reached.

Here, on the city perimeters, where the caravans often used to assemble, are the ironmongers, blacksmiths and the other craftsmen and vendors serving the caravan trade. Among them are the saddlers, suppliers of sacking and string, tents and whatever else the traveller might need in preparation for a long journey.

Furthest afield are the potteries and the tanneries, usually exiled to beyond the city walls because of the noxious odours and smoke they produce.

Funduqs Muslim civilisations have always been mobile. Arab conquerors were originally nomadic; huge Muslim armies were constantly on the move, and students and scholars undertook long journeys to sit at the feet of famous masters. From the earliest days of Islam, pilgrims travelled long distances

Funduq
1 Shops, mills, warehouses, bakeries, teashops & stabling (ground floor); pilgrim's cells (second floor)
2 Peristyle
3 Courtyard
4 Doorway
5 Mosque

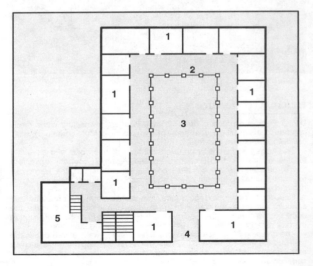

for the *hajj* (pilgrimage) to Mecca. Above all, there was the strong tradition of trade, with merchants travelling vast distances to buy and sell goods. This led to the creation of caravanserais, known in Tunisia as *funduqs*, which sprang up at regular intervals along the major trade routes of the entire Islamic world.

Their function was similar to that of modern-day motels or motorway cafes, providing food and accommodation for both traveller and their transport, usually camels, mules or horses.

In general, they were unremarkable architecturally. An unadorned façade provided a doorway wide enough to allow camels or heavily laden beasts to enter. The central courtyard was usually open to the sky and was surrounded by a number of similar stalls, bays or niches, usually arranged over two floors. The ground floor housed shops, warehouses, tea shops and stabling for the animals, and the second floor accommodated the travellers.

Funduqs were once found in all Tunisia's major towns. At Houmt Souq, on the island of Jerba, four of the town's old funduqs have been converted into tourist accommodation and are well worth seeking out.

Hammams Another essential feature of Islamic towns and societies is the *hammam* or public bath. Although serving a mundane function, the hammam can be a surprisingly impressive architectural structure. Most commonly, however, they are identifiable only by the smoking chimney and low, glass-studded dome.

The Muslim hammam is directly descended from the baths of classical times, although with time the emphasis shifted from social and sporting purposes to the Muslim concern with cleanliness.

Traditionally, the hammam consists of a spacious, domed disrobing room, with a pool in the centre. Next in the bathing sequence is the cold room, an elongated room with three domes, which is furthest from the heating room. Afterwards comes the warm room, larger and more elaborately constructed and decorated than the cold room, with niches in the four corners of the chamber where the bather can recline.

The hot or steam room is the next stop and is the simplest room with a low, domed ceiling. A final stop is made in the warm room where the bather can be cleansed and massaged, soaped, shampooed and rinsed by bath attendants.

Frances Linzee Gordon
David Willett

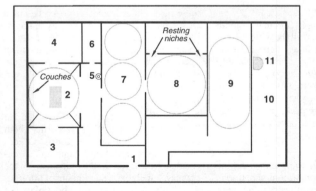

Hamman
1 Entrance (zigzag design)
2 Disrobing room with pool plus couches to rest on; tea, coffee or sherbet is served after bathing
3 Attendant's room
4 Relaxing room
5 Fountain
6 Toilet
7 Cold room, traditionally with three domes
8 Warm room with niches for reclining bathers; bath attendants assist with washing, massage and rinsing
9 Hot room
10 Heating room
11 Boiler & furnace

Facts for the Visitor

PLANNING
When to Go
Tunisia's tourism year peaks in July and August when about two million Northern European holiday-makers descend on the country in search of guaranteed sunshine. This makes it a good time to stay away. Hotels prices go up, rooms can be hard to find and public transport gets packed out. It's also too hot for serious activity between 10 am and 6 pm, which places considerable restrictions on activities like visits to ancient sites.

The best time to visit is between mid-March and mid-May. The spring days are pleasantly warm and the countryside is at its prettiest after the winter rains. By the middle of May, the summer heat has arrived and doesn't start to relent until the middle of September. From mid-September until the beginning of December, conditions are again ideal for touring around.

Winter is wet and dreary in the north, but it is the best time to see the migratory birds at Lake Ichkeul. It's also the perfect time to visit the Saharan south.

What Kind of Trip?
How Long? Most people find that a month is long enough to take in all the major places of interest without rushing themselves off their feet. Tunisia is also a perfect place to go for a short break from Europe, perhaps as an impulse holiday to get away from whatever the latest weather atrocity might be. The country's huge package tourism industry means that cheap tickets are always available with the charter airlines.

Packages Unless you want to stay on the coast in the high season, accommodation is readily available and you need do no more than turn up. Some first-time visitors opt to buy a flight/accommodation package with the idea of using the hotel as a base, but it's not worth it. Such accommodation is always in some giant resort hotel on one of the many tourist strips. You're better off avoiding them and looking for your own accommodation in the local towns; all the major towns have a range of places to choose from. If you want a base, most hotels will be happy to store baggage for you while you tour around. It's not particularly important where you fly to – nowhere is more than nine hours by bus from Tunis.

Travelling Companions Travelling alone is much easier for single men than for single women (see also the Women Travellers section later in this chapter). Travelling with a friend or a group of friends has the advantage of enabling you to share the cost of a hire car, which then opens up a whole new range of possibilities for exploring off the beaten track.

If you decide to travel with others, bear in mind that travel can put relationships to the test in a way that few other experiences can. Many a long-term friendship has collapsed under the strain of constant negotiations on where to stay and eat, what to do and where to go next. Other friendships become much closer than before – there's no way of knowing until you try it. It's a good idea to agree on a rough itinerary before you go, and to be operating with similar budgets. Above all, you need to be flexible.

Maps
The government-run Office National du Tourisme Tunisien (ONTT) has offices both in Tunisia and abroad (see Tourist Offices later in this chapter) and hands out a reasonable free 1:1,000,000 road map of the country. It includes a fair amount of information, in English and French, about places of interest, but it is a long time since it was updated. A lot of new roads have been built in the interim, and many roads in the south

that previously could be tackled only by 4WD have been upgraded or sealed.

If you are planning on travelling off the beaten track, you'll need to buy something better. It's hard to find too much wrong with Michelin's *Algeria-Tunisia*, except that you're unlikely to find much use for the Algerian section. No 958 is the most recent edition, last published in 1995. The previous edition, No 972, is still on sale in some places. Michelin maps are sold at bookshops in Tunisia, unlike those of its competitor Freytag & Berndt. Its 1:800,000 map of Tunisia is the most comprehensive map available, but you will need to buy it before you travel.

What to Bring

Bring the minimum. When you have gathered all the stuff you think you're going to need, throw half of it out and you'll probably be close to a sensible amount. There is nothing worse than having to lug loads of excess stuff around. Unless it's essential, leave it at home!

A rucksack is far more practical than an overnight bag and more likely to stand up to the rigours of travel. It is worth paying for a good one. Buckles and straps soon start falling off cheap rucksacks and before long all you have is a worthless bit of junk. What type of pack you take is a matter of personal preference. Berghaus, Lowe and Karrimor are three recommended brands, and one of the best stockists in London is the YHA Adventure Centre, 14 Southampton St, London WC2E 7HA (☎ (0171) 836 8541).

Your clothing needs depend on the time of year and where you are going. In summer, you need little more than light cotton clothes on the coast, but you will need to pack a light sweater if you are planning on venturing into the interior. The nights are cool in the mountains even in summer, and it gets surprisingly cold in the Sahara. In winter, you need to pack for all climates; rainproof clothing is a good idea as it can get quite wet.

Also bear in mind the clothing guidelines outlined in the Society & Conduct section in the Facts about the Country chapter.

For most of the year, a hat, sunglasses and sunscreen are useful, and they are indispensable in the desert. Other handy items include a Swiss Army knife, compass (especially in the desert and mountains), a torch (flashlight), a universal sink plug, a few metres of nylon cord (in case you need to rig up a washing line), earplugs (to aid sleep in the noisier cheapies), a small sewing kit and a medical kit (see the Health section later in this chapter for more details).

Most toiletries – soap, shampoo, toothpaste, toilet paper, washing powder – are available all over Tunisia, although tampons are usually only found in supermarkets. Condoms are cheap and readily available over the counter at pharmacies.

SUGGESTED ITINERARIES

The following itineraries are designed to help travellers to make the most of their time in Tunisia.

If you are in Tunisia for only a week, it's best to stick to exploring one area. There is a choice of one week itineraries based on arrival at each of the country's three major international airports – Tunis, Monastir and Jerba. There is also a choice of two week itineraries, which combine regions, and finally a four week grand tour that takes in all the highlights.

One Week

Northern Tunisia Start in Tunis, visit the Bardo Museum, the medina and Carthage (two days); then catch an early bus to Dougga and explore the site on the way to Le Kef (one day). Catch an early bus to Jendouba and visit Bulla Regia then continue to 'Ain Draham (one day). Travel slowly down to the coast at Tabarka, stopping for a walk through the cork forest on the way (one day); relax on the beach in Tabarka (one day), before returning to Tunis.

Central Tunisia Start in Sousse and visit the medina and the museum (two days). Visit Kairouan (one day) and head south to Sfax, stopping on the way at El-Jem (one day). Explore the medina in Sfax (one day), then

HIGHLIGHTS
Chapter locations are given in brackets

Archaeological

Bulla Regia *(Northern Tunisia)*
Famous as the site where the Romans went underground, building their villas with a subterranean level to escape the heat.

Carthage *(Tunis)*
The Romans did such a thorough job of levelling ancient Carthage that little remains. Nonetheless, history buffs will want to stand on top of the Byrsa Hill and survey the setting of the city that once dominated the western Mediterranean.

Dougga *(Northern Tunisia)*
This hill-top site is the best preserved of the many Roman towns in Tunisia. The star attraction is the magnificent capitol, which is one of the country's most photographed monuments.

El-Jem *(Central Tunisia)*
The enormous colosseum built by the Romans at El-Jem was the third largest in the Roman Empire. It rises spectacularly above the modern town, and can be seen for miles across the flat surrounding plains.

Sbeitla *(Central Tunisia)*
You'll need to be up with the birds to see the magnificent Roman temple complex at Sbeitla (Roman Sufetula) at its best; the temples glow a glorious orange in the early morning light.

Medinas

Kairouan *(Central Tunisia)*
Kairouan is Tunisia's holy city and its medina houses some of the country's finest examples of early Islamic architecture, especially the magnificent Great Mosque.

Mahdia *(Central Tunisia)*
The medina at Mahdia dates back to the 10th century when the town was founded as the capital of the Fatimid caliphs. It is a rare example of a medina that remains alive and well as a residential area. It's a fascinating place to explore, and the tourist shops have yet to take over.

Sfax *(Central Tunisia)*
For some reason, the country's mass tourism industry continues to bypass Sfax. The narrow, winding streets are the perfect place to get lost in for a few hours.

Tunis *(Tunis)*
Touristy or not, the medina of Tunis is a veritable treasure trove of Islamic architecture dating back over the centuries and should not be missed.

Museums

Bardo Museum *(Tunis)*
Foremost among the nation's museums, the Bardo is famous for its collection of Roman mosaics. It also houses the cream of the other finds from Tunisia's many ancient sites.

Sousse Museum *(Central Tunisia)*
Housed in the city's impressive kasbah, the museum has a good collection of mosaics as well as finds dating back to Punic times.

Dar Charait Museum *(Southern Tunisia)*
This private museum in the oasis town of Tozeur has some very well-presented scenes of Tunisian life past and present, ranging from the bedroom of the last bey to a traditional Berber tent. It also has an interesting collection of modern Tunisian paintings.

Activities

Bird-Watching *(Northern Tunisia)*
The World Heritage Listed Ichkeul National Park, near Bizerte, is an important wildlife sanctuary and a prime bird-watching site. Between November and March, the park is a wintering ground for a long list of migratory birds from all over Europe.

head north to visit Mahdia (one day) before returning to Sousse.

Southern Tunisia Start in Jerba and explore Houmt Souq and surrounds (one day). Travel south to Tataouine and then charter a *louage*
(shared taxi) out to Ksar Ouled Soltane (one day). Charter another louage to visit Douiret or Chenini, then head to Matmata via Gabès (one day). Return to Gabès and travel west across the Chott el-Jerid to Tozeur (two days). Catch an early bus to Douz and go on

Ballooning
(Southern Tunisia)

You can recreate the celebrated 'flying over the desert' scenes from the film *The English Patient* with AerOasis, which operates balloon trips over the desert from its base in Tozeur.

Trekking
(Northern Tunisia)

The forests of the Kroumirie Mountains around 'Ain Draham have enormous potential as a trekking destination. The region is stunningly beautiful and conditions are perfect for walking in spring and autumn. At present, however, the potential is limited by the absence of the sort of detailed local maps you need in order to venture off the beaten track.

Camel Trekking
(Southern Tunisia)

Camel trekking in the Sahara Desert around Douz is an experience not to be missed. Go for three or four days and you'll get a real taste of desert adventure, sleeping out under the stars around a fire.

Landscapes

Chott el-Jerid
(Southern Tunisia)

The largest of Tunisia's salt lakes, the Chott el-Jerid stretches into the distance south of the causeway linking Kebili and Tozeur. The causeway is lined with great drifts of salt that could easily be mistaken for snow were it not for the heat. The setting is especially beautiful beneath a full moon.

Palmeraie
(Southern Tunisia)

The palmeraie (palm groves) of the southern oases rank among Tunisia's more remarkable sights. Abundant ground water has been used to create veritable gardens of Eden in the middle of the harsh, surrounding desert. Flourishing beneath the shade of tall palms is an astonishing assortment of fruit and vegetables – everything from bananas and grapes to carrots and lettuce. The best examples are at Douz and Tozeur.

Berber Architecture

Chenini & Douiret
(Southern Tunisia)

The crumbling ruins of these stunning hill-top Berber villages are well worth the effort entailed in getting there from Tataouine. Both were abandoned relatively recently and are fascinating places to scramble around.

Ksar Ouled Soltane
(Southern Tunisia)

They've been heavily restored for the benefit of the tourist industry, but all the same the four-storey high ghorfas at Ksar Ouled Soltane are a remarkable sight.

Matmata
(Southern Tunisia)

The thousands of tourists who pour through here don't come without good reason. It's an amazing place – a surreal, lunar landscape dotted with the troglodyte pit homes of its Berber inhabitants. You'll enjoy Matmata more if you arrive late in the afternoon to avoid the crowds and spend a night at one of the troglodyte hotels.

Relaxation

Beaches

The beaches are the reason most tourists come to Tunisia. The best beaches are in the north around Tabarka and Bizerte and at Sidi Ali el-Mekki. The best of the rest are the sheltered (but very crowded) town beach at Monastir, and the beach at Aghir, on the island of Jerba.

Food & Wine

One speciality of Tunisian cuisine that's not to be missed is the curious *briq à l'oeuf*, a deep-fried triangle of crisp, wafer-thin pastry filled with an egg. They are yummy, and it doesn't matter if you get egg on your face. Connoisseurs can move on to deluxe versions like *briq aux fines herbes* (with herbs) or *briq aux crevettes* (with shrimp). Wash them down with one of Tunisia's excellent wines, such as Vieux Magon, a delicious full-bodied red.

---

an overnight camping trip into the desert (one day), before returning to Jerba.

Two Weeks
Northern & Central Tunisia Start in Tunis and visit the Bardo Museum, the medina,

Carthage and Sidi Bou Saïd (three days). Catch the train north to Bizerte (one day), then travel west along the north coast to Tabarka (one day). Travel slowly up to 'Ain Draham, stopping for a walk in the cork forest on the way (one day), then visit Bulla

Regia and continue via Jendouba to Le Kef (one day). Explore Le Kef and make a day trip to Dougga (two days), then travel southeast to Kairouan, stopping at Makthar on the way (one day). Explore Kairouan before heading to Sousse (one day); visit the Sousse medina and museum (one day). Head to Nabeul and use it as a base for a side trip to Kelibia and El-Haouaria (two days); then return to Tunis.

Central & Southern Tunisia Start your trip in Sousse and visit the medina and the museum (two days) there. Take a day trip to Monastir and then go to Kairouan (one day). Explore Kairouan before travelling on to Sbeitla (one day) to visit the Roman ruins at Sufetula. Then travel to Gafsa (one day) and ride the *Lezard Rouge* train through the Seldja Gorge (which requires advance planning) and continue to Tozeur (one day). Explore Tozeur (two days), then head across the Chott el-Jerid to Gabès. Travel out to Matmata (one day) before going on to Sfax (one day) via Gabès. Visit Mahdia (one day) and return to Sousse via El-Jem (one day).

Southern Tunisia Start off in Jerba; explore Houmt Souq and surrounds (two days) before travelling south to Tataouine. Charter a louage out to Ksar Ouled Soltane (one day); charter another louage for an early morning visit to Douiret or Chenini, then head to Ghomrassen and Ksar Haddada (one day). Visit Matmata via Gabès (one day) before returning to Gabès and travelling to Douz. Go camel trekking (two days) around Douz. Visit Tozeur (two days) and use it as a base for a side trip to the mountain oases of Chebika, Midès and Tamerza (one day). Organise a train ride through the Seldja Gorge on the way from Tozeur to Gafsa (one day), then travel via Gabès to Matmata (one day). Visit one of the villages around Matmata, before travelling to Medenine. Stay in Metameur (one day), then return to Jerba.

Four Weeks
Start in Tunis: visit the Bardo Museum, the medina, Carthage and Sidi Bou Saïd (three days). Catch the train north to Bizerte (one day) then travel west along the north coast to Tabarka (one day). Travel slowly up to 'Ain Draham, stopping for a walk in the cork forest on the way (one day). Visit Bulla Regia and continue via Jendouba to Le Kef (one day). Explore Le Kef and make a day trip to Dougga (two days); then travel southeast to Kairouan, stopping at Makthar on the way (one day).

Explore Kairouan early and then travel to Sbeitla (one day), where you can visit the Roman ruins at Sufetula. Travel to Gafsa (one day) and organise a ride on the *Lezard Rouge* train through the Seldja Gorge. Continue to Tozeur (one day); explore Tozeur (one day) and use it as a base for a side trip to the mountain oases of Chebika, Midès and Tamerza (one day). Travel across the Chott el-Jerid to Douz and go camel trekking (two days). Visit Matmata (one day) and one of the villages around Matmata before going on to Medenine and Metameur. Stay overnight

---

The Best & the Worst
Top 10

- The friendly people you meet when you travel alone
- Early morning visits to the *ksour* around Tataouine
- Oasis greenery
- The mountain oases west of Gafsa
- Islamic architecture in Kairouan, Mahdia and Tunis
- The colosseum at El-Jem
- Roman ruins at Dougga
- Walking in the forest around 'Ain Draham
- Spicy *chorba* (soup)
- Vieux Magon (red wine)

Bottom 10

- High season crowds
- Boring food at resort hotels
- Inadequate labelling at museums
- Matmata after 9 am
- Metlaoui
- Polluted waterways in Gabès
- The toilets at Ksar Ghilane
- The Tijani Zoo in Tozeur
- Carpet touts in Kairouan
- The cost of car hire

in Metameur (one day), then travel south to Tataouine and charter a louage out to Ksar Ouled Soltane (one day). Charter another louage for an early morning visit to Douiret or Chenini, then head to Ghomrassen and Ksar Haddada (one day). Travel via Medenine to Houmt Souq and use it as a base to explore Jerba (two days) before going up the coast to Sfax (one day). Continue to Mahdia (one day); and then travel via El-Jem to Sousse (one day). Visit the Sousse medina and museum before returning to Tunis (one day).

TOURIST OFFICES

The government-run Office National du Tourisme Tunisien (ONTT) handles tourist information. It has a network of offices throughout Tunisia as well as overseas.

Local Tourist Offices

The standard of service varies from super efficient (Sousse) to totally apathetic (Tunis). Most offices can supply no more than glossy brochures in half a dozen languages and a map. Some can supply a list of hotels and prices, and one or two have transport information. ONTT offices in Tunisia include the following:

Bizerte
    (☎ (02) 432 897) 1 Rue de Constantinople
Douz
    (☎ (05) 470 351) Place des Martyrs
Gabès
    (☎ (05) 270 254) Ave Hedi Chaker
Gafsa
    (☎ (06) 221 664) Place des Piscines Romaines
Hammamet
    (☎ (02) 280 423) Ave Habib Bourguiba
Jerba
    (☎ (05) 650 016) Rue Ulysse, Houmt Souq
Kairouan
    (☎ (07) 221 797) Ave de la République
Mahdia
    (☎ (03) 681 098) Rue el-Moez
Monastir
    (☎ (03) 461 960) Rue de l'Indépendance
Nabeul
    (☎ (02) 286 800) Ave Taieb Mehiri
Sfax
    (☎ (03) 211 040) Ave Mohammed Hedi Khefecha

Sousse
    (☎ (03) 225 157) 1 Ave Habib Bourguiba
Tabarka
    (☎ (08) 643 496) 2 Rue de Bizerte
Tozeur
    (☎ (06) 454 088) Ave Abdulkacem Chebbi
Tunis
    (☎ (01) 341 077) 1 Ave Mohammed V

Some towns have municipal tourist offices, called *syndicat d'initiative*, which tend to open only in the high season.

Tourist Offices Abroad

ONTT's foreign representatives tend to be much better equipped, and more enthusiastic, than their domestic counterparts. They include the following:

Austria
    (☎ (1) 408 39 60) Landesgerichstr 22, 1010 Vienna
Belgium
    (☎ (2) 511 11 42) Galerie Ravenstein 60, 1000 Brussels
Canada
    (☎ (514) 397-1182) 1253 McGill College, Montreal, Quebec H3A 3B6
France
    (☎ 04 78 52 35 86) 12, rue de Séze, 69006 Lyon; (☎ 01 47 42 72 67) 32, ave de l'Opéra, 75002 Paris
Germany
    (☎ (30) 8 85 04 57) Kurfuerstendamm 171, 10707 Berlin; (☎ (211) 8 42 18) Steinstrasse 23, 40210 Dusseldorf; (☎ (69) 23 18 91/2) Am Hauptbahnhof 6, 6329 Frankfurt am Main 1
Italy
    (☎ (2) 86 45 30) Via Baracchini 10, 20123 Milan; (☎ (6) 482 3665) Via Sardegna 17, 00187 Rome
Netherlands
    (☎ (20) 622 49 71) Muntplein 2, 1012 WR Amsterdam
Spain
    (☎ (3) 488 0182) C-/Consejo de Ciento, 08016 Barcelona; (☎ (1) 548 1435) Torre de Madrid 18, 28008 Madrid
Sweden
    (☎ (8) 678 06 45) Stureplan 15, 11145 Stockholm
Switzerland
    (☎ (1) 211 48 30) Bahnhofstrasse 69, 8001 Zürich
UK
    (☎ (0171) 224 5561; fax 224 4053) 77A Wigmore St, London W1H GLJ

VISAS & DOCUMENTS
Passport
Your most important travel document is your passport. Before you go, make sure that it is valid until well after your planned return. If there's any danger that it might expire while you're away, renew it before you go. Renewing a passport overseas can be a hassle and involve days of waiting. Even at home it can be a slow business, so don't leave it until the last minute. You can usually speed the process up by doing things in person rather than relying on the mail or on agents.

Once you start travelling, carry your passport at all times and guard it carefully. Hotels sometimes want to hold onto your passport, which can be inconvenient. You can usually get round this by paying for your room in advance or by offering a driving licence as an alternative.

Visas
A visa is a stamp in your passport (or sometimes a separate piece of paper) that permits you to enter the issuing country for a specified period of time. Fortunately, visas are not a problem for most visitors to Tunisia. Nationals of most western European countries can stay for up to three months without a visa – you just roll up and collect a stamp in your passport. Americans, Canadians, Germans and Japanese can stay for up to four months.

The situation is a bit more complicated for other nationalities but most visitors do not require a visa if arriving on an organised tour. Australians and New Zealanders travelling independently can get a two week visa at the airport for TD3, although some travellers have reported being given a month. South Africans can stay a month. Travellers wanting to stay longer should get a three month visa (TD6) before they arrive; these are available wherever Tunisia has diplomatic representation.

Israeli nationals are not allowed into the country.

Visa Extensions It is unlikely that you will need to extend your visa because a month in Tunisia is ample time for most people. If you

do, applications can be made only at the Interior Ministry on Ave Habib Bourguiba in Tunis. They cost TD3, payable only in revenue stamps (available from post offices), take up to 10 days to issue, and require two photographs, bank receipts and a *facture* (receipt) from your hotel. It may sound simple, but the process is more hassle than it's worth.

Photocopies
The hassles created by losing your passport, travellers cheques and other important documents can be reduced considerably if you take the precaution of having photocopies. It is a good idea to have photocopies of the passport pages that cover personal details, issue and expiry dates and the current entry stamp or visa. Other documents worth photocopying are airline tickets, credit cards, driving licence and insurance details. You should also keep a record of the serial numbers of your travellers cheques, crossing them off as you cash them.

This emergency material should be kept separate from the originals, so that hopefully they won't both get lost (or stolen) at the same time. Leave an extra copy with someone you can rely on at home just in case.

Travel Insurance
It is sensible to take out travel insurance. This not only covers you for medical expenses and luggage theft or loss, but also for cancellation or delays in your travel arrangements. (You could fall seriously ill a few days before departure, for example.) Cover depends on the type of insurance and the type of airline ticket, so ask both your insurer and your ticket-issuing agency to explain exactly where you stand and check the small print. Ticket loss is also covered by travel insurance. Some policies specifically exclude 'dangerous activities', which can include scuba diving, motorcycling, and even trekking. A locally acquired motorcycle licence is not valid under some policies.

You may prefer a policy which pays doctors or hospitals directly rather than you having to pay on the spot and claim later. If you have to claim later make sure you keep all documentation. Some policies ask you to call back (reverse charges) to a centre in your home country where an immediate assessment of your problem is made. Check that the policy covers ambulances or an emergency flight home.

Buy travel insurance as early as possible. You may find, for instance, that if you buy it at the last minute you are not covered for problems caused by strikes or other industrial action that started, or had been threatened, before you took out the insurance.

The best places to seek good insurance deals are travel agents specialising in youth or student travel, but make sure that the package you buy meets your needs. Ask, for example, about refund limits for special items like cameras and computers.

Paying for your airline ticket with a credit card sometimes provides limited travel insurance, and you may be able to reclaim the payment if the flight operator doesn't deliver. In the UK, institutions issuing credit cards are required by law to reimburse consumers if a company goes into liquidation and the amount in contention is more than UK£100. Ask your credit card company what it covers.

Driving Licence & Permits
If you plan to hire a car or motorbike of more than 50cc, you will need to bring your national driving licence, which you must have held for at least one year. International driving permits are also acceptable.

Hostel Card
You need to be a member of Hostelling International (HI) if you want to stay at any of the four affiliated hostels (see Hostels under Accommodation later in this chapter for more details). You can join on the spot at the hostel in Tunis (☎ (01) 567 850), which is at 25 Rue Saida Ajoula in the medina.

Student & Youth Cards
There are no advertised discounts for student cards – although it never hurts to ask. One traveller reported being given free admission

to some of the ancient sites on flashing a student card – probably because the site guardian mistook the card for some sort of official document.

Seniors' Cards
There are no special discounts for older travellers in Tunisia – holders of seniors' cards have as much chance of finding a discount as holders of student cards. See also the Senior Travellers section later in this chapter.

International Health Card
You'll need this little yellow booklet only if you're coming from parts of Africa where yellow fever has been reported. See the Health section later in this chapter for further details.

EMBASSIES
As a tourist, it's important to realise what your own embassy – the embassy of the country of which you are a citizen – can and can't do. Generally speaking, they won't help much in emergencies if the trouble you're in is remotely your own fault. Remember that you are bound by the laws of the country you're in. Embassies will not be sympathetic if you end up in jail after committing a crime locally, even if such actions are legal in your own country. In genuine emergencies you might get some assistance, but only if other channels have been exhausted. For example, if you need to get home urgently, a free ticket home is exceedingly unlikely – the embassy would expect you to have insurance. If you have all your money and documents stolen, they might assist with getting a new passport, but a loan for onward travel is out of the question.

Embassies used to keep letters for travellers or have a small reading room with home newspapers, but these days the mail-holding service has been stopped, and even their newspapers tend to be out of date.

On the more positive side, if you are heading into very remote or politically volatile areas, you might consider registering with your embassy so they know where you are, but make sure you tell them when you come back too. Some embassies post useful warning notices about local dangers or potential problems. The US embassies are particularly good for providing this information and it's worth scanning their notice boards for 'travellers advisories' about security, local epidemics, and dangers to lone travellers.

Tunisian Embassies

Following is a list of Tunisian embassies abroad which issue visas:

Algeria
(☎ (2) 69 20 857) Rue Ammar Rahmani, El-Biar, 16000 Algiers
Austria
(☎ (1) 581 52 81/2) Ghaegastrasse 3-4, 1030 Vienna
Belgium
(☎ (2) 771 7395) 278 Ave De Tervueren, 1150 Brussels
Canada
(☎ (613) 237-0330/2) 515 O'Connor St, Ottawa, Ontario K1S 3P8
Egypt
(☎ (2) 340 4940) 26 Rue el-Jazirah, Zamalek, 11211 Cairo
France
(☎ 04 78 93 42 87) 14. ave du Maréchal Foch, 69412 Lyon; (☎ 04 91 50 28 68) 8, blvd d'Athènes, 13001 Marseilles; (☎ 04 93 96 81 81) 18, ave des Fleurs, 66000 Nice; (☎ 01 45 53 50 94) 17-19, rue de Lubeck, 75016 Paris; (☎ 05 61 63 61 61) 19, allé Jean Jaurès, 3100 Toulouse
Germany
(☎ (30) 4 72 20 64/7) 110 Esplanade 12, 1100 Berlin; (☎ (211) 37 10 07) 7-9 Graf Adolf Platz, 4000 Düsseldorf; (☎ (40) 2 20 17 56) Overbeckstrasse 19, 2000 Hamburg 76; (☎ (89) 55 45 51) Adimstrasse 4, 8000 Munich 19
Greece
(☎ (1) 671 7590) Ethnikis Antistasseos 91, 15231 Halandri, Athens
India
(☎ (11) 688-5346) 23 Olaf Palam Marg, Vavant Vihar, 110057 New Delhi
Italy
(☎ (6) 860 42 82) Via Asmara 5, 00199 Rome; (☎ (91) 32 89 26) 24 Piazza Ignazio Florio, 90100 Palermo
Japan
(☎ (3) 3353-4111) 1-18-8 Wakaba Cho, Shinjuku-Ku, 160 Tokyo

Libya
(☎ (21) 607161) Ave Jehara, Sharia Bin 'Ashur, 3160 Tripoli
Malta
(☎ 435 175) Quormi Rd, Attard, Valetta
Morocco
(☎ (7) 730576) 6 Rue de Fès, Rabat
Netherlands
(☎ (70) 351 22 51) Gentestraat 98, 2587 HX The Hague
Norway
(☎ (22) 8319 17) Grand Hôtel, Oslo
Poland
(☎ (2) 282 586) Ul Mysliweicka 14, 00-459 Warsaw
Portugal
(☎ (1) 301 0330) Rua de Alcolena, 35 Restele, 1004 Lisbon
Russia
(☎ (95) 291 28 69) 28/1 Rue Katchalova, Moscow
South Africa
(☎ (12) 342 6283) 850 Church St, Arcadia, 0007 Pretoria
Spain
(☎ (1) 447 35 08) Plaza Alonzo Martinez 3, 28004 Madrid
Sweden
(☎ (8) 663 53 70) Drottningatan 73C, 11136 Stockholm
Switzerland
(☎ (31) 352 8226) Kirchenfeldstrasse 63, 3005 Bern
Turkey
(☎ (212) 152 8618/9) Cumhuriyet Caddesi 169/1, El-Madaq, 80230 Istanbul; (☎ (312) 37 77 20) Cayhane Sokak 40, Gazi Osmane Paza, 06700 Ankara
UK
(☎ (0171) 584 8117) 29 Prince's Gate, London SW7 1QG
USA
(☎ (202) 862-1850) 1515 Massachusetts Ave NW, Washington DC 20005

Australia has an Honorary Tunisian Consulate in Sydney (☎ (02) 9363 5588) which sends out visa application forms. The address is GPO Box 801, Double Bay, NSW 2028.

Foreign Embassies in Tunisia

Foreign embassies are concentrated in the capital, Tunis (telephone area code 01), and include the following. Australians should note that the Canadian Embassy in Tunis handles consular affairs in Tunisia for the Australian government.

Algeria
Embassy: (☎ 780 055; fax 790 852) 18 Rue du Niger, 1002 Tunis
Consulate: (☎ 287 139) 83 Ave Jugurtha, 1002 Tunis

Austria
(☎ 751 091; fax 751 094) 6 Rue Ibn Hamdiss, 1004 El-Menzah

Belgium
(☎ 781 655; fax 792 797) 47 Rue du 1 Juin, 1002 Tunis

Canada
(☎ 796 577; fax 792 371) 3 Rue du Sénégal, 1002 Tunis

Denmark
(☎ 792 600; fax 793 804) 5 Rue de Mauritanie, 1002 Tunis

Egypt
(☎ 791 181; fax 792 233) Ave Mohammed V, 1002 Tunis

France
Embassy: (☎ 347 838; fax 354 388) Place de l'Indépendance, Ave Habib Bourguiba, 1000 Tunis
Consulate: (☎ 333 027; fax 351 967) 1 Rue de Hollande, 1000 Tunis

Germany
(☎ 786 455; fax 788 242) 1 Rue el-Hamra, 1002 Tunis

Greece
(☎ 288 411; fax 789 518) 9 Impasse Antelas, 1002 Tunis

India
(☎ 891 006; fax 783 394) 4 Place Didon, Notre Dame, 1002 Tunis

Italy
(☎ 341 811; fax 354 155) 3 Rue de Russie, 1000 Tunis

Japan
(☎ 791 251; fax 792 363) 10 Rue Mahmoud el-Matri, 1002 Tunis

Libya
Embassy: (☎ 781 913; fax 780 866) 48 Rue du 1er Juin, 1002 Tunis
Consulate: (☎ 285 402; fax 280 586) 74 Ave Mohammed V, 1002 Tunis

Morocco
Embassy: (☎ 782 775; fax 787 103) 39 Rue du 1er Juin, 1002 Tunis
Consulate: (☎ 784 442; fax 783 627) 26 Rue Ibn Mandhour, Notre Dame, 1002 Tunis

Netherlands
(☎ 799 442; fax 785 557) 8 Rue de Meycen, 1002 Tunis

Norway
(☎ 802 158; fax 801 944) 20 Rue el-Kahena, 1002 Tunis

Palestine
(☎ 784 725; fax 785 973) 17 Rue Dr Ernest Conseil, 1002 Tunis

Poland
(☎ 286 237; fax 795 118) 4 Rue Sophonisbe, 1002 Tunis

Spain
(☎ 782 217; fax 786 267) 22 Rue Dr Ernest Conseil, 1002 Tunis

South Africa
(☎ 798 449; fax 796 742) 7 Rue Achtart, 1002 Tunis

Sweden
(☎ 795 433; fax 788 894) 87 Ave Taieb Mehiri, 1002 Tunis

Switzerland
(☎ 783 997; fax 788 796) 10 Rue Ech-Chenkiti, 1002 Tunis

UK
Embassy: (☎ 341 444; fax 354 877) 5 Place de la Victoire, 1000 Tunis
Consulate: (☎ 793 322; fax 792 644) 141-143 Ave de la Liberté, 1002 Tunis

USA
(☎ 782 566; fax 789 719) 144 Ave de la Liberté, 1002 Tunis

CUSTOMS
The duty free allowance is 400 cigarettes, 2L of wine, 1L of spirits and 250ml of perfume. It is advisable to declare valuable items (such as cameras) on arrival to ensure a smooth departure.

MONEY
Costs
Tunisia is a cheap country to travel in, especially for western visitors. It's usually possible to find a clean room for about TD5 per person, main meals in local restaurants seldom cost more than TD3.500, and transport is cheap. If you're fighting to keep costs down, you can get by on TD20 a day. You'll have more fun with a budget of about TD30 per day and can be quite lavish for TD50.

Carrying Money
The safest way of carrying cash and valuables (passport, travellers cheques, credit cards etc) is a favourite topic of travel conversation. The simple answer is that there is

no foolproof method. The general principle is to keep things out of sight. The front pouch, for example, presents an obvious target for a would-be thief – it's only marginally less inviting than a fat wallet bulging in your back pocket.

The best place to keep your valuables is under your clothes in contact with your skin where, hopefully, you will be aware of an alien hand before it's too late. Most people opt for a money belt, while others prefer a leather pouch hung around the neck. Another option is to sew a secret stash pocket into the inside of your clothes. Whichever method you choose, put your valuables in a plastic bag first – otherwise they will get soaked in sweat as you wander around in the heat of the day and after a few soakings they'll end up looking like they've been through the washing machine.

Cash

Nothing beats cash for convenience – or for risk. If you lose it, it's gone for good and very few travel insurers will come to your rescue. Those who do will normally limit the amount to about US$300. It's best not to carry too much cash on you at any one time – use travellers cheques or your automated teller machine (ATM) card to withdraw as much cash as you think you'll need for a few days at a time.

It's also a good idea to set aside a small amount of cash, say US$50, as an emergency stash.

Travellers Cheques

The main reason for carrying your funds as travellers cheques rather than cash is the protection they offer against theft. They are, however, losing popularity as more and more travellers opt to leave their money in a bank at home and withdraw it at ATMs as they go along.

American Express (Amex), Visa and Thomas Cook cheques are all widely accepted and have efficient replacement policies. Maintaining a record of the cheque numbers and when you use them is vital when it comes to replacing lost cheques. Keep this record separate from the cheques themselves. US dollars are a good currency to use, since US$1 is about TD1.

Tunisian banks will want to see your passport when you change money. The Banque Nationale Agricole (BNA) also insists on being shown the customer purchase record.

ATMs

ATMs are found in almost every town large enough to support a bank – and certainly in all the tourist areas. If you've got Master-Card or Visa, there are plenty of places to withdraw money.

Automatic foreign exchange machines (AFEMs) are starting to make an appearance. They take all the major European currencies, US dollars and Japanese yen.

Credit Cards

Credit cards are now an accepted part of the commercial scene in Tunisia, especially in major towns and tourist areas. They can be used to pay for a wide range of goods and services such as upmarket meals and accommodation, car hire and souvenir shopping.

If you are not familiar with the card options, ask your bank to explain the workings and relative merits of the various schemes: cash cards, charge cards and credit/debit cards. You should explain what you want to do with the card and push for a credit limit that meets your needs. Ask whether the card can be replaced in Tunisia if it gets stolen, and ask what happens if a card issued in Europe gets swallowed by a Tunisian ATM.

The main credit cards are MasterCard and Visa (Access in the UK), both of which are widely accepted in Tunisia. They can also be used as cash cards to draw Tunisian dinars from the ATMs of affiliated Tunisian banks in the same way as at home. Daily withdrawal limits are set by the issuing bank. Cash advances are given in local currency only. Both companies say they can replace a lost card in Tunisia within 24 hours, and will supply you with a phone number in your home country that you can call reverse charge in an emergency.

The main charge cards are Amex and Diners Club, which are widely accepted in tourist areas but unheard of elsewhere.

Currency

The unit of currency is the Tunisian dinar (TD), which is divided into 1000 millimes (mills). There are 5, 10, 20, 50, 100 and 500 mills coins and 1 dinar coins. There are also 5, 10, 20 and 30 dinar notes. Changing the larger notes is not a problem.

Currency Exchange

The TD is a soft currency, which means that exchange rates are fixed artificially by the government. The dinar cannot be traded on currency markets and it's illegal to import or export it, so you won't be able to equip yourself with any local currency before you arrive. It is not necessary to declare your foreign currency on arrival.

Within the country, all the major European currencies are readily exchangeable, as well as US and Canadian dollars and Japanese yen. Australian and NZ dollars and South African rand are not accepted. Exchange rates are regulated, so the rate is the same everywhere. Banks charge a standard 351 mills commission per travellers cheque and the larger hotels take slightly more. Post offices will change cash only. There is no black market. When leaving the country, you can re-exchange up to 30% of the amount you changed into dinar, up to a limit of TD100. You need to produce bank receipts to prove you changed the money in the first place.

Exchange Rates

Exchange rates for the major currencies are:

Australia	A$1	=	TD0.751
Canada	C$1	=	TD0.805
France	1FF	=	TD0.190
Germany	DM1	=	TD0.639
Italy	L1000	=	TD0.648
Japan	¥100	=	TD0.923
New Zealand	NZ$1	=	TD0.670
UK	UK£1	=	TD1.938
US	US$1	=	TD1.159

These exchange rates were correct at the time of writing, but check with your bank for the latest rates.

Tipping & Bargaining

Tipping is not a requirement. Cafes and local restaurants put out a saucer for customers to throw their small change into, but this is seldom more than 50 mills. Waiters in tourist restaurants are accustomed to tips: 10% is plenty. Taxi drivers do not usually expect tips from locals, but often round up the fare for travellers.

Handicrafts are about the only items you may have to bargain for in Tunisia. To be good at bargaining, you need to enjoy the banter. If you don't, you're better off buying your souvenirs from one of the government fixed-price Office National de l'Artisanat Tunisien (ONAT) craft shops or SOCOPA (Société de Commercialisation des Produits de l'Artisanats) stores. It's a good idea to go there anyway just to get an idea of prices.

POST & COMMUNICATIONS
Post Offices

Post offices are known as PTTs. Opening hours are a little confusing. They differ between city and country areas – most places you are likely to visit will be keeping city hours – and the hours change again in summer (July and August) and during Ramadan (see Public Holidays later in this chapter).

Most of the year, city post offices are open Monday to Saturday from 8 am to 6 pm and Sunday from 9 to 11 am; in summer, they open Monday to Saturday from 7.30 am to 1.30 pm while Sunday hours are unchanged. Country offices usually open Monday to Thursday from 8 am to noon and 3 to 6 pm, and Friday and Saturday from 7.30 am to 1.30 pm; in summer, they open Monday to Saturday from 7.30 am to 1.30 pm.

During the Ramadan month, post offices are open Monday to Saturday from 7.30 am to 1.30 pm.

Postal Rates

Air mail letters cost 650 mills to Europe and 700 mills to Australia and the Americas;

postcards are 100 mills cheaper. You can buy stamps at post offices, major hotels and some general stores and newsstands.

Sending Mail
The Tunisian postal service is slow but reliable. Letters from Europe generally take about a week to arrive; letters from further afield take about two weeks. Delivery times are similar in the other direction. If you want to ensure that your mail gets through quickly, the Rapide Poste service guarantees to deliver anywhere in Europe within two working days (TD10), or within four working days to the Americas, Asia and Oceania (TD16). The service is available from all post offices.

Parcels weighing less than 2kg can be sent by ordinary mail. Larger parcels should be taken, unwrapped for inspection, to the special parcel counter. Indicate clearly if you want to send something surface mail.

Receiving Mail
Mail can be received poste restante at any post office in the country. It should be addressed clearly, with your family name in capitals. Ask the clerks to check under your given name as well if you think you are missing mail. There is a collection fee of 180 mills per letter.

Telephone
Local Calls The Tunisian telephone system is modern and efficient. Public telephones, known as Taxiphones, are everywhere and it's rare to find one that doesn't work. Most places have Taxiphone offices, readily identified by their yellow signs, with several booths and attendants to give change. Some shops have public phones, usually indicated by a blue sign, and you'll normally find a public phone at post offices. Many households do not have a phone, so public phones are always busy.

Phones are equipped to take 100 mills, 500 mills and TD1 coins. Local calls cost 100 mills for two minutes, so you'll need a few to have a conversation.

Taxiphone offices keep a copy of the recently updated national telephone directory, published in both Arabic and French, as well as having information on international area codes and charges. The number for directory information is ☎ 120.

Area Codes	
Tunis region	01
Bizerte, Hammamet & Nabeul	02
Sousse & Monastir	03
Sfax	04
Gabès & Jerba	05
Tozeur & Gafsa	06
Kairouan	07
Tabarka & Le Kef	08

International Calls Making an international call is straightforward but expensive. Almost all public phones are equipped for international direct dialling. You just feed them dinar coins instead of 100 mills coins. To dial out, phone the international access code (00), followed by the country code, then the local code and number. If you're calling Tunisia from abroad, the country code is 216. International codes and charges per minute are listed in the table below.

International Codes & Charges		
Country	*Code*	*Cost (TD)*
Algeria	213	0.720
Australia	61	1.750
France	33	0.980
Germany	49	0.980
Italy	39	0.980
Morocco	212	0.720
New Zealand	64	1.750
Poland	48	1.920
UK	44	0.980
USA/Canada	1	1.500

Fax, Telegraph & Email
Faxes are all the rage in Tunisia, and almost every classified hotel has a fax machine. Most major hotels also offer telex facilities. It will cost you less to use the public facilities available at the telephone offices in major

towns. Telegrams can be sent from any post office. There are no places in Tunisia as yet where you can send or receive emails, except from private offices and companies.

BOOKS

Unless you want your literary diet to consist of nothing but expensive English newspapers, bring enough books to keep yourself busy. Bookshops, although common, do not stock anything in English. There are a couple of exceptions to this rule, see under Children later in this section, but they're not worth hanging out for. The best solution is to look out for fellow travellers with books to swap.

Books that deal solely with Tunisia are few and far between. If your French is up to book standard you have a far better chance of finding something. See also Literature under Arts in the Facts about the Country chapter.

Most books are published in different editions by different publishers in different countries. As a result, a book might be a hardcover rarity in one country while it's readily available in paperback in another. Fortunately, bookshops and libraries search by title or author, so your local bookshop or library is best placed to advise you on the availability of the recommendations listed below.

Lonely Planet

For travellers on wider-reaching trips, Lonely Planet publishes *Mediterranean Europe on a shoestring*, which has chapters on the countries around the Mediterranean, and *Africa on a shoestring*, which covers the whole continent. It also publishes a wide range of language guides, including French and Egyptian Arabic.

Travel

Many of the early European travellers were stiff-upper-lip colonialist types who wrote about the 'natives' with barely disguised contempt. About the most bigoted of the lot was Norman Douglas, who passed through south-western Tunisia in 1912 and wrote about his experiences in *Fountains in the Sand*. His account is entertaining enough – as long as you can ignore his intolerance of Arabs in general and everything Tunisian in particular.

Paul Theroux visited Tunisia during his grand tour of the Mediterranean in the early 1990s that resulted in *The Pillars of Hercules*. The chapter on Tunisia includes an amusing account of an encounter with a carpet tout in Tunis as well as descriptions of his visit to Sfax and the Kerkennah Islands.

History & Politics

Peter Mansfield offers an excellent insight into the Arab psyche in *The Arabs*, widely regarded as providing the best available explanation of the many forces at work in this complicated part of the world. It includes a section on Tunisia. *Crossroads*, by David Pryce-Jones, is a good introduction to the modern Islamic world in general.

If you're interested in Roman history, Susan Raven's *Rome in Africa* provides a good account of Rome's tussle with Carthage and the subsequent conquest of North Africa.

The Sultan's Admiral by Ernie Bradford is a lively biography of the famous 16th century pirate Khair ed-Din, who terrorised Christian shipping in the western Mediterranean and paved the way for the Ottoman conquest of North Africa.

Novels

Salammbô by Gustave Flaubert is a historical epic set at the time of the mercenaries' rebellion against Carthage in the 3rd century BC. It claims to be based on fact, but any fact that might have crept in is buried beneath a more than adequate quota of violence and sex.

Aldous Huxley fans will be disappointed by the patronising tone of *In a Tunisia Oasis*, set around Nefta in the 1930s. It features in a collection of his short stories titled *The Olive Tree*, published in 1939.

Katy in Tunisia by Katy Hounsell-Robert tells of Katy's time spent sharing a house in Tunisia with a woman artist friend during the late 1980s.

Children

Editions Alif does an excellent series of pop-up books about Tunisian and regional life. The series includes only one title in English, *A Walk Through an Arab City: the Tunis Medina*, which is also published in German and French. The other books in the series are in French, and they look at oasis life, ancient Carthage and Mediterranean life in 1492 AD. The books have two levels of appeal: children like them for their pop-up features, and adults will find a wealth of information that is hard to find elsewhere.

Editions Alif has a retail outlet in Tunis on the corner of Rue d'Allemagne and Rue de Hollande. The shop at the Dar Charait Museum in Tozeur also stocks the full range.

Both outlets also stock a series of books about Tunisian crafts by author/illustrator May Angeli. The titles are *Attia Chouraqi: Jeweller in Mahdia*; *Marcus Magonius: Mosaicist at Carthage*; *Ali al-Andaloussi: Ceramist in Tunis*; and *Saliha Karoui: Weaver in Kairwan*. They all cost TD4, and are published in English, French and German. They are aimed at seven to 10-year-olds. If you can't track them down, publishers Sérès Productions can be contacted in Tunis on ☎ (01) 787 516.

ONLINE SERVICES

The Internet was launched in Tunisia in the middle of 1997, but the amount of information about the country that can be gleaned from the web is fairly limited. Many sites visited were still under construction at the time of writing. The Tunisian National Tourist Organisation's web site (www.tourismtunisia.com) is more advanced than most, but offers little more than you'll find in their glossy brochures.

A more interesting site to explore is www.tunisiaonline.com, where you can read the Tunisian newspapers. You'll find *La Presse* and *Le Temps* in French, and the Arabic dailies *Essahafa* and *Assabah*, all available on the day of publication.

A bit of searching around on the web turns up all sorts of oddities, such as the home page

of soccer club Sportif Sfaxien located under www.geocities.com.

NEWSPAPERS & MAGAZINES

You can buy two-day-old English, German, Italian and French newspapers in all the major centres. International current affairs magazines such as *Time* and *Newsweek* are also readily available.

The weekly *Tunisian News* is the only locally produced publication in English. It costs TD1 and usually includes a few interesting feature articles about Tunisia together with some very unexciting local news stories that read like ministerial press releases.

La Presse and *Le Temps* are the main French-language papers. They offer very similar fare. Both are published daily, and both include a couple of pages of international news and local service information such as train, bus and flight times; both cost 300 mills. Arabic daily newspapers include *Assabah* and *Al-Houria*.

RADIO & TV

There is a French-language radio station broadcasting on (or around) FM 98. It broadcasts in English from 2 to 3 pm, in German from 3 to 4 pm and in Italian from 4 to 5 pm. A much better source of English-language

Starring Tunisia

Tunisia was a popular spot for international film makers even before the enormous success of *The English Patient*, which scooped a remarkable nine Oscars at the 1997 Academy Awards. The ribat in Monastir was used by the Monty Python team as a setting in *The Life of Brian* and the Hotel Sidi Driss in Matmata was used for the intergalactic bar scene in *Star Wars*.

In *The English Patient*, the desert scenes were shot around the edge of the Chott el-Jerid, west of Tozeur; the scene purporting to be the souq in Cairo was shot in Sfax; the seafront in Mahdia was used for the German invasion of Benghazi; and the Christmas party scene was shot in Tunis. You probably won't hear it mentioned elsewhere, but Tunisians feel they were sufficiently involved in the production process to claim some of the credit. ■

radio is the BBC World Service, which can be picked up on 15.070 and 12.095 MHz SW.

The French-language TV station has half an hour of news, with lots of foreign news and sport, at 8 pm every night. Most of the regular TV programs are mindless game shows (which you wind up watching in cheap restaurants), although they do sometimes have decent movies on Friday night. Some of the more upmarket hotels offer satellite TV, allowing guests to tune in to CNN news.

VIDEO SYSTEMS

If you want to record or buy video tapes to play back home, you won't get a picture unless the image registration systems are the same. Like Europe and Australia, Tunisia uses PAL, which is incompatible with the North American and Japanese NTSC system.

PHOTOGRAPHY & VIDEO
Photography

The main problem facing the photographer is the brilliant sunlight. If you don't take suitable precautions, your holiday snaps will all end up over-exposed – pale and washed out. You can get around the problem either by using a polarising filter or by restricting your photography sessions to the times of the day when the light is best, generally early morning and late evening.

Name-brand film such as Kodak and Fuji is widely available, but don't expect any bargains: it will cost you at least as much as it does at home. The Monoprix supermarket chain sells 24-exposure 100 ASA Fuji film for TD3.850 and 36-exposure film for TD4.900. It is harder to find slides and film of other speeds outside the main tourist areas. There are quick-processing labs which can develop any type of print film in all the main tourist areas.

Video

Properly used, a video camera can give a fascinating record of your holiday. As well as videoing the obvious things, remember to record some of the ordinary everyday details of life in the country. Often the most inter-

esting things occur when you're actually intent on filming something else. Remember too that, unlike still photography, video 'flows' – so, for example, you can shoot scenes of countryside rolling past the train window, which gives an overall impression that isn't possible with ordinary photos.

Video cameras these days have amazingly sensitive microphones, and you might be surprised how much sound will be picked up. This can also be a problem if there is a lot of ambient noise – filming by the side of a busy road might seem OK when you do it, but viewing it back home might simply give you a deafening cacophony of traffic noise.

One good rule to follow for beginners is to try to film in long takes, and don't move the camera around too much. Otherwise, your video could well make your viewers seasick! If your camera has a stabiliser, you can use it to obtain good footage while travelling on various means of transport, even on bumpy roads. And remember, you're on holiday – don't let the video take over your life and turn your trip into a Cecil B de Mille production.

Make sure you keep the batteries charged and have the necessary charger, plugs and transformer for the country you are visiting. In most countries, it is possible to obtain video cartridges easily in large towns and cities, but make sure you buy the correct format. It is usually worth buying at least a few cartridges duty-free to start off your trip.

Finally, remember to follow the same rules regarding people's sensitivities as for a still photography – having a video camera shoved in their face is probably even more annoying and offensive for locals than a still camera. Always ask permission first.

Restrictions

It is forbidden to take photographs of airfields, military installations, police stations and government buildings.

Photographing People

You should always ask permission before taking photographs of people. While Tunisians expect every tourist to carry a camera, most do not like to have the lens turned on them. This applies particularly to Tunisian women and to people in rural areas.

TIME

Tunisia is one hour ahead of GMT/UTC from October to April, and two hours ahead of GMT/UTC from May to September.

ELECTRICITY

Most of the country is on 220V but the occasional hotel in Tunis and some of the smaller towns in the south are still on 110V. Check before plugging in any appliance. The supply is reliable and uninterrupted. As in Europe, wall plugs have two round pins.

WEIGHTS & MEASURES

Tunisia uses the metric system, with weights expressed in kilograms and distances in metres. Basic conversion charts are given on the inside back cover of this book.

LAUNDRY

Laundrettes don't exist in the western sense, and they barely exist in any other sense. There are a couple of places in Tunis filled with washing machines and driers where you can pay for washing to be done by the kilogram. You just drop off a load and collect it later.

The only other option is to ask about laundry at your hotel, although this can prove expensive. To have a shirt washed and ironed will cost about 500 mills at a rated hotel.

Tourist areas and most larger towns have dry-cleaning shops. Some typical prices include the following: shirt TD1, silk shirt TD1.300, trousers TD1.200, jeans TD1.700, cloth jacket TD1.800, and women's skirt and jacket TD2.800.

HEALTH

Travel health depends on your predeparture preparations, your daily health care while travelling and how you handle any medical problem that develops. While the potential dangers can seem quite frightening, in reality few travellers experience anything more than an upset stomach.

Predeparture Planning

Immunisations For some countries no immunisations are necessary, but the further off the beaten track you go the more necessary it is to take precautions. Be aware that there is often a greater risk of disease with children and in pregnancy.

Plan ahead for getting your vaccinations: some of them require more than one injection, while some vaccinations should not be given together. It is recommended you seek medical advice at least six weeks before you travel.

Record all vaccinations on an International Health Certificate, available from your doctor or government health department.

Discuss your requirements with your doctor, but you should consider the following vaccinations for Tunisia:

- **Hepatitis A** This is the most common traveller's illness after diarrhoea and can put you out of action for weeks. Havrix 1440 and Vaqta are vaccines which provide long term immunity (possibly more than 10 years) after an initial injection and a booster at six to 12 months.

  Gamma globulin is ready-made antibody collected from blood donations. It should be given close to departure because, depending on the dose, it only protects for two to six months.

  A combined hepatitis A and hepatitis B vaccination, Twinrix, is also available. This combined vaccination is recommended for people wanting protection against both types of viral hepatitis. The course involves having three injections over a six month period.
- **Typhoid** This is an important vaccination to have where hygiene is a problem. Available either as an injection or oral capsules.
- **Diphtheria & Tetanus** Diphtheria is a potentially fatal throat infection and tetanus a potentially fatal wound infection. Everyone should have these vaccinations. After an initial course of three injections, boosters are necessary every 10 years.
- **Hepatitis B** This disease is spread by blood or by sexual activity. Travellers should consider a hepatitis B vaccination, especially if they are planning to visit countries where blood transfusions may not be adequately screened or where sexual contact is a possibility. It involves three injections, the quickest course being over three weeks with a booster at 12 months.

- **Polio** Polio is a serious, easily transmitted disease which is still prevalent in many developing countries. Everyone should keep up to date with this vaccination. A booster every 10 years maintains immunity.
- **Rabies** Vaccination should be considered by those who are planning to spend a month or longer in Tunisia, especially if they are cycling, handling animals, caving or travelling to remote areas, and also for children (who may not report a bite). Pretravel rabies vaccination involves having three injections over 21 to 28 days. If someone who has been vaccinated is bitten or scratched by an animal, they will require two booster injections of vaccine, those not vaccinated require more.

Health Insurance Make sure that you have adequate health insurance. See the Travel Insurance section under Visas & Documents in this chapter for more details.

Other Preparations Make sure you're fit and healthy before you start travelling. If you are going on a long trip make sure your teeth are OK. If you wear glasses take a spare pair and your prescription.

If you require a particular medication take an adequate supply, as it may not be available locally. Take part of the packaging showing the generic rather than brand name, which will make getting replacements easier. To avoid any problems, it's a good idea to have a legible prescription or letter from your doctor to show that you legally use the medication.

Basic Rules

Food There is an old colonial adage which says: 'If you can cook it, boil it or peel it you can eat it ... otherwise forget it'. Vegetables and fruit should be washed with purified water or peeled where possible.

Beware of ice cream which is sold in the street or anywhere else it might have been melted and refrozen; if there's any doubt (eg a power cut in the last day or two) steer well clear.

Shellfish such as mussels, oysters and clams should be avoided as should undercooked meat, particularly in the form of mince. Steaming does not make shellfish safe for eating.

Medical Kit Check List

Consider taking a basic medical kit including:

- ☐ **Aspirin** or paracetamol (acetaminophen in the USA) – for pain or fever.
- ☐ **Antihistamine** (such as Benadryl) – useful as a decongestant for colds and allergies, to ease the itch from insect bites or stings, and to help prevent motion sickness. Antihistamines may cause sedation and interact with alcohol so care should be taken when using them; take one you know and have used before, if possible.
- ☐ **Antibiotics** – useful to have if you're travelling well off the beaten track, but they must be prescribed; carry the prescription on you.
- ☐ **Loperamide** (eg Imodium) or Lomotil for diarrhoea; prochlorperazine (eg Stemetil) or metaclopramide (eg Maxalon) for nausea and vomiting.
- ☐ **Rehydration mixture** – for treatment of severe diarrhoea; particularly important for children.
- ☐ **Antiseptic** such as povidone-iodine (eg Betadine) – for cuts and grazes.
- ☐ **Multivitamins** – especially useful for long trips when your dietary vitamin intake may be inadequate.
- ☐ **Calamine lotion** or **aluminium sulphate spray** (eg Stingose) – to ease irritation from bites or stings.
- ☐ **Bandages** and Band-Aids.
- ☐ **Scissors, tweezers** and a **thermometer** (note that mercury thermometers are prohibited by airlines).
- ☐ **Cold and flu tablets** and **throat lozenges**.
- ☐ **Insect repellent, sunscreen, lip salve** and **water purification tablets**.
- ☐ **Syringes**, in case you need injections in a country with medical hygiene problems. Ask your doctor for a note explaining why they have been prescribed.

If a place looks clean and well run and the vendor also looks clean and healthy, then the food is probably safe. In general, places that are packed with travellers or locals will be fine, while empty restaurants are more doubtful. The food in busy restaurants and eateries is cooked and eaten quite quickly with little standing around and is probably not reheated.

Water The tap water is safe to drink in most parts of Tunisia, although it often doesn't taste too good. Bottled mineral water is widely available if you prefer it.

Nutrition

If your food is poor or limited in availability, if you're travelling hard and fast and therefore missing meals, or if you simply lose your appetite, you can soon start to lose weight and place your health at risk.

Make sure your diet is well balanced. Cooked eggs, beans, lentils and nuts are all safe ways to get protein. Fruit you can peel (bananas, oranges or mandarins for example) is usually safe and a good source of vitamins, although melons can harbour bacteria in their flesh and are best avoided. Try to eat plenty of grains (including rice) and bread. Remember that although food is generally safer if it is cooked well, overcooked food loses much of its nutritional value. If your diet isn't well balanced or if your food intake is insufficient, it's a good idea to take vitamin and iron pills.

In hot climates make sure you drink enough – don't rely on feeling thirsty to indicate when you should drink. Not needing to urinate or small amounts of very dark yellow urine is a danger sign. Always carry a water bottle with you on long trips. Excessive sweating can lead to loss of salt and muscle cramps. Salt tablets are not a good idea as a preventative but in places where salt is not used much, adding salt to food can help. ■

Medical Problems & Treatment

Self-diagnosis and treatment can be risky, so you should always seek medical help. Although we do give drug dosages in this section, they are for emergency use only. Correct diagnosis is vital.

An embassy, consulate or five star hotel can usually recommend a good place to go for advice. In some places standards of medical attention are so low that for some serious medical problems the best advice is to get on a plane and go somewhere else. Ideally, antibiotics should be administered only under medical supervision. Take only the recommended dose at the prescribed intervals and use the whole course, even if the illness seems to be cured earlier. Stop immediately if there are any serious reactions and don't use the antibiotic at all if you are unsure that you have the correct one. Some people are allergic to commonly prescribed antibiotics such as penicillin or sulpha drugs; you should carry this information on you (eg on a bracelet) when travelling.

Travel Health Guides

If you are planning to be away or travelling in remote areas for a long period of time, you might like to consider taking a more detailed health guide. Recommended guides include:

Staying Healthy in Asia, Africa & Latin America, Dirk Schroeder, Moon Publications, 1994. Probably the best all-round guide to carry; it's compact, detailed and well organised.

Travellers' Health, Dr Richard Dawood, Oxford University Press, 1995. Comprehensive, easy to read, authoritative and highly recommended, although it's rather large to lug around.

Where There is No Doctor, David Werner, Macmillan, 1994. A very detailed guide intended for someone, such as a Peace Corps worker, going to work in an underdeveloped country.

Travel with Children, Maureen Wheeler, Lonely Planet Publications, 1995. Includes advice on travel health for younger children.

There are also a number of excellent travel health sites on the Internet. From the Lonely Planet home page there are links at lonelyplanet.com/weblinks/wlprep.htm to the World Health Organisation and the US Center for Diseases Control & Prevention.

Environmental Hazards

Fungal Infections Fungal infections, such as ringworm, occur more commonly in hot weather and are usually found on the scalp, between the toes or fingers, in the groin and on the body. You get ringworm from infected animals or other people. Fungal infections thrive in moist conditions.

To prevent fungal infections wear loose, comfortable clothes, avoid artificial fibres, wash frequently and dry yourself carefully. If you do get an infection, wash the infected area at least daily with a disinfectant or medicated soap and water, and rinse and dry well. Apply an antifungal cream or powder like tolnaftate (Tinaderm). Try to expose the infected area to air or sunlight as much as possible and wash all towels and underwear in hot water, change them often and let them dry in the sun.

Heat Exhaustion Dehydration and salt deficiency can cause heat exhaustion. Take time to acclimatise to high temperatures, drink sufficient liquids and do not do anything too physically demanding.

Salt deficiency is characterised by fatigue, lethargy, headaches, giddiness and muscle cramps; salt tablets may help, but adding extra salt to your food is better.

Anhydrotic heat exhaustion, caused by an inability to sweat, is quite rare. It is likely to strike people who have been in a hot climate for some time, rather than newcomers.

Heatstroke This serious, occasionally fatal, condition can occur if the body's heat-regulating mechanism breaks down and the body temperature rises to dangerous levels. Long, continuous periods of exposure to high temperatures and insufficient fluids can leave you vulnerable to heatstroke.

The symptoms are feeling unwell, not sweating very much (or at all) and a high body temperature (39°C to 41°C or 102°F to 106°F). Where sweating has ceased the skin becomes flushed and red. Severe, throbbing headaches and lack of coordination will also occur, and the sufferer may be confused or aggressive. Eventually the victim will become delirious or convulse. Hospitalisation is essential, but in the interim get victims out of the sun, remove their clothing, cover them with a wet sheet or towel and then fan continually. Give fluids if they are conscious.

Hypothermia Too much cold can be just as dangerous as too much heat. Although most people usually associate Tunisia with heat and sunshine, it gets very cold in winter in the north and nights in the desert can get surprisingly chilly, even in summer.

Hypothermia occurs when the body loses heat faster than it can produce it and the core temperature of the body falls. It is surprisingly easy to progress from very cold to dangerously cold due to a combination of wind, wet clothing, fatigue and hunger, even if the air temperature is above freezing. It is best to dress in layers; silk, wool and some of the new artificial fibres are all good insulating materials. A hat is important, as a lot of heat is lost through the head. A strong, waterproof outer layer (and a 'space' blanket for emergencies) are essential. Carry basic supplies, including food containing simple sugars to generate heat quickly and fluid to drink.

The symptoms of hypothermia include exhaustion, numb skin (particularly toes and fingers), shivering, slurred speech, irrational or violent behaviour, stumbling, dizzy spells, lethargy, muscle cramps and violent bursts of energy. Irrationality may take the form of sufferers claiming they are warm and trying to take their clothes off.

To treat mild hypothermia, first get the person out of the wind and/or rain, remove their clothing if it's wet and replace it with dry, warm clothing. Give them hot liquids – not alcohol – and some high-kilojoule, easily digestible food. Do not rub victims, instead allow them to slowly warm themselves. This should be enough to treat the early stages of hypothermia. The early recognition and treatment of mild hypothermia is the only way to prevent severe hypothermia, which is a critical condition.

Jet Lag Jet lag is experienced when a person travels by air across more than three time zones (each time zone usually represents a one hour time difference). It occurs because many of the functions of the human body (such as temperature, pulse rate and emptying of the bladder and bowels) are regulated by internal 24-hour cycles. When we travel long distances rapidly, our bodies take time to adjust to the 'new time' of our destination, and we may experience fatigue, disorientation, insomnia, anxiety, impaired concentration and loss of appetite. These effects will usually be gone within three days of arrival, but the following measures may minimise the impact of jet lag.

- Rest for a couple of days prior to departure.
- Try to select flight schedules that minimise sleep deprivation; arriving late in the day means you can go to sleep soon after you arrive. For very long flights, try to organise a stopover.
- Avoid excessive eating (which bloats the stomach) and alcohol (which causes dehydration) during the flight. Instead, drink plenty of non-carbonated, non-alcoholic drinks such as fruit juice or water.

- Avoid smoking.
- Make yourself comfortable by wearing loose baggy clothes and perhaps bringing an eye mask and ear plugs to help you sleep.
- Try to sleep at the appropriate time for the time zone you are travelling to.

Motion Sickness Eating lightly before and during a trip will reduce the chances of motion sickness. If you are prone to motion sickness try to find a place that minimises movement – near the wing on aircraft, close to midships on boats, or near the centre on buses. Fresh air usually helps; reading and cigarette smoke don't. Commercial motion-sickness preparations, which can cause drowsiness, have to be taken before the trip commences. Ginger (in capsule form) and peppermint (including mint-flavoured sweets) are natural preventatives.

Prickly Heat Prickly heat is an itchy rash caused by excessive perspiration trapped under the skin. It usually strikes people who have just arrived in a hot climate. Keeping cool, bathing often, drying the skin and using a mild talcum or prickly heat powder or resorting to air-conditioning may help.

Sunburn The intensity of the sun is by far the biggest health risk in Tunisia. You can get sunburnt surprisingly quickly, even through cloud. Use a sunscreen, hat, and barrier cream for your nose and lips. Calamine lotion or Stingose is good for mild sunburn. Protect your eyes with good sunglasses, particularly if you are near water, sand or snow.

Infectious Diseases

Diarrhoea Simple things like a change of water, food or climate can all cause a mild bout of diarrhoea, but a few rushed toilet trips with no other symptoms is not indicative of a major problem.

Dehydration is the main danger with any diarrhoea, particularly in children or the elderly as dehydration can occur quite quickly. *Fluid replacement* (at least equal to the volume being lost) is the most important thing to remember in all circumstances. Weak black tea with a little sugar, soda water,

---

Everyday Health
Normal body temperature is 37°C or 98.6°F; more than 2°C (4°F) higher indicates a fever. The normal adult pulse rate is 60 to 100 per minute (children 80 to 100, babies 100 to 140). As a general rule the pulse increases about 20 beats per minute for each °C (2°F) rise in fever.

Respiration (breathing) rate is also an indicator of illness. Count the number of breaths per minute: between 12 and 20 is normal for adults and older children (up to 30 for younger children, 40 for babies). People with a high fever or serious respiratory illness breathe more quickly than normal. More than 40 shallow breaths a minute may indicate pneumonia. ■

---

or soft drinks allowed to go flat and diluted 50% with purified water are all good.

With severe diarrhoea a rehydrating solution is preferable to replace minerals and salts lost. Commercially available oral rehydration salts (ORS) are very useful; add them to boiled or bottled water. In an emergency you can make up a solution of six teaspoons of sugar and a half teaspoon of salt to a litre of boiled or bottled water.

You need to drink at least the same volume of fluid that you are losing in bowel movements and vomiting. Urine is the best guide to the adequacy of replacement – if you have small amounts of concentrated urine, you need to drink more. Keep drinking small amounts often. Stick to a bland diet as you recover.

Lomotil or Imodium can be used to bring relief from the symptoms, although they do not actually cure the problem. Only use these drugs if you do not have access to toilets, for example if you *must* travel. For children under 12 years Lomotil and Imodium are not recommended. You should not use these drugs if you have a high fever or are severely dehydrated.

In certain situations antibiotics may be required: diarrhoea with blood or mucus (dysentery), any diarrhoea with fever, watery diarrhoea with fever and lethargy, persistent diarrhoea not improving after 48 hours and severe diarrhoea. In these situations gut-paralysing drugs like Imodium or Lomotil should be avoided.

A stool test is necessary to diagnose which kind of dysentery you have, so you should seek medical help urgently. Where this is not possible the recommended drugs for dysentery are norfloxacin 400mg twice daily for three days or ciprofloxacin 500mg twice daily for five days. These are not recommended for children or pregnant women. The drug of choice for children would be co-trimoxazole (Bactrim, Septrin, Resprim) with dosage dependent on weight. A five day course is given. Ampicillin or amoxycillin may be given in pregnancy, but medical care is necessary.

Amoebic dysentery is gradual in onset and fever may not be present. It will persist until treated and can recur and cause other health problems.

Giardiasis is another type of diarrhoea. The parasite causing this intestinal disorder is present in contaminated water. The symptoms are stomach cramps and bloating, nausea, watery, foul-smelling diarrhoea and frequent gas. Giardiasis can appear several weeks after you have been exposed to the parasite. The symptoms may disappear for a few days and then return; this can go on for several weeks. Tinidazole, known as Fasigyn, or metronidazole (Flagyl) are the recommended drugs. Treatment is a 2g single dose of Fasigyn or 250mg of Flagyl three times a day for five to 10 days.

Hepatitis Hepatitis is a general term for inflammation of the liver. It is a common disease worldwide. The symptoms are fever, chills, headache, fatigue, feelings of weakness and aches and pains, followed by loss of appetite, nausea, vomiting and abdominal pain. Signs to look out for include dark urine, light-coloured faeces, jaundiced (yellow) skin and yellowing of the whites of the eyes.

Hepatitis A is transmitted by contaminated food and drinking water and poses a real threat to western travellers. You should seek medical advice, but there is not much you can do apart from rest, drink lots of fluids, eat lightly and avoid fatty foods. People who have had hepatitis should avoid alcohol for some time after the illness, as the liver needs time to recover.

Hepatitis E is transmitted in the same way; it can be very serious in pregnant women.

There are almost 300 million chronic carriers of hepatitis B in the world. It is spread through contact with infected blood, blood products or body fluids, for example through sexual contact, unsterilised needles and blood transfusions, or contact with blood via small breaks in the skin. Other risk situations include having a shave, tattoo, or having your body pierced with contaminated equipment. The symptoms of hepatitis B may be more severe and may lead to long term problems.

Hepatitis D is spread in the same way, but the risk is mainly from shared needles.

Hepatitis C can lead to chronic liver disease. The virus is spread by contact with blood – usually via contaminated transfusions or shared needles. Avoiding these is the only means of prevention.

HIV & AIDS Infection with the human immunodeficiency virus (HIV) may develop into the acquired immune deficiency syndrome (AIDS), which is a fatal disease. HIV is a major problem in many countries and Tunisia (where AIDS is known by its French acronym SIDA) is no exception. Any exposure to blood, blood products or body fluids may put the individual at risk. The disease is often transmitted through sexual contact or dirty needles – vaccinations, acupuncture, tattooing and body piercing can be potentially as dangerous as intravenous drug use. HIV/AIDS can also be spread through infected blood transfusions; some developing countries cannot afford to screen blood used for transfusions.

If you do need an injection, ask to see the syringe unwrapped in front of you, or take a needle and syringe pack with you.

Remember that fear of HIV infection should never preclude treatment for serious medical conditions.

Sexually Transmitted Diseases Gonorrhoea, herpes and syphilis are among these diseases; sores, blisters or rashes around the genitals, discharges or pain when urinating are common symptoms. With some STDs, such as wart virus or chlamydia, symptoms may be less marked or not observed at all, especially in women. Syphilis symptoms eventually disappear but the disease continues and can cause severe problems in later years. While abstinence from sexual contact is the only 100% effective prevention, using condoms is also effective. The treatment of gonorrhoea and syphilis is with antibiotics. The different sexually transmitted diseases each require specific antibiotics. There is no cure for herpes or AIDS.

Typhoid Typhoid fever is a dangerous gut infection caused by contaminated water and food. Medical help must be sought.

In its early stages sufferers may feel they have a bad cold or flu on the way, as early symptoms are a headache, body aches and a fever which rises a little each day until it is around 40°C (104°F) or more. The pulse is often slow relative to the degree of fever present – unlike a normal fever where the pulse increases. Additional symptoms include vomiting, abdominal pain, diarrhoea or constipation.

In the second week the high fever and slow pulse continue and a few pink spots may appear on the body; trembling, delirium, weakness, weight loss and dehydration may also occur. Complications include pneumonia, perforated bowel or meningitis. The fever should be treated by keeping the person cool and giving them fluids; watch for dehydration. Ciprofloxacin 750mg twice a day for 10 days is good for adults.

Chloramphenicol is recommended in many countries. The adult dosage is two 250mg capsules, four times a day. Children aged between eight and 12 years should have half the adult dose; younger children should be given one-third of the adult dose.

Cuts, Bites & Stings
Rabies is passed through animal bites. See under Less Common Diseases for more details.

Bedbugs & Lice Bedbugs live in various places, but particularly in dirty mattresses and bedding, revealed by spots of blood on bedclothes or on the wall. Bedbugs leave itchy bites in neat rows. Calamine lotion or Stingose spray may help.

All lice cause itching and discomfort. They make themselves at home in your hair (head lice), your clothing (body lice) or in your pubic hair (crabs). You catch lice through direct contact with infected people or by sharing combs, clothing and the like. Powder or shampoo treatment will kill the lice and infected clothing should then be washed in very hot, soapy water and left in the sun to dry.

Insect Bites & Stings Although there are lots of bees and wasps in Tunisia, their stings are usually painful rather than dangerous. Calamine lotion or Stingose spray will give relief and ice packs will reduce the pain and swelling. However, people who are allergic to bee stings may develop severe breathing difficulties, requiring urgent medical care.

Scorpions are common in the south of Tunisia. Scorpion stings are notoriously painful and can sometimes be fatal. Scorpions often shelter in shoes or clothing.

There are various fish and other marine creatures which can sting or bite dangerously or which are dangerous to eat. Seek local advice.

Cuts & Scratches Wash well and treat any cut with an antiseptic such as povidone-iodine. Where possible avoid bandages and Band-Aids, which can keep wounds wet.

Sea Urchins & Jellyfish Watch out for sea urchins around rocky beaches; if you get their needles embedded in your skin, olive oil will help to loosen them. If they are not removed they will become infected. Be wary also of jellyfish, particularly during the months of September and October. Although they are not lethal, their stings can be painful. Dousing in vinegar will deactivate any stingers which have not 'fired'. Calamine lotion, antihistamines and analgesics may reduce the reaction and relieve the pain.

Snakes There are lots of snakes, including the poisonous horned viper, in Tunisia, especially in the south.

To minimise your chances of being bitten always wear boots, socks and long trousers when walking through undergrowth where snakes may be present. Don't put your hands into holes and crevices, and be careful when collecting firewood.

Snake bites do not cause instantaneous death and antivenenes are usually available. Immediately wrap the bitten limb tightly, as you would for a sprained ankle, and then attach a splint to immobilise it. Keep the victim still and seek medical help, if possible keeping the dead snake for identification. Don't attempt to catch the snake if there is a possibility of being bitten again. Tourniquets and sucking out the poison have now been comprehensively discredited as methods of treatment.

Less Common Diseases

The following diseases pose a small risk to travellers, and so are only mentioned in passing. Seek medical advice if you think you may have either of these diseases.

Rabies Rabies is a fatal viral infection found in many countries, including Tunisia. Many animals can be infected (such as dogs, cats, bats and monkeys) and it is their saliva that is infectious. Any bite, scratch or even lick from a warm-blooded, furry animal should be cleaned immediately and thoroughly. Scrub with soap and running water, and then apply alcohol or iodine solution. Medical help should be sought promptly to receive a course of injections to prevent the onset of symptoms.

Tetanus Tetanus occurs when a wound becomes infected by a germ which lives in soil and in the faeces of horses and other animals. It enters the body via breaks in the skin. All wounds should be cleaned promptly and adequately and an antiseptic cream or solu-

tion applied. Use antibiotics if the wound becomes hot, throbs or pus appears. The first symptom may be discomfort in swallowing, or stiffening of the jaw and neck; this is followed by painful convulsions of the jaw and whole body. The disease can be fatal.

Women's Health

Gynaecological Problems Sexually transmitted diseases are a major cause of vaginal problems. Symptoms include a smelly discharge, painful intercourse and sometimes a burning sensation when urinating. Medical attention should be sought and male sexual partners must also be treated. Remember that, in addition to these diseases, HIV or hepatitis B may also be acquired during exposure. Besides abstinence, the best thing is to practise safe sex using condoms.

Antibiotic use, synthetic underwear, sweating and contraceptive pills can lead to fungal vaginal infections when travelling in hot climates. Maintaining good personal hygiene and wearing loose-fitting clothes and cotton underwear will help to prevent these infections.

Fungal infections, characterised by a rash, itch and discharge, can be treated with a vinegar or lemon juice douche, or with yoghurt. Nystatin, miconazole or clotrimazole pessaries or vaginal cream are the usual treatment.

Pregnancy It is not advisable to travel to some places while pregnant as some vaccinations normally used to prevent serious diseases are not advisable in pregnancy eg yellow fever. In addition, some diseases are much more serious for the mother (and may increase the risk of a stillborn child) in pregnancy eg malaria.

Most miscarriages occur during the first three months of pregnancy. Miscarriage is not uncommon, and can occasionally lead to severe bleeding. The last three months should also be spent within reasonable distance of good medical care. A baby born as early as 24 weeks stands a chance of survival, but only in a good modern hospital. Pregnant women should avoid all medication that is not absolutely necessary; however, vaccinations and malarial prophylactics should still be taken where necessary. Additional care should be taken to prevent illness and particular attention should be paid to diet and nutrition. Alcohol and nicotine, for example, should be avoided.

TOILETS

You will still come across the occasional squat toilet, but most places frequented by tourists have western-style, sit-down toilets – as do most modern Tunisian homes.

Public toilets are almost unheard of, except in places like airports and major bus and train stations. If you're caught short, the best bet is to go to a cafe, but you will be expected to buy something for the privilege of using their facilities.

WOMEN TRAVELLERS

Women travellers face an additional problem that is unlikely to be encountered by male travellers – the threat of sexual harassment. Fortunately, the situation in Tunisia is nothing like as bad as in other North African and Middle Eastern countries. The harassment is more likely to take the form of being stared at, harmless banter or proposals of marriage and declarations of undying love (or considerably less noble suggestions). Physical harassment is very rare; it may happen in a crowded medina, but it's unlikely to occur elsewhere. Most women report no problems at all.

Prior to marriage, Tunisian men have very little opportunity to meet and get to know women. Western women exist outside the Tunisian social structure and are seen as almost a different species – not bound by the laws of Islam, excitingly independent, somewhat exotic and possibly even available. Be warned that the country's beach resorts are the territory of gigolos, who spend their summers attempting to charm their way into the bedrooms of female tourists.

Women can reduce their chances of being hassled by taking a few basic precautions. Modest dress is the first and most obvious thing, particularly in more conservative rural

Poor Thing

Tunisian women love a good laugh and it doesn't take much to make them laugh. I remember my Tunisian mother-in-law collapsing with laughter when I imitated a donkey braying or when I played 'this little piggie went to market'. They also enjoy cake and gelati. If you are on the skinny side, you will be called *miskin*, 'poor thing', and they will attempt to feed you until you explode. Even if you have a strapping, healthy physique, they will feed you even more and praise Allah for your good health.

Tunisian women like to have 'foreign friends' because it makes them appear exotic. They will often try to show you off, which can be fun. My mother-in-law and I sometimes pretend to talk to each other in a made-up language, just to exaggerate it even more!

Young Tunisian men tend to make wild assumptions, based on Hollywood films, that all western women are fair game. Your best bet is to ignore all advances. It may seem rude, but it will save you much hassle. Of course, you may be persuaded to talk to one of them, in which case you might just end up marrying him, like I did!

Jamila Keppie

areas. Even in the height of summer keep shoulders, upper arms and legs covered – and not with skin-tight apparel. If you dress modestly, you will be treated with respect, largely left alone and, especially in times of trouble, helped a great deal more. Avoid eye contact with Tunisian men – dark sunglasses may help. Some travellers have reported that a headscarf can come in handy in remote areas as proof of modesty. A wedding ring can also be a useful accessory for discouraging unwelcome attention. If you are not married but are travelling in male company, say you are married rather than girlfriend/boyfriend. If you are travelling alone or in female company, a photo of some unsuspecting boyfriend or male friend also helps and, for extra kudos, you could carry a picture of your 'child'.

Women travelling alone are strongly advised not to hitchhike. They should also avoid the cheap medina hotels, which are totally unsuitable for women, and stick to the hotels recommended in the course of this book – although a recommendation is unfortunately not a guarantee against predatory staff.

The best place for women travellers to meet and talk to local women is at a hammam (public bathhouse), although you will need to speak either French or Arabic if you want to converse. See under the Activities section later in this chapter for more information on hammams.

On a more mundane level, toiletries, cosmetics, tampons etc are widely available from shops and supermarkets.

GAY & LESBIAN TRAVELLERS

While the lifestyle in Tunisia is liberal by Islamic standards, society has yet to come to terms with overt homosexuality. Homosexuality is illegal under Tunisian law.

DISABLED TRAVELLERS

If mobility is a problem and you wish to visit Tunisia, the hard fact is that most hotels, museums and sites are not wheelchair accessible. If you are determined, then take heart in the knowledge that disabled people do come to Tunisia. The trip will need careful planning, so get as much information as you can before you go. The British-based Royal Association for Disability and Rehabilitation (RADAR) publishes a useful guide called *Holidays & Travel Abroad: A Guide for Disabled People*. It's available from RADAR (☎ (0171) 637 5400) at 25 Mortimer St, London W1N 8AB.

SENIOR TRAVELLERS

Older travellers who are reasonably fit should have no problems in Tunisia, as most of the sites do not involve strenuous exertion. Avoiding the heat of the summer is advice that holds good for any age. There are no special discounts available for older travellers in Tunisia.

There are several UK tour operators who do accommodation and flight packages for the over-50s. These include Cadogan (☎ (01703) 332661), Airtours (☎ (01706) 260000) and Thomson (☎ (0121) 2523669).

Panorama Holidays (☎ (01273) 206531), 29 Queens Road, Brighton BN1 3YN, also offer bridge, painting, golf, sequence dancing and bridge holidays. Several companies offer special interest archaeology, desert safari and bird-watching tours that are suitable for older travellers, including the following:

Wigmore Holidays (☎ (0171) 486 4425), 122 Wigmore St, London, are Tunisia specialists who offer four and seven-day archaeology tours and a seven day bird-watching tour, as well as tailor-made holidays.
Explore Worldwide (☎ (01252) 319448; fax 343170), 1 Frederick St, Aldershot, Hants GU11 1LQ, has a 15 day tour that includes a camel safari and visits to Carthage and Kairouan.

See also the Organised Tours section in the main Getting There & Away chapter for more information on tours to Tunisia.

TRAVEL WITH CHILDREN

With war-torn Algeria next door, it's hardly surprising that Tunisia puts a lot of effort into promoting itself as a safe family holiday destination – which it definitely is. Most families stick to the beach resorts, probably because most children prefer playing on the beach to touring Roman ruins, but travellers who have struck out on their own have nothing but good things to report. Tunisians seem to love making a fuss of children. Baby food, nappies and other requirements are available at supermarkets everywhere.

A useful tip when travelling with children is to stick to using buses and trains – children under five travel free on buses and trains, while children under 15 pay half fare. Children are charged the full fare on louages.

Lonely Planet's *Travel with Children* is full of useful tips for parents.

DANGERS & ANNOYANCES

Probably the worst hassles you will encounter are the carpet touts of Kairouan, but they are persistent rather than threatening. There have been isolated reports of beach thefts, but they are normally the result of carelessness. Crimes such as mugging are extremely rare.

BUSINESS HOURS
Banks

From July to September, opening times for banks are 7.30 to 11 am weekdays; for the rest of the year, the hours are Monday to Thursday 8 to 11 am and 2 to 4.15 pm and Friday from 8 to 11 am and 1 to 3.15 pm. In tourist areas, one bank is rostered to open on Saturday morning. Ask at the local tourist office.

Offices

These are open Monday to Thursday from 8.30 am to 1 pm and 3 to 5.45 pm, and Friday and Saturday from 8.30 am to 1.30 pm. In summer, offices do not open in the afternoon at all.

Shops

Generally, shops are open Monday to Friday from 8 am to 12.30 pm and 2.30 to 6 pm, and from 8 am to noon on Saturday. Summer hours are usually 7.30 am to 1 pm. These hours vary slightly from place to place, especially in the south, where the weather is more extreme in summer. Souvenir shops tend to stay open as long as there are tourists around.

PUBLIC HOLIDAYS

Public holidays are primarily religious celebrations or festivities which mark the anniversary of various events in the creation of the modern state. Some of these holidays, such as Women's Day and Evacuation Day (see the table below), pass without notice. On others, everything comes to a halt and absolutely nothing happens (although transport still runs). On some long weekends, such as the 'Eid al-Fitr (celebrating the end of Ramadan, see below), public transport gets strained to the limit as everyone tries to get home for the festival.

As the Gregorian (western) and Islamic calendars are of different lengths, the Islamic holidays fall 10 days earlier every western calendar year. For more details on the Islamic calendar and holidays, see under Religion in the Facts about the Country chapter. Ramadan is the main holiday to watch out for, because for a month the opening hours of everything are disrupted.

ACTIVITIES
Ballooning

Tozeur-based AerOasis (☎ (06) 452 361) is the only company in Tunisia offering balloon flights. It operates year-round and charges TD80 for a one hour flight, travelling as far afield as Douz in search of the right conditions.

Bird-Watching

Tunisia is a good place to see an interesting variety of birds, ranging from rarities such as

---

Holidays
Dates of the Islamic holidays are as follows:

Hejra Year	New Year	Prophet's Birthday	Ramadan Begins	'Eid al-Fitr	'Eid al-Adha
1419	28.04.98	06.07.98	19.12.98	18.01.99	28.03.99
1420	17.04.99	26.06.99	09.12.99	08.01.00	16.03.00
1421	06.04.00	14.06.00	27.11.00	27.12.00	06.03.01
1422	26.03.01	12.06.01	17.11.01	16.12.01	23.02.02

Other public holidays in Tunisia are:

New Year's Day	1 January	Republic Day	25 July
Independence Day	20 March	Public Holiday	3 August
Youth Day	21 March	Women's Day	13 August
Martyrs' Day	9 April	Evacuation Day	15 October
Labour Day	1 May	Anniversary of Ben Ali's Takeover	7 November

Festivals

Numerous festivals are held throughout the year in Tunisia. Although most are staged with the tourist trade foremost in the minds of the organisers, they are worth a look if you are in the area. The main ones are:

December/January
   Sahara Festival (Douz & Tozeur) – this has everything from camel races to traditional marriages
April
   Nefta Festival – features parades and folkloric events
May
   Monastir Festival – more parades!
June-July
   Festival of Malouf (Testour) – performances of Tunisia's musical emblem, malouf
July-August
   Carthage International Festival – Tunisia's cultural event of the year, with music, poetry and theatre performances at the Roman theatre at Carthage
   Dougga Festival – floodlit performances of classical drama in the restored theatre at Dougga
   El-Jem International Symphonic Music Festival – candle-lit performances of works by composers such as Mozart, Bach and Bizet at El-Jem's famous colosseum
   Siren Festival (Kerkennah Islands) – more folkloric favourites for the tourists
   Hammamet Festival – this is a serious arts festival, in spite of the location and timing, with musical and cultural events
   Tabarka Festival – music and theatre, and a coral exhibition
   Ulysses Festival (Jerba) – strictly for the tourists this one, right down to the Miss Ulysses competition
August
   Baba Aoussou Festival (Sousse) – another event for the tourists
September
   Grombalia Wine Festival – this sounds more promising than the month's other candidate, the *Wheat Festival* at Beja
October
   Carthage International Film Festival – biennial, even-numbered years, every other year it is held in Ouagadougou (Burkina Faso); two weeks of films from around the world, with an emphasis on Arab and African cinema
November
   Festival of the Ksour (Ksar Ouled Soltane) – performances of traditional dance etc in the courtyard of the Ksar Ouled Soltane

Audouin's gull to local specialities such as Levaillant's woodpecker and Moussier's redstart. Although Tunisia doesn't have many resident species, it is an important stopover for migratory birds. Spring and autumn are therefore the best times to see a wide range of birds. Ichkeul National Park, in the north, is a prime bird-watching site. For more information, see the illustrated Flora & Fauna of Tunisia section in the Facts about the Country chapter.

Camel Trekking

Camel trekking has become big business in recent years. The place to head for is the village of Zaafrane, 12km south-west of Douz, where you can organise anything from a one hour ride (TD3.500) to an eight day, oasis-hopping trek to Ksar Ghilane and back (TD30 per day).

Diving & Watersports

The best place to go diving is Tabarka on the north coast. The Club de Plongée (☎ (08) 644 478), at the marina, organises trips, rents equipment and runs courses for beginners. Other centres include Centre International de Plongée (☎ (03) 614 799) in Port el-Kantaoui and Ecole de Plongée de Monastir (☎ (03) 661 156) in Monastir.

The beaches of the big tourist resorts (Hammamet, Sousse, Monastir and Jerba) are the places to go for watersports. You'll find a whole range of activities such as windsurfing, waterskiing and parasailing.

Dune Skiing

The Hôtel Faouar (☎ (05) 491 531; fax 491 295), 30km south-west of Douz at the tiny oasis village of El-Faouar, includes dune skiing on its list of activities.

Golf

Tunisia has six golf courses, none built with local players in mind. They are at Hammamet (☎ (02) 282 722), Monastir (☎ (03) 461120), Skanes (☎ (03) 461 833), Tabarka (☎ (08) 644 321) and Tunis (☎ (01) 765 919). The Tunis course is at La Soukhra, north of the airport.

Hammams

Hammams (public bathhouses) are one of the focal points of life in every Tunisian town, as they are just about everywhere in the Middle East and North Africa. They are much more than just a place to go and clean up. In the Roman fashion, they are places to go to unwind and socialise. Every town has at least one hammam, with separate admission times for men and women, while the bigger towns have separate ones for each sex. Some resort towns have unisex hammams for the benefit of the tourists. Hammams are recommended as a good way to get a glimpse of Tunisian life.

Men don't need to take anything along. The standard TD1.500 charge includes a *fouta* (cotton bath towel), which is worn around the waist while you move about the hammam (don't walk around naked). The charge also includes a rubdown with a *kassa*, a coarse mitten that is used to remove the grime and dead skin after your stint in the steam room. It is usually possible to have a massage as well.

Women are not issued with a fouta and so will need to bring along a towel. The idea is to wear a pair of underpants while washing, so you'll need to bring a dry pair to change into. Be warned: a rubdown with the kassa is not for for the faint-hearted – it can be quite rough.

Land Yachting

Air Tropic (see Scenic Flights following) rents out the only land yachts in the country, for TD10 per hour. The sand flats south of Aghir on the island of Jerba stretch for miles and are a perfect location for this activity.

Scenic Flights

Scenic flights are a very recent addition to the activity list. The only place offering flights is Jerba, where Air Tropic (☎ (09) 723 344) charges TD30 for a 30 minute ride in one of its tiny Petrel hydroplanes. It operates from the sand flats south of Aghir on the east coast of the island.

Swimming

The best beaches are in the north of Tunisia. Many Tunisians rate the beach at Sidi Ali el-Mekki, in the north-east near Ghar el-Melh, as the best beach in the country. There are more good beaches on the north coast around Tabarka and Bizerte. These are much less crowded than the beaches of the major resorts, such as Hammamet, Sousse and Monastir.

The beaches further south look attractive enough in the glossy tourist brochures, but are not much good for swimming. The sea is so shallow around the Kerkennah Islands and Gabès that you have to walk out hundreds of metres just to get your knees wet. The best beach in the south is at Aghir, on the east coast of Jerba.

Trekking

Tunisia is only just starting to wake up to the possibilities for trekking. The forests of the Kroumirie Mountains around 'Ain Draham have enormous potential as a trekking destination. The region is stunningly beautiful and conditions are perfect for walking in spring and autumn. The potential is limited by the absence of the sort of detailed local maps you need in order to venture off the beaten track by yourself.

The Hôtel Rihana (☎ (08) 655 391; fax 655 396) in 'Ain Draham offers a range of guided treks for small groups for about TD40 per day.

Yachting

Tourist authorities have taken to promoting the country as a destination for yachting people. The main attraction seems to be the price of winter berthing compared with prices in the trendy northern Mediterranean. The largest yachting marinas are at Monastir, Port el-Kantaoui, Sidi Bou Saïd, Tabarka and Zarzis.

LANGUAGE COURSES

The Institut Bourguiba des Langues Vivantes (☎ (01) 282 418; fax 780 398), 47 Ave de la Liberté, 1002 Tunis Belvedere, offers summer and year-long courses in standard

Arabic and Tunisian Arabic (see the Language Appendix for information about these two forms of Arabic).

ACCOMMODATION
Camping
Camping has not caught on in the same way as it has in other parts of the Mediterranean. There are few official camp sites, and facilities tend to be pretty basic. Most charge about TD2.500 per person.

Camp sites apart, it should be possible to camp anywhere as long as you get the permission of the landowner. We have not heard of any readers having problems camping.

Sleeping out on the beach is the accepted thing in the north at Raf Raf and Ghar el-Melh, near Bizerte, and the same applies to the remote beaches of the north coast. The same does not apply, however, to the beaches in the resort areas of the Cap Bon Peninsula, Jerba and Sousse.

Hostels
Hostels fall into two categories. There are the *auberges de jeunesse*, affiliated to Hostelling International, and there are the government-run *maisons des jeunes*. They couldn't be more different.

The auberges de jeunesse are thoroughly recommended. Most have prime locations, such as a converted palace in the Tunis medina and a fascinating old funduq (caravanserai) in Houmt Souq on Jerba. Others are located at Remel Plage outside Bizerte and at the beach in Nabeul. See Places to Stay under the individual town entries for more details.

They generally charge about TD3.500 per night, with breakfast available for TD1 and other meals for TD3 each. Their popularity means that they impose a three night limit during the high season.

There's no reason for anyone to introduce any time limits at the maisons des jeunes. Almost without exception (see the one at 'Ain Draham), they are characterless concrete boxes with all the charm of an army barracks. They are run along the same lines. Almost every town has one, normally stuck way out in the middle of nowhere. They are

used mainly for holiday camps for school kids, or to accommodate visiting sporting teams. The only reason to mention them is that in some towns they are the only budget accommodation option. They all charge TD4 for a dormitory bed. Breakfast is served only for groups of 10 or more.

There are a couple of places where the maison des jeunes concept has evolved into a grander scheme called *centre des stages et vacances*, which are holiday camps that combine hostel and camp site. These are located right on the beach at Aghir on Jerba, in the oasis at Gabès and north of Kelibia on Cap Bon (see the relevant chapters for more details). Camping charges are TD2 per person and 500 mills per tent. Power and hot showers are available.

Hotels
Hotel prices are controlled by the government and hotels must display the tariff by the reception desk.

Tunisian hotels fall into two main categories: classified hotels, which have been awarded between one and five stars under the government's rating system; and non-classified hotels, which haven't. They are indicated by the initials NC (*non-classifié*) on the accommodation lists handed out by tourist offices.

The fact that a hotel has not been classified does not mean it is no good – the majority of the budget places recommended in this book are non-classified. You can normally find reasonable singles/doubles with shared bathroom for around TD8/14, sometimes less. Hot showers normally cost extra.

Gambling

If you like a flutter, Tunisia has Promosport, its version of the soccer pools. It involves selecting the results (home win, away win or draw) of 14 games. You need to get at least 12 correct to win. Tickets are available from all cafes and cost 500 mills for four bets or TD1 for eight, plus 50 mills commission. The cut-off day is Thursday. ■

The cheapest rooms are found at the non-classified hotels in the medinas of the major cities. They are basic, often with no showers, and you pay for a bed in a shared room. The price ranges from TD2.500 to TD5 per person, depending on the level of facilities. If you want the room to yourself, you will normally be asked to pay for all the beds. Note that these hotels are not generally recommended for westerners and they are totally unsuitable for women travellers.

The majority of hotels are classified. The one and two star hotels tend to be smaller, older hotels, often built in colonial times. They are generally clean, if a little shabby, and are popular with local business travellers and tourists who want a decent double room with private bathroom and hot water. A three star rating usually indicates a hotel built to cater for tour groups. Four and five star hotels are of international standard with all the usual facilities.

A word of warning – at the time of going to press, the prices of some middle to top range hotels appeared to be on the increase, by up to 20%. Prices are normally listed according to three seasons – high (*haute*), middle (*moyenne*) and low (*basse*). The high season runs from 1 July to 15 September, low season is from 1 November to 15 March, and the rest is middle season. Typical high-season charges for single and double rooms in these categories are: one star – TD21/35; two star – TD30/45; three star – TD50/75; four star – TD65/90; and five star – TD100/130. There can be huge price differences between seasons, especially in resort areas. In Hammamet, for example, prices for singles/doubles at the four star Sheraton Hôtel fall from TD66.500/92 in high season to TD52/ 76 in middle season and a bargain TD26/39 in low season.

Most hotels serve breakfast. At classified hotels, the room rates include breakfast; at non-classified hotels, breakfast is often quoted separately, so ask. A typical hotel breakfast consists of coffee, French bread, butter and jam. Occasionally, you may be lucky enough to be offered a croissant instead of the French bread.

ENTERTAINMENT
Cinemas
Cinemas are everywhere in Tunisia and are a popular form of entertainment. The film posters point to lots of Rambo-style action, all in French or Arabic. A ticket costs between TD1.200 and TD2.

The Carthage International Film Festival, which shows films from around the world, with an emphasis on Arab and African cinema, is held in October in even-numbered years.

Discos
Discos exist basically for the benefit of tourists and are virtually always associated with big hotels in the main tourist areas.

SPECTATOR SPORT
Soccer
When Tunisians say football, it's soccer they're referring to. It's the country's most popular sport. After school, every side street and patch of wasteland is taken over by kids kicking a ball around.

Tunisia fields one of the strongest teams in Africa, and will be one of the five African representatives at the 1998 World Cup finals in France. It will be the country's second appearance in the finals; the first was in 1978 when the team failed to advance beyond the group stage despite defeating Mexico 3-1 and holding West Germany to a 0-0 draw.

Tunisia enhanced its reputation as one of Africa's leading soccer nations by producing a stirring performance to reach the final of the 1996 African Nations Cup, eventually losing 2-0 to host nation South Africa. Hopes that the team could go one step better in 1998 were dashed when the team failed to make it past the quarter finals.

Tunisia's club teams are also among the best on the continent, with Club Athlétique Bizertin (Bizerte), Club Africain (Tunis) and Etoile Sportif du Sahel (Sousse) all winning African Cup competitions in recent years.

Domestically, the nation's top teams play in a 14 club first division. The competition runs from early October until the end of

March, with matches played on Sunday afternoon starting at 2 pm.

At the time of writing, the first division was as follows: Avenir Sportif de la Marsa (ASM), Club Africain (CA), Club Sportif de Hammam Lif (CSHL), CO Transport (COT), Espérance Sportive de Tunisie (EST) – all from Tunis; Etoile Sportif du Sahel from Sousse; Club Sportif Sfaxien from Sfax; Olympique du Kef (OK) from Le Kef; Club Olympique Medenine (COM); Espérance Sportive de Zarzis (ESZ); and Club Athlétique Bizertin (CAB).

The top clubs are joined by teams from the lower divisions to contest the Tunisian Cup, a knock-out competition which is played midweek.

Athletics
Like its North African neighbours, Algeria and Morocco, Tunisia has a history of producing good middle and long distance runners. You'll see plenty of budding young athletes out pounding the streets in the early hours of the day, no doubt dreaming of emulating the feats of the country's greatest runner, Mohammed Gammoudi, who won medals at three Olympic Games. Gammoudi started with silver in the 10,000m at the Olympic Games in Tokyo, struck gold over 5000m in Mexico City in 1968 and then collected another silver over the same distance in Munich in 1972.

Volleyball
Volleyball is also popular. At the time of writing, the national team was ranked No 16 in the world after winning the 1997 African Championships in Lagos, defeating Cameroon 3-0 in the final. The papers indicate that this is also the most popular women's sport, although they don't give any details of when or where matches are played. There are national volleyball competitions for both men and women.

Handball
While something of a curiosity to many westerners, handball is taken very seriously in Tunisia. The national men's team is ranked

among the best in the world, and the national competition gets a lot of press coverage.

THINGS TO BUY
Rugs & Carpets
These are among the most readily available souvenirs and, although they are not cheap, there are some really beautiful ones for sale. The main carpet-selling centres are Tunis, Kairouan, Tozeur and Jerba.

There are two basic types of carpet: knotted and woven. The traditional (pre-Islamic conquest) carpet industry was based on the weaving of *mergoums* and *kilims*. Mergoums feature very bright, geometric designs, with bold use of reds, purples, blues and other vivid colours. Kilims use traditional Berber motifs on a woven background. Both are reasonably cheap to buy – you can reckon on paying about TD60 per sq metre.

Allouchas are a type of thick-pile Berber woven rug, spun by hand in wool. They feature natural tones and are decorated with simple traditional Berber motifs. Look for them in 'Ain Draham, where they are produced by a small women's cooperative called Les Tapis de Kroumirie. (See under

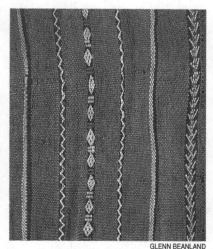

GLENN BEANLAND
Flatwoven Berber rug, with traditional motifs.

'Ain Draham in the Northern Tunisia chapter for more details.) They are also sold in Tunis at Main des Femmes, above the Banque de l'Habitat in Ave Habib Bourguiba.

The best known of the knotted carpets are the classical (Persian-style) Kairouan carpets. This style of carpet-making was first introduced to Tunisia by the Turks. Legend has it that the first knotted carpet to be made in Tunisia was by the daughter of the Turkish governor of Kairouan. Whatever the truth might be, today Kairouan is the carpet capital of the country.

Knotted carpets are priced according to the number of knots per sq metre. A carpet with 40,000 knots per sq metre costs around TD130 per sq metre; a fine carpet with 250,000 knots per sq metre can cost up to TD1500. The Berber *guetiffa* is a another type of knotted carpet. It is a thick-pile carpet, normally cream coloured, with Berber motifs.

All these types of carpets are on sale at ONAT emporiums in all the major tourist centres. They will all have been inspected by ONAT and classified according to type and number of knots. They come with an affixed label giving this information. At the time of research, ONAT shops were being replaced in most towns by SOCOPA shops, so it's worth keeping a look out for both.

The different qualities are ordinary (*deuxième choix*) – up to 40,000 knots per sq metre; fine (*premier choix*) – up to 90,000 knots per sq metre; and superfine (*qualité supérieure*) – up to 250,000 knots per sq metre. Prices are fixed at ONAT shops and are slightly higher than those elsewhere.

Many of the carpets on sale elsewhere have also been inspected by ONAT and come with a label of authenticity attached. There are also a great many carpets on sale that have not been classified by ONAT. The prices will be cheaper, but the quality may be suspect – the only safeguard is to know your product.

Pottery

Tunisia has a long connection with the art of pottery. The main centre is Nabeul, partly because of the number of tourists that pass through there; Guellala on the island of Jerba is another.

Leather

There is plenty of leatherwork for sale in the souq in Tunis, and some of it is really fine work. Much of it comes from Morocco, however, and is not all that cheap.

Leatherwork that originates in Tunisia often comes from Kairouan. Articles for sale include traditional pieces such as camel and donkey saddles, water skins and cartridge pouches, as well as more mundane objects like wallets and belts.

Copper & Brass

Beaten copper and brass items are also popular and are widely available. Beaten plates, which range in size from a saucer to a coffee table, make good souvenirs, although transporting the larger ones can be a problem.

Jewellery

Arabic jewellery (and particularly gold jewellery) is often too gaudy and ornate for western tastes.

The hand of Fatima (daughter of the Prophet) or *khomsa* is a traditional Arabic design; it can be found in varying sizes, from small earrings to large neck pendants, and is usually made of silver. In pre-Islamic times this same design represented Baal, the protector of the Carthaginians.

Other traditional pieces of jewellery include the *hedeyed*, which are finely engraved, wide bracelets made of gold or silver, and the *kholkal*, which are similar, but worn around the ankle. In Carthaginian times the kholkal were a sign of chastity; today they are still a symbol of fidelity and are often part of a bride's dowry.

The quality of pure silver and gold jewellery can be established by the official stamps used to grade all work. The quality of unstamped items is immediately suspect. The stamps in use are: the horse's head – used to mark all 18 carat gold jewellery (the horse's

Take five – the hand of Fatima is a traditional, and ubiquitous, design motif.

head was the Carthaginian symbol for money); the scorpion – used on all nine carat gold jewellery; grape clusters – used on silver graded at 900 mills per gram; and the Negro head – used on poorer quality silver graded at 800 mills per gram.

Miscellaneous
Chechias *Chechias* are the small, red felt hats worn by older Tunisian men. The chechia souq in Tunis is the obvious place to look for them. Quality varies, but an average price is around TD5.

Esparto Goods Rectangular, woven esparto baskets are practical and cheap. Some are pretty awful, with pictures of camels and 'typical desert scenes' woven into them, but there are plenty of other more simple designs. Hats and fans are other popular goods. Most of the esparto items come from Gabès and Jerba in the south of the country.

Perfume Cheap scented oils are sold everywhere. Bottle sizes range from a tiny 5ml (TD1.500) up to a whopping 500ml.

Sand Roses You'll find these for sale all over the country, and in fact all over the Maghreb. They are formed of gypsum, which is present in the sand and has been dissolved and then dehydrated many times. When it crystallises, beautiful patterns are formed.

They are most prominent in Southern Tunisia, and range from about 5cm in diameter up to the size of a large watermelon. They do make good cheap souvenirs but, unless you have a vehicle, carting around a great load of gypsum for days or weeks on end isn't much fun.

Chichas The ubiquitous water pipes come in all shapes and sizes and are readily available from souqs and tourist shops, ranging in price from TD4 for a small cheap one up to TD70 for a good quality, full-size version.

Stuffed Camels It seems that in Arabic desert countries you can tell how well developed the tourist industry is by the number of stuffed camels for sale – and Tunisia is way out in front in this field. Every souvenir shop has a selection, ranging from pocket size right up to about one-third full size. Prices start at TD1.500.

Jigsaws Editions Alif (see under Children in the Books section earlier in this chapter) produces a range of jigsaws for various age groups. There are 100-piece maps of both Tunis and the Tunis medina (TD6), a 50 piece puzzle of a mosaic of two fighting cocks (TD4.800) and several mini-puzzles for TD1.500. They are available from the Editions Alif outlet in Tunis and the shop at the Dar Charait Museum in Tozeur.

More widely on sale are 200-piece jigsaws of Sidi Bou Saïd, Carthage, Jerba and the Kerkennah Islands. Monoprix supermarkets stock the full range for TD10.400. They cost a couple of TD less from tourist stalls such as those in the middle of Ave Habib Bourguiba in Tunis.

Markets

Town and village life often revolves around the weekly markets. Market day is a good day to be in a town, as it will be far more lively than usual and, apart from the itinerant merchants selling fairly mundane household goods, there will be other local people who have travelled in from the outlying districts.

Some markets have become real tourist traps, and for that reason are crowded and worth avoiding; nevertheless, it is on market days that there is the best selection of stuff for sale. Nabeul is one that fits into this category.

Market Days

Day	Location
Monday:	'Ain Draham, El-Jem, Houmt Souq, Kairouan and Tataouine
Tuesday:	Beja, Ghardimao and Kasserine
Wednesday:	Jendouba and Sbeitla
Thursday:	Douz, Gafsa, Nefta and Tebersouk
Friday:	Mahdia, Mateur, Midoun, Nabeul, Sfax, Tabarka, Zaghouan and Zarzis
Saturday:	Ben Guerdane, El-Fahs and Monastir
Sunday:	Hammam Lif and Sousse

Tunisian Cuisine

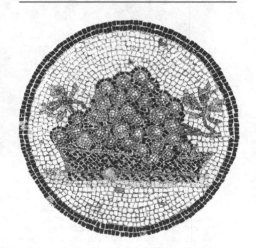

Title page: Basket of grapes – detail of a mosaic from the House of Africa (El-Jem Museum).

FOOD

Tunisia's national dish is *couscous* (semolina granules) which, together with bread, is the main staple of the diet. Couscous is not a separate grain, as is often thought, but is derived from durum wheat. It's thought to have been originally created by the Berbers, and primitive coucous steamers have been found in tombs in the Maghreb dating back to 200 BC. Couscous is usually served in a large bowl with a stew and the ubiquitous *harissa* (spicy chilli sauce) poured over it, and is found everywhere in Tunisia. There are said to be more than 300 ways of preparing it – sweet as well as savoury. A bowl served with stew costs about TD3 in local restaurants.

DAMIEN SIMONIS

Rice, couscous, pasta and dried pulses are readily available from shops and stalls, like this one in the medina at Kairouan.

Couscous is sold everywhere in a pre-cooked or instant form that takes a couple of minutes to prepare. This is quite a recent invention; traditionally, all couscous was made by hand by the women of the household. This was an arduous daily task which involved rubbing semolina grains, flour and salted water together by hand until all the grains were coated with flour. Pre-cooked couscous, with its political implications for the emancipation of women, is claimed as a Tunisian invention.

Couscous, home-made or pre-cooked, is usually steamed over the stew as it cooks, traditionally in a special *couscoussier*. This quintessentially North African piece of equipment consists of a large vessel (made of tin, aluminium, stainless steel or earthenware) with two parts: a lower part in which the stew is cooked and an upper part which holds the couscous. The removable upper part has a perforated base, allowing steam from below to permeate and flavour the couscous.

Other popular Tunisian dishes include:

briq
This curiosity of Tunisian cuisine consists of a crisp, very thin deep fried pastry envelope which comes with a range of fillings always including egg.
chorba bil djej
Thick spicy chicken soup with rice-shaped pasta.
harissa
A fiery red chilli paste that comes as a side-serve with almost everything.
kammounia
Meat stew made with lots of cumin.

lablabi
A chickpea broth which is doled out on a bed of broken bread and spiced up with harissa.

mloukhia
Similar to kammounia, except that it's made with a blend of dried herbs. Cuts of lamb or beef are simmered until they almost disappear into the rich, green sauce.

salade mechouia
A very spicy mixture of grilled tomato, capsicum and chilli, which is served as an accompaniment to dishes such as roast chicken.

salade tunisienne
Finely diced salad vegetables mixed with a dressing of lemon juice and olive oil.

shakshuka
A thick vegetable soup based on onions and green peppers. Unfortunately for vegetarians, it's normally made from a meat stock.

ojja
Sometimes described as Tunisian scrambled eggs, ojja is spicy tomato sauce with eggs stirred in at the end.

tajine
The Tunisian version is no relation to its Moroccan namesake. It's similar to quiche and is normally served cold with chips and salad.

One lasting legacy of the days of the French protectorate is the excellent bread. Baguettes, the long, crusty loaf revered by the French, are the main form of bread. It's the mainstay of the Tunisian diet, and is available at bakeries and shops everywhere for a standard 160 mills. A basket of bread comes free with your meal at all restaurants.

DAMIEN SIMONIS

Although instant couscous has made the arduous task of grinding semolina granules a thing of the past in towns and cities, it's still part of the daily ritual for many women in the more remote areas of the country, especially in the south.

Vegetarian

Vegetarians are in for a hard time. Tunisians love their meat and can't understand why anyone would want to give it up. There are very few dishes that don't contain meat in some form. Even seemingly safe dishes such as salade tunisienne and salade mechaouia normally come garnished with tuna, while soups and stews use a meat stock.

The result is that vegetarians will need to do a fair amount of self catering (see also under Self Catering later in this section). If you eat dairy products, these can be a good fallback. You'll find a good range of local cheeses at supermarkets, and yoghurt is available everywhere. Fruit is also plentiful and cheap.

Fast Food

Almost every town has a shop selling *casse-croûtes*, half a French loaf stuffed with a choice of fillings – fried egg, chips and harissa is a favourite, known as *khaftegi*. Western-style fast food is also becoming popular. Pizza parlours and hamburger joints can be found in most of the major towns. Pizza is very popular. It is normally made in large trays, then cut up and sold by weight (from TD6 per kg). After a couple of days in Tunisia it will come as no surprise to discover that tuna is the most popular topping.

Sweets & Pastries

Sweet-toothed travellers have quite a line-up of treats to look forward to. The French left their mark with their patisseries. The best are on Ave Habib Bourguiba in Tunis, where you'll find shop after shop selling

TUNISIAN RECIPES

Harissa

Harissa is widely used throughout the Maghreb for flavouring cous-cous, stews and soups.

Ingredients
100g hot, dried red chilli peppers
6 cloves of garlic
4 tbsp sea salt
6 tbsp coriander seeds
4 tbsp cumin seeds
10 tbsp of olive oil

Method
Peel the garlic. Using a mortar and pestle, pound the garlic with the salt until smooth, and set aside. Remove the seeds and stems from the chillies and soak them in hot water until soft. Crush the drained chillies in the mortar with another two tablespoons of salt. Add to the garlic paste. Place the coriander and cumin seeds in the mortar and use the pestle to pound them to a powder. Add the garlic and chilli paste and a little olive oil and pound until smooth. Continue this process, adding up to 10 tablespoons of olive oil, until the sauce is well blended.

Salade Mechouia

This spicy vegetable mixture is popular as a dip, mopped up with crusty bread, or as an accompaniment to otherwise bland meals like chicken and chips.

Ingredients
Serves four
4 large ripe tomatoes
2 large green capsicums
3 or 4 green chillies
1 garlic clove, crushed
pinch of salt
1 tsp ground caraway seeds
juice of half a lemon
olive oil
tuna chunks, boiled egg and black olives, to decorate

Method
Grill the tomatoes, capsicums and green chillies until the skins are blistered and charred. Allow to cool for a few minutes then peel off the skins, rinse and pat dry. Remove the seeds and dice. Mash the diced vegetables with the garlic, salt, caraway seeds and lemon juice. Spread out on a serving plate, sprinkle liberally with good quality olive oil and decorate with chunks of tuna, slices of boiled egg and black olives.

Ojja

This dish is delicious at any time of day, including breakfast. Some Tunisians swear that it's the ultimate hangover cure!

Ingredients
Serves four
2 large, very ripe tomatoes
5 tbsp olive oil
4 green chillies, finely chopped
4 tbsp tomato paste
4 cloves garlic, crushed
1 tsp harissa
1 tsp ground caraway seeds
½ cup of water
6 eggs

Method
Chop the tomatoes and fry them in the olive oil until they start to disintegrate. Stir in the green chillies, tomato paste, garlic, harissa, ground caraway seeds and water and bring to the boil. Simmer for 10 minutes then add two eggs and mix them into the sauce until they set. Add four more eggs around the pan, cover and poach until set.
   Serve with chunks of fresh, crusty bread.

Chorba bil Djej

This thick, spicy soup is delicious on cold winter days, accompanied by plenty of fresh, crusty bread. *Chorba* – the ingredient that gives the dish its name – is a locally produced rice-shaped pasta.

Ingredients
Serves six
1kg chicken pieces (or 500g chopped chicken fillet)
salt and pepper to taste
2 tbsp tomato paste
½ tsp harissa
2 tbsp chopped parsley
1 stick celery, chopped
6 cups water
250g chorba (rice-shaped pasta)

Method
Season the chicken with salt and pepper and brown the pieces in a large pan. Add the tomato paste, harissa, parsley, celery and sufficient water to cover. Bring to the boil and simmer for 30 minutes – or until the chicken is well cooked. Add six cups of water and return to the boil before adding the chorba (*rizini* makes a good substitute if you're unable to find chorba); simmer until the pasta is cooked.

Baklava is only one of a range of yummy treats to tempt the sweet-toothed traveller.

delicious chocolate and almond croissants and a colourful assortment of cakes overloaded with chocolate.

The Turks brought their range of goodies, too. Favourites include *baklava* (layers of pastry filled with crushed nuts and honey) and *loukoum* (Turkish delight). The best loukoum comes from Kairouan, which is also famous for its *makhroud* – small cakes made from semolina and dates.

The *corne de gazelle*, a pastry horn filled with chopped nuts and drowned in honey, is a speciality of southern Tunisia.

Fruit

Tunisia is a great place for fruit eaters. There's always fresh, locally grown fruit of some description to be found at the markets.

Spring is the only time of year when the pickings are a bit slim, but you'll still find fresh oranges. The first fruit of the new season are medlars (also known as loquats). They are closely followed by cherries, apricots, plums and other stone fruit, melons and watermelons.

Grapes make their first appearance on the scene in late June, but the best eating varieties don't reach the markets until the end of August. Look out for the delicious white muscats from around Kelibia and *razzegoui*, a large white grape that ripens to a pink blush. August is also the month for figs and peaches.

Prickly pears, also known as barbary figs or cactus fruit, are very popular. Their season is from October until December, when you'll see street vendors pushing around barrows of the plump, orange/red fruit. The vendors will peel them for you, so you don't have to contend with the prickles. You should never touch the unpeeled fruit with bare hands. The prickles are so fine as to be virtually invisible – but you'll soon know all about them if you pick one up. It's a mistake that most people only make once.

October is the time of year when pomegranates start to make their appearance. These beautiful ruby-red fruit are a colourful addition to the marketplace – and they taste as good as they look. November is the start of the date season. The best variety is *deglat ennour* (finger of light), so called because of the delicate, translucent quality of the flesh. Tunisia also produces a lot of citrus fruit, particularly oranges and mandarins. The season starts in December and extends through until March.

Bananas are available all year round. Most are imported from South America, but some are grown locally. The bananas from around El-Haouaria (Cap Bon) and the southern oases are smaller and sweeter than the imported varieties and worth seeking out.

DAMIEN SIMONIS

Souqs are the best places to pick up fresh fruit and vegetables.

Restaurants

Restaurants can be divided into three broad categories:

gargottes
   This is where you'll find most of the food mentioned above. Gargottes vary from very basic to slightly upmarket. Generally a main dish and salad won't cost much over TD3.500. Many serve fish, lamb cutlets and kebabs.

rôtisseries
   These are easy to spot because they normally have a rotating spit of roast chickens outside. That's about all they serve, usually with chips and salad. Prices start at TD1.700 for a quarter of a chicken.

tourist restaurants
   Many serve what they like to call Franco-Tunisienne cuisine. If you can avoid lobster, most meals cost under TD15. Tourist restaurants normally sell alcohol – unlike the others.

Glossary of Food Terms

The Arabic and French terms listed below will help you negotiate your way through Tunisia's markets and eateries to chop-licking satisfaction. See also the Language Appendix for a more general list of Arabic and French terms.

English	Arabic	French
Soup	**Chorba**	**Potage**
spicy lentil soup	harira	soupe aux lentilles
Vegetables	**Khadrawaat**	**Légumes**
carrots	kheezoo gazar	carottes
cucumber	khiyaar	concombre
green beans	loobeeya	haricots verts
haricot beans	fasooliya	haricots blancs
lentils	'aads	lentilles
olives	zeetoun	olives
onion	besla	oignon
peas	zelbana/bisila	petits pois
potatoes	batatas	pommes de terre
tomato	mataisha/tamatim	tomate
Meat	**Lehem**	**Viande**
camel	lehem jemil	chameau
chicken	farooj/dujaj	poulet
kidneys	kelawwi	rognons
lamb	lehem ghenmee	agneau
liver	kebda	foie
Fish	**Samak**	**Poisson**
lobster	laangos	homard
red mullet	trilya	rouget
shrimp	qaimroon	crevette
tuna	ton	thon
Fruit	**Fakiya**	**Fruits**
apple	teffah	pomme
apricot	mesh-mash	abricot
banana	banan/moz	banane
dates	tmer	dattes
figs	kermoos	figues
grapes	'eineb	raisins
orange	portaghal	orange
pomegranate	remman	grenade
watermelon	dellah	pastèque
Miscellaneous		
bread	khubz	pain
butter	zebda	beurre
cheese	fromaj	fromage
chips	ships	frites
eggs	bayd	oeufs
oil	zit	huile
pepper	filfil/lebzaar	poivre
salt	melha	sel
sugar	sukur	sucre
yoghurt	zabadee/laban danoon	yaourt

BETHUNE CARMICHAEL

If your tannin and sugar levels need a turbo boost, try a drop of Tunisian-style tea.

Self Catering

Self caterers will find supermarkets in all the major towns and resort areas, although Tunisian supermarkets are very poorly stocked by western standards. In fact, they are more like budget department stores and often have very little space devoted to food. What they do normally have, however, is a good dairy produce section with cheese, yoghurt and (occasionally) fresh milk. The country's biggest supermarket chain is Monoprix, which has branches in all the major towns. Monoprix supermarkets also stock a good range of local wines.

Supermarkets don't sell fruit and vegetables, which are readily available from shops and stalls. Major towns have special produce markets.

DRINKS

Nonalcoholic Drinks

Tunisians are great coffee drinkers, and great coffee is only as far away as the nearest cafe. Most cafes have an espresso machine and offer a choice of styles. The most popular is *exprès*, which equates to a short black. A *capucin* bears absolutely no resemblance to a cappucino; it's a short black with a barely detectable dash of milk. The closest thing to a cappucino is a *café direct*, which is served with milk foamed in the espresso machine. They also serve Turkish coffee, called *café turc*. Upmarket cafes in tourist areas also sell filtered coffee.

Tea is also popular, but most westerners have trouble with the Tunisian way of drinking it. All types of tea – black, green and mint – are treated in the same way: almost equal quantities of tea leaves, sugar and water are boiled up to produce something with a viscosity similar to tar. It is then sipped from very small cups. Mint tea normally comes served with a sprig of fresh mint, which makes it look attractive at least.

English-style tea is known as *thé au lait* and is available only from tourist cafes and hotels. Unfortunately UHT milk is used. You'll occasionally find fresh milk in supermarkets, but don't count on it. UHT milk is available everywhere.

Bottled mineral water is cheap and available everywhere. Safia is the most popular brand. Coca-Cola and all the others are here in force. They are known collectively as *boissons gazeuses* (carbonated drinks). Freshly squeezed orange juice is readily available in season. You can find packaged juices in supermarkets, but they are expensive.

Alcoholic Drinks

Drinking alcohol is forbidden by Islam, but that doesn't stop a lot of Tunisians from indulging in the odd tipple. Alcohol is readily available. It is sold at bars and some restaurants as well as from supermarkets. Supermarkets sell alcohol from midday to 6.30 pm only, and not on Friday. Alcohol you have bought from a supermarket should be carried discreetly, preferably in a closed bag.

Celtia is the only beer in Tunisia. A 330ml bottle sells for TD1.400 at bars in Tunis, and for as little as TD1.200 outside the capital. Supermarkets stock only 300ml cans, which sell for 730 mills.

Thibarine is a local curiosity produced in the village of Thibar (in the Tebersouk Mountains near Dougga). It's made according to a secret recipe dreamt up last century by French monks from the order of the White Fathers. Supposedly a digestive, it tastes like herbal cough mixture. The only local spirit is a fiery product called *boukha*, made from

Quench your thirst and feast your eyes at one of these exquisite lemonade stands.

figs. It is generally consumed with a mixer. If you are curious, a small bottle costs TD2.800.

Bars

Bars can be found in all the major towns. They are generally hard-drinking, smoke-filled, male preserves. Travellers, particularly women, may feel more comfortable drinking at the resort hotels.

Tunisian Wine

Wine was first produced in Tunisia in the times of the Phoenicians, although the modern industry is descended from French and Italian plantings during the 19th and 20th centuries. In the 1950s Tunisia, along with Algeria and Morocco, accounted for two-thirds of the international wine market, most of it flowing north across the Mediterranean to France. Nowadays, Tunisian wine is probably not about to threaten Bordeaux, but there are quite a few moderately priced, medium-dry wines that may pleasantly surprise you.

Wine production has fallen steadily since independence, and of the 28,000 hectares still under vine today, about half are dedicated to wine production. Although drinking alcohol is prohibited by Islam, only about one-third of the annual vintage is exported. The industry is regulated by the government *Office du Vin*, which lays down Tunisia's wine regions in a quality designation system based on the one used in France, the *appellations controlées*.

The main wine-producing areas are Cap Bon and Nabeul, with smaller amounts of wine produced at Zaghouan, Bin Arus, Bizerte and Aryanah. Growers are generally grouped into cooperatives rather than selling wine individually. Some of the better-known independent producers include Tardi, Château Feriani and the Société Lomblot.

The main grape varieties are mostly stalwarts from southern France, such as alicante bouschet (a tough and early ripening variety with a mediocre reputation for quality) and carignan (another high-yielding but unsubtle red), cabernet sauvignon and cinsault.

Full-bodied acidic reds are the staple of the industry, although lighter rosés and a few whites are produced. Most wines sell for under TD5 at supermarkets. White wines mostly rely on the inferior quality Muscat of Alexandria grape variety, which thrives in hot climates and produces a strong and very sweet *vin ordinaire*. It's better known as an eating grape. However, there are some drier whites on the market – look out for labels such as Sidi Rais, Domaine de Karim and the unusual Muscat Sec de Kelibia. The latter is quite unlike any other muscat you will have tasted – a delicious fruity white that should be served chilled. It can be hard to find so is worth grabbing if you see it.

Tunisian rosé is probably the best bet, as it's generally the most consistent in quality. Gris de Hammamet is one of a number of very similar rosés that retail for under TD4, or try the relatively expensive Château Mornag. Among the cheaper reds, you may find some more to your liking than others, as they can be quite acidic, but the moderately priced Magon Rouge is usually safe. Vieux Magon is the top of the range, a very passable full-bodied red that is great value at TD7.600 from supermarkets. Budget hunters and drinkers who like to work their way up the quality scale could start with Vieux Thibar.

Richard Plunkett

Getting There & Away

AIR

Airports & Airlines

Most of the four million tourists who travel to Tunisia each year arrive by air. The three main airports for international flights are Tunis-Carthage, Monastir and Jerba. The airports at Tozeur and Tabarka also handle a few international flights.

Tunisia's national airline is Tunis Air, which operates a fleet of European Airbuses (A320 and A300) and Boeing 737s to a wide range of destinations in Europe, the Middle East and North Africa. It normally shares the route with the national airline of the country concerned. There are no direct flights between Tunisia and North or South America, Asia or Oceania.

Buying Tickets

If you are flying to Tunisia from outside Europe, the plane ticket will probably be the most expensive item on your budget and buying it can be an intimidating business. There will be a multitude of airlines and

travel agents hoping to separate you from your money, and it's well worth taking time to research the options. Start early: some of the cheapest tickets have to be bought months in advance, and popular flights tend to sell out early. Generally speaking, the cheapest tickets are for travel during the low season, which runs from January to February, and the most expensive tickets are for travel during the high season, which is from June to August.

Discounted tickets fall into two categories: official and unofficial. Official discount schemes include advance-purchase excursion (Apex) tickets, Super-Apex, budget fares and a few other variations on the theme. These tickets can be bought from travel agents or direct from the airline. They often have restrictions on them – payment a certain time in advance is the usual one. Others are restrictions on the minimum and maximum period you must be away, such as a minimum of 14 days and a maximum of one year. Unofficially discounted tickets are simply discounted tickets that the airlines release through selected travel agents. Don't go looking for these from the airlines because they are available only through travel agents. Airlines can supply information on routes and timetables; however, except at times of inter-airline war they do not supply cheapest tickets.

Return tickets always work out much cheaper than two one-way tickets; in some cases, *cheaper* than a one way ticket. Generally, you can find discounted tickets at prices as low, or even lower, than Apex or budget tickets. Phone around the travel agents for bargains.

Use the fares quoted in this book as a guide only. They are approximate and based on the rates advertised by travel agents at the time of going to press. Quoted air fares do not necessarily constitute a recommendation for the carrier. If you are travelling from the UK or the USA, you will probably find that the cheapest flights are being advertised by obscure bucket shops whose names haven't yet reached the telephone directory. Many such firms are honest and solvent, but there are a few rogues who will take your money and disappear, to reopen elsewhere a month or two later under a new name. If you feel suspicious about a firm, don't give them all the money at once - leave a deposit of 20% or so and pay the balance when you get the ticket. If they insist on cash in advance, go somewhere else. And once you have the ticket, ring the airline to confirm that you are actually booked on the flight.

You may decide to pay more than the rock-bottom fare by opting for the safety of a better known travel agent. Firms such as STA Travel, which has offices worldwide, Council Travel in the USA or Travel CUTS in Canada are not going to disappear overnight, leaving you clutching a receipt for a nonexistent ticket, and they do offer good prices to most destinations.

No matter what kind of ticket you buy, make sure you take out travel insurance. For more information, see Travel Insurance under the Visas & Documents section of the Facts for the Visitor chapter earlier.

It's a good idea to buy travel insurance as early as possible. If you buy it just before you fly, you may find that you're not covered for problems such as delays caused by industrial action. Paying for your ticket by credit card sometimes provides limited travel insurance, and you may be able to reclaim the payment if the operator doesn't deliver. In the UK, for instance, credit-card providers are required by law to reimburse consumers if a company goes into liquidation and the amount in contention is more than UK£100. Ask your credit-card company what it covers.

Travellers with Special Needs

Airlines are well used to dealing with customers with a range of special needs. The most common of these is special diets. Airlines can offer a huge range of different meals: kosher, halal, vegetarian (western or Indian), seafood, white meat only etc. You should let the airline know of your requirements as soon as possible – preferably when booking your ticket. Check that your request has been registered when you reconfirm your booking (at least 72 hours before departure) and again when you check in at the airport. Airlines do not carry special meals unless they have been ordered.

The same rules apply to travellers with a disability. If you've broken a leg, or you're travelling in a wheelchair, let the airline know as soon as possible. Most international airports will provide escorts from the check-in desk to the plane where needed, and there should be ramps, lifts, accessible toilets and reachable phones. Aircraft toilets, on the other hand, could present a problem; travellers should discuss this with the airline at an early stage and, perhaps, with their doctor.

Guide dogs for the blind will often have to travel in a specially pressurised baggage compartment with other animals, away from their owner; smaller guide dogs may be admitted to the cabin. All guide dogs will be subject to the same quarantine laws (six months in isolation etc) as any other animal when entering or returning to countries currently free of rabies, such as Australia. Deaf travellers can ask for airport and in-flight announcements to be written down for them.

Airlines have special deals for children. Children under two years of age travel for 10% of the standard fare (or free, on some airlines) as long as they don't occupy a seat. The flip side of this deal is that they do not get a baggage allowance. Airlines can normally provide 'Skycots' if requested in advance; these will take a child weighing up to about 10kg. Most airlines charge two-thirds of the adult fare for accompanied children aged between two and 12 years, who will get a baggage allowance. Push-chairs can often be taken as hand luggage.

The USA

There are no direct flights between the USA and Tunisia, but other options are as follows.

Scheduled Flights New York has both the cheapest air fares and the largest choice of

Air Travel Glossary

Apex Apex, or 'advance purchase excursion', is a discounted ticket which must be paid for in advance. There are penalties if you wish to change it.

Baggage Allowance This will be written on your ticket and usually includes one 20kg item to go in the hold, plus one item of hand luggage.

Bucket Shops These are unbonded travel agencies specialising in discounted airline tickets.

Budget Fares These can be booked at least three weeks in advance, but the travel date is not confirmed until seven days prior to travel.

Cancellation Penalties If you have to cancel or change an Apex or other discounted ticket, there are often heavy penalties involved; insurance can sometimes be taken out against these penalties. Some airlines impose penalties on regular tickets as well, particularly against 'no-show' passengers.

Check-in Airlines ask you to check in a certain time ahead of the flight departure (usually one to two hours on international flights). If you fail to check in on time and the flight is overbooked, the airline can cancel your booking and give your seat to somebody else.

Confirmation Having a ticket written out with the flight and date you want doesn't mean you have a seat until the agent has checked with the airline that your status is 'OK' or confirmed. Meanwhile you could just be 'on request'.

Courier Fares Businesses often need to send urgent documents or freight securely and quickly. Courier companies hire people to accompany the package through customs and, in return, offer a discount ticket which is sometimes a phenomenal bargain. In effect, what the companies do is ship their freight as your luggage on the regular commercial flights. This is a legitimate operation, but there are two shortcomings – the short turnaround time of the ticket (usually not longer than a month) and the limitation on your luggage allowance. You may have to surrender all your allowance and take only carry-on luggage.

Discounted Tickets There are two types of discounted fares – officially discounted (such as promotional fares) and unofficially discounted. The lowest prices often impose drawbacks like flying with unpopular airlines, inconvenient schedules or unpleasant routes and connections. Discounted tickets only exist where there is fierce competition.

Economy-Class Tickets Economy-class tickets are usually not the cheapest way to go, though they do give you maximum flexibility and they are valid for 12 months. If you don't use them, most are fully refundable, as are unused sectors of a multiple ticket.

Full Fares Airlines traditionally offer 1st class (coded F), business class (coded J) and economy class (coded Y) tickets. These days there are so many promotional and discounted fares available that few passengers pay full economy fare.

ITX An ITX, or 'independent inclusive tour excursion', is often available on tickets to popular holiday destinations. Officially it's a package deal combined with hotel accommodation, but many agents will sell you one of these for the flight only and give you phoney hotel vouchers in the unlikely event that you're challenged at the airport.

Lost Tickets If you lose your airline ticket an airline will usually treat it like a travellers cheque and, after inquiries, issue you with another one. Legally, however, an airline is entitled to treat it like cash and if you lose it then it's gone forever. Take good care of your tickets.

MCO An MCO, or 'miscellaneous charge order', is a voucher that looks like an airline ticket but carries no destination or date. It can be exchanged through any IATA (International Association of Travel

---

airlines. Royal Air Maroc can get you to Tunis via Casablanca for US$818 return in low season, rising to around US$1200 in high season. With British Airways, the fare ranges from US$846 in low season to US$1250 in high season. From the west coast, the simplest way to travel is to fly via Europe using one of the major European airlines with regular flights to Tunis. Air France, Lufthansa and British Airways are the best. Fares start from US$1000 in low season to US$1475 in high season.

Cheap Flights There are cheaper ways of getting to Tunisia from the USA, but they involve considerably more time and effort. The cheapest option is to buy a discount ticket to Europe and then to shop around, but there's not much point in doing this unless you want to spend a few days hanging around. London is the best place to head for.

The North Atlantic is the world's busiest long-haul air corridor, and the flight options to Europe are bewildering. Microsoft's popular Expedia web site (www.msn.com)

Agents) airline for a ticket on a specific flight. It's a useful alternative to an onward ticket in those countries that demand one, and is more flexible than an ordinary ticket if you're unsure of your route.

No-Shows No-shows are passengers who fail to show up for their flight. Full-fare passengers who fail to turn up are sometimes entitled to travel on a later flight. The rest are penalised (see Cancellation Penalties).

On Request This is an unconfirmed booking for a flight.

Open Jaw Tickets These are return tickets where you fly out to one place but return from another. If available, this can save you backtracking to your arrival point.

Overbooking Airlines hate to fly empty seats and since every flight has some passengers who fail to show up, airlines often book more passengers than they have seats. Usually excess passengers make up for the no-shows, but occasionally somebody gets bumped. Guess who it is most likely to be? The passengers who check in late.

Point-to-Point Tickets These are discount tickets that can be bought on some routes in return for passengers waiving their rights to a stopover.

Promotional Fares These are officially discounted fares like Apex fares, available from travel agents or direct from the airline.

Reconfirmation At least 72 hours prior to departure time of an onward or return flight, you must contact the airline and 'reconfirm' that you intend to be on the flight. If you don't do this the airline can delete your name from the passenger list and you could lose your seat.

Restrictions Discounted tickets often have various restrictions on them – Apex is the most usual one. Others are restrictions on the minimum and maximum period you must be away, such as a minimum of 14 days or a maximum of one year.

Round-the-World Tickets RTW tickets are just that. You have a limited period in which to circumnavigate the globe and you can go anywhere the carrying airlines go, as long as you don't backtrack. These tickets are usually valid for one year, the number of stopovers or total number of separate flights is worked out before you set off and they often don't cost much more than a basic return flight.

Stand-by This is a discounted ticket where you only fly if there is a seat free at the last moment. Stand-by fares are usually only available on domestic routes.

Tickets Out An entry requirement for many countries is that you have a ticket out of the country. If you're unsure of your next move, the easiest solution is to buy the cheapest onward ticket to a neighbouring country or a ticket from a reliable airline which can later be refunded if you do not use it.

Transferred Tickets Airline tickets cannot be transferred from one person to another. Travellers sometimes try to sell the return half of their ticket, but officials can ask you to prove that you are the person named on the ticket. This is unlikely to happen on domestic flights, but on an international flight tickets may be compared with passports.

Travel Agencies Travel agencies vary widely and you should choose one that suits your needs. Some simply handle tours, while full-service agencies handle everything from tours and tickets to car rental and hotel bookings. If all you want is a ticket at the lowest possible price, then go to an agency specialising in discounted tickets.

Travel Periods Some officially discounted fares, Apex fares in particular, vary with the time of year. There is often a low (off-peak) season and a high (peak) season. Sometimes there's an intermediate or shoulder season as well. Usually the fare depends on your outward flight – if you depart in the high season and return in the low season, you pay the high-season fare.

gives a good idea of the possibilities. Other sites worth checking out are ITN (www.itn.net) and Travelocity (www.travelocity.com).

The *New York Times*, the *San Francisco Chronicle Examiner*, the *LA Times* and the *Chicago Tribune* all publish weekly travel sections in which you'll find any number of travel agents' advertisements. Council Travel (www.ciee.org/travel) and STA (www.statravel.com) have offices in major cities nationwide. One-way fares can work out

very cheap on a stand-by basis. One company that specialises in this sort of thing is Airhitch (☎ (212) 864-2000; email airhitch@netcom.com); it can get you to Europe for US$175 one way from the east coast or US$269 from the west coast.

Courier flights are another possibility. Discount Travel International in New York (☎ (212) 362-3636; fax 362-3236) offers New York-London for US$299 in summer and Los Angeles-London for US$399 one way. Call two or three months in advance, at the beginning of the month. The *Travel Unlimited* newsletter, PO Box 1058, Allston, MA 02134, publishes details of the cheapest airfares and courier possibilities from the USA and other countries, including the UK, to destinations all over the world. It's a treasure trove of information. One monthly issue costs US$5, and a year's subscription costs US$25, or US$35 for subscribers outside the USA.

Canada

There are no direct flights to or from Canada to Tunisia, which means that Canadians are faced with a similar range of alternatives to Americans. You can either use one of the major European airlines and take a connecting flight to Tunis, or fly to Europe as cheaply as possible and then shop around.

Travel CUTS has offices in all major cities including Toronto (☎ (416) 798-2887), Vancouver (☎ (604) 681-9136) and Edmonton (☎ (403) 488-8487). It can get you to Tunis from Toronto or Montreal for about C$1200 or from Vancouver for C$1500. The *Globe & Mail*, the *Toronto Star* and the *Vancouver Province* all carry ads for cheap tickets.

For courier flights to Europe, contact FB On Board Courier Services in Montreal (☎ (514) 631-2677) or Vancouver (☎ (604) 278-1266). Return fares to London are C$525 from Montreal or Toronto and C$570 from Vancouver.

The UK

London has long been Europe's major centre for discounted fares, including some very good deals on flights to Tunisia. The following are some of the leading travel agencies selling discount tickets:

Campus Travel
    (☎ (0171) 730 3402; web site www.campustravel. co.uk) 52 Grosvenor Gardens, London SW1 0AG (tube station: Victoria)
STA
    (☎ (0171) 361 6262; web site www.statravel. co.uk) 86 Old Brompton Rd London SW7 3LQ (tube station: South Kensington)

Trailfinders
    (☎ (0171) 937 5400) 194 Kensington High St, London W8 (tube station: High St Kensington)

You'll also find ads for cheap fares in *Time Out*, the Sunday papers, the *Evening Standard* and *Exchange & Mart*. Some of the free magazines and newspapers available in London are worth checking out. These include *TNT*, *Footloose*, *Southern Cross*, *Supertravel Magazine* and *Trailfinder* – you can pick them up outside the main train and tube stations.

Scheduled Flights GB Airways, a subsidiary of British Airways, and Tunis Air both operate scheduled flights from London to Tunis. You'll find the best deals with GB Airways (☎ 0990 444 000), which flies from Gatwick three times a week on Monday, Wednesday and Thursday. The price of a one month excursion ticket ranges from UK£165 in low season (January 1 to February 28) to UK£219 in high season (July 1 to October 31). GB Airways also has same-day connecting flights from Manchester and Glasgow. The low/high-season excursion fares from Manchester are UK£283/337 and from Glasgow, UK£331/385. The airline also offers special deals, which it calls World Offers. These deals are usually announced between four and six weeks before departure, and you'll see them advertised in the press and at travel agents.

Tunis Air (☎ (0171) 734 7644) flies from Heathrow three times a week on Tuesday, Friday and Sunday. The one month excursion fare is UK£215.40 year-round. Tunis Air doesn't offer special deals.

Charter Flights Contrary to popular perception, charter flights are not much cheaper than the one month excursion deals available on scheduled flights, unless you are prepared to hunt around for a last minute deal. One advantage of using charter flights is that they offer a much wider choice of departure points. The options include departures from Bristol, Birmingham, East Midlands, Gatwick, Glasgow, Luton and Manchester. The biggest disadvantage is the restriction on the length of time you can stay away, which ranges from one to three weeks. Most tickets are for a two week stay. Two of the biggest British charter operators are Thomson Holidays (☎ 0990 502555) and Thomas Cook (☎ 0990 666222). The Tunisian National Tourist Office (☎ (0171) 224 5561; fax 224 4053), 77A Wigmore St, London W1H 9LJ, has a list of all the operators.

You can also contact the Air Travel Advisory Bureau (☎ (0171) 636 5000; www. tcol.co.uk/orgs/atab/atab.html) for information about charter flight bargains. Typical high-season return fares include Gatwick to Monastir for UK£216, and Glasgow to Monastir for UK£278. The return fare from Gatwick to Monastir drops to UK£189 in low season, but you should be able to pick up a discount ticket for half that if you shop around.

Continental Europe

France Not surprisingly, France has better flight connections to Tunisia than anywhere else in Europe. Air France and Tunis Air both have at least two flights a day from Paris to Tunis. Advance purchase fares start at around 2500FF return. Tunis Air also flies from Paris to Tozeur twice a week. The routes from other French airports to Tunisia are shared by Tunis Air and Air Inter Europe. Each has a daily flight from Marseille to Tunis (from 2000FF), while Tunis Air has weekly flights from Marseille to Jerba and Monastir. Other airports with flights to Tunis are Bordeaux, Lyon and Nice. Charter flights are much cheaper. You'll pay around 1700FF in high season for a return flight from Paris to Tunis or Jerba, and 2500FF to Tozeur. In low season, return fares to Tunis fall below 1000FF; the corresponding fares to Jerba and Tozeur are 1350FF and 1650FF, respectively. Return flights from Marseille to Tunis range from 1400FF in high season to 1200FF in low season. Reliable travel agents include:

Council Travel
   (☎ 01 44 55 55 44) 22, rue des Pyramides, 75001 Paris

Nouvelles Frontières
   (☎ 01 41 41 58 58) 87, boulevard de Grenelle, 75015 Paris
Planète Havas
   (☎ 01 53 29 40 00) 26, ave de l'Opéra, 75001 Paris
Usit Voyages
   (☎ 01 42 34 56 90) 6, rue de Vaugirard, 75006 Paris

Germany For cheap air tickets in Frankfurt, try SRID Reisen (☎ (069) 43 01 91), Berger Strasse 118. In Berlin, Alternativ Tours (☎ (030) 8 81 20 89), Wilmersdorfer Strasse 94 (U-Bahn: Adenauerplatz), specialises in discounted fares to just about anywhere in the world. SRS Studenten Reise Service (☎ (030) 2 83 30 94), at Marienstrasse 23, near Friedrichstrasse station, offers flights with discounted student (aged 34 or less) or youth (aged 25 or less) fares. Travel agents offering unpublished cheap flights advertise in *Zitty*, Berlin's fortnightly entertainment magazine.

Greece Tunis Air flies from Athens to Tunis on Tuesday and Thursday. There are plenty of bucket shops offering cheap fares in the Plaka area and around Syntagma Square in Athens; try ISYTS (☎ (1) 322 1267), 2nd Floor, Odos Nikis, Syntagma.

The Netherlands Reliable travel agents in Amsterdam include:

Budget Air
   (☎ (020) 627 12 51) Rokin 34
ILC Reizen
   (☎ (020) 620 51 21) NZ Voorburgwal 256
Malibu Travel
   (☎ (020) 626 66 11) Damrak 30
NBBS Reizen
   (☎ (020) 624 09 89) Rokin 38
   (☎ (020) 638 17 36) Leidsestraat 53

Australia

There are no direct flights between Australia and Tunisia. The easiest option is to travel to Europe with one of the major European airlines with good connections to Tunisia, and then fly to Tunis as a side trip. STA Travel and Flight Centres International are major dealers in cheap air fares. Check the travel agents' ads in the Yellow Pages and ring around. KLM-Royal Dutch Airlines has some very good deals: it can get you to Tunis from the east coast of Australia for A$1630 to A$2170 return, depending on the season. Flights from Australia to Tunis via Amsterdam are handled by KLM subsidiary Transavia, which flies the route twice a week – requiring an overnight stop in Amsterdam in each direction.

Lufthansa is more convenient but more expensive, with ticket prices starting at A$1990. It has daily flights from Frankfurt to Tunis. Lufthansa no longer flies into Australia; it uses Thai International for the Sydney-Bangkok leg

New Zealand
As in Australia, two popular travel agents are STA Travel and Flight Centres International. There are no direct flights from New Zealand to Tunisia. The quickest way to get there is to fly Thai International/Lufthansa to Frankfurt and connect with the daily Lufthansa flight to Tunis.

Africa
Egypt EgyptAir and Tunis Air both operate between Cairo and Tunis. The one month excursion fare is TD399.800.

Morocco Royal Air Maroc and Tunis Air share the route between Tunis and Casablanca. The one month excursion fare from Tunis is TD351.800.

LAND
Although you are unlikely, for the foreseeable future anyway, to be taking your own vehicle into Tunisia from either Libya or Algeria, crossing by ferry from Italy or France is a popular option (see the Sea section later in this chapter for details of ferry timetables and fares). Drivers of cars and riders of motorbikes will need the vehicle's registration papers, liability insurance and an international drivers' permit in addition to their domestic licence. Beware: there are two

kinds of international permits, one of which is needed mostly for former British colonies. There is no need for a *carnet de passage en douane* (which is effectively a passport for the vehicle and acts as a temporary waiver of import duty) when taking your car into Tunisia. However, this document is required in many other African countries and would be worth getting if you think you'll be driving on beyond Tunisia, Algeria or Morocco. Contact your local automobile association for details about all documentation required.

Liability insurance is not available in advance for many out-of-the-way countries but has to be bought when crossing the border. The cost and quality of such local insurance varies wildly, and you will find in some countries that you are effectively travelling uninsured.

Anyone who is planning to take their own vehicle with them needs to check in advance what spares and petrol are likely to be available. Lead-free petrol is not widely available in Tunisia, and neither is every little part for your car. See also Car & Motorcycle in the Getting Around chapter.

Cycling is a cheap, convenient, healthy, environmentally sound and above all fun way of travelling. One note of caution: before you leave home, go over your bike with a fine-toothed comb and fill your repair kit with every imaginable spare. As with cars and motorbikes, you won't necessarily be able to buy spares for your machine if it breaks down in the middle of nowhere.

You can take your bicycle by air. You can take it to pieces and put it in a bike bag or box, but it's much easier simply to wheel your bike to the check-in desk, where it should be treated as a piece of baggage. You may have to remove the pedals and turn the handlebars sideways so that it takes up less space in the aircraft's hold; check all this with the airline well in advance. See also the Bicycle section in the Getting Around chapter, following.

Algeria
It's years now since the last recorded crossing of this border by a tourist. Algeria has

been effectively out of bounds to travellers since the start of the civil war in early 1993. There is little likelihood of this changing in the foreseeable future. At the time of writing, the SNTRI bus service between Tunis and Annaba had been suspended. The Trans Maghreb Express train, *Al-Maghreb al-Arabi*, which once linked Tunisia with Morocco via Algiers, is another war victim – suspended until further notice. For the record, the main crossing points between Tunisia and Algeria are at Babouch (between 'Ain Draham and Annaba), Ghardimao (Jendouba and Souq Ahras), Sakiet Sidi Youssef (Le Kef and Souq Ahras), Bou Chebka (Kasserine and Tébessa) and the desert post at Hazoua between Nefta and El-Oued.

Louage The only form of public transport still operating between the two countries are *louages* (shared taxis). They operate from Place Sidi Bou Mendil in the Tunis medina to Annaba (TD28) and Constantine (TD35).

Libya

Tunisia has become Libya's lifeline to the outside world in the wake of the international air embargo imposed on Libya following its refusal to hand over two suspects accused of planting the bomb that destroyed a Pan Am jet over Lockerbie in 1992. As a result, the road from Tunis to Tripoli has never been busier. The main crossing point is Ras Ajdir, on the coast 33km east of Ben Guerdane.

There's another border post in the south between Dehiba (Tunisia) and Wazin, but Libyan immigration officials have a habit of sending people back up to Ras Ajdir. Unfortunately, obtaining a tourist visa remains as difficult as ever. It's almost impossible for an individual to get a visa. The best approach is to go through one of the tour companies specialising in trips to Libya.

Bus There are daily buses to Tripoli from the southern bus station in Tunis, departing at 5 pm. The trip takes 11½ hours and costs TD27.600. There are also daily services from Sfax (seven hours, TD17.350).

Louage Louages are faster and more convenient than the buses. There are regular services to Tripoli from many Tunisian towns, including Tunis, Sfax, Gabès, Medenine, Houmt Souq and Ben Guerdane.

SEA
Italy

There are year-round ferry connections between Tunis and the Italian ports of Trapani (in Sicily) and Genoa, and summer connections between Tunis and Naples. The ferries are heavily booked in summer, so it is essential to book well in advance if you want to take a car or camper van across. The fares quoted below are for one way travel in economy class, which gets you an aircraft-type reclining seat. There are all sorts of

Ferry Timetables & Fares				
Route	Journey Length	Timetable	Fares (TD; one way)	Operator
Trapani-Tunis	8 hours	Year-round service; leaves Trapani 8 am Monday, returns from Tunis 8 pm Monday	65	Tirrenia Navigazione
Genoa-Tunis	24 hours	Year-round service; four per month in winter 11 per month in July and August	140	CTN
Naples-Tunis	14 hours	Weekly service June to September	87	CTN
Marseille-Tunis	24 hours	Year-round service; varies seasonally but at least twice weekly	180	CTN, SNCM

discounts, starting from about 15% on return tickets. Children aged under four travel free, and children aged four to 15 pay half the fare. Students (with cards) aged 15 to 25 also qualify for discounts of up to 50%.

For more information about these services and bookings, contact the following shipping agents:

Tunisia
　　Compagnie Tunisienne de Navigation (☎ (01) 322 775/802; fax 354 855), 122 Rue de Yougoslavie, Tunis
Italy
　　Tirrenia Navigazione (☎ (0923) 218 96), Salvo Viaggi, Corso Italia 48, Trapani; Tirrenia Navigazione (☎ (010) 275 80 41; fax 269 82 55), Stazione Marittima Ponte Colombo, Genoa; Tirrenia Navigazione (☎ (081) 761 36 88), Sezione Marittima molo Angioino, Naples
UK
　　Southern Ferries (☎ (0171) 491 4968), 5th Floor, 179 Picadilly, London W1V 9DB; Serena Holidays (☎ (0171) 373 6548), 40-42 Kenway Rd, London SW5 0RA

Trapani–Tunis Italian company Tirrenia Navigazione runs a weekly service between Trapani and La Goulette (Tunis). The trip takes eight hours and costs TD65 one way. The boat leaves Trapani at 8 am on Monday morning and Tunis at 8 pm the same day.

There used to be a hydrofoil service between Trapani and Kelibia on the Cap Bon Peninsula, but, at the time of writing, this was no longer running. For more information contact the Compagnie Tunisienne de Navigation (CTN).

Genoa–Tunis The route between Tunis and the northern Italian port of Genoa is operated by the CTN. The frequency of services to Genoa varies between four a month in winter and 13 a month in July and August. The trip takes 24 hours and costs TD140 one way.

Naples–Tunis CTN also runs a weekly service between Tunis and Naples from the beginning of June until the end of September. The trip takes 14 hours and the one way fare is TD87.

France
Both CTN and French company SNCM operate a ferry service all year round between Marseille and Tunis. Between them there are at least two ferries a week, even in the middle of winter. There are sailings almost every day between late June and the middle of November. The boats are usually packed, so you will need to book well ahead if you want to take a vehicle across. The trip takes 24 hours and costs TD180 one way.

For more information about these services and bookings, contact the following shipping agents:

Tunisia
　　Compagnie Tunisienne de Navigation (☎ (01) 322 775/802; fax 354 855), 122 Rue de Yougoslavie, Tunis; SNCM (☎ (01) 336 536), 47 Ave Farhat Hached, Tunis
France
　　SNCM (☎ 04 91 56 30 10; fax 04 91 56 35 86), 61, boulevard des Dames, Marseille
UK
　　Southern Ferries (☎ (0171) 491 4968), 5th Floor, 179 Picadilly, London W1V 9DB

DEPARTURE TAX

There is no departure tax to be paid when leaving the country. A TD8 airport tax is included in the price of an air ticket, and a similar TD2 port tax is included in the price of ferry tickets.

ORGANISED TOURS

Nearly every European country has travel companies specialising in hotel and airfare packages to Tunisia. British operators have some of the cheapest deals. Thomas Cook (☎ 0990 666222), for example, offers a week's holiday (half board) at a three star hotel in Hammamet in July for UK£569 or two weeks for UK£789. These prices drop dramatically in winter when the same hotel in Hammamet costs UK£199 for one week or UK£359 for two weeks. Similar deals are available at other resorts.

The Tunisian Travel Bureau (☎ (0171) 373 4411), at 305 Old Brompton Rd, London, UK, has the biggest range of destinations. These include Bizerte, Kerkennah, Mahdia, Nefta,

Tabarka and Tozeur, as well as the standard beach resorts such as Hammamet-Nabeul, Sousse-Monastir and Jerba.

In addition to the standard package tours, a number of tour operators run specialist tours to Tunisia, ranging from traditional art and archaeology tours of the classical sites to bird-watching, golfing and even thalassotherapy tours. They tend to be at the upper end of the price range and generally speaking the itineraries on these trips are quite tight, leaving little time for roaming around on your own. But if your time is short and purse long, they may be the deal for you.

The following information is intended as a guide only and is not a recommendation of these operators over others. Examples of some specialist tours from the UK to Tunisia include:

Andante Travels (☎ (01980) 610555), The Old Telephone Exchange, Winterbourne Dauntsey, Salisbury SP4 6EH, does an eight day archaeological tour of Carthage and northern Tunisia for UK£820.

Martin Randall Travel (☎ (0181) 742 3355), 10 Barley Mow Passage, Chiswick, London W4 4 PH, offers eight-day tours of the Roman sites, accompanied by a lecturer. Prices range from UK£945 to UK£980.

Prospect Music and Art Tours (☎ (0181) 995 2151), 454-458 Chiswick High Rd, London W4 5TT, does an eight day accompanied cultural tour, including the main Roman sites as well as Tunis and Monastir, for UK£995.

Branta Travel (☎ (0171) 635 5812), 7 Wingfield St, London SE15 4LN, runs bird-watching tours to Lake Ichkeul and the south. Prices are from UK£895.

Wigmore Holidays (☎ (0171) 486 4425; fax 486 3559), 122 Wigmore St, London W1H 9FE, is a Tunisia specialist who offers four and seven day archaeology tours and a seven day bird-watching tour, as well as tailor-made holidays.

Swan Hellenic (☎ (0171) 800 2200), 77 New Oxford St, London WC1A 1PP, runs cruises in the Mediterranean that include stopovers in Tunisia. You'll need to start saving your pennies, though: prices start at a staggering UK£2705.

Other tour operators who go to Tunisia include: Explore Worldwide (☎ (01252) 319448/344161), 1 Frederick St, Aldershot, Hants GU11 1LQ (15-day camel safari, including visits to Carthage and Kairouan); Club Golf (☎ (01293) 723134) British Airways Holidays, Astral Towers, Betts Way, London Rd, Crawley, West Sussex RH10 2XA (golfing holidays); and Thermalia Travel (☎ (0171) 483 1898/586 7725), 12 New College Parade, Finchley Rd, Swiss Cottage, London NW3 5EP (thalassotherapy holidays).

There are many tour operators and travel agencies in France offering tours to Tunisia, including Voyageurs au Proche Orient et au Maghreb (☎ 01 42 86 17 90), 55, rue Sainte-Anne, 75002 Paris. See also under France in the Air section earlier in this chapter.

The London office of the Tunisian National Tourist Office (☎ (0171) 224 5561; fax 224 4053), 77A Wigmore St, has a list of all UK companies offering holidays in Tunisia. You'll find similar lists at Tunisian tourist offices in other countries. See the Tourist Offices section in the Facts for the Visitor chapter for a list of addresses.

Getting Around

Tunisia has a well developed transport network. It's a small country, and just about every town of any consequence has daily connections with the capital, Tunis.

For most of the year public transport copes easily with the demand, but things get pretty hectic during August and September and on public holidays. At these times, book ahead if possible.

AIR

Tunisia's domestic air network is fairly limited – there just aren't many places that are far enough from Tunis to warrant catching a plane.

Domestic flights are operated by Tunis Air subsidiary Tuninter, which uses the strangely inappropriate flight code UG. It operates to a summer timetable from April to October, and to a slightly curtailed winter schedule for the rest of the year. Four airports service domestic routes: Tunis, Jerba, Sfax and Tozeur. There are no domestic flights to either Monastir or Tabarka.

By far the most popular route is between Tunis and Jerba, with seven flights a day each way in summer and six in winter. The flight takes an hour and costs TD50.500 one way or TD99.300 return. There are also five flights a week between Tunis and Tozeur (one hour, TD48.500/94.150), and four a week between Tunis and Sfax (45 minutes, TD42.500/82.800).

The only route that doesn't involve Tunis is Jerba-Tozeur. There are two flights a week, on Tuesday and Saturday. The trip takes 45 minutes and the one way/return fares are TD27.800/53.150.

BUS
National Buses

The national bus company, the Société Nationale du Transport Interurbain, is always referred to as SNTRI – pronounced 'sintry'. It operates daily air-conditioned buses to just about every town in the country. The frequency of services ranges from one bus to smaller towns to half a dozen to major cities like Sousse and Sfax. The green-and-white buses run pretty much to schedule, and they're fast, comfortable and not too expensive. Some sample one-way fares include TD5.930 for Tunis to Sousse and TD16.550 for Tunis to Tozeur.

In summer, many of the long distance departures are at night to avoid the heat of the day, which means you don't get to see anything of the country you are travelling through. It's a good idea to book in advance at this time, especially if you are planning to leave from Tunis.

All buses originating or terminating in Tunis stop en route to pick up and set down passengers, so you don't have to be going all the way to or from Tunis to use them. If you pick one up en route, however, there is no guarantee that seats will be available.

For details of intercity bus services, see the Getting There & Away sections for individual towns and cities.

Regional Buses

In addition to the national company, SNTRI, there are regional bus companies which operate services within a particular region and to nearby cities just outside the region. They often also operate services to Tunis.

Domestic Flight Routes & Fares (TD)			
Route	Journey Length	Frequency	Fares (one way/return)
Tunis to Jerba	1 hour	daily (summer)	50.500/99.300
Tunis to Tozeur	1 hour	5/week	48.500/94.150
Tunis to Sfax	45 minutes	4/week	42.500/82.800
Jerba to Tozeur	45 minutes	Tuesday & Saturday	27.800/53.150

The buses are reliable enough but often they are getting on a bit; they are also slow and are never air-conditioned. Coverage of routes is good and services are frequent enough to meet the demand most of the time. Booking in advance is both impossible and unnecessary. The only way to be sure of bus schedules is to go to the bus station and ask. Most depots do not have timetables displayed; those that do, have them in Arabic only – with the exception of Houmt Souq on Jerba. The bulk of departures tend to be early in the day. If seeking directions to the bus station, ask for the *gare routière*.

One catch to be aware of is that some towns are served by two or three regional companies. Generally they share depots, but in some places (eg Tabarka) each company has its own. Officials from one company never know about the schedules of another, so always ask if there is more than one company in town.

TRAIN

Trains are run by the Société Nationale des Chemins de Fer Tunisiens (SNCFT). The rail network is a long way short of comprehensive. What there is, however, is modern and efficient – and the trains do run on time. (I'm sure there must be a connection between a country's system of government and the punctuality of its trains!)

The main train line runs north-south between Tunis and Gabès, via Sousse and Sfax. There are at least eight trains a day as far as Sousse, six to Sfax and three to Gabès. One train per day branches off at Mahrès, south of Sfax, to Gafsa and Metlaoui. There are also lines to Bizerte, via Mateur; Ghardimao (near the Algerian border), via Jendouba; and Kalaat Khasba (halfway between Le Kef and Kasserine). Branch lines run between Bir Bou Rekba and Nabeul, and from Sousse to Monastir and Mahdia. Both these lines are linked to the main north-south line and offer at least one direct train to Tunis every day. Other rail lines shown on maps are for freight only.

Passenger trains offer three classes: 2nd, 1st and *confort*. Second class costs about the same as a bus, and is normally packed – with everything from people and produce to livestock. It's a circus that can be fun to experience for a short journey. Unless you get on at the point of origin, there's little chance of finding a seat.

You're better off travelling 1st class, which costs about 40% more than 2nd class. There are reclining, upholstered seats, and every chance of getting to sit in one. Confort costs a bit more again, but doesn't offer much extra apart from a smaller, slightly more exclusive compartment. Most mainline trains have a restaurant car, which sends out a regular supply of sandwiches, soft drinks and coffee.

See the Getting There & Away section of the Tunis chapter for a table of train fares from Tunis and see also the Getting There & Away sections for individual towns for more details of fares and timetables.

For train enthusiasts, the *Lezard Rouge* (Red Lizard) is a restored beylical train that runs between Metlaoui and Redeyef daily, offering great views of the Seldja Gorge. For more details, see the Around Gafsa section in the Southern Tunisia chapter later in this book.

LOUAGE

Tunisia's shared, long-distance taxis are called *louages*. Most of them are old white Peugeot 404 station wagons with an extra seat in the back. The newer ones are Peugeot 504 or 505 wagons, usually with a distinctive red stripe. They all take five passengers and leave when full. They are the fastest way to get around, as it never takes long for them to fill up, and they are generally quite comfortable because the five person limit is strictly adhered to. Fares are only slightly higher than for buses.

The louage 'station' in most towns is usually just a convenient gathering point – a vacant lot or other open space – close to the town centre.

The louages themselves are instantly recognisable by their roof racks with white identification signs on the front and back. These have a town name on them (in Arabic

Louage Fares (TD) from Tunis	
Bizerte	2.800
Tabarka	6.700
'Ain Draham	7.300
Jendouba	6.700
Le Kef	6.850
Hammamet	3.000
Sousse	6.200
Kairouan	6.800
Sfax	10.650
Mahdia	7.600
Gafsa	14.000
Houmt Souq	17.800
Tozeur	15.850

or English or both) but this sign does not tell you where the vehicle is going – just where it's licensed. There's always someone calling out destinations and directing people to louages. A foreigner is sure to be asked their destination and given assistance. It's a good idea to ask the fare before you get in. If you think you are being ripped off, ask to see the list of tariffs (set by the government) that all drivers are required to carry.

At certain times, particularly during the summer, public transport is in high demand and competition for seats in louages can be fierce. You may find it necessary to be fairly ruthless when it comes to the battle for a seat or you will simply not get a ride. The tactic is to grab onto a door handle as the louage arrives. Fortunately, this situation does not arise very often.

CAR & MOTORCYCLE

Tunisia has an excellent road network. All but the most minor roads are tar sealed and well maintained. Potholes are almost unheard of. Many of the roads which are marked as unsealed on older maps have now been sealed. There is one toll road (*péage*) in Tunisia – the new A1 expressway between Tunis and Sousse. At the time of writing, the toll gates were in place but the toll had yet to be introduced.

There are still a lot of unsealed roads in the desert areas of the south, but these are graded regularly and can usually be negotiated easily enough with a conventional vehicle. The worst road you are likely to

encounter is the back road from Matmata to Medenine. People will tell you it's for 4WDs only, but it can be negotiated with caution in even the smallest Fiats and Citroens.

Tunisian drivers are generally well behaved, and drive fairly predictably and safely. For someone used to driving in western Europe, the worst thing is not the cars but the thousands of moped riders, who weave suicidally in and out of the traffic, and the pedestrians, who think they have an inalienable right to walk on the road regardless of traffic conditions.

There are police and National Guard checkpoints all over the country; although officials are not too bothered with checking foreigners, it's best to make sure you have your passport handy at all times.

Road Rules

The road rules in Tunisia are basically the same as in continental Europe. You drive on the right and overtake on the left. The speed limits are 50km/h in built-up areas and 90km/h on the open road. The only exception is on the toll road from Tunis to Sousse, where the speed limit is 110km/h.

The regulation that causes the most problems for tourists is the one giving priority to traffic coming from the right in built-up areas. This also extends to roundabouts, where you are obliged to give way to traffic approaching from the right even if you are already on the roundabout.

The special intersections for turning left off major roads are another curiosity of Tunisian driving. Instead of using a turning lane in the centre of the road, the Tunisian system involves a special lane leading off to the right which loops back and crosses the main road at right angles. It can be very confusing if you're driving along looking for a sign pointing to the left and then find a sign telling you to turn right!

Tunisia seems to have a lot of traffic police, and the road rules are strictly enforced – for locals anyway. It's almost unheard of for a tourist to be booked – unless the infringement causes an accident, when the police are obliged to act. The rest of the time they are unlikely to do more than check your driving licence and passport, which you should carry with you at all times.

Fuel Prices
Fuel is cheap by European standards and prices are the same everywhere: 310 mills/L for diesel, 570 mills/L for super (high octane), 530 mills/L for regular (low octane) and 650 mills/L for two-stroke mix. Unleaded fuel (620 mills/L) is still something of a rarity outside the major towns.

Licence Requirements
To drive a car or motorcycle of more than 50cc, you must be over 21 and hold a valid licence in your country of residence or an international licence.

Automobile Clubs
The Touring Club de Tunisie (☎ (01) 323 114; fax 324 834), 15 Rue d'Allemagne, Tunis 1000, has a reciprocal rights arrangement with many European automobile clubs, including the UK's Automobile Association. If your car conks out, they can direct you to an affiliated breakdown service.

Car Rental
Hire cars can be a great way to see the country in more detail, but they are so expensive that they're not a realistic option unless you have a fat wallet or are travelling in a small group.

Typical rental charges for the smallest cars (Renault Esp or Citroen C15) start at about TD22 per day plus 220 mills per kilometre. It is cheaper to take one of the unlimited kilometre deals, which start at about TD350 per week. On top of these rates you'll have to pay 17% tax, insurance at about TD10 per day, contract fees etc. By the time you've filled up at the petrol station at 570 mills/L, your wallet will be a lot lighter.

All the major international operators have offices in the larger towns – see under individual town entries for addresses of local and international car rental companies. Rental conditions are fairly straightforward. If you are paying by cash, a deposit of roughly the equivalent of the rental is required. Credit cards don't have the same restriction.

In summer, particularly on Jerba and in Tunis, it's almost impossible to get a car straight away. You may have to wait up to a week unless you are prepared to take a larger and more expensive model. Book as early as possible and check with the company every day to make sure they don't forget your booking, as this does happen. Out of season, when things are much quieter, you can easily get a small car and it is even sometimes possible to bargain a bit on the rates, especially if you are paying cash.

Road Distances (km) between Cities & Towns											
	Tunis	Bizerte	Tabarka	Nabeul	Sousse	Kairouan	Gafsa	Sfax	Gabès	Tataouine	Tozeur	Houmt Souq
Tunis	0	66	175	64	142	154	343	266	375	497	436	481
Bizerte	66	0	147	130	208	220	409	332	441	563	502	547
Tabarka	175	147	0	239	317	277	347	441	496	672	440	602
Nabeul	64	130	239	0	96	114	323	220	357	479	416	463
Sousse	142	208	317	96	0	68	277	127	264	259	370	132
Kairouan	154	220	277	114	68	0	209	136	215	337	302	321
Gafsa	343	409	347	323	277	209	0	197	149	271	93	255
Sfax	266	332	441	220	127	136	197	0	137	259	290	243
Gabès	375	441	496	357	264	215	149	137	0	122	242	106
Tataouine	497	563	672	479	259	337	271	259	122	0	364	118
Tozeur	436	502	440	416	370	302	93	290	242	364	0	348
Houmt Souq	481	547	602	463	132	321	255	243	106	118	348	0

Rental companies require that drivers be aged over 21 and hold a driving licence which has been valid for at least a year.

When you hire the car, make sure that an accident report form has been included with the car's papers. If you have an accident while driving a hire car, both parties involved must complete the form. If the form is not completed, you may be liable for the costs, regardless of whether you have paid for insurance or not.

Motorcycle Rental

The short distances and reasonably good road conditions make motorbikes an ideal way of making the most of Tunisia. Unfortunately, there is only one motorbike rental agency in the country – Holiday Bikes on Jerba. It has 80cc scooters for TD45 per day and 125cc Yamaha trail bikes for TD65, fully inclusive. Another company in Houmt Souq, Raïs Rentals, rents out mopeds but not larger machines. No licence or insurance is required for a moped, but to rent a motorbike you need to be over 21 and to have held a valid motorbike licence for more than a year.

If you are bringing your own motorbike make sure you carry some basic spare parts. These are virtually impossible to find within the country, as people just don't own motorbikes in Tunisia.

BICYCLE

Cycling is also an excellent way to see the country, providing you pick the right time of year. It's too hot to cycle around in summer and it can get very cold in winter in the north, but for the rest of the year conditions are ideal. It's also possible to put a bike on the train if you want to skip a long stretch or get yourself back to Tunis.

There are a few places where you can rent bicycles, but they are quite expensive by Tunisian standards with rates starting from TD8 per day. A lot of the bikes are horrible old rattlers that leave you tired and sore at the end of the day. Where possible, check through the bikes to find the best one – and make sure that the brakes work. Hire places seem to be concerned only about whether the

bike goes or not and aren't too bothered about how to stop it! Maintenance is done on a very casual basis – when something breaks it gets patched up, but nothing is done that might prevent the thing from failing in the first place. See also under Land in the Getting There & Away chapter.

HITCHING

The following information is intended solely as an explanation of how hitching works in Tunisia, not as a recommendation. Although many people do hitch, it is not an entirely safe method of transport and you do so at your own risk. It is strongly recommended that women do not attempt to hitch without a male companion.

Conditions for hitching vary throughout the country. The south is easiest as there is a great deal more tourist traffic – either people who hire cars on Jerba or overlanders heading for Tozeur and the Sahara. You shouldn't have to wait more than a couple of hours for a lift. In the north, people seem less inclined to pick up hitchers, particularly in the summer when there are so many tourists in the country.

Between small towns, *camionnettes*, or pick-ups, are the usual means of transport and hitching on these is a standard way of getting around, although you will normally be expected to pay the equivalent of the bus fare. Try to establish what the locals are paying before you set out to hitch. If in doubt, check before you get in whether the driver expects payment or not.

WALKING

Most visitors confine their walking to what is required to get around town and check out the sights. In summer, walking is really only a viable option in the cool of the early morning and evening. See also Trekking under Activities in the Facts for the Visitor chapter.

BOAT

There are two regular scheduled ferry services in the country. The first connects Sfax with the Kerkennah Islands, which lie about 25km off the coast. In summer, there are up

BETHUNE CARMICHAEL

BETHUNE CARMICHAEL

DAMIEN SIMONIS

BETHUNE CARMICHAEL

BETHUNE CARMICHAEL

Tunisia is a craft-buyer's paradise: specialities include gorgeously patterned plates (top left), cosy camel-skin shoes (top right), a huge variety of brassware (middle right), practical and decorative woven esparto baskets (bottom right) and totally impractical but irresistable blue and white wire birdcages.

BETHUNE CARMICHAEL

BETHUNE CARMICHAEL

BETHUNE CARMICHAEL

BETHUNE CARMICHAEL

FRANCES LINZEE GORDON

BETHUNE CARMICHAEL

The souq (bottom middle) is *the* place to shop for souvenirs. A brass (top left) or earthenware (top right) couscoussier is a must for any couscous afficionado. Pottery (middle) has a long history in Tunisia dating back to pre-Roman times while intricate floral-patterned tiles (bottom left and right) are the product of Tunisia's Islamic heritage.

to eight crossings daily, dropping to four in winter. The trip takes 1½ hours and costs 570 mills one way for passengers without vehicles. It costs TD4 to take a car across, and you need to get in the queue well before the first departure at 7.30 am to be assured of getting across that morning.

The second service runs from Jorf on the mainland to Ajim on the island of Jerba. The crossing takes 15 minutes and the ferries run throughout the day and night. The fare is 600 mills one way for a car. Passengers travel free. See the Jerba section in the Southern Tunisia chapter for more details.

LOCAL TRANSPORT

Most towns are compact enough to get around on foot. The problem comes in summer, when it is too hot to walk far during the day. Taxis are the best alternative. They can be found in most towns and are reasonably cheap. Flagfall is 280 mills, and fares work out at about 500 mills/km. Major towns like Sousse, Sfax and Tunis have local bus networks. Tunis also has a modern *métro léger* (tram) network as well as a suburban train line (TGM) connecting the city centre with the northern suburbs.

Towns without taxis will normally have a camionnette working a specific route or available for charter. Some towns, including Gabès, Houmt Souq, Nabeul and Tozeur, have *calèches* (horse-drawn carriages) for hire. Prices start at about TD10 per hour.

See the Getting Around sections for the individual town entries for more details of local transport options.

ORGANISED TOURS

If you are very short of time, organised tours are one option. It's possible to get just about anywhere in Tunisia by tour bus or 4WD. You can expect to pay about TD30 to TD35 for a half day tour, TD55 to TD60 for a full day and about TD80 per day for tours that also include accommodation.

The biggest operators in the north are Carthage Tours and Transtours. Carthage Tours has offices at 59 Ave Habib Bourguiba, Tunis (☎ (01) 347 015), Place Farhat Hached, Sousse (☎ (03) 227954) and Rue Dag Hammarskjoeld, Hammamet (☎ (02) 281 926). Transtours is at 14 Ave de Carthage, Tunis (☎ (01) 256806), 7 Rue d'Alger, Bizerte (☎ (02) 432 174), and 63 Ave Habib Bourguiba, Sousse (☎ (03) 227 282).

Their offerings range from half-day tours of Carthage to week-long nationwide extravaganzas. One tour that might appeal is the package that includes the Roman sites of Dougga (Northern Tunisia) and Bulla Regia (Central Tunisia), which require quite an effort to reach independently.

Saharan 4WD safaris are the name of the game in the south, and the main players are Douz Voyages (☎ (05) 495 315) and Abdelmoula Voyages (☎ (05) 495 484), both based in Douz. They can take you into the Sahara for any length of time, from eight hours to a week. Many of the tours include camel riding and camping in the desert.

These tours take you to some spectacular and otherwise inaccessible (except to about a hundred other 4WDs) places, but they generally involve hours bouncing around in the desert crammed into a vehicle with 10 other tourists. See the Southern Tunisia chapter for more details.

The half-day tours from Tozeur to the mountain oases at Chebika, Midès and Tamerza are worth considering, again because of the difficulty in getting there independently. Tour operators in Tozeur include: Abdelmoula Voyages (☎ (06) 451 130), Route de Degache and Tunisie Voyages (☎ (06) 452 404), Route de Nefta.

Tunis

Pop 1.5 million ☎ *Area code 01*

Tunisia's capital comes as a pleasant surprise to most western visitors. Compared with the mega-cities found elsewhere in the world, Tunis is little more than a large country town.

The city centre is compact and easy to negotiate, and there are enough attractions to warrant stopping here for a few days. The medina (Arab quarter) is a treasure trove of Islamic architecture dating back more than a thousand years, while the Bardo Museum has a superb collection of Roman mosaics. The ruins of ancient Carthage lie just a few kilometres north-east of the city, across Lake Tunis.

Tunis is a very liberal city by Islamic standards, and it's an easy place to make the adjustment from west to east. Wandering around the new city, it is hard to tell that you are in a Muslim country, let alone in Africa.

HISTORY

Tunis (ancient Tynes) has existed since the earliest days of Carthaginian expansion into the hinterland. The name features on maps of the region dating from the 5th century BC, although nothing else is known about the place at this time.

The first medina, which occupied a narrow band of high ground flanked by the Sebkhet Sejoumi (salt lake) to the south-west and Lake Tunis to the east, was built as a defensive position by the Arabs at the end of the 7th century AD. It wasn't until the 9th century, when Aghlabite ruler Ibrahim ibn Ahmed II moved his court to Tunis, that the city took on any significance.

It fell from favour under the Fatimids, who chose Mahdia as their capital in the 10th century, but escaped the subsequent ravages of the Hilalian invasion in the 11th century. It emerged once again as the capital following the conquest of North Africa by the Almohads in 1160.

The city flourished under the Hafsids, who ruled from 1229 to 1574 – a period

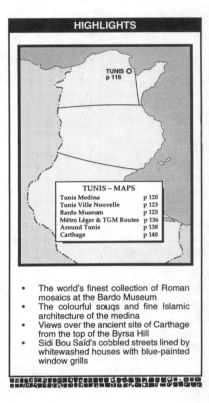

HIGHLIGHTS

TUNIS ✪
p 116

TUNIS – MAPS

Tunis Medina	p 120
Tunis Ville Nouvelle	p 123
Bardo Museum	p 125
Métro Léger & TGM Routes	p 136
Around Tunis	p 138
Carthage	p 140

- The world's finest collection of Roman mosaics at the Bardo Museum
- The colourful souqs and fine Islamic architecture of the medina
- Views over the ancient site of Carthage from the top of the Byrsa Hill
- Sidi Bou Saïd's cobbled streets lined by whitewashed houses with blue-painted window grills

regarded as the city's golden age. The population more than tripled (to about 60,000) during this time. Souqs, mosques and *medersas* (Qur'anic schools) were built, trade with Europe flourished and one of the great Islamic universities was established in the heart of the medina at the Zitouna Mosque, also known as the Great Mosque.

Tunis suffered badly during the power struggle between the Ottoman Turks and Spain that unseated the Hafsids. Much of the city was destroyed and the population fled as the city changed hands repeatedly. Tunis was finally secured for the Ottomans by Sinan Pasha in 1574, and the population began to return. Their number was swollen by the arrival of large numbers of Andalusian refugees fleeing religious persecution in Spain, and a similar exodus of Jews from Livorno in Italy. The newcomers included many fine artisans who played an important role in the rebuilding of the city.

The medina remained very much the centre of things until the arrival of the French in 1881. The French wasted no time in stamping their influence on the place, building their *ville nouvelle* (new town) directly to the east of the medina on land reclaimed from Lake Tunis.

This new city, laid out on a grid, is very much the heart of modern Tunis; it has a distinctly European feel, with its wide main boulevard, street cafes and some fine examples of 1920s colonial architecture.

ORIENTATION

Few cities in the world are as easy to find your way around as Tunis. Almost everything of importance to travellers is within the compact ville nouvelle and the straightforward grid layout makes it hard to get lost.

The main thoroughfare of the ville nouvelle is Ave Habib Bourguiba, which runs east-west from Lake Tunis to Place de l'Indépendance. Ave Habib Bourguiba is lined with an assortment of banks, cinemas, hotels, travel agencies, restaurants, patisseries and fast-food joints, and the shady, tree-filled central strip is a favourite spot for well-dressed Tunisians to strut their stuff.

The western extension of Ave Habib Bourguiba between Place de l'Indépendance and the medina is Ave de France. It terminates in front of the Bab Bhar, also known as the Porte de France. This huge freestanding arch was once the eastern gateway to the medina – until the surrounding walls were demolished to create Place de la Victoire. The two main streets of the medina lead off the western side of this square: Rue de la Kasbah cuts straight through the medina to

Place du Gouvernement, while Rue Jemaa Zitouna leads to the Zitouna Mosque.

A causeway at the eastern end of Ave Habib Bourguiba carries road and light-rail traffic across Lake Tunis to the port suburb of La Goulette, and north to the affluent beach suburbs of Carthage, Sidi Bou Saïd and La Marsa. The lake itself is not a thing of beauty, although in November and December there are often small flocks of pink flamingos on the edge of the causeway.

The main north-south thoroughfare of the ville nouvelle is the street known as Ave de Carthage to the south of Ave Bourguiba and as Ave de Paris to the north. Ave de Carthage leads to Place Barcelone, hub of the city's excellent *métro léger* (tram) network. The train station is on the southern side of the square. Ave de Paris leads to a chaotic five-way intersection known as Place de la République. République station, on the northern side of this intersection, is another important stop on the métro léger network (see Getting Around later in this section).

Maps

The best available map of Tunis is the free map handed out by the tourist office (see following section). There is no A-Z street map of Tunis or equivalent.

INFORMATION
Tourist Offices

The tourist office (☎ 341 077) is on Ave Habib Bourguiba, at Place du 7 Novembre 1987, with its large roundabout and clock tower. This is the head office of the tourist authority, but the service is largely restricted to handing out glossy brochures full of flowery descriptions of places of interest. Getting more information out of them can be like pulling teeth – slow and painful. The office does, however, hand out a good map of Tunis and useful brochures on the medina and Carthage. The staff speak Arabic, English, French and German.

The office is open Monday to Saturday from 8 am to 1.30 pm in summer, and from 8 am to noon and 3 to 6 pm in winter. It's closed Sunday and public holidays.

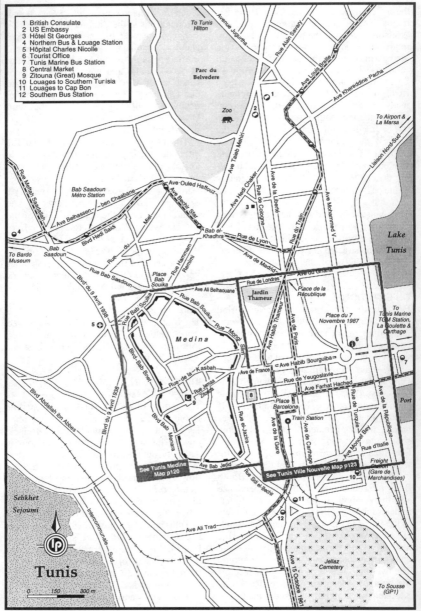

1 British Consulate
2 US Embassy
3 Hôtel St Georges
4 Northern Bus & Louage Station
5 Hôpital Charles Nicolle
6 Tourist Office
7 Tunis Marine Bus Station
8 Central Market
9 Zitouna (Great) Mosque
10 Louages to Southern Tunisia
11 Louages to Cap Bon
12 Southern Bus Station

To Tunis
Hilton

Avenue Juguria

Rue Alain Savary

Rue Louis Braille

Parc du
Belvedere

Ave Khereddine Pacha

Zoo

To Airport &
La Marsa

Ave Taïeb Mehri

Liaison Nord-Sud

Rue Mattah Saadallah

Ave Ouled Haffouz

Rue Hedi Chaker

Ave de la Liberté

Rue de Cologne

Ave Mohammed V

Lake
Tunis

Bab Saadoun
Métro Station

ben Chaabane

Ave Bechir Sfar

Ave Belhassen

Miel

Bab el-
Khadhra

Rue de Lyon

Rue du Train

Ave Hedi Saïdi

Bab
Saadoun

Rue du

Rue Hammam
Remini

Rue de Madrid

To Bardo
Museum

Rue Bab Saadoun

Place
Bab
Souika

Ave du Ghana

Rue de Londres

Blvd Hedi Saïdi

Ave Ali Belhaouane

Jardin
Thameur

Place de la
République

Blvd du 9 Avril 1938

Rue Bab Souika

Rue Bab Souika — Rue — Mongi

Ave Habib Thameur

Place du 7
Novembre 1987

To
Tunis Marine
TGM Station,
La Goulette &
Carthage

Medina

Slim

Ave de Paris

Blvd Bab Bnet

Rue de la Kasbah

Ave de France

Ave Habib Bourguiba

Rue de Yougoslavie

Ave Farhat Hached

Ave de la République

Blvd du 9 Avril 1938

Rue Jemaa
Zitouna

Place
Barcelone

Port

Blvd Abdallah ben Abbes

Blvd Bab Menara

Rue el-Jazira

Train Station

Ave de Carthage

Rue de Turquie

Ave Mongi Bey

Rue d'Italie

See Tunis Medina
Map p120

Ave Bab Jedid

Ave de la Gare

See Tunis Ville Nouvelle Map p123

Rue Sidi el-Bechir

Freight
Station
(Gare de
Marchandises)

Sebkhet
Sejoumi

Intercommunale — Sud

Ave Ali Trad

Ave 15 Octobre 1961

Jellaz
Cemetery

Tunis

To Sousse
(GP1)

0   150   300 m

There is another branch of the tourist office at the train station; it hands out train timetables, among other things. Yet another branch can be found on the mezzanine level at the airport.

Foreign Embassies
Tunis has a large number of embassies and consulates. See under Embassies in the Facts for the Visitor chapter for a full list of embassies in Tunis.

Money
There are branches of all the major banks on Ave Habib Bourguiba. The branch of the STB next to the Hôtel Africa Méridien is open until 6 pm daily, including weekends, for foreign exchange.

A couple of banks have 24-hour automated exchange machines for banknotes; these include the branch of the UIB at the corner of Ave Habib Bourguiba and Rue de Hollande and the Banque de l'Habitat at the corner of Ave Habib Bourguiba and Ave de Paris.

There are also banks at the airport, including a branch of the STB inside the arrivals hall before customs. It is supposed to be open to meet all incoming flights, but if you arrive late at night you will probably have to wait for someone to come and open it up.

American Express (☎ 347 381) is represented by Carthage Tours, 59 Ave Habib Bourguiba. Thomas Cook no longer has representation in Tunis.

Post & Communications
The main post office (PTT) is the cavernous old building on Rue Charles de Gaulle, between Rue d'Espagne and Rue d'Angleterre. The poste restante counter is well organised, but it will hold mail for two weeks only. There is a charge of 200 mills for each letter.

For most of the year, the post office is open Monday to Saturday from 8 am to 6 pm and Sunday from 9 to 11 am. The exception is during July and August, when it's open Monday to Saturday from 7.30 am to 1.30 pm only and closed Sunday.

There are plenty of Taxiphone offices dotted around town.

Travel Agencies
There are lots of travel agencies around the city centre offering tickets, tours and hotel bookings. Carthage Tours (☎ 347 015; fax 352 740), at 59 Ave Habib Bourguiba, and Transtours (☎ 346 035; fax 347 782), at 14 Ave de Carthage, are two of the biggest.

Bookshops
There are very few places that stock English-language books. For novels, try Librairie Claire Fontaine, just off Ave Habib Bourguiba at 14 Rue d'Alger. It has a small English-language section that includes the Penguin Classics. The second-hand bookshop on Rue d'Angleterre, opposite the main post office, has a couple of piles of books in English. Most of them are trash, but there's the odd decent novel among them. The owner will also buy or exchange books. Novels in French are readily available from any of the many bookshops in central Tunis, especially on Ave de France.

Editions Alif, on the corner of Rue de Hollande and Rue d'Allemagne, is worth checking out for its range of publications about Tunisia (see also under Books in the Facts for the Visitor chapter).

The bookshop in the lobby of the Hôtel Africa Méridien has a selection of glossy coffee-table books. If that's what you are interested in, check the stalls in the centre of Ave Habib Bourguiba, as they often have the same books at much lower prices.

International Newspapers & Magazines
The stalls in the middle of Ave Habib Bourguiba stock day-old English newspapers (such as the *Times*, the *Guardian*, the *Sun* and the *Sunday Times*) as well as the *International Herald Tribune, USA Today, Time* and *Newsweek*. They also sell Italian, German and French newspapers. If you're looking for back copies, try the bookshop in the lobby of the Hôtel Africa Méridien.

Cultural Centres

The British Council, next to the British Embassy on Place de la Victoire, has a good library. Visitors can go in and browse, but you need to become a member before you can borrow books. It's not worth the trouble unless you're resident in Tunis.

The US Cultural Centre, at 14 Rue Yahia Ibn Omar, also requires visitors to become a member before they can come in and browse through the US papers etc. You'll need your passport and a couple of passport photos. The Goethe Institut (☎ 799 131) is at 14 Rue Ibn Jazzar and the Centre Culturel Français (☎ 783 355) is at 87 Ave de la Liberté.

Laundry

The Lavarie Tahar, 15 Rue d'Allemagne, charges TD5.500 to wash and dry 5kg of clothes, which are returned neatly folded.

Film & Photography

There are numerous shops in the city centre which sell and process print film. The one on the corner of Ave Habib Bourguiba and Rue de Rome also does passport photos on the spot. Typical prices are TD2 for developing plus 80 mills for each 10cm x 15cm print.

Emergency

The following phone numbers may be useful in case of emergency:

Ambulance & Doctor (☎ 341 250 or 341 280)
Hôpital Charles Nicolle (☎ 664 209)
Poisons Centre (☎ 245 075)
Police & Fire Brigade (☎ 197)

The inside back pages of the local papers, *La Presse, Le Temps* and *Tunisia News*, all have the addresses and phone numbers of late-night chemists.

Lost passports and travellers cheques etc should be reported to the police as soon as possible. The nearest police station to the central hotel district is on Rue Jamel Abdelnasser, just south of the PTT building. A couple of the officers speak English. Be sure to ask for a copy of the police report. You should report the loss of your passport to

your embassy. Lost travellers cheques should be reported to the company concerned – see Money earlier in this section for details of American Express and Thomas Cook representatives in Tunis.

Dangers & Annoyances

Tunis is a very safe city. The only annoyance worth mentioning is the touts working for some of the carpet dealers in the medina. They have come up with a string of ingenious lines to lure potential customers into their employers' clutches, frequently involving no mention of carpets or shops. The touts who hang around the Zitouna Mosque, for example, will ask if you would like a rooftop view of the mosque. It sounds innocent enough – until you realise that getting to the rooftop entails walking through a carpet shop! Travel writer Paul Theroux came away very impressed by his encounter with a Tunis carpet tout, and wrote about it at length in *The Pillars of Hercules*.

It's easy enough to turn down the touts, who are normally polite and (apparently) helpful, but the carpet dealers can be very hard to shake once you step through their doors.

MEDINA

The medina is the historical and cultural heart of the modern city of Tunis and is the ideal place to get a feel for the Tunisian way of life.

It was founded at the end of the 7th century AD (shortly after the Arab conquest), and was the focal point of the city for more than a thousand years. In fact, for most of that time the city existed solely within its walls. At the start of the French protectorate (1881-1956), it housed a population of about 100,000.

When the French arrived and built their ville nouvelle, the medina lost its importance as a commercial centre and slipped into a steady decline. Less than 15,000 people live in the medina today, and souvenir shops provide the main commercial activity – catering for the thousands of tourists who pour through here each summer.

Large parts of the northern section of the medina were demolished in the 1930s and 40s under a program of slum demolition that was designed to create vehicle access to the medina. Fortunately, the demolition days are over and conservation is now the order of the day. The conservation effort is led by the Association de Sauvegarde de la Medina (☎ 560 896; fax 560 965), based at the Dar Lasram palace in the northern part of the medina at 24 Rue du Tribunal. As a result of the association's efforts, the medina was added to the UN's World Heritage List in 1981.

The southern part of the medina remains pretty much in its original condition and houses the majority of the attractions described in this section.

The best way to see the medina is on foot. The following three walking tours are marked on the Tunis medina map on the next page. Only three sites charge for admission: the Zitouna Mosque, the Dar Ben Abdallah Museum and the Tourbet el-Bey. You used to be able to get a multiple entry ticket for all three sites, but now you have to buy separate tickets. Admission to each of the three sites is TD1.600.

Walking Tour 1

This walk starts and finishes at the Bab Bhar, on the eastern side of the medina, and follows a route designed by the Association de Sauvegarde de la Medina to include the cream of the medina's attractions. The route is indicated with faded orange arrows along the way and is also marked on the free medina map available from the tourist office on Ave Habib Bourguiba in the ville nouvelle. The walk itself takes about 45 minutes, but this can easily stretch to four hours by the time you've checked out the various attractions along the way. It's best to start early – both to beat the heat and to ensure you reach the Zitouna Mosque before it closes at noon.

From the Bab Bhar, head into the medina along Rue Jemaa Zitouna, which is packed solid with tourist shops selling everything from tacky T-shirts and stuffed camels to high-quality handicrafts. The storekeepers

can be very persistent. If you're tempted to buy, bargain hard as the prices quoted here are some of the highest in Tunisia.

Rue Jemaa Zitouna eventually emerges at the main entrance of the **Zitouna Mosque** (Mosque of the Olive Tree), which is also known as the Great Mosque. The first mosque to occupy this site was built in 698 AD, at the time the medina was founded, but it was completely rebuilt in the 9th century by the Aghlabite ruler Ibrahim ibn Ahmed (856-63) – in typically austere Aghlabite fashion. The builders recycled 200 columns salvaged from the ruins of Roman Carthage for the central prayer hall.

The mosque's theological faculty was an important centre of Islamic learning until it was closed down by Bourguiba shortly after independence as part of a campaign to reduce the influence of religion on society. The faculty, known as Zitouna University, was reopened in 1987. Non-Muslims are allowed in as far as the courtyard of the mosque between 8 am and noon every day except Friday; modest dress is compulsory.

Turn right at the Zitouna Mosque, and then left into the covered **Souq el-Attarine**. Your nose will tell you before your eyes that this is the Perfume Makers' Souq. The shops here sell a range of essential oils, some blended to imitate well known brands of perfume.

The Souq el-Attarine leads into the **Souq el-Trouk**, the Turkish Sailors' Souq. The main point of interest here is an old Turkish cafe, Café M'Rabet, that has been maintained in authentic condition. It's a good excuse to stop for a coffee.

Continuing west from the Café M'Rabet, the Souq el-Trouk finishes in front of the **Mosque of Youssef Dey**. Built in 1616, this was the first Ottoman-style mosque to be built in Tunis. It was designed by the Andalusian architect Ibn Ghalib and is a colourful combination of styles. Look out for the octagonal minaret crowned with a miniature green-tiled pyramid for a roof.

Turn right at the end of Souq el-Trouk and walk along Souq el-Bey until you come out at Place du Gouvernement, a shady square

TUNIS

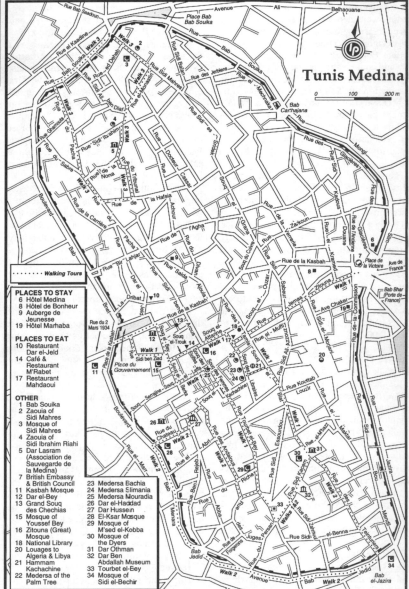

Tunis Medina

0   100   200 m

on the western edge of the medina. The **Dar el-Bey**, on the southern side of the square, is a former palace guesthouse that now houses the prime minister's office. The guards are quite a sight in their red uniforms, but photographs are not permitted.

West of the Dar el-Bey is the **Place de la Kasbah**. Now an enormous open square, beautifully paved with local granite, it was once overlooked by the old kasbah (citadel), which was destroyed by the French in 1883. The **Kasbah Mosque**, to the south-west, dates from the 13th century. The call to prayer is signalled by a white flag hung from the pole on the minaret. You have to be quick to spot it as it is only displayed for a minute or two.

From here, head back to the Mosque of Youssef Dey via Rue Sidi ben Ziad, and turn right into the **Souq el-Berka**. In Ottoman times, this was the slave souq where prisoners, taken at sea by the Muslim corsairs, were brought to be sold into slavery.

Keep going south through the Souq el-Berka and turn left into Souq el-Leffa, which runs downhill to the Souq des Étoffes, on the western side of the Zitouna Mosque. Behind the ornately studded door of No 37 is the **Medersa Mouradia**, a former Islamic college built in 1673 on the ruins of a Turkish barracks destroyed during a rebellion. Today, it is used to train apprentices in traditional crafts and is open Monday to Saturday from 9 am to 4.30 pm.

The tour now heads for the southern section of the medina via the Souq des Femmes, which leads into Rue Tourbet el-Bey – one of the main thoroughfares. The discreet little mosque on the right at No 41 is the **Mosque of M'sed el-Kobba**. The famous historian Ibn Khaldoun (1332-1406) was born just along the street at No 33 and taught briefly at the mosque before leaving Tunis to further his career in Cairo. Accordingly, the mosque is also known as the Kouttab Ibn Khaldoun (*kouttab* is a Qur'anic primary school).

Keep heading south along Rue Tourbet el-Bey for another 100m and you'll come to the building that gives the street its name, the **Tourbet el-Bey**. This huge mausoleum was built during the reign of Ali Pasha II (1758-82) and became the final resting place of many of the subsequent Husseinite beys, together with various princesses, ministers and trusted advisers. The caretaker is keen to show visitors around the funerary chambers and to point out the salient features of the ornate marble sarcophagi.

The Tourbet el-Bey is open Monday to Saturday from 9.30 am to 4.30 pm. Admission used to be covered by a medina multiple entry ticket, but now you have to buy a separate ticket for TD1.600.

Turn left after the Tourbet el-Bey onto Rue Sidi Kacem, cross Rue Sidi Zahmoul and you'll see a sign on the right pointing to the **Dar Ben Abdallah Museum**, on Impasse Ben Abdallah.

Built in 1796, this former palace now houses the Centre for Popular Arts and Traditions. Four of the rooms have been used to create scenes of bourgeois life in 19th century Tunis, using dummies dressed in traditional costumes. Another room has a very detailed map of the medina with all the hammams, mosques, souqs and other points of interest shown on it.

The building itself is probably of more interest than the museum: it has an unusual, highly ornate entrance leading to a marble courtyard complete with fountains and sculptures. The museum is open Tuesday to Saturday from 9.30 am to 4.30 pm. Admission is TD1.600.

Continue to the end of Rue Sidi Kacem and turn left onto Rue des Teinturiers (the Street of the Dyers). The octagonal minaret on the corner marks the extravagant **Mosque of the Dyers**, built in 1716 by Hussein ben Ali, founder of the Husseinite line of beys.

Opposite the mosque, an archway leads to Rue el-M'Bazz and the **Dar Othman**. Built by Othman Dey at the beginning of the 17th century, the palace is an excellent example of period architecture, distinguished by its magnificent façade. The palace is under restoration after suffering years of neglect under Bourguiba.

Return to Rue des Teinturiers and keep heading north for about 150m, then turn left into Souq el-Kachachine and take the first right into the Souq des Libraires (the Booksellers' Souq). The western side of the souq is lined with a series of medersas formerly linked to the theological faculty of the Zitouna Mosque. The oldest of them is the **Medersa of the Palm Tree** at No 11, which was built in 1714 on the site of a former *funduq* (travellers' inn) and is named after a palm tree that once occupied its central courtyard. It still serves as a Qur'anic school and is closed to the public. The **Medersa Bachia**, at No 19, is identifiable by the small public fountain beside the entrance. It was built in 1752 by the Husseinite bey Ali Pasha and now houses a school for apprentice artisans. The **Medersa Slimania**, at the corner of Souq des Libraires and Souq el-Kachachine, was also built by Ali Pasha. It was constructed in 1754 in memory of Ali Pasha's son Suleiman, who was poisoned by his brother. It is now occupied by the Tunisian Medical Association.

The Souq des Libraires continues north and emerges in front of the Zitouna Mosque. The Restaurant Mahdaoui, on Rue Jemaa Zitouna near the mosque, claims to be the oldest restaurant in Tunis. A bowl of couscous here is the perfect way to finish your tour before heading back along Rue Jemaa Zitouna to the Bab Bhar.

Walking Tour 2

This walk takes in some of the quieter areas of the southern medina, as well as some of the major attractions. Start at the medina's south-eastern gate, the **Bab el-Jazira**, and follow Rue des Teinturiers to the **Dar Othman**. A left turn here into Rue Sidi Kacem takes you past the **Dar Ben Abdallah Museum** and the **Tourbet el-Bey**. Other points of note on the walk are the **Dar Hussein**, which houses the National Museum of Archaeology and Art, and the **El-Ksar Mosque**. A short detour also takes in the **Dar el-Haddad**, one of the medina's oldest dwellings. The walk back to Bab el-Jazira along Blvd Bab Menara and Ave Bab Jedid takes you through the bustling local **market** around Bab Jedid. The huge mosque at Bab

el-Jazira is the 14th century **Mosque of Sidi el-Bechir**.

Walking Tour 3

This walk covers the main sites of interest in the northern medina. Start at the main northern entrance to the medina, **Bab Souika**, and follow Rue Sidi Mahres past the **Mosque of Sidi Mahres** – the building opposite is the Zaouia of Sidi Mahres. Then take Rue el-Monastiri and cross into Rue Sidi Ibrahim, then turn south into Rue du Tribunal opposite the Zaouia of Sidi Ibrahim Riahi. Rue du Tribunal is home to the **Dar Lasram**, a former palace that now houses the Association de Sauvegarde de la Medina – the group responsible for preserving the medina's heritage. At the southern end of Rue du Tribunal, a right turn into Rue de la Hafsia (named after the medina's old Jewish quarter) leads to Rue du Pacha – the main street of the Turkish elite in Ottoman times. The walk is completed by following Rue du Pacha north to Rue Bab Souika.

VILLE NOUVELLE

The streets of the ville nouvelle are lined with old French buildings with louvred windows and balconies with wrought-iron railings. This gives the whole place a very European feel, which is heightened by the pavement cafes and the numerous patisseries selling all manner of both sweet and savoury pastries.

There are few points of interest apart from some fine examples of colonial architecture. You'll find a selection of styles, ranging from the exuberant to the bizarre. The only way to describe the **Cathedral of St Vincent de Paul**, which faces the French Embassy on Place de l'Indépendance, is bizarre. Built in 1883, the cathedral incorporates an extraordinary collection of clashing styles – part-Gothic, part-Byzantine and part-North African. The main doors are normally locked, but there is a side entrance on Rue d'Alger. The statue opposite the cathedral is of Ibn Khaldoun, the great Islamic teacher and philosopher who was born in Tunis.

continued on page 126

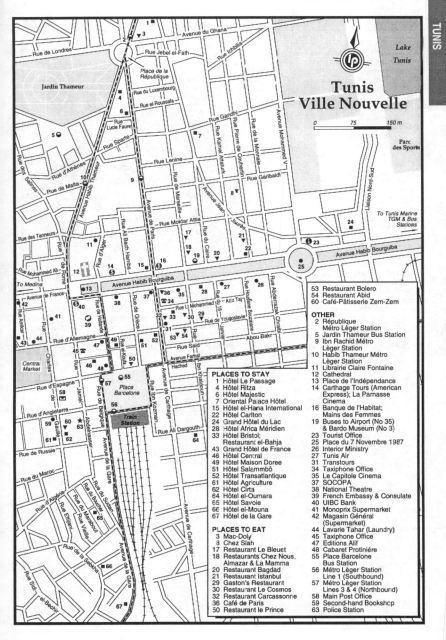

Tunis
Ville Nouvelle

Lake
Tunis

Parc
des Sports

0   75   150 m

To Tunis Marine
TGM & Bus
Stations

Jardin Thameur

To Medina

Central
Market

PLACES TO STAY
1 Hôtel Le Passage
4 Hôtel Ritza
6 Hôtel Majestic
7 Oriental Palace Hôtel
15 Hôtel el-Hana International
22 Hôtel Carlton
24 Grand Hôtel du Lac
28 Hôtel Africa Méridien
33 Hôtel Bristol;
    Restaurant el-Bahja
43 Grand Hôtel de France
46 Hôtel Central
49 Hôtel Maison Doree
51 Hôtel Salammbô
52 Hôtel Transatlantique
61 Hôtel Agriculture
62 Hôtel Cirta
64 Hôtel el-Oumara
65 Hôtel Savoie
66 Hôtel el-Mouna
67 Hôtel de la Gare

PLACES TO EAT
3 Mac-Doly
8 Chez Slah
17 Restaurant Le Bleuet
18 Restaurants Chez Nous,
    Almazar & La Mamma
20 Restaurant Bagdad
21 Restaurant Istanbul
29 Gaston's Restaurant
30 Restaurant Le Cosmos
32 Restaurant Carcassonne
36 Café de Paris
50 Restaurant le Prince

53 Restaurant Bolero
54 Restaurant Abid
60 Café-Pâtisserie Zem-Zem

OTHER
2 République
   Métro Léger Station
5 Jardin Thameur Bus Station
9 Ibn Rachid Métro
   Léger Station
10 Habib Thameur Métro
   Léger Station
11 Librairie Claire Fontaine
12 Cathedral
13 Place de l'Indépendance
14 Carthage Tours (American
   Express); La Parnasse
   Cinema
16 Banque de l'Habitat;
   Mains des Femmes
19 Buses to Airport (No 35)
   & Bardo Museum (No 3)
23 Tourist Office
25 Place du 7 Novembre 1987
26 Interior Ministry
27 Tunis Air
31 Transtours
34 Taxiphone Office
35 Le Capitole Cinema
37 SOCOPA
38 National Theatre
39 French Embassy & Consulate
40 UIBC Bank
41 Monoprix Supermarket
42 Magasin Général
   (Supermarket)
44 Lavarie Tahar (Laundry)
45 Taxiphone Office
47 Editions Alif
48 Cabaret Protinière
55 Place Barcelone
   Bus Station
56 Métro Léger Station
   Line 1 (Southbound)
57 Métro Léger Station
   Lines 3 & 4 (Northbound)
58 Main Post Office
59 Second-hand Bookshop
63 Police Station

Bardo Museum

The Bardo is the best museum in the country. It houses the most important finds from Tunisia's many ancient sites. Even if you are normally bored silly by museums, you'll be missing out badly if you don't pay at least a brief visit to the Bardo.

The Bardo would be worth a visit even without its exhibits. Located in the suburb of Le Bardo, about 4km west of the city centre, it occupies the former Bardo Palace – official residence of the Husseinite beys. The first palace to be built on the site was commissioned by the Hafsid sultan El-Mustansir (1249-77). He was responsible for restoring and diverting the Zaghouan to Carthage aqueduct to supply the palace and the medina with water. The present palace was built at the end of the 17th century, and was steadily en-

Keep an eye out for this magnificent mosaic of Neptune, god of the sea.

larged by a succession of Husseinite occupants until it became a museum in 1888.

The museum is organised into sections which cover the Carthaginian, Roman, early Christian and Arab-Islamic eras. The Roman section contains one of the finest collections of Roman mosaics anywhere in the world – just when you think you have seen the best, another room reveals something bigger and better. (See also the boxed text on mosaics in the Arts section of the Facts about the Country chapter.) There are so many mosaics that they are overwhelming, and excellent pieces that would stand out on their own elsewhere get lost in the floor-to-ceiling displays. It is worth making a couple of half-day trips to the museum if you are keen, rather than trying to do it all in one hit and becoming so saturated that it is hard to appreciate yet another mosaic.

The best mosaics include the depiction of the poet Virgil flanked by the muses of literature and drama in Room 15 and the monumental Triumph of Neptune in Room 10. Room 15 is quite something in its own right. It was formerly the palace harem, and the four smaller corner rooms were occupied by the ruler's favourite wives. In Room 6, the statues from the Temple of Apollo at Bulla Regia are another highlight.

Also not to be missed is the haul from the wreck of a boat which came to grief off the coast at Mahdia in the 1st century BC. It was carrying a load of marble and bronze statuary, and this adds some welcome variety to the museum. The exhibits from the wreck are displayed in Rooms 17 to 22.

The Islamic section is somewhat overshadowed by the other exhibits.

The Bardo is open Tuesday to Sunday from 9 am to 5 pm in summer, and from 9.30 am to 4.30 pm in winter. It's open on all the public holidays except for the 'Eid al-Fitr festival at the end of Ramadan (see Public Holidays in the main Facts for the Visitor chapter for a table of dates). Entry is TD3.150, plus a further TD1 if you want to take photos.

Getting There & Away There are several transport options for getting to the museum (see the Around Tunis map later in this chapter). The simplest is to take a taxi, which costs about TD2.500 from the city centre. It's also possible to get there by métro léger (tram). The museum is a short walk from Le Bardo station, two stops west of Bab Saadoun on métro léger line 4. The museum entrance is on the northern side of the museum on Rue Mongi Slim, while the station is on the southern side of the museum on Boulevard du 20 Mars 1956. There ia a signpost at the station pointing the way.

The third option is to catch yellow city bus No 3 from Tunis Marine, which terminates just around the corner from the museum entrance on Ave de l'Union de Maghreb Arabe. You can catch this service from the bus stop opposite the Hôtel Africa Méridien. ∎

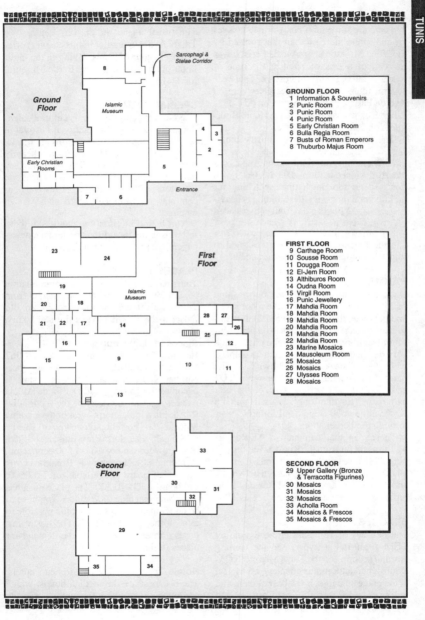

Sarcophagi & Stelae Corridor

Ground Floor

Islamic Museum

Early Christian Rooms

Entrance

GROUND FLOOR
1 Information & Souvenirs
2 Punic Room
3 Punic Room
4 Punic Room
5 Early Christian Room
6 Bulla Regia Room
7 Busts of Roman Emperors
8 Thuburbo Majus Room

First Floor

Islamic Museum

FIRST FLOOR
9 Carthage Room
10 Sousse Room
11 Dougga Room
12 El-Jem Room
13 Althiburos Room
14 Oudna Room
15 Virgil Room
16 Punic Jewellery
17 Mahdia Room
18 Mahdia Room
19 Mahdia Room
20 Mahdia Room
21 Mahdia Room
22 Mahdia Room
23 Marine Mosaics
24 Mausoleum Room
25 Mosaics
26 Mosaics
27 Ulysses Room
28 Mosaics

Second Floor

SECOND FLOOR
29 Upper Gallery (Bronze & Terracotta Figurines)
30 Mosaics
31 Mosaics
32 Mosaics
33 Acholla Room
34 Mosaics & Frescos
35 Mosaics & Frescos

continued from page 122
There are some fabulously ornate façades around, none more so than that sported by the Hôtel Majestic at 36 Ave de Paris. It was in need of a coat of paint at the time of research but was still impressive. There are several more good examples elsewhere on Ave de Paris and further north on Ave de la Liberté, as well as south of Ave Habib Bourguiba on Rue de Yougoslavie.

The formidable Interior Ministry building, which occupies a whole block at the eastern end of Ave Habib Bourguiba, was clearly designed to intimidate. It's best if you don't spend too much time searching for architectural nuances – the building is heavily guarded 24 hours a day, and is barricaded off to prevent pedestrians wandering past. Other grand structures like the post office and the French Embassy were designed to impress through their size and grandeur.

HAMMAMS
If you are staying in a hotel without washing facilities, or if you just feel like a hot sauna and massage, there are numerous hammams in the medina. The Dar Ben Abdallah Museum (see the Medina section earlier) has a very detailed map of the medina on display, which has all the hammams shown on it. The hammams generally charge between TD1 and TD1.500 per person. One of the best hammams (for men only) is the Hammam Kachachine at 30 Souq des Libraires; enter through the barber shop.

There's another hammam at 11 Rue el-Methira, not far from the Rue des Teinturiers, but you'll have to ask for directions. It's open all day and is reserved for women between 1 and 3 pm. The hammam at 64 Rue des Teinturiers is for men only; a visit here costs TD1.

BEACHES
The beaches of Tunis are all accessible by TGM (light-rail network; see the Getting Around section and the Tunis Metro & TGM Routes map later in this chapter). La Marsa, at the end of the line, is the best of them and is less crowded than those at Carthage and La Goulette.

ORGANISED TOURS
The travel agents in the city centre (see Travel Agencies earlier in this chapter) offer a half day tour of Tunis, taking in the highlights of the medina and the Bardo Museum, for TD15.

SPECIAL EVENTS
The main event on the Tunis cultural calendar is the Carthage International Festival in July and August – two months of music, dance and theatre held at Carthage's heavily restored Roman theatre. The biennial Carthage International Film Festival is next due in October 1999. The two week festival concentrates on Middle Eastern and African cinema.

You'll find information about both these festivals in the local French-language newspapers. Tickets are sold at the door.

PLACES TO STAY
Tunis has a good choice of accommodation for all budgets. The options range from youth hostel accommodation in an old palace to the latest in modern five star luxury.

Places to Stay – budget
Hostels The *Auberge de Jeunesse* (☎ 567 850), which is affiliated to Hostelling International (HI), is a good place to stay. It occupies the 150-year-old Dar Saida Ajoula palace, right in the heart of the medina on Rue Saida Ajoula, north-west of the Zitouna Mosque. The hostel is signposted off Rue de la Kasbah. The dorms are quite good, if a little crowded, and cost TD4.500 per person, including a free hot shower. Breakfast costs TD1. Half board is available for TD7.500; full board is TD 10.500. The place even has a washing machine (500 mills). You have to be an HI member to stay, but it's possible to join on the spot for TD12. The hostel imposes a three-night limit if the demand for places is high.

Hotels Tunis has dozens of cheap hotels. The cheapest are the medina hotels, which are found either within the medina or in the streets immediately surrounding it. Most of them are set up with visiting labourers in mind, not western tourists. They charge by the bed in a shared room, which means that if you want your own room, you will have to pay for all the beds in it. A typical example of this style of hotel is the grubby *Hôtel de Bonheur*, on the southern side of Rue de la Kasbah, about 100m from Place de la Victoire, where you'll pay TD3 per person in a shared room. Unless you are down to your last few dinars, you should avoid these places like the plague. They are totally unsuitable for women.

There are a couple of better medina places that are worth considering. The *Hôtel Medina* (☎ 255 056), on Place de la Victoire at the entrance to the medina, has clean doubles for TD10, but no singles. Hot showers cost TD1 – a trip to a nearby hammam is much better value. Unlike many of the cheapies, it has a few windows and doesn't get quite as stuffy as the others in summer, although the location means that it is fairly noisy. The *Hôtel Marhaba* (☎ 343 118), on the opposite side of the square at 5 Rue de la Commission, has single/double rooms for TD7.500/8 and charges 500 mills for a hot shower.

Most travellers opt to stay outside the medina in the area south of Ave Habib Bourguiba. A popular choice is the *Hôtel Bristol* (☎ 244 836), off Ave de Carthage on Rue Lt Mohammed Aziz Taj. It has the best budget rooms in town with singles/doubles for TD4.900/7.800. Breakfast is available at the Restaurant el-Bahja next door for TD1 per person.

The *Hôtel Cirta* (☎ 321 584), at 42 Rue Charles de Gaulle, is another favourite with travellers. The place looks a bit shabby from the outside, but the rooms are kept spotlessly clean and the management are friendly. It charges TD7/12 for singles/doubles with shared bathroom. Hot showers cost an extra TD1.

Another possibility is the *Hôtel Central* (☎ 240 433) on Rue de Suisse, a quiet side street running between Rue de Hollande and Rue Jamel Abdelnasser. It has rooms for TD9/12 and charges a hefty TD1.500 for a shower.

If you have an early morning bus to catch, the closest hotel to the southern bus station is the *Hôtel de la Gare* (☎ 256 754). It's a lot better inside than its shabby exterior indicates. Singles/doubles cost TD7/12, plus TD1 for a shower. A nearby alternative is the *Hôtel el-Mouna* (☎ 343 375) in Rue de la Sebkha, which has large doubles with en suite shower for TD12.

Places to Stay – middle

Most of the hotels that fall into this category are old-style French hotels that date back to the 1930s and 40s. In their prime, they ranked as the best hotels in town; these days, they have been relegated to the ranks of the also-rans. They include some good places and generally have much more character than their modern counterparts. The streets south of Ave Habib Bourguiba are where to start looking.

The pick of bunch is the two star *Hôtel Maison Doree* (☎ 332 401), 6 Rue el-Koufa, just north of Place Barcelone off Rue de Hollande. Opened in 1940, it has been maintained in tip-top condition by the French family who run it. It even has a lift. Comfortable single/double rooms cost TD19.100/22.350 with washbasin or TD23.650/25.900, with shower and toilet. The best rooms cost TD29.750/32.700, and come with bath and toilet. All the rooms have central heating in winter, and air-conditioning is available in summer for an additional TD2.500. The prices listed include breakfast of coffee and croissants.

If those prices sound too steep, try the *Hôtel Salammbô* (☎ 334 252; fax 337 498), a block to the east of the Maison Doree at 6 Rue de Grèce. It's a one star version of the Maison Doree – it has a huge old timber staircase instead of a lift, for example. The staff are friendly and efficient, and the whole place is kept spotlessly clean. It also offers a wide choice of rooms, starting with a couple of basic singles without facilities for TD11. Singles/doubles with shower and toilet are TD15.500/24, or TD16.500/25 with bath. Prices include breakfast – bread and jam, not croissants.

The *Hôtel Transatlantique* (☎ 240 680), at 106 Rue de Yougoslavie, is another fine old place, its name emblazoned in mosaic on the corner of Ave de Carthage. Its prices are similar to those at the Salammbô. The splendid-sounding *Grand Hôtel de France* (☎ 245 876; fax 343 314), just south of Place de la Victoire at 8 Rue Mustapha Mbarek, is another reasonable place, with similar prices.

The *Hôtel Agriculture* (☎ 326 394), at 25 Rue Charles de Gaulle south of the post office, has undergone a complete transformation in the last couple of years. The new owners have gutted the interior of this former cheapie and have converted it into a comfortable mid-range hotel. Singles/doubles with bathroom are TD14/24, and breakfast costs TD1.200 per person.

There are also a few mid-range hotels in the streets north of Ave Habib Bourguiba. The *Hôtel Ritza* (☎ 245 428), just south of Place de la République on Ave Habib Thameur, charges TD14.500 per person, including breakfast, for singles/doubles. You'll need to be a heavy sleeper – the hotel is right next to one of the busiest intersections in town. No matter how much traffic noise there might be, you're better off at the Ritza than at the *Hôtel Savoie*, a rock-bottom dump off Ave de la Gare on Rue du Boucher which charges TD2.500 per person.

You'll struggle to find a quieter location than that of the *Hôtel St Georges* (☎ 781 029), tucked away at 16 Rue de Cologne about 500m north of Place de la République. It's the hotel that time forgot. The two star rating must be based on something other than the cracking, pre-independence vinyl furniture. Still, it is quiet, and TD19/25 is a reasonable price for singles/doubles with bathroom, including breakfast.

The *Hôtel Le Passage* (☎ 335 855; fax 337 202), at 68 Ave Jean Jaurès, is a comfortable, modern two star hotel charging TD26/35 for good singles/doubles with bathroom and breakfast. All rooms come with air-con and satellite TV.

The *Hôtel Majestic* (☎ 332 848; fax 336 908), at the northern end of Ave de Paris, is a splendid piece of fading grandeur with one of the finest French colonial façades in town. Singles/doubles here cost TD35/48 with breakfast. Air-conditioning is available for an extra TD3.500 in summer.

Places to Stay – top end

For those with the money and the inclination, Tunis has its full quota of expensive hotels. At the last count, there were at least 20 hotels in town rating three stars or more – and there were a dozen more by the beach at Gammarth, north of Carthage (see the Around Tunis section later in this chapter for details).

The *Hôtel Carlton* (☎ 330 664; fax 338 168), 31 Ave Habib Bourguiba, represents one of the best deals around. Right in the heart of town, this small, immaculately maintained three star hotel has all the comforts (including satellite TV and air-con) you could want at a price that won't break the bank. It charges TD41/62, including breakfast, for singles/doubles.

The *Hôtel el-Oumara* (☎ 333 122; fax 338 030) is a brand new three star establishment on Rue Ali Dargouth, five minutes walk from the train station. It charges TD50/65 for large, well-appointed singles/doubles with breakfast.

The bizarre inverted pyramid behind the tourist office at the eastern end of Ave Habib Bourguiba is the *Grand Hôtel du Lac* (☎ 258 322; fax 342 759), the city's leading architectural curiosity. You're better off looking at it from the outside. Singles/doubles cost TD52/77 with breakfast.

You won't have any trouble locating the five star *Hôtel Africa Méridien* (☎ 347 477; fax 347 432), 50 Ave Habib Bourguiba – it's the only high-rise building on the whole street. Naturally enough, the rooms have great views over the city. It charges TD131/148 for singles/doubles, or you can lash out TD420 on the presidential suite.

Rather more discreet is the stylish *Oriental Palace Hôtel* (☎ 342 500; fax 350 327), at 29 Ave Jean Jaurès, with its array of clocks showing the time in most of the world's capital cities. Five star treatment here costs TD105/115 for rooms with breakfast.

Hilton-hoppers will be happy to find their favourite here too, on Ave de la Ligue Arabe on the northern edge of the Parc de Belvedere, 10 minutes by taxi from the centre of town and the airport. The *Tunis Hilton* (☎ 782 100; fax 781 713) prices its rooms according to what you can see. Rooms with a 'limited view' cost TD110/120, including breakfast, while rooms with a 'panoramic view' go for TD130/140.

The smartest rooms in town are at the swank *Hôtel Abou Nawas Tunis* (☎ 350 355; fax 352 882), behind Parc Kennedy on Ave Mohammed V. Prices start at TD160/170 for predictably plush singles/doubles, including breakfast.

PLACES TO EAT

The city centre is dotted with dozens of restaurants, cafes and fast-food joints. Although at first glance there appears to be plenty of variety, they have remarkably similar menus, with about a dozen standard dishes. Service, prices and décor are the major variables.

Restaurants – budget

There's no shortage of cheap places serving good local food. The best deal around is to be found at the long-time travellers' favourite, the *Restaurant Carcassonne*, 8 Ave de Carthage. The value offered by its TD3.500 four course menu is little short of remarkable, even if the meat dishes are not exactly enormous. The crème caramel is a nice touch. The place also has welcome ceiling fans and fast, friendly service. It's not hard to understand why it's popular with tourists and locals alike.

The Carcassonne is not the cheapest place around. That title goes to the *Restaurant Istanbul*, just north of Ave Habib Bourguiba on Rue Pierre de Coubertin. It charges just TD3 for four courses.

The *Restaurant le Prince* is a popular cafeteria-style eatery on Place Barcelone that offers three courses for TD2.950 from noon to 2 pm on weekdays.

The only problem with these set menus is that the choice is limited to dishes that are cheap and easy to prepare. You'll find a

much better range of dishes at the *Restaurant Abid*, 98 Rue de Yougoslavie. It has a selection of daily specials, each for TD3 or less. The *Restaurant el-Bahja*, next to the Hôtel Bristol on Rue Lt Mohammed Aziz Taj, is also recommended.

The *Restaurant Mahdaoui*, opposite the Zitouna Mosque on Rue Jemaa Zitouna, claims to be the oldest restaurant in Tunis. It's the perfect place for medina visitors to stop for lunch. It has a daily menu of traditional dishes, each for about TD3.500, and specialises in couscous. The restaurant is closed in the evening.

Restaurants – middle

There are stacks of more upmarket restaurants around the ville nouvelle. The main concentrations are south of Ave Habib Bourguiba around the junction of Rue de Yougoslavie and Rue Ibn Khaldoun, and on the southern reaches of Ave de Paris and Rue de Marseille. Many restaurants in this category also have live entertainment, and are covered in the Entertainment section later in this chapter. All the restaurants listed in this section serve alcohol.

The *Restaurant Bolero* (☎ 245 928), at 6 Passage el-Guattar, is a great favourite with Tunis residents. It specialises in grilled meats and seafood, and boasts an extensive wine list. A hearty meal for two with wine costs from TD25. Passage el-Guattar is a small side street running south off Rue de Yougoslavie between Ave de Carthage and Rue Ibn Khaldoun.

The *Restaurant Bagdad*, opposite the Hôtel Africa Méridien, at 29 Ave Habib Bourguiba, is a good place to try more typically Tunisian dishes like fish chorba for TD2.900 or couscous with lamb for TD7.

The *Restaurant Le Cosmos* (☎ 241 610), at 7 Rue Ibn Khaldoun, is a place that has built up a solid reputation for good French-style food and reasonable prices. You can amuse yourself by studying the pretty awful paint job of the universe on the ceiling and the collection of kitsch around the walls.

The French connection at the Hôtel Maison Doree (see Places to Stay earlier in this chapter) extends to the hotel's excellent *Restaurant Margaritas* (☎ 240 632). The three course set menu is very good value at TD5.500. The restaurant entrance is at 6 Rue de Hollande.

Chez Nous (☎ 243 043), 5 Rue de Marseille, makes a meal of all the celebrities who have graced its tables. The walls are decked with photos of the likes of Michael York and Mohammed Ali having a good time. Most people ignore the overpriced à la carte menu, opting instead for the TD12 three course menu.

Restaurants – expensive

Top of the range for Tunisian food is the *Restaurant Dar el-Jeld* (☎ 560 916), on the western side of the medina in Rue Dar el-Jeld. It's probably the best restaurant in town, and it certainly has the best setting. The Dar el-Jeld is the palatial former home of a wealthy bourgeois family, and the dining room and table settings are quite magnificent. There's a three course menu for TD18; otherwise expect to pay about TD30 per person, plus wine. The wine list includes imported French champagne (from TD185 per bottle). The restaurant is open Monday to Saturday for lunch and dinner. Bookings are essential.

Chez Slah (☎ 258 588), 14 Rue Pierre de Coubertin, is rated by many as the best French-style restaurant in town.

Cafes

Cafes are an essential part of life in Tunis. Most of them are small, neighbourhood places, but a couple have achieved celebrity status.

The *Café de Paris*, on the corner of Ave Habib Bourguiba and Ave de Carthage, is the trendy spot to be seen in. It's expensive – prices start at TD1.200 for an exprès coffee – but it's a convenient meeting place and a good spot for people watching. It must be just about the only cafe in the country that serves beer (TD1.800).

The *Café M'Rabet*, right in the heart of the medina in the Souq el-Trouk, is an old Ottoman cafe that has been maintained in

authentic condition. The restaurant upstairs is used for performances of Tunisian music and dance in the evenings (see the Entertainment section, following). The entrance to the cafe is hard to spot; look for the old wrought-iron street lamp outside.

Fast Food

Rôtisseries are at the bottom of the cheap-eats scale and are found all over the city. They specialise in grilled chicken with chips, either to eat in or to take away. Most of them charge around TD1.800 for a quarter chicken with chips, which comes with a handful of salad and a chunk of bread.

Pizza parlours are the most popular form of western food outlet. There are several places on Ave Habib Bourguiba, opposite the Hôtel Africa Méridien, that sell a range of pizzas by the slice. Prices start at 650 mills for 100g – you can just point to a slice, which is then weighed and priced accordingly, or you can specify the amount you want in grams. *La Mamma*, 10-11 Rue de Marseille, has individual pizzas priced from TD4, and a range of pasta dishes from TD3.

Burgers haven't achieved anything like the popularity of pizzas, but they can be found. Addicts can be sure of getting a fix at the quaintly named *Mac-Doly* on Ave du Ghana, just off Place de la République. Offerings include a basic burger for TD1.200, Big Dolys for TD1.750 and a Mac Senior for TD2.100.

Patisseries

The French left their mark in the shape of the many patisseries in the ville nouvelle. They stock a mouth-watering array of sweet cakes and croissants, as well as small pizzas, savoury pastries and crêpes (pancakes) – perfect for breakfast or lunch. There is nearly always a cafe at the back of these places, where you can get a coffee to have with your snack.

You'll find the best selection of goodies at the big patisseries opposite the Hôtel Africa Méridien on the northern side of Ave Habib Bourguiba. There are more places on Rue Charles de Gaulle, including the excellent

Café-Patisserie Zem-Zem, two doors north of the Hôtel Cirta. Fresh is the operative word here: it has freshly squeezed orange juice (500 mills), freshly ground coffee and a good range of cakes, croissants and other pastries.

Self Catering

The central *market* on Rue Charles de Gaulle is the best place to stock up on food. You'll find a wide selection of local cheeses and yoghurts, cold meats, fresh bread, olives and pickles as well as fresh fruit and vegetables. The fish section is on the northern side of the market and has its own entrance on Rue d'Allemagne.

The main supermarkets in the city centre are *Monoprix*, on Rue Charles de Gaulle, and the *Magasin Général* on Ave de France. Both stock a good range of local wines as well as food, toiletries etc.

ENTERTAINMENT
Cinemas

Tunis residents are obviously keen cinema-goers, if the large number of cinemas in the ville nouvelle is anything to go by. Most of them show action movies in Arabic, but you'll also find the latest Hollywood box office hits, dubbed into French.

You'll find the cinema listings in the entertainment pages of the local French-language papers. Admission prices are TD1.200 at smaller cinemas, rising to TD2.500 at plush, modern, air-conditioned cinema centres like *La Parnasse*, inside the arcade on Ave Habib Bourguiba between Rue d'Alger and Rue Ali Bach Hamba, and *Le Capitole*, next to the Café de Paris on Ave Habib Bourguiba.

Discos

Discos don't feature prominently on the local entertainment scene. They are found in the big hotels, and exist primarily for the benefit of tourists and the Tunisian jet set. The main ones in the city centre are the *Jockey Club*, at the Hôtel el-Hana International, and *Club Shehrazade*, at the Hôtel Abou Nawas.

Traditional Music & Dance

The best-known venue is the *Restaurant M'Rabet* (☎ 261 729), in the medina's Souq el-Trouk, above the Café M'Rabet. There is a range of set meals for TD7 to TD24, plus an extra TD5 per person for the show. It features traditional folk music, displays of Berber dance and a brief appearance by a belly dancer. The place is open every night and is very popular with tour groups.

Locals prefer to head for Rue de Marseille in the ville nouvelle, where several of the restaurants have live music. The *Restaurant Almazar* (☎ 257 417), at No 11, has music every night from 6 to 8.30 pm, while the action continues until the small hours at No 23, *Le Bleuet* (☎ 349 280). There's no cover charge for the show in these places, but most customers give generously when the hat is passed around. Neither restaurant is particularly cheap – allow at least TD30 for two, plus wine. *Gaston's*, at 73 Rue de Yougoslavie, has music on Tuesday, Friday and Saturday evenings.

Bars

The bars in Tunis are serious drinking dens. The *Bar Coquille*, next to the Restaurant Carcassonne on Ave de Carthage, is a typical one and charges TD1.450 for a beer, the most popular drink. These bars are not suitable for women travellers, who may feel more comfortable going to the bars at the bigger hotels. The bar at the *Hôtel Maison Doree* is worth trying.

Nightclubs

The *Cabaret Protiniére*, just to the north of Place Barcelone at 11 Rue de Hollande, is an archetypal Middle Eastern nightclub. You'll find pouting belly dancers and crooning singers – barely visible through the dense cigarette haze – and groups of increasingly animated men drinking Johnny Walker Red Label by the bottle at TD120 a throw. It's an interesting place to check out, if only to confirm that such places do exist outside the movies – but definitely not recommended for single women looking for a quiet night out. The Protiniére is open daily from 10 pm to 4 am. The entry charge of TD6 includes your first (soft) drink.

SPECTATOR SPORT
Horse Racing
There's horse racing every Sunday afternoon at L'Hippodrome de Kassar Saïd, about 10km west of the city centre. The six-race card normally starts at about 1 pm, and includes events for Arab horses as well as for imported thoroughbreds. There is computerised betting, both on local races and on racing from France. Entry is 500 mills. Buses to Kassar Saïd (620 mills) leave from the Jardin Thameur bus station. A taxi from the city centre costs about TD5.

Soccer
Six of the 14 teams in the Tunisian first division are from Tunis, including arch rivals Club Africain and Espérance Sportive de Tunisie. Both use the Stade Olympique in El-Menzah as a home ground, and play there on alternate weeks. Matches are played on Sunday starting at 2 pm. Admission prices start at 800 mills for the cheapest terrace tickets. To get there, take métro léger line 2 from République and get off at the Cité Sportive stop.

You'll find details of fixtures in the Saturday French-language papers. The teams are usually referred to by their initials – CA for Club Africain, and EST for Espérance Sportive de Tunisie. The other clubs from around Tunis are Stade Tunisien (ST), Avenir Sportif de La Marsa (ASM), Club Sportif de Hammam Lif (CSHL) and CO Transport (COT) from the western suburbs.

THINGS TO BUY
Although Tunis is not noted for its handicraft production, the shops of the Tunis medina offer everything the souvenir hunter could desire.

Rue Jemaa Zitouna is packed solid with shops selling everything from tacky T-shirts adorned with cartoons of copulating camels to top-quality handicrafts. There are more souvenir shops on Rue de la Kasbah and in the souqs around the Zitouna Mosque. Prices start high, so be prepared to haggle like hell if you want to buy anything.

If you don't enjoy bargaining, you're better off heading for the new Société de Commercialisation des Produits de l'Artisanats (SOCOPA) store on the corner of Ave Habib Bourguiba and Ave de Carthage. It has a huge selection of crafts from all over the country, the quality is good and prices are clearly marked. Even if you don't buy here, you can get a good idea of the quality and price of the best stuff available before you start bargaining with the shop owners in the medina.

Another good place to buy handicrafts is Mains des Femmes, above the Banque de l'Habitat at 47 Ave Habib Bourguiba. The shop is the sales outlet for handicrafts produced by a variety of women's cooperatives in poor rural areas.

It has a good selection of carpets, woven rugs, including *kilims* and *mergoums*, embroidered blankets, wooden toys, dolls and jewellery. Prices are very reasonable, and the money goes to a good cause. The shop is open Monday to Saturday from 9.30 am to 1 pm and 3 to 6.30 pm.

GETTING THERE & AWAY
Air
The domestic airline Tuninter flies at least six times a day to Jerba and less frequently to Tozeur and Sfax. It can be difficult to get a booking in the middle of summer. See the Air section of the main Getting Around chapter for details of times and prices.

Tickets can be bought from the Tunis Air office (☎ 330 100) at 48 Ave Habib Bourguiba, on the corner of Ave Habib Bourguiba and Rue 18 Janvier, or from any travel agent (see Travel Agencies under Information earlier in this chapter). Tuninter also has a special reservations service on ☎ 701 111.

For details of international flights to and from Tunis, see the main Getting There & Away chapter at the beginning of this book. International airline offices in Tunis include the following:

Aeroflot
(☎ 340 844) 24 Ave Habib Thameur
Air Algérie
(☎ 341 888) 26 Ave de Paris
Air France
(☎ 341 578) 1 Rue d'Athènes
Alitalia
(☎ 331 377) 17 Ave Habib Thameur
EgyptAir
(☎ 341 182) 1st Floor, Complexe el-Hana International, 49 Ave Habib Bourguiba
GB Airways
(☎ 330 046) 17 Ave Habib Bourguiba
KLM (Transavia)
(☎ 341 309) 6 Rue Lucie Faure
Lufthansa
(☎ 793 515) Complexe el-Mechtel, Ave Ouled Haffouz
Middle East Airlines
(☎ 341 206) Hôtel Africa Méridien, 50 Ave Habib Bourguiba
Royal Air Maroc
(☎ 351 377) 16 Ave Habib Bourguiba
Sabena
(☎ 259 845) Hôtel Abou Nawas Tunis, Ave Mohammed V
Tunis Air
(☎ 330 100) 48 Ave Habib Bourguiba

Bus

Tunis has two intercity bus stations – one for departures to the south of Tunis and another for departures to the north.

The French-language papers, *La Presse* and *Le Temps*, carry details of SNTRI departures from both bus stations every day. It should be noted that these schedules list only final destinations and not the places passed through en route. Thus Sousse and Kairouan seldom get a mention, even though all buses heading south pass through one of them.

Southern Bus Station Buses to the south leave from the Gare Routière Sud de Bab el-Fellah (☎ 495 255), situated just south of the city centre opposite the huge Jellaz Cemetery. It's 10 minutes walk south of Place Barcelone, beyond the flyover at the end of Ave de la Gare. Alternatively, you can catch métro léger line 1 heading south and get off at the first stop, Bab Alioua, which is 200m beyond the bus station.

The bus station is well organised and easy to work out. Arrival and departure times are clearly indicated on large information boards. The staff at the information kiosk speak minimal English, but are friendly and will do their best to help.

The following table lists the journey times, one way fares (in TD) and frequency of services to selected destinations:

Destination	Duration	Fare	Frequency
Ben Guerdane	8½ hours	19.900	1/day
Douz	9 hours	19.240	1/day
El-Jem	3 hours	8.150	5/day
Gabès	6½ hours	13.420	10/day
Gafsa	6 hours	13.450	8/day
Hammamet	1½ hours	2.800	hourly
Jerba	7-8 hours	17.760	4/day
Kairouan	2¼ hours	6.500	hourly
Makthar	3 hours	6.670	1/day
Matmata	7½ hours	15.210	3/day
Medenine	7½ hours	17.300	6/day
Nabeul	1½ hours	2.700	hourly
Nefta	7½ hours	17.250	2/day
Sbeitla	3¾ hours	9.350	3/day
Sfax	4 hours	10.260	5/day
Sousse	2 hours	5.930	10/day
Tamerza	8 hours	18.360	2/day
Tataouine	8½ hours	19.380	2/day
Tozeur	7 hours	16.550	2/day
Zarzis	8½ hours	17.990	2/day

Northern Bus Station Buses to the north leave from the Gare Routière Nord de Bab Saadoun (☎ 562 299), about 2km north-west of the city centre.

The easiest way to get there is by métro léger line 3 or 4 to Bab Saadoun station (310 mills) from Place Barcelone or République stations. The métro station is about 300m east of the bus station – just follow the tram lines west and you will get there. Alternatively, take a No 3 bus from Tunis Marine bus station or from Ave Habib Bourguiba opposite the Hôtel Africa Méridien, and get off at the first stop after Bab Saadoun (which you can't miss – it's a massive, triple-arched gate in the middle of a roundabout); the bus station is 100m over to the right.

The table over the page lists the journey times, one way fares (in TD) and frequency of services to selected destinations:

TUNIS

Destination	Duration	Fare	Frequency
'Ain Draham	3¾ hours	6.900	3/day
Bizerte	1¾ hours	2.900	half-hourly
Jendouba	3 hours	5.650	5/day
Kalaat Kasba	4½ hours	7.870	2/day
Le Kef	3½ hours	6.200	8/day
Tabarka	3¼ hours	6.370	9/day
Tebersouk	2¼ hours	3.820	8/day

Destination	2nd Class	1st Class	Confort
Bizerte	2.250	–	–
El-Jem	6.700	8.900	9.450
Gabès	11.550	15.550	16.550
Hammamet	2.700	3.700	3.900
Jendouba	5.050	6.350	6.800
Kalaat Khasba	9.800	–	–
Mahdia	6.700	8.900	9.450
Nabeul	2.700	3.700	3.900
Sfax	7.950	10.650	11.350
Sousse	4.850	6.500	6.900

Train

The trains are the way to travel. The train station is modern and efficient; it's on Place Barcelone, conveniently close to the hotels of the ville nouvelle.

Scheduled departures and arrivals are displayed on a huge electronic board in the terminal building. The staff at the small information kiosk can help with queries – provided you can speak enough Arabic or French to ask.

The most useful route is the main line south to Sousse, Sfax and beyond. There are at least eight trains a day to Sousse (two hours), leaving between 7.10 am and 9.20 pm. Four of these services continue to El-Jem (three hours) and Sfax (four hours). The 7.10 am service keeps going down the coast from Sfax to Gabès (7¼ hours), while the 9.20 pm service branches inland to Gafsa (eight hours) and Metlaoui (8½ hours).

There are also at least two trains a day (9.05 am and 12.05 pm) to Monastir (2¾ hours), and one a day (12.05 pm) to Mahdia.

Trains to Hammamet (one hour) and Nabeul (1¼ hours), via Bir Bou Rebka, have all but been phased out. There's one daily train Monday to Saturday but no trains run on Sunday.

Other services from Tunis include five trains a day to Bizerte (1½ hours); five a day to Jendouba (2¾ hours) and Ghardimao (3¼ hours); and one a day to Kalaat Khasba (five hours).

The trains can get very crowded in summer, especially on the main line south. If you want a guaranteed seat, it's a good idea to make a reservation at the station the day before you travel. There's a discount of 15% on return tickets.

The following table lists one way fares (in TD) from Tunis to various destinations:

Louage

Tunis has three main louage stations. Louages to Cap Bon leave from opposite the southern bus station (see Bus earlier in this section), and services to other southern destinations leave from the station at the eastern end of Rue al Aid el-Jebbari, off Ave Moncef Bey. Louages to the north leave from outside the northern bus station. Although a bit more expensive, the louages are a good alternative to the buses, as the services are more flexible.

The louage station at Place Sidi Bou Mendil in the medina is for services to Algeria and Libya.

Car Rental

All the major companies have offices at the airport and in town, including:

Avis
    (☎ 782 017) 90 Ave de la Liberté
    (☎ 782 112) Tunis Hilton lobby
Azur
    (☎ 782 224) 59 Ave Hedi Chaker
Europcar
    (☎ 340 303) 17 Ave Habib Bourguiba
Express
    (☎ 259 954) 39 Ave Farhat Hached
Garage Lafayette
    (☎ 287 284) 84 Ave de la Liberté
Hertz
    (☎ 248 559) 29 Ave Habib Bourguiba
Topcar
    (☎ 285 003) 7 Rue de Mahdia

Boat

The ferries from Europe arrive at the port at La Goulette, at the eastern end of the causeway across Lake Tunis. A taxi from here to the city centre costs about TD5.500, and can be considered a good investment compared with the effort involved in walking to La

Goulette Vieille station and catching a TGM train to Tunis (see the Getting Around section below).

Getting a booking on a ferry out of Tunis can be a problem in summer – travellers have reported having to wait for up to 10 days to get a place. Make your reservations as early as possible, especially if you want to take a vehicle.

The Compagnie Tunisienne de Navigation (CTN; ☎ 322 775/802; fax 354 855) office at 122 Rue de Yougoslavie handles tickets for all the ferries. It can be a real bun fight here, with people doing battle for tickets. Turn up first thing in the morning when things are marginally less frantic.

See the Getting There & Away chapter earlier in this book for full details of ferry services to and from France (Marseilles) and Italy (Genoa, Naples and Trapani).

GETTING AROUND
To/From the Airport
Tunis-Carthage airport is 8km north-east of the city centre. Yellow city bus No 35 runs there from the Tunis Marine terminus every 30 minutes or so from 6 am to 9 pm. You can also pick it up at the stop opposite the Hôtel Africa Méridien. The trip takes about 25 minutes and costs 620 mills. Coming from the airport, the bus stop is on the right just outside the terminal.

A taxi to the city centre from the airport costs about TD5.

Warning L'Aeroport station, on the TGM line from Tunis Marine to La Marsa, is nowhere near the airport.

Bus
Yellow city buses operate to all parts of the city, but you should have little cause to use them other than for getting to the airport, the Bardo Museum or the northern bus station. The destination, point of origin and route number are displayed in Arabic on a board by the entry door at the rear of the vehicle. Routes that are of interest to tourists have the destination marked in Latin script as well. The number is also displayed in the front

window. The basic fare is 250 mills on most routes. You buy your ticket on the bus.

There are three main terminuses for the buses: Tunis Marine, which is near the TGM station at the causeway end of Ave Habib Bourguiba; Place Barcelone; and Jardin Thameur, just off Ave de France. The No 3 bus to the Bardo Museum and the No 35 to the airport both leave from Tunis Marine.

Métro Léger
The smart new métro léger tram network is much easier to use than the buses. There are five main routes running to various parts of the city – see the Métro Léger & TGM Routes map on the following page. There are route maps in both Arabic and French inside the trams which show the order of the stations.

Tickets are sold at the small kiosks at the entrance to each station, and must be bought before you travel. The basic fare is 250 mills.

Line 1 runs from Tunis Marine to the southern suburb of Ben Arous via Place Barcelone. Bab Alioua, one stop south of Place Barcelone, is the closest stop to the southern bus and louage stations.

Line 2 runs from République to the northern suburb of Ariana. Useful stops include Palestine (US Embassy and the British Consulate) and Cité Sportive (Stade Olympique soccer stadium).

Line 3 runs from Place Barcelone to Ibn Khaldoun via République. This line services the Tunis University campus north-west of the city centre. It also stops at Bab Saadoun, the closest station to the northern bus and louage stations.

Line 4 runs from Tunis Marine to the western suburb of Den Den via République. Useful stops include Bab Saadoun (northern bus and louage stations) and Le Bardo (Bardo Museum).

Line 5 runs from Ibn Khaldoun to El-Intilaka. This line is no more than an extension of line 3. It services the modern residential area suburbs beyond the university.

TGM
The TGM is the light-rail system that connects central Tunis with the beachside suburbs of La Goulette, Carthage, Sidi Bou Saïd and La Marsa. It is fast, cheap and convenient, although it can get crowded during the rush hour from 7.30 to 8.30 am and 5 to 6 pm. The first train leaves Tunis Marine at 3.42 am, and the last train at 12.30 am. The

TUNIS

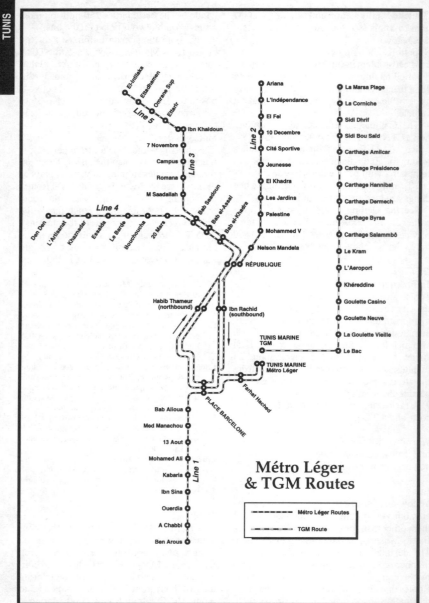

Métro Léger & TGM Routes

	Métro Léger Routes
	TGM Route

last train back from La Marsa leaves at midnight. Departures range from every 12 minutes during peak hours to every 40 minutes at the beginning and end of the day.

There seems to be little point in forking out the extra for 1st class, although it is less crowded. The 2nd class fares are: 330 mills from Tunis to La Goulette (20 minutes); and 530 mills to Carthage (30 minutes), Sidi Bou Saïd (35 minutes) and the end of the line, La Marsa (45 minutes).

Taxi

Taxis are amazingly cheap by European standards. Flagfall is 280 mills and the meter ticks over subsequently at about 500 mills per kilometre – which makes it hard work to run up a fare of more than TD5! Other than at the airport, where some drivers are intent on negotiating a set fare, drivers always use the meter. Taxis are especially good if you are visiting embassies, as the drivers always know where the embassies are and can save you a good deal of foot slogging. The only problem with taxis is that there aren't enough of them. During peak hours this is a real problem; you just have to be patient and lucky. One of the best places to pick one up

is by the railway station on Ave de la Gare; Ave Habib Bourguiba is one of the worst places. Taxis can also be booked by phone – very handy when you're trying to get to the airport with a mountain of baggage. Ask at your hotel reception.

Around Tunis

There are quite a few places within day-trip distance of Tunis. Strictly speaking, the beach suburbs of Carthage, Sidi Bou Saïd and La Marsa are part of Tunis, but it takes a day trip to visit any or all of them.

CARTHAGE

Despite Carthage's fascinating history and the position of dominance it held in the ancient world, the Romans did such a thorough demolition job on it that the ruins today are a something of a disappointment. Most of the little there is to see is of Roman origin.

History

Archaeologists and historians continue to debate the exact origins of the ancient city of

---

Elissa the Wanderer

The legend surrounding the founding of Carthage in 814 BC evolved from the efforts of Greek and Roman writers to come up with a suitably aristocratic background for one of the great cities of the ancient Mediterranean world. They based the story on the few facts known to them about Carthage's Phoenician origins, and emphasised the blue-blooded nature of the link. The best known version features in Virgil's epic poem, *The Aeneid*.

The story begins in the Phoenician capital of Tyre in the time of King Pygmalion. According to Virgil, Pygmalion coveted the wealth of the high priest Sichaeus, who was married to his sister, Princess Elissa. Pygmalion arranged for Sichaeus to be murdered and, concealing his involvement from Elissa, attempted to lay his hands on the loot. The ghost of Sichaeus, however, told Elissa what had happened and advised her to flee – as well as revealing the location of his treasure. Elissa decided to take his advice, and tricked Pygmalion into providing her with ships on the pretext of moving to a new palace down the coast, away from the memory of her husband. Thus she was able to load up all her belongings without raising Pygmalion's suspicions. At the last moment, she was joined by 80 noblemen, including her brother Barca.

They fled first to Cyprus, where they were joined by 80 suitable wives and the island's high priest, before setting sail for North Africa. By now Elissa had become Elissa Didon, meaning 'the wanderer' in Phoenician. On arriving in North Africa, Elissa set about the job of acquiring land on which to found the city that would become Carthage. She struck a deal with the locals whereby she could have as much land as could be covered with an ox hide. The wily Elissa cut the hide into thin strips, which she used to surround the hill that became the Byrsa. (This final part of the legend is seen by many as a snide Roman dig at the Carthaginians' reputation for sharp business practices.) ∎

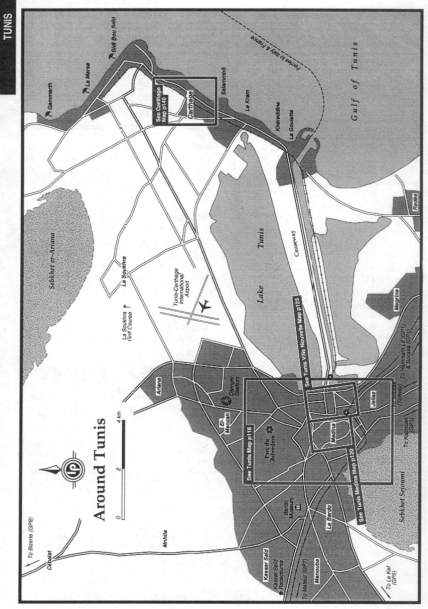

Carthage, the former Phoenician colony that rose to become the dominant power of the Western Mediterranean in the 5th century BC and arch rival of Rome in the 3rd and 2nd centuries BC. Attempts to date the city vary widely. The Greek writer Euripides reckoned that Carthage was already in existence at the time of the Trojan wars in the 12th century BC. This is somewhat at odds with the evidence provided by pottery remains, the earliest of which date to around 750 BC.

It seems likely that the legendary foundation date of 814 BC (see the boxed text on page 137) is not far off the mark. Phoenician power, based in the city of Tyre in modern Lebanon, was at its peak at this time, and the Phoenicians appeared to have founded Carthage with the aim of consolidating their hold on North Africa established by smaller, earlier settlements.

Its Phoenician name Qart Hadasht means 'new city', which suggests that from the very outset it was intended to be more than just another trading post. The location was ideal for a seafaring empire – a narrow, hilly promontory flanked by the sea on three sides (the Sebkhet er-Ariana, the salt lake to the north of Tunis, was connected to the sea at this time).

The first settlement was limited to the coastal strip now occupied by the modern suburb of Dermech and the lower slopes of the Byrsa Hill. The summit of the Byrsa is thought to have been a temple district, all evidence of which was later destroyed when the Romans cut the top off the hill to create a suitable space for their own temples.

Tyre came under increasing threat from the Assyrians in the course of the 7th century BC, and Carthage took over as the major city of the Phoenician world. Its rise to become the main power of the Western Mediterranean and its epic conflict with Rome are covered in the history section of the Facts about the Country chapter at the beginning of this book.

Things to See

There are six main sites: Byrsa Hill and the National Museum of Carthage; the Roman amphitheatre; the Roman theatre and villas; the Antonine Baths; the Sanctuary of Tophet; and the Punic ports. The biggest problem for the visitor is that they are spread over a wide area. It's 2km from the Sanctuary of Tophet in the south to the Antonine Baths in the north. You can overcome this to a certain extent by making use of the TGM (light rail) line which runs right through the middle of the area, but seeing everything still requires a good deal of walking. In the heat and humidity of summer, this is more hassle than it's worth. If you have only a few hours, your best bet is to limit yourself to the museum and the surrounding Punic ruins on the slopes of the Byrsa Hill. With half a day you could also see the Antonine Baths, the Punic ports and the theatre, and in a whole day you could see the lot.

It is possible to get a multiple entry ticket that covers all the sites at Carthage. It costs TD4.100, plus TD1 to take photos, and it's available only at the museum, the Antonine Baths and the Roman villas. All sites are open daily from 8 am to 7 pm from April 1 to September 15, and from 8.30 am to 5.30 pm for the rest of the year.

Byrsa Hill The Byrsa is the best place to start. The hill dominates the area and the whole site is visible from the summit.

To get to the top, head uphill from Carthage Hannibal TGM station along Avenue de l'Amphithéatre, past the plush diplomats' residences, and then go up the stairs to the left at the top of the hill, just near the sign for the Hôtel Reine Elyssa Didon. The entrance is around to the right at the top of the steps, next to the **Cathedral of St Louis**.

The cathedral is visible for miles around. Built by the French in 1890, and an eyesore of truly massive proportions, it was dedicated to the 13th-century French saint-king who died on the beach at Carthage in 1270 during the ill-fated 8th Crusade (see the boxed text on page 141). The cathedral has been deconsecrated and was closed for years. It has now been restored and is open to the public. Admission is covered by the multiple entry ticket.

TUNIS

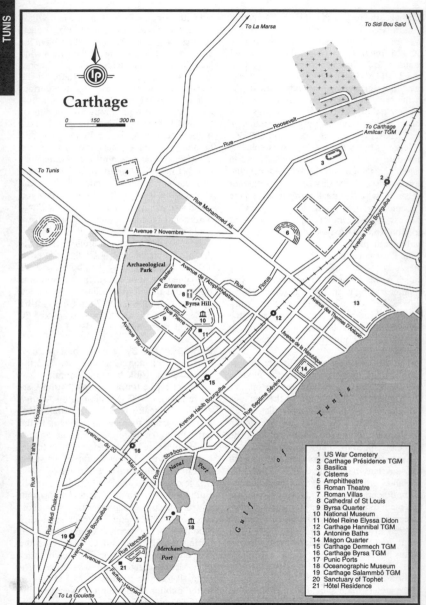

Carthage

0   150   300 m

To La Marsa

To Sidi Bou Saïd

To Carthage
Amilcar TGM

To Tunis

Rue   Roosevelt

Rue Mohammed Ali

Avenue 7 Novembre

Archaeological
Park

Rue Pasteur

Entrance

Byrsa Hill

Rue Pierre

Avenue de l'Amphithéâtre

Rue Florus

Avenue Habib Bourguiba

Avenue des Thermes D'Antoni

Avenue de la République

Avenue Tite-Live

Avenue Habib Bourguiba

Rue Septime Sévère

Avenue du 20

Mars 1934

Rue Strabon

Rue Taha   Houssine

Rue Hédi Chaker

Avenue Habib Bourguiba

Avenue

Rue Hannibal

Farhat   Hached

Naval   Port

Merchant
Port

Gulf   of   Tunis

To La Goulette

1   US War Cemetery
2   Carthage Présidence TGM
3   Basilica
4   Cisterns
5   Amphitheatre
6   Roman Theatre
7   Roman Villas
8   Cathedral of St Louis
9   Byrsa Quarter
10 National Museum
11 Hôtel Reine Elyssa Didon
12 Carthage Hannibal TGM
13 Antonine Baths
14 Magon Quarter
15 Carthage Dermech TGM
16 Carthage Byrsa TGM
17 Punic Ports
18 Oceanographic Museum
19 Carthage Salammbô TGM
20 Sanctuary of Tophet
21 Hôtel Residence

Louis IX and the 8th Crusade

The arrival of the 8th and final Crusade at Tunis on 18 July 1270 was one of the stranger episodes in Tunisian history. The Crusades had been going on for the best part of 200 years by this time, and people had become increasingly cynical about the motivation behind them. The noblemen who led these assaults on the Holy Land appeared to be more interested in getting rich than in religion.

This was confirmed once and for all by the Tunis venture, which was basically a scam organised by Charles of Anjou, younger brother of the French saint-king, Louis IX. Charles was King of Sicily, and thought that North Africa would make a nice little addition to his domains. Louis, for his part, had long been planning to send another crusade to atone for the disasters of the 7th Crusade, which had been all but wiped out by the Mameluke armies in Egypt. Charles managed to persuade him that Tunis was a better target than Jerusalem. He explained that the Hafsid ruler of Tunis, El-Mustansir, was prepared, given a nudge, to convert to the cross, and painted a picture of a Christian North Africa harking back to the days of St Augustine.

The Crusade was a fiasco from start to finish. Everything was ready to roll by the beginning of 1270, but Louis spent so long stopping at monasteries to pray that his troops started fighting among themselves. It was July before the fleet finally set out from France. The crusaders landed without much trouble, but soon discovered that it's too hot to do anything in Tunisia in summer – let alone dress up in armour and fight. The residents of Tunis simply withdrew behind their walls and watched as the crazy foreigners wilted in the heat. By the end of August, the crusading army was in tatters, enfeebled by the sun, lack of water and the effects of poor sanitation. By the time Charles showed up with reinforcements, Louis IX was on his deathbed. Charles succeeded in making his troops look sufficiently threatening to extract a payment of 94,500kg of gold from El-Mustansir and headed home, running into a crashing storm on the way. ■

The **National Museum** is the large white building at the back of the cathedral. Its displays have recently been revamped, with Canadian and US assistance, and they are well worth a look. The Punic displays upstairs are especially good. The Byrsa Quarter (in the museum grounds) has the only Carthaginian ruins of any consequence. The Romans levelled off the top of the hill, burying the Carthaginian houses under the rubble. The area has been well excavated and the finds are described in full (in French) in the museum.

Amphitheatre The Roman amphitheatre is on the western side of the Byrsa, about 15 minutes walk from the museum. It was supposedly one of the largest in the Roman Empire, but not much remains today. Most of its stones were pinched for other building projects in later centuries. The outer circle is hard to distinguish, and the limited excavations and reconstructions date from 1919.

Cisterns The collection of huge cisterns north-east of the amphitheatre were the main water supply for Carthage during the Roman

times. The cisterns were fed by an aqueduct which carried mountain spring water from Zaghouan, 55km to the south. They are now ruined and not worth the scramble through the prickly pears to inspect.

US War Cemetery & Basilica The detour out to the war cemetery and the basilica is only for the dedicated. The cemetery contains row upon row of neat tombstones marking the graves of 2840 Americans who died in North Africa during WWII. The names of 3724 others are listed on a remembrance wall. The Byzantine basilica across the field amounts to nothing more than a few piles of stones.

Roman Theatre & Villas The theatre has been completely covered in concrete and obscured with lighting towers and equipment for the annual Carthage International Festival (see Special Events in the main Tunis section earlier in this chapter for more details). It really has very little going for it.

The same applies to the Roman Villas Archaeological Park (called the Villa de la Volière on the ticket), just downhill from the theatre. The villa in question looks like it was reassembled on a concrete block.

Antonine Baths The Antonine Baths are right down on the waterfront and are impressive more for their size and location than for anything else. At the top of the steps just inland from the baths is a marble slab with a diagram which helps to give some idea of just how big they used to be.

The entrance is about 100m from the sea. From Carthage Hannibal TGM station, take the main road (Ave Habib Bourguiba) and turn right at the intersection which features an enormous capital (headstone of a pillar) from the baths.

Magon Quarter The Magon Quarter is another archaeological park, this time down by the water, a few blocks south of the Antonine Baths along Rue Septime Sévère (the street opposite the entrance to the baths). It has recently been excavated by a team of

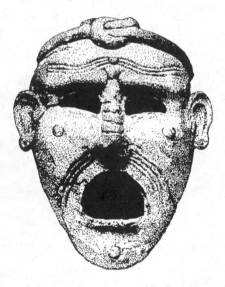

Crying out to be seen – one of the Punic clay masks on display at the National Museum in Carthage.

German archaeologists whose work has revealed a residential area. It is mildly interesting and the multiple ticket gets you in. If you don't have this ticket, don't bother.

Sanctuary of Tophet The Tophet (sacrificial area), on Rue Hannibal just east of Carthage Salammbô TGM station, created a great deal of excitement when it was first excavated in 1921. The amateur French archaeologists responsible for the dig were curious about the source of a number of ancient grave stelae that were being offered for sale. Their excavations uncovered a sacrificial site and associated burial ground where the children of Carthaginian nobles were sacrificed to the deities Baal Hammon and Tanit. More than 20,000 urns have been discovered at the site, each containing the remains of a burnt child and marked with a stele. The majority of them have been dated to the period between the 4th and 2nd centuries BC when Carthage was embroiled in numerous wars and rebellions – and the need to appease the gods was at its greatest.

Among their discoveries was the famous priest stele, now in the Bardo Museum in Tunis, showing a priest holding an infant who is presumably about to be sacrificed. Most of the victims were newborns, but some are thought to have been as old as four. Just how these children died remains uncertain, although the uncertainty hasn't stopped some writers coming up with dramatic versions of the ceremony.

French scholar James Février, writing in 1960, provides a particularly vivid account. He describes an eerie night-time scene with a great bronze statue of the Carthaginian god Baal Hammon standing, glowing, on the edge of a sacred fire pit, its arms stretched out over the flames. Flute and tambourine players set up a deafening din as the parents of the victim hand their child to a priest, who then ceremonially cuts its throat before placing it in the arms of Baal Hammon – from where it slips into the fire.

Février writes of multiple sacrifices, and describes how a swaying crowd surrounding the fire pit, 'crazed by the noise and the

Around Tunis – Carthage 143

odour of burnt flesh', is whipped into a mounting frenzy by the tambourine players as each new victim is offered up.

Unfortunately, the site itself is far less exciting than the prose it has inspired. It's little more than a small patch of overgrown weeds with a few excavated pits. If you don't have a multiple ticket, it's not worth paying to get in – you can see almost as much from the outside.

Punic Ports Although they don't look very impressive today, these two ports were the basis of Carthage's power and prosperity. The northern basin was the navy base and was originally circular with a diameter of about 300m. It is said that it could hold as many as 220 warships, although it's hard to work out how. The harbour was surrounded by a high wall on the landward sides. The island in the centre held the naval headquarters, while the southern harbour was for commercial shipping. The two harbours were linked, and the entrance was by a channel to the sea south of the commercial port. It was filled in by Scipio after the destruction of Carthage in 146 BC.

Oceanographic Museum Situated on the island which separates the ports, this sorry display of fish and things nautical is a total waste of time. Entry is only 600 mills, however, so it won't break the bank if you feel like a wander around. It is open Tuesday to Sunday from 4.30 to 7.30 pm, and also Sunday morning from 10 am to noon; it's closed Monday.

Places to Stay & Eat
There are a couple of hotels, both at the more expensive end of the market. The three star *Hôtel Reine Elyssa Didon* (☎ (01) 733 433; fax 732 599), named after the Phoenician queen who founded Carthage (see the boxed text 'Elissa the Wanderer', earlier), has a magnificent location on top of the Byrsa Hill, right next to the museum grounds. It's worth visiting for the view alone. Single/ double rooms cost TD59/78 in summer, dropping to TD42/60 in winter, including

breakfast . It's popular at lunch time for its TD9 set menu.

The other place is the *Hôtel Residence* (☎ (01) 731 072; fax 353 057), 100m from the Tophet site at 16 Rue Hannibal. Singles/ doubles cost TD24.500/39 in summer and TD6 per person less in winter.

Getting There & Away
There is no need to consider any options other than the train. The journey from Tunis Marine to any of the six Carthage TGM stations costs 530 mills and takes about 20 minutes. See the Tunis Getting Around section and the Métro Léger & TGM Routes map earlier in this chapter for more details.

SIDI BOU SAÏD
Sidi Bou Saïd is a pretty little whitewashed village set high on a cliff overlooking the Gulf of Tunis, about 10km north-east of Tunis. It's a delightful place to go for stroll in the maze of narrow cobbled streets with old stone steps. Gleaming whitewashed walls are dotted with the ornate, curved window grills that are a local trademark, all painted the same deep blue, and colourful arched doorways that open onto small courtyards which are filled with geraniums and bougainvillea. The style is so reminiscent of the Greek islands that you could be forgiven for expecting to stumble upon a small Orthodox church or shrine. Instead you may come across the Mosque and Zaouia of Sidi Bou Saïd, the 13th century Sufi saint after whom the place is named.

The lighthouse above the village stands on the site of an ancient *ribat* (fort), built at the beginning of the 9th century as part of a coastal early-warning system that included the ribats of Sousse and Monastir (see the Central Tunisia chapter).

The centre of activity is the small, cobbled main square, Place Sidi Bou Saïd, which is lined with cafes, sweet stalls and souvenir shops. Watching the shopkeepers leap into action when the tour buses pull up can be fun; Sidi Bou Saïd is included with Carthage on a popular half-day tour.

The street heading off to the right at the top end of the main square takes you to the top of a steep path leading down to a small and relatively uncrowded beach. From here it is possible to follow the road around and back up the hill to bring you out at Carthage Amilcar TGM station. The walk from Sidi Bou Saïd takes about an hour.

Places to Stay

There are some good places to stay in Sidi Bou Saïd. The *Hôtel Sidi Bou Fares* (☎ (01) 740 091) is signposted up some cobbled stairs to the west of the main square. The rooms are small but clean and pleasant, set around a traditional courtyard full of flowering shrubs and vines. Singles/doubles with breakfast cost TD11.500/20. This place is very popular and is invariably full, so it's a good idea to phone first.

The two star *Hôtel Dar Saïd* (☎ (01) 740 215; fax 740 741) is something special; it occupies a beautiful old palace just beyond the northern end of the square. It was closed for renovations at the time of research, but was scheduled to reopen in early 1998. Expect to pay around TD20/30 for singles/doubles with breakfast. Some rooms have views over the Gulf of Tunis.

The upmarket option is the flash four star *Hôtel Sidi Bou Saïd* (☎ (01) 740 411; fax 745 129) about 1km north of Sidi Bou Saïd off the road to La Marsa. It charges TD73/106 for singles/doubles. Facilities include tennis courts and a swimming pool.

Places to Eat

The cheaper places to eat are around Place du 7 Novembre, which is the large roundabout just uphill from the Sidi Bou Saïd TGM station. There are several small places here selling sandwiches and pizza by the slice. The *Restaurant La Bagatelle* (☎ (01) 741 116), 100m south of Place du 7 Novembre on Ave Habib Bourguiba, does excellent Tunisian food and fish and has a three course menu for TD7.500. An added attraction is that it's run by a colourful character with an impressive waxed moustache.

There are more places around the cobbled square that is the focal point of Sidi Bou Saïd. The *Café des Nattes* is probably the most expensive cafe in the country, but it's worth spending TD2 on a coffee for the opportunity to study its elaborate Moorish-style decor at your leisure. For a meal, the *Restaurant Le Chargui*, at the northern end of the square, has a pleasant open-air court-yard and reasonable prices. You'll pay a lot more for a bit more style at the *Restaurant Dar Zarouk*, opposite the Hôtel Dar Saïd.

Getting There & Away

Sidi Bou Saïd is on the TGM line and it takes about 30 minutes to get there from Tunis (530 mills). It's a 15 minute walk from the station up to the top of the hill and the centre of the old part of the village.

LA MARSA

La Marsa is an exclusive beachside suburb at the end of the TGM line from Tunis. There is no reason to come here other than to visit the beach, which is arguably the best on this stretch of coast. It stretches north around a great sweeping bay that finishes beneath the cliffs of the five star resort village of Gammarth. The beach is relatively uncrowded during the week, but gets packed out at weekends when the wealthy set emerge to work on their suntans. There is a cluster of cafes and restaurants around the TGM station, and a couple of fish restaurants on the beach during the summer months. There are no places to stay in La Marsa itself; the hotels are in the nearby suburb of Gammarth (see the following section).

GAMMARTH

Gammarth, 2km north of La Marsa, was once a pretty little seaside village nestled beneath the cliffs of Cap Gammarth. These days it has been transformed into a play-ground for the rich and famous and is packed solid with five star resort hotels and expensive restaurants. The latest addition is the opulent *Hôtel Le Palace* (☎ (01) 748 445; fax 748 442), which is home to Tunisia's first

FRANCES LINZEE GORDON

PETER PTSCHELINZEW

Top: Is this the oldest minaret in the world? The minaret of the Great Mosque in Kairouan dates back to 728 AD.
Bottom: The narrow streets of the medina in the ancient fortress town of Le Kef make it a great place to explore for a couple of days.

FRANCES LINZEE GORDON

ONTT

JON DAVISON

FRANCES LINZEE GORDON

Top Left: Traditional music, or malouf, is an important part of Tunisia's national identity.
Top Right: Savour the Greek-island charm of Sidi Bou Saïd.
Bottom Left: Built to deter – the impressive 8m high walls of Sousse's medina.
Bottom Right: Art out of the mundane – a pile of terracotta squid pots, Kerkennah Islands.

casino. It also has the most expensive rooms in the country, with singles/doubles for TD210/380. Most people arrive here in their private limos. The less well-heeled can catch bus No 20B from Jardin Thameur, or walk around the bay from La Marsa. The walk takes about 45 minutes, unless you take your togs and stop for a swim on the way.

HAMMAM LIF

Tunis has steadily expanded to the south-east in recent years and has now absorbed the small seaside town of Hammam Lif, 17km from the city centre. Nothing very much happened in Hammam Lif until it became the home-in-exile of the Palestine Liberation Organisation (PLO) in the early 1980s after the PLO was forced out of Lebanon by the Israelis. The town hit the headlines in 1985 when Israeli jets swooped in low from the Gulf of Tunis and destroyed several Palestinian houses in the beachside district of Hammam Plage in retaliation for the killing of three Israelis on Cyprus. Trains between Tunis and Sousse stop at Hammam Lif and take 20 minutes.

Cap Bon Peninsula

This fertile peninsula stretches out into the Mediterranean Sea to the north-east of Tunis, forming the eastern shore of the Gulf of Tunis. The rugged hills that form the backbone of Cap Bon represent the eastern end of the Tunisian Dorsale, the country's main mountain range. Geologists speculate that the peninsula once extended all the way to Sicily, providing a land link between Europe and Africa that disappeared beneath the rising waters of the Mediterranean some 30,000 years ago.

The peninsula has been an important agricultural region since Carthaginian times. It was one of the main areas of European settlement during the French protectorate, and the countryside is dotted with the ruins of old, red-tiled farmhouses and their outbuildings. The French developed the large areas of citrus groves in the south-western corner of the peninsula around Hammamet and Nabeul, as well as the vineyards around Grombalia. The area's farms are still major suppliers of fruit and vegetables.

Today, Cap Bon – particularly the beaches around Hammamet and Nabeul – is Tunisia's number one destination for package tourists. The pace slowly slackens as you head northeast along the coast to Kelibia, with its small port overlooked by an ancient fortress. The area around the small town of El-Haouaria, at the northern tip of the peninsula, is also worth exploring. Much of the stone used in the construction of Roman Carthage was quarried from the caves on the coast just west of town. Halfway between Kelibia and El-Haouaria are the ruins of Kerkouane, the best preserved of Tunisia's Carthaginian sites.

The west coast of Cap Bon is far more rugged. The main road runs a couple of kilometres inland for most of its length, leaving the coast virtually inaccessible. Settlement is confined to scattered small villages. The only place of any interest is the small town of Korbous, which is famous for its hot springs.

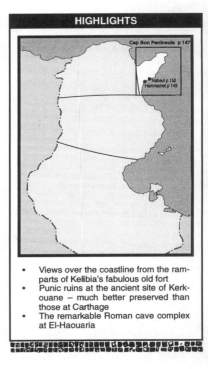

HIGHLIGHTS

Cap Bon Peninsula p 147

Nabeul p 152
Hammamet p 149

- Views over the coastline from the ramparts of Kelibia's fabulous old fort
- Punic ruins at the ancient site of Kerkouane – much better preserved than those at Carthage
- The remarkable Roman cave complex at El-Haouaria

History

The hills of Cap Bon were clearly visible across the Gulf of Tunis from ancient Carthage, and the peninsula was firmly under Carthaginian control by the beginning of the 5th century BC. Kerkouane was established at this time, as were the larger settlements of Clypea (Kelibia), Neapolis (Nabeul) and Thinissut (Bir Bou Rebka). These towns were razed by Rome in the course of the various Punic wars. The Romans occupied Clypea and Neapolis, but made little attempt to settle the rest of the peninsula. Clypea later became a Byzantine stronghold that held out against the Arabs until the end of the 7th

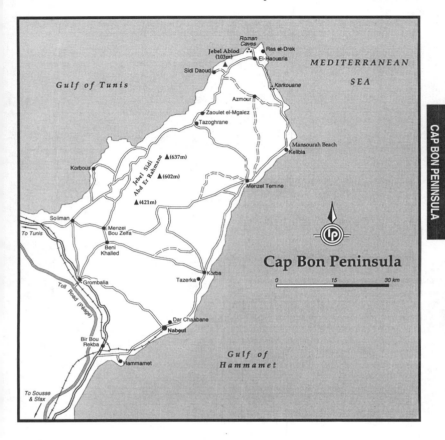

century AD, long after the rest of Tunisia had fallen to the invaders. In the 16th century, Cap Bon was under constant threat from the Spanish, forcing many coastal communities to shift away from the sea. This is the reason why the centres of towns like Nabeul and Kelibia are located well away from the coast.

HAMMAMET
Pop 20,000 ☎ Area code 02

No town in Tunisia has given itself over to the dictates of the package tourism industry more totally than Hammamet, 70km southeast of Tunis. A staggering 30% of all tourists

to Tunisia wind up here, staying at one of the huge hotel complexes that line the coast. A walk down the main street during summer is likely to turn up about 10 tourists to every local – and the pace barely slackens except in the middle of winter.

It's not hard to see why Hammamet is so popular. It has a prime position at the northern end of the Gulf of Hammamet, with an old medina overlooking a great expanse of sandy beach. It's also a lively town, brimming with discos, restaurants and colourful souvenir shops – everything that a holiday-maker could want.

The hotels themselves are remarkably discreet – considerably more so than their guests! Standing on top of the walls of the medina, it's hard to believe that there are more than 30 giant hotels hidden away among the trees behind the beach that curves away to the north-west. None of them are built above tree height; this is a remarkable piece of environmental awareness given that many of the hotels were built back in the 1960s and 70s.

Hammamet's transition from quiet fishing village to resort began in the 1920s when it was discovered by the European jet set, led by Romanian millionaire George Sebastian. The palatial villa that Sebastian built himself by the beach, 3km north-east of town, was used as a regional headquarters by German forces during WWII. It is now home to Hammamet's International Cultural Centre.

Orientation
Hammamet is an easy place to negotiate. The town centre is around the medina, which stands overlooking the sea on a small spit of land jutting out into the Gulf of Hammamet. Most things of importance to travellers are located nearby on one of the two main streets, Ave Habib Bourguiba and Ave de la République. Ave Habib Bourguiba runs north from the medina and links up with the roads to the beach hotels, Sousse and Tunis, while Ave de la République heads north-east from the medina and becomes the main road to Nabeul.

Information
Tourist Office The tourist office (☎ 280 423) is near the centre of town on Ave Habib Bourguiba. It hands out a good map of Hammamet and Nabeul, and can supply you with a list of the latest accommodation prices, which can be useful for finding special deals in winter. There's usually someone around who can speak enough English to answer questions.

The office is open Monday to Thursday from 8.30 am to 1 pm and 3 to 5.45 pm, and Friday and Saturday until 1.30 pm. During July and August, it's open Monday to Saturday from 7.30 am to 7.30 pm.

Money The challenge is to find somewhere that won't change money. The banks are concentrated around the junction of Ave Habib Bourguiba and Ave de la République, opposite the medina.

Post & Communications The main post office is on the Nabeul road, Ave de la République, near the centre of town. There are Taxiphone offices everywhere, although it seems there are never enough phones to meet demand. The Taxiphone office at the south-eastern end of Rue Ali Belhouane is one place where you can normally avoid queueing.

Medina
Hammamet's pocket-sized medina was built by the Hafsids between 1463 and 1474 AD on the site of an earlier structure built by the Aghlabites at the end of the 9th century AD. Its main feature is the heavily restored kasbah in the north-western corner. The main reason for visiting the kasbah is for the views from its ramparts. It's open daily from 8.30 am to 8.30 pm from May to September, and until 6 pm for the rest of the year; admission is TD1.

The old souqs around the kasbah have been taken over by souvenir shops, but the residential district in the southern part of the medina remains surprisingly unspoiled.

International Cultural Centre
The celebrated villa built by millionaire George Sebastian in the 1920s was purchased by the state after independence and converted into the town's grandly titled International Cultural Centre, complete with the addition of a Roman-style open-air theatre. It is used during July and August to stage Hammamet's annual International Cultural Festival, which features everything from classical theatre to Arabic music. The events are heavily promoted around town, and you can get a copy of the program from the

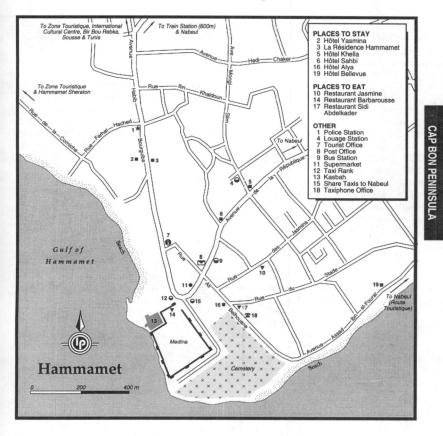

tourist office. Tickets are sold at the tourist office and at the door.

The centre is 3km north-west of the town centre, clearly signposted off Ave des Nations Unies – the western extension of Ave du Koweit. The villa and grounds are open from 8 am to 6 pm in summer and from 9 am to 3 pm in winter. Admission is free.

Beaches
Hammamet is first and foremost a beach resort. The best beach is the main beach stretching north-west from the medina. It is much prettier, more sheltered and better maintained than the beach running north-east towards Nabeul.

Places to Stay – budget
Camping The town's only camp site has now closed, leaving *Camping Les Jasmins* at Nabeul (see under Places to Stay in the Nabeul section following) as the closest option for campers.

Hotels There are no budget hotels in town. It's a case of least expensive rather than cheap, and that honour goes to the two star

Hôtel Sabhi (☎ 280 807; fax 280 134), about 400m north-east of the medina on Ave de la République. It has comfortable singles and doubles with bathroom plus breakfast for TD24/38 in summer and TD16/22 in winter – but it's hardly a backpackers' haunt.

The *Hôtel Khella* (☎ 283 900; fax 283 704), a further 150m north on Ave de la République, charges TD36/50 in summer, dropping to TD18.500/25 in winter.

Another option is the *Hôtel Alya* (☎ 280 218; fax 282 365), right in the middle of town on Rue Ali Belhouane. The rooms are large and airy with generous balconies, and those away from the road have good views of the medina. Rates drop from TD40/50 in summer to a bargain TD13/20 in winter.

You'll find very similar prices at the *Hôtel Bellevue* (☎ 281 121; fax 283 156), overlooking the beach on Ave Assad Ibn el-Fourat.

Places to Stay – middle & top end

You're wasting your breath asking for a room at any of the big resort hotels in summer. They are all block-booked by package tour companies and are outrageously expensive anyway. Prices plummet in winter, when you can take your pick from dozens of places offering singles/doubles with breakfast for around TD20/30. The tourist office can give you a list with all the prices.

Two places worth checking out are *La Résidence Hammamet* (☎ 280 406; fax 280 396), 600m north of the medina on Ave Habib Bourguiba. It has a range of studio apartments with kitchen facilities for up to four people. Singles/doubles with breakfast cost TD44/73 in summer, dropping to TD14/22 in winter. Opposite is the beachfront *Hôtel Yasmina* (☎ 280 222; fax 280 593), which has singles/doubles for TD54/90 in summer and TD22/38 in winter.

Probably the best winter deal of the lot is to be found at the stylish four star *Hammamet Sheraton* (☎ 226 555; fax 227 301). It slashes its summer prices of TD79/106 to a bargain TD26/39 in winter. The Sheraton is by the beach, about 5km north-west of town, signposted off the road to Sousse.

Places to Eat

The seafront along Ave Habib Bourguiba is just about a solid wall of tourist restaurants, hamburger joints, pizza parlours, patisseries and ice cream shops.

For a cheap meal, try the *Restaurant Jasmine* on Rue des Jasmins. It does grilled fish for TD3.500, plus salads and casse-croûtes (French bread sandwiches). The *Restaurant Sidi Abdelkader*, opposite the Hôtel Alya, is another good place. It does a large bowl of couscous with chicken for TD3.200, and couscous with fish for TD4. It also does a three course menu of the day for TD6.500.

The main attraction at the *Restaurant Barbarousse* is that seating is on the ramparts of the medina. Prices reflect this; expect to pay around TD30 for two people, plus wine. The entrance to the restaurant is inside the medina, opposite the gateway to the kasbah.

Self caterers can stock up at the *supermarket* at the medina end of Ave de la République. It also sells a good range of local wines.

Entertainment

The entertainment season peaks during the International Cultural Festival in July and August. For the rest of the year, the action is focussed on the discos of the resort hotels. Most of them are at the hotels along the main beach to the north-west of town, including the *Tropicana Club* at the Hôtel Regency and the *Boule d'Argent* at the Hôtel Les Charmes. Both are far enough out of town to warrant taking a taxi. There are no discos in the town centre.

Getting There & Away

Bus All buses leave from a small vacant lot about 200m from the medina on Ave de la République. There are buses to Nabeul (30 minutes, 500 mills) every half-hour, hourly buses to Tunis (1½ hours, TD2.800) and three buses a day to Sousse (1½ hours, TD3.090).

Train Train services from Hammamet are of little more than academic interest. There's one train a day to Tunis at 6 am, returning at

2.20 pm. The fares are TD2.700 in 2nd class, TD3.700 in 1st class and TD3.900 in *confort*. The station is about 1.5km from the centre of town at the northern end of Ave Habib Bourguiba.

Louage Louages leave from Ave Mongi Slim, about 100m north of the Hôtel Khella. The only destinations are Tunis (TD3) and Sousse (TD4). There are yellow share taxis to Hammamet from the parking lot east of the medina. If you don't want to hire the whole cab, make sure that the driver understands you're only paying for one seat *(une place)*, which costs 800 mills.

Car Rental The agencies with offices in Hammamet include: Avis (☎ 280 303), Rue de la Gare; Europcar (☎ 280 146), Ave des Hôtels; Hertz (☎ 280 187), Ave des Hôtels; and Topcar (☎ 280 767), Ave du Koweit.

Getting Around
Taxis are the only alternative to walking. The main taxi rank is at the large roundabout just north of the medina.

NABEUL
Pop 40,000 ☎ Area code 02
Nabeul, 18km north of Hammamet, is the main town and administrative centre of the Cap Bon Peninsula. It was an important town long before the advent of mass tourism, and it continues to earn the bulk of its income from its traditional role as a service centre for the region.

Tourism has become a major player in recent years, and in summer the streets are almost as packed with sunburnt Europeans as with Hammamet residents. Most tourists stay at the growing line-up of beach resort hotels that stretches south along the coast towards Hammamet. The biggest difference between Hammamet and Nabeul is that Nabeul has a good range of budget accommodation, including the best organised camping area in the country. Even in the middle of summer it is possible to find a room for a price that won't break the bank.

Orientation
Nabeul is spread out over a wide area. The town centre is about 1.5km inland – a legacy of the time during the 16th century when Christian forces terrorised the Cap Bon coast, forcing towns to relocate away from the sea. The town has slowly spread back towards the coast in modern times, but it's a fair hike between the beach hotels and the shops and services in the town centre.

The two areas are linked by the main street, Ave Habib Bourguiba, which runs roughly north-south through the middle of town. It comes into the north-west of town as the road from Tunis, and finishes down by the beach. The town centre is around the intersection of Ave Habib Bourguiba with Ave Habib Thameur and Ave Farhat Hached. Ave Habib Thameur leads south-west past the main bus and louage stations and becomes the road to Hammamet, while Ave Farhat Hached goes north-east through the old part of town and links up with the road to Kelibia.

Information
Tourist Office The ONTT office (☎ 286 800) is on Ave Taieb Mehiri between the beach and the centre of town. It has a good brochure with maps of Nabeul and Hammamet and other information. Even when it's closed, bus, train and accommodation information is posted outside the office.

The office is open Monday to Thursday from 8.30 am to 1 pm and 3 to 5.45 pm, and Friday and Saturday until 1.30 pm. During July and August, it's open Monday to Saturday from 7.30 am to 7.30 pm.

Money There are plenty of banks ready to take your money, mostly along Ave Farhat Hached and Ave Habib Bourguiba.

Post & Communications The main post office is on Ave Habib Bourguiba, 200m north of the intersection with Ave Farhat Hached.

Medical Services The huge regional hospital (☎ 285 633) occupies a whole block on

Nabeul

PLACES TO STAY
1 Pension el-Habib
2 Hôtel & Camping Les Jasmins
3 Pension Les Oliviers
4 Hôtel Fakir
8 Pension Les Hafsides
12 Pension Les Roses
17 Pension Mustapha
26 Hôtel Kheops
27 Maison des Jeunes
29 Auberge de Jeunesse
30 Hôtel Nabeul Plage
31 Hôtel Les Pyramides

PLACES TO EAT
18 Restaurant Carthage
20 Restaurant L'Olivier

OTHER
5 Neapolis (Roman Ruins)
6 ONAT
7 Main Bus & Louage Station
9 Hospital
10 Tunis Air
11 Main Post Office
13 Grand Mosque
14 Daily Market
15 Cap Bon Buses & Louages; Friday Market
16 Cap Bon Buses & Louages (Friday)
19 Touta Supermarket
21 Police
22 Train Station
23 Museum
24 Supermarket
25 Tourist Office
28 Stadium

Gulf of Hammamet

To Tunis
To Hammamet
To Kélibia
To Jardin Neapolis

the northern side of Ave Habib Thameur, just west of Ave Habib Bourguiba.

Market

Nabeul's Friday market has become one of the major tourist events in the country, although quite why is a bit of a mystery. The crowds need to be seen to be believed. The tour buses descend from as far afield as Sousse and Monastir, disgorging thousands of day-trippers for a few hours of frantic souvenir shopping. Not surprisingly, prices are sky high; stall-holders are used to people paying top dollar, and have little time for people who want to haggle.

The town centre is chaotic on market day, when Ave Farhat Hached is closed to traffic between Ave Habib Bourguiba and Ave Habib el-Karma. The whole stretch is packed with tourists and traders. The markets continue north-east of Ave Farhat Hached along Rue el-Arbi Zarrouk, occupying the bus and louage stations. The markets are at their busiest between 9 am and noon. By 2 pm, life is slowly returning to normal.

Beaches

Most of Nabeul's beaches are in a disgraceful state, littered with all sorts of detritus (mainly rusting beer cans and plastic bottles). They are kept clean only in front of the resort hotels, so it makes sense to take advantage of this and make discreet use of the beach umbrellas etc.

Museum

Opposite the railway station on Ave Habib Bourguiba, Nabeul's small archaeological museum is only for the real enthusiast. It houses a few pieces of Punic pottery from a range of sites around Cap Bon and a couple of mosaics from Roman Neapolis. It's open daily from 8 am to 7 pm in summer and from 8.30 to 5.30 pm in winter. Admission is TD1.100, plus a further TD1 if you want to take photos.

Neapolis

The site of ancient Neapolis lies about 1.5km south-west of the town centre, opposite the Hôtel Fakir on the Route Touristique that runs along the coast to Hammamet. The original Carthaginian settlement, established in the 5th century BC, was destroyed by Roman forces in 148 BC during the closing stages of the Third Punic War. It was later re-established as a Roman town, best known as a producer of a disgusting-sounding fish-paste called *garum* – made from putrefied fish guts. Several amphorae full of the stuff were unearthed when the site was excavated in the 1960s.

The site was locked up at the time of research and looked heavily overgrown, although the tourist office reckons it's open.

Places to Stay – budget

Camping *Camping Les Jasmins* (☎ 285 343; fax 285 073) is an excellent little camp site in the grounds of the Hôtel Les Jasmins, about 1.5km south-west of town on the way to Hammamet. The hotel is clearly signposted on the left, 200m beyond the Oued Souhil on Ave Habib Thameur. The camping area has shady sites beneath some large old olive trees, and charges TD1.900 per person, TD1.300 for a tent, TD1.500 for caravans and camper vans, TD1.700 for power and TD2 for a hot shower.

The place is well situated, just five minutes walk from the beach; the extra bit of distance between it and Nabeul means that the beach is relatively uncrowded. On the beach is a small cafe, which has some welcome umbrellas and serves cold drinks and sandwiches.

Hostels Nabeul has both a maison des jeunes and an HI-affiliated auberge de jeunesse. The only things they have in common are that they are both cheap and they are both likely to be fully booked in summer.

The no-frills *Maison des Jeunes*, towards the beach on Ave Taieb Mehiri, could easily be mistaken for a detention centre. It charges the standard TD4. The *Auberge de Jeunesse* (☎ 285 547), right on the beach at the end of Ave Mongi Slim, is a bit on the primitive side, but the location is great and the manager is friendly and enthusiastic. Dormitory accommodation, including breakfast, costs TD3.500, or TD6 for half board and TD8 for full board.

Hotels There is a good choice of budget accommodation, starting with the friendly *Pension Les Roses* (☎ 285 570), right in the middle of town on Ave Farhat Hached. It has clean, comfortable singles/doubles for TD9/16 in summer, falling to TD7/12 in winter. Cold showers are free and hot showers cost 500 mills. The pension can be hard to find; it's tucked away on the western side of the small open square where Ave Farhat Hached makes a dogleg in the centre of town.

Another good place is the *Pension Mustapha* (☎ 222 729), on the corner of Ave Habib el-Karma and Ave Ali Belhaouane. It charges TD11.500/20 in summer, TD9/15 in winter. The rooms have showers and hot water, and prices include breakfast.

You'll find similar prices at the *Pension Les Hafsides* (☎ 285 823), behind the hospital on Rue Sidi Maaouia, and the *Pension el-Habib* (☎ 287 190), south-west of town just beyond the Oued Souhil.

Places to Stay – middle
There is a cluster of good places to the south-west of town between Ave Habib Thameur and the Route Touristique, starting with the *Hôtel Les Jasmins* (☎ 285 343; fax 285 073). Unfortunately, it's often fully booked in summer, when singles/doubles with breakfast cost TD28/50, but it never hurts to ask. In winter, the rates drop to TD20/30. All rooms come with toilet and either shower or bath.

The friendly, family-run *Pension Les Oliviers* (☎ 286 865), signposted down a small lane opposite the entrance of the Hôtel Les Jasmins, is a great little place surrounded by olive and citrus groves. It charges TD29/37 in summer and TD15/20 in winter for immaculate rooms with shower, toilet and washbasin, plus breakfast. The owners are high-school teachers, and both husband and wife speak excellent English.

Between the Hôtel Les Jasmins and the beach is another possibility, the *Hôtel Fakir* (☎ 285 477; fax 287 616), which has a grand,

spiral staircase and large, airy rooms which cost TD32.500/48 in summer, dropping to TD23/30 in winter, including breakfast.

Places to Stay – top end
The situation with the big resort hotels is much the same as in Hammamet: they are booked out by tour groups in summer, and offer some astonishingly cheap deals in winter. The giant three star *Hôtel Les Pyramides* (☎ 285 444; fax 287 461), by the beach at the southern end of Ave Habib Bourguiba, leads the way among the price-cutters. Singles/doubles that are listed at TD47/66 in summer are slashed to TD12/18 in winter, which includes a buffet breakfast. Facilities include tennis courts, swimming pools and a disco.

The difference isn't quite as radical at the *Hôtel Nabeul Plage* (☎ 285 008; fax 286 429), set back from the beach on Rue Jardin Neapolis. It cuts its rates from TD54/90 in summer to a more modest TD27.500/39 in winter. The smartest hotel in town is the four star *Hôtel Kheops* (☎ 285 555; fax 286 024), just north of the Hôtel Les Pyramides on Ave Habib Bourguiba. In summer, it charges a whopping TD88/116, dropping to TD28/32 in winter, including breakfast.

Places to Eat
There are several good, cheap restaurants around the town centre. The restaurant attached to the *Pension Mustapha* is as good as any. It has briq à l'oeuf (filled pastry triangle) for 800 mills, salads from TD1.200 and a variety of main dishes from TD2.500. There are numerous cafes and small restaurants along Ave Farhat Hached. The *Restaurant de la Jeunesse* and the *Restaurant du Bonheur*, on either side of the Pension Les Roses, are both reasonable. The *Restaurant Carthage*, on Ave Hedi Chaker, does excellent couscous with lamb for TD2.700. The restaurant at the *Hôtel Les Jasmins* does a very popular three course menu for TD6, while the *Hôtel Fakir* charges TD7.500 for similar fare in more refined surroundings.

If money is no object, you could try *Restaurant L'Olivier* (☎ 286 613), Nabeul's top restaurant, at the junction of Ave Hedi Chaker and Ave Habib Bourguiba. A meal for two costs about TD30, plus wine.

Self caterers should head for the large *Touta supermarket* on Ave Hedi Chaker, which is also the place to buy wine. There is another large *supermarket* on Ave Habib Bourguiba next to the Hôtel Imeme, halfway between the town and the beach. For fresh fruit and vegetables, check out the colourful daily *markets* at the northern side of town on Rue de France.

Things to Buy

Nabeul has long been famous for its pottery, and likes to think of itself as the national centre of the craft – a title it disputes with the town of Guellala, on Jerba. The potters of Nabeul turn out an amazing range of styles to meet the demands of the tourist trade. Traditionally, they were known for their Punic and Roman-influenced pots and vases, and for the ornate decoration introduced by Andalusian immigrants in the 17th century. There are some beautiful examples of traditional work in the shops around town. The interesting stuff, though, is outnumbered by the tacky stuff – amphorae covered with tacky scenes of camels and palm trees, and gaudily decorated dinner sets that bear little relation to anything remotely Tunisian.

If you want to buy some pottery but you're unsure of how much you should be paying, check out the prices at the ONAT emporium on Ave Habib Thameur first to get an idea. You'll find the biggest choice of pottery at the Friday market, but no bargains.

Getting There & Away

Air The Tunis Air (☎ 285 092) office is at 145 Ave Habib Bourguiba, opposite the main post office. The nearest airport is at Tunis.

Bus There are two bus stations in Nabeul. The main bus station is near the centre of town on Ave Habib Thameur. It has departures to Hammamet (30 minutes, 500 mills) every half-hour from 5.30 am to 7 pm, and hourly buses to Tunis (1½ hours, TD2.700). Other services include three buses a day to

Zaghouan (two hours, TD2.950), Sousse (two hours, TD3.590) and Kairouan (2¼ hours, TD4.280).

Buses for Kelibia and the rest of Cap Bon leave from the site of the Friday market on Rue el-Arbi Zarrouk on the other side of town. On Friday, the buses move to a vacant lot just opposite. There are 16 services a day to Kelibia (1¼ hours, TD2.050), the last bus leaving at 6.15 pm. The 10.30 am and 6.15 pm services continue to El-Haouaria (1¾ hours, TD2.880); otherwise, catch any bus to Kelibia and change there. The last bus back from Kelibia is at 6.45 pm.

Train The station is conveniently close to the centre of town at the junction of Ave Ali Belhaouane and Ave Habib Bourguiba. Unfortunately, services from Nabeul have all but been phased out. The only departure is the 5.50 am train to Tunis (1½ hours), which is unlikely to be of much interest to tourists. It stops at Hammamet, Bir Bou Rebka and Grombalia on the way. The fare to Tunis is TD2.700 in 2nd class, TD3.700 in 1st class and TD3.900 in confort. The return service departs from Tunis at 2.20 pm.

Louage There are two louage stations, next to the respective bus stations. Tunis (TD2.900) is by far the most popular destination from the station on Ave Habib Thameur. From here there are also occasional louages to Zaghouan, Sousse and Kairouan. Services to Cap Bon, including Kelibia (TD2.400), El-Haouaria (TD3.500) and Soliman (TD3), leave from next to the bus station on Rue el-Arbi Zarrouk. The vacant lot opposite, which is used by buses and louages on market day (Friday), is the departure point for share taxis to Hammamet. A seat costs 800 mills, although drivers often ask for far more if they spot a tourist.

Car Rental Half a dozen agencies are represented in Nabeul, including Avis (☎ 286 555) at the Hôtel Kheops, Hertz (☎ 285 327) out towards Hammamet on Ave Habib Thameur and Nova Rent (☎ 222 072) at 54 Ave Habib Bourguiba.

Getting Around

Nabeul is reasonably spread out, and in summer it's a major effort to walk the kilometre or so from the main street to the beach. A taxi costs about 500 mills and can be a life-saver; otherwise you can take one of the many horse-drawn *calèches* (carriages), but bargain hard and agree on a price before setting off.

KELIBIA
Pop 18,000 ☎ Area code 02

By the time you get to Kelibia, 58km north of Nabeul, you'll have left the worst of the commercialism far behind. What you'll find instead is a small town that continues to survive mainly on its fishing fleet and as a service centre for the surrounding farmland. The town centre is a couple of kilometres inland and has nothing to recommend it. The attractions are all on the coast at the eastern edge of town, where you'll find a small sheltered beach, the port and a few fairly low-key resort hotels – all overlooked by a picturesque old fort.

Orientation & Information

Most travellers will arrive in town at the bus and louage station on Ave Ali Belhouane, which is the name of the main coast road during its run through town. The town centre is just east of here around the junction of Rue Ibn Khaldoun and Ave Habib Bourguiba. To get there, head north along Ave Ali Belhouane (towards El-Haouaria) from the bus and louage stations, and then turn right into Rue Ibn Khaldoun. There are a couple of banks and a supermarket on Rue Ibn Khaldoun, and the post office is on Ave Habib Bourguiba. There is no tourist office. The fort and port are 2km east of here along Ave des Martyrs.

Fort

Kelibia's main attraction is the fabulous old fort that overlooks the harbour. Almost 2500 years of history are contained within its walls. The first fort to occupy this site was built by the Carthaginians in the 5th century BC to defend the ancient town of Clypea. The foundations of this structure are still visible below the square tower in the south-western corner. The structure that stands today was built by the Byzantines in the 6th century AD, modified during a brief period of Spanish occupation in the middle of the 16th century AD and further modified by the Turks. The most recent additions are gun emplacements, which were built by German forces during WWII.

A road leads up to the fort from opposite the maison des jeunes on the Mansourah road, which runs north from just past the port. The fort is open every day from 8 am to 7 pm in summer, and from 8.30 am to 5.30 pm in winter. Admission is TD1.100. The caretaker and his extended family live on the site, and the whole area is something of a farmyard, with chickens and cows. It's still a restricted area of some sort, so it's advisable to ask permission before taking photos and to heed the *accès interdit* (no entry) signs. The views over the coastline from the ramparts are magnificent.

Beaches The best beach is at Mansourah, 2km to the north of town along the road past the fort. The beach at Kelibia itself is very small and not that flash.

Places to Stay

Hostel The *Maison des Jeunes* (☎ 296 105), down past the harbour on the Mansourah road, is the usual masterpiece of architectural innovation and excellence for the usual TD4 a night. The staff usually let people camp in the grounds.

Hotels Kelibia has a limited choice of hotels, most of them out at the beach by the harbour. The one star *Hôtel Florida* (☎/fax 296 248), built in 1946, is an old favourite; it has a nice shaded terrace by the water's edge. Room rates range from TD12 per person in winter to TD15 in summer, including breakfast.

Next door to the Florida is the *Hôtel Palmarina* (☎ 274 062; fax 274 055), a smart new three star place with a swimming pool and its own small patch of beach. It charges a hefty TD53/76 for single/double rooms in summer, dropping to a bargain TD24/36 in winter.

Location is the only black mark against the friendly *Pension Anis* (☎ 295 777), half-way between the beach and the town on Ave Erriadh. Spotless rooms cost TD17.500/27 in summer, dropping to TD13/20 in winter, including breakfast. Ave Erriadh forks south off Ave des Martyrs about 500m of the town centre and also runs down to the coast. It emerges near the *Hôtel Mamounia* (☎ 296 088; fax 296 858), a big beach resort to the south-west of the port. Rates range from TD49/70 in summer to TD29/38 in winter.

Out at Mansourah Beach, the *Hôtel Mansourah* (☎ 295 992) is a village-style package resort that was touted as the first phase of a major development proposed for this stretch of coast when it opened in 1995. Nothing has happened since.

Places to Eat
The *Restaurant de la Jeunesse*, opposite the Hôtel Florida, is the main budget option. It serves up a generous turkey cutlet, chips and salad for TD2.800. The restaurant at the *Hôtel Florida* is very popular. It does a three course meal for TD6, and has outdoor seating on its small terrace overlooking the sea.

The *Restaurant el-Mansourah* has a magnificent setting on a small headland at the southern end of Mansourah Beach. It's worth the trip for the view alone. Prices reflect this, with meals from TD15, plus wine. To get there, follow the road that leads out to Mansourah Beach from the port.

Back in town, the restaurant at the *Pension Anis* is well worth a visit. A plate of fresh grilled rouget (red mullet), chips and salad costs TD6.

Getting There & Away
Bus & Louage Buses and louages leave from Ave Ali Belhouane, which is the main road through town. There are 16 buses a day south to Nabeul (1¼ hours, TD2.050), the last bus leaving at 6.45 pm, and 10 a day north to El-Haouaria (40 minutes, 830 mills) between 6 am and 2.45 pm. There are also regular louages to both destinations.

The sign of Tanit, the main Carthaginian female deity, is seen on many stelae.

Hydrofoil The international hydrofoil service that once operated between Kelibia and the port of Trapani in Sicily (Italy) had been cancelled at the time of writing. There appeared to be little prospect of the service resuming. For more information, contact the shipping operator, Compagnie Tunisienne de Navigation (☎ (01) 322 775/802; fax 354 855), 122 Rue de Yougoslavie, Tunis.

Getting Around
The bus station is a solid 2.5km from the harbour and beach. A taxi to the bus station costs about TD1.500.

KERKOUANE
Halfway between Kelibia and El-Haouaria is the relatively unheralded Carthaginian site of Kerkouane. Its location makes it a bit of an effort to get to unless you have your own transport, but it's well worth a visit. The town was founded during the 6th century BC and existed for less than 300 years before it was destroyed by Roman forces under Regulus in 256 BC. The site was excavated in 1962, revealing a neatly laid-out small town within a semicircular outer wall.

It's easy to spend a couple of hours wandering around the wide streets. The citizens appear to have lived very comfortably, judging by the well-appointed courtyard-style houses. Evidence found at the site suggests that the main activity at Kerkouane was the manufacture of a rich purple dye produced from *Murex*, a species of shellfish that was once plentiful along the coast. The dye was known as Tyrian purple (after the Phoenician capital, Tyre) and was highly prized in Carthaginian and Roman times.

The museum at the site houses some interesting finds uncovered during excavation. Its star attraction is the 'Princess of Kerkouane', a wooden sarcophagus cover carved in the shape of the goddess Astarte. There are also some beautiful pieces of jewellery and delicate funerary statues discovered at grave sites around Kerkouane. Opening hours are Tuesday to Sunday from 8 am to 7 pm in summer, and from 8.30 am to 5.30 pm in winter. Entry is TD2.100, plus another TD1 to take photos.

Getting There & Away

The site is easy to find if you're driving your own vehicle, being clearly signposted off the road between Kelibia and El-Haouaria. It's also possible to catch a bus or louage (or hitch) to the turn-off and walk the remaining 1km to the site. Another option is to lash out about TD20 for a return taxi fare from Kelibia, plus waiting time while you explore.

EL-HAOUARIA
Pop 2500 ☎ *Area code 02*

This small town is tucked beneath the mountainous tip of Cap Bon. It's a quiet spot with a couple of good beaches, especially at **Ras el-Drek** on the southern side of the point. The main attraction, though, are the **Roman Caves** on the coast 3km to the west of town. There are also some good walks from the town up to nearby Jebel Abiod, where other caves are home to thousands of small bats.

El-Haouaria has a tradition of falconry, and it stages an annual festival in mid-June. It's also a good place to see migrating birds of prey in the spring (for more information

Murex

The famous purple dye so highly prized in ancient times by the Carthaginians and Romans came from two kinds of mollusc: the *Murex* and the *Buccinum*. They both have a long sac or vein filled with a yellowish fluid that turns purple when exposed to light.

A myth surrounds the origin of the discovery of the dye in Phoenicia, and goes as follows. Melkart, a Phoenician god, was walking on the beach one day with his lover, a nymph called Tyrus, and his dog. The dog bit into one of the murex shells and its muzzle became stained with a purple dye. When she saw the beautiful colour, Tyrus demanded that Melkart make her a garment of purple. So Melkart gathered a quantity of the shellfish to dye a gown which he presented to her.

This romantic tale hides the fact that production of the dye was a smelly, messy business, which involved a great deal of hard work. The molluscs were gathered in deep water by dropping narrow-necked baskets baited with mussels and frog meat. Once harvested the shellfish were hauled off to dye pits where their sacs were removed, pulped and heated in huge lead vessels. All the extraneous matter was skimmed off and the resulting dye fixed.

The dye pits were placed downwind of the residential areas to avoid the noxious smell. With practice the dyers could produce a variety of colours from pale pink to deep violet by mixing the *Murex* and *Buccinum* fluids in different quantities. The dye industry was on such a large scale that the farming of the molluscs caused them to become almost extinct.

Ann Jousiffe

on bird-watching in Tunisia see the illustrated Flora & Fauna of Tunisia section in the Facts about the Country chapter).

The town now has a choice of two hotels, and there are a couple of banks on the main street. There is no tourist office.

Roman Caves

Much of the stone used for the building of ancient Carthage and other towns of the region was cut from the remarkable complex of caves on the coast west of El-Haouaria. The cliffs along here are formed of a beautiful, easily worked yellow sandstone that was highly prized by the builders of the ancient world. Although signs on the way to the caves refer to them as the Grottes Romaines (Roman Caves), they were in fact begun by the Carthaginians in the 6th century BC.

The quarriers discovered that the quality of the stone was much better at the base of the cliff than on the surface, and opted to tunnel into the cliffs rather than to cut down. The end result after almost 1000 years of quarrying was an extraordinary network of caves stretching almost 1km along the coast. It was a highly sophisticated operation, with frequent light wells to the surface from the roofs of the pyramid-shaped caves. The cut stone was dragged out through the caves and loaded onto ships for transportation.

The caves are open every day from 8 am to 7 pm in summer, and from 8.30 am to 5.30 pm in winter. Admission is TD1.100, plus TD1 to take photos. The official guide, complete with brass nameplate, is keen to show people around.

The caves are clearly signposted 3km west of town. It takes about 45 minutes to walk there, but there's plenty of passing traffic as the caves are a popular attraction. The road ends at the Café des Grottes, next to the entrance to the site.

Places to Stay & Eat

The *Pension Dar Toubib* (☎ 297 163) promises much with its blue-tiled entrance, but the rooms are no more than pokey little boxes. Singles/doubles are TD14/20 in summer, or TD8/12 in winter; breakfast is an additional TD2.500. To get there, follow the 'Hotel' signs from the main square out towards the mountain. It's a 10 minute walk. The two star *Hôtel L'Epervier* (☎ 297 017; fax 297 258)

is a comfortable, if overpriced, modern place on the main street in the middle of town. Rooms with breakfast are TD38/60, falling to a more manageable TD26/36 in winter. The hotel restaurant does a good three course menu for TD7.500, but it's often booked out by tour groups at lunch time. If you decide to eat here, don't miss the owner's Muscat d'Epervier, delicious served chilled with a slice of lemon. The tiny *Restaurant de la Jeunesse*, opposite L'Epervier, is the only other eating option in town.

The *Café des Grottes*, out by the caves, has a lovely position overlooking the sea. It's a good place to sit and linger over a bowl of fish chorba (soup; TD2.400).

El-Haouaria is one of the few places in Tunisia where bananas are grown. The local fruit is smaller and sweeter than its imported rivals.

Getting There & Away

There are regular buses (830 mills) and louages (950 mills) to Kelibia, and occasional buses and louages to Soliman and Tunis. Hitching between El-Haouaria and Kelibia is very easy, but there is very little traffic on the other side of the peninsula.

AROUND EL-HAOUARIA
Sidi Daoud

Much of the ubiquitous canned tuna served up in the nation's restaurants and casse-croûte shops originates from the small and otherwise unremarkable fishing village of Sidi Daoud, 7km south-west of El-Haouaria. The place used to be famous – or infamous – for the spectacular 'harvest' carried out in May, when the fish congregate off the coast to breed. These days the Tunisian authorities are a bit sensitive about the image created by blood-splattered fishermen slaughtering vast numbers of the giant fish, and the harvest is conducted away from the prying eyes of tourists.

There is no public transport to Sidi Daoud.

Northern Tunisia

Most visitors to Tunisia head for the Sahara and the beach resorts south of Tunis, leaving the north virtually undiscovered.

The beaches at Raf Raf and Sidi Ali el-Mekki, between Tunis and Bizerte, are some of the best in the country. They are a favourite summer destination for Tunisian holiday-makers and scores of weekend trippers from Tunis, but foreign tourists are relatively rare. There are more good beaches along the north-west coast around the small resort town of Tabarka.

Inland from Tabarka, perched high in the forests of the Kroumirie Mountains, the town of 'Ain Draham is high enough to get snow in winter – and to remain pleasantly cool in summer while the rest of the country swelters.

The north's most-visited attractions are the Roman sites of Bulla Regia and Dougga. Less heralded but equally worth visiting is the ancient fortress city of Le Kef.

BIZERTE
Pop 110,000 ☎ Area code 02
The port of Bizerte, 66km north of Tunis, is the largest city in Northern Tunisia. It sees very few tourists, which is one reason why it's worth a visit. There are a few reasonable beaches north and east of town, but the main attraction is the architecture of the unspoiled traditional quarter around the old port.

History
Just a few kilometres south of Cap Blanc (the northernmost tip of the African continent), Bizerte's strategic location has assured it an eventful history.

It was founded by the Phoenicians in the 8th century BC as Hippo Zarytus, one of their chain of ports along the North African coast. It was further developed by the Carthaginians, who built the first canal connecting Lake Bizerte to the sea – opening up one of the finest harbours in the Western Mediterranean. The Punic city was destroyed

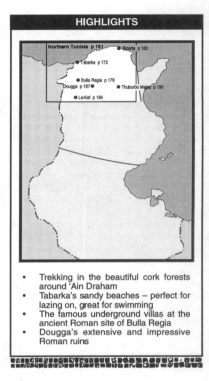

HIGHLIGHTS

- Trekking in the beautiful cork forests around 'Ain Draham
- Tabarka's sandy beaches – perfect for lazing on, great for swimming
- The famous underground villas at the ancient Roman site of Bulla Regia
- Dougga's extensive and impressive Roman ruins

by the Romans in 146 BC in reprisal for supporting Carthage in the Punic Wars. It was rebuilt 100 years later as the Roman town of Hippo Diarrhytus, and later occupied by the Vandals and the Byzantines.

The name stuck until 678 AD when the town was captured by the Arabs and renamed Bizerte. The Spanish occupied the town from 1535 to 1570, when it fell to the Ottomans and became the principal port for the Muslim corsairs who preyed on Christian shipping in the Mediterranean. (See also the boxed text 'Pirates of the Barbary Coast' under Around Bizerte later in this chapter.)

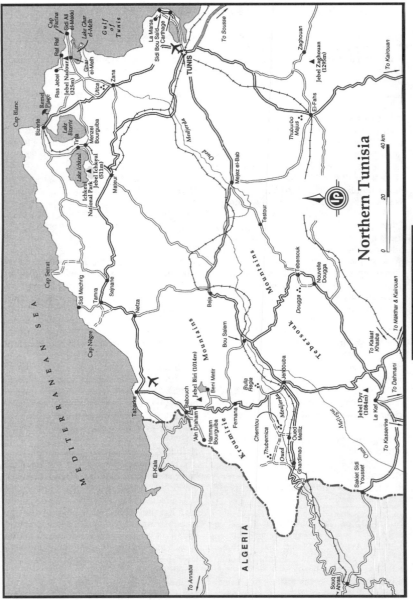

Northern Tunisia

During the French occupation, Bizerte was developed into a major military and naval base (at nearby Menzel Bourguiba, on the south-western edge of Lake Bizerte). They dug a new canal, completed in 1895, to handle modern shipping and filled in the old canal, dug by the Carthaginians, to build their *ville nouvelle* (new town).

Such was the French attachment to Bizerte and its harbour facilities that they refused to abandon it after granting independence to the rest of the country in 1956. More than 1000 Tunisian lives were lost in the attempt to oust the French before they finally withdrew on 15 October 1963. The day is no longer a public holiday, but it is still marked with speech-making and the laying of wreaths.

Orientation

The centre of the modern city is the French ville nouvelle, built on reclaimed land north of the shipping canal. For some reason the town planners broke away from the standard grid system used everywhere else in Tunisia and added a couple of diagonal streets for good measure.

The shipping canal is spanned by a modern bridge with a central section which can be raised to allow larger vessels to pass through. The main road south to Tunis crosses the bridge.

The old Arab quarter is immediately north of the ville nouvelle and borders the old harbour – which is all that remains of the original canal built by the Carthaginians.

Boulevard Hassen en-Nouri runs north from the ville nouvelle to the beaches of the Corniche.

Information

Most facilities of importance to tourists are in the ville nouvelle.

Tourist Office There is an ONTT office (☎ 432 897) on the corner of Quai Tarak ibn Ziad and Ave Taieb Mehiri. Its usefulness can be judged by the fact that the free map of Bizerte was produced back in the days before the bridge across the shipping canal was built. It still shows the ferry crossings!

You may be able to get your hands on a copy of the latest accommodation prices for selected places in the northern region. Opening hours are Monday to Thursday from 8.30 am to 1 pm and 3 to 5.45 pm, and Friday and Saturday from 8.30 am to 1.30 pm.

Money The banks are clustered around Place du 7 Novembre 1987 in the ville nouvelle.

Post & Communications The main post office is on Ave d'Algérie. There are lots of Taxiphone offices in the ville nouvelle.

Travel Agencies There are no ferries from Bizerte, but the Compagnie Tunisienne de Navigation (☎ 431 257) in Place Tarak ibn Said, near the main bus station, can arrange ferry bookings for departures from Tunis.

Kasbah

The enormous kasbah is the most impressive structure in the old town, with its massive walls towering over the northern side of the entrance to the old harbour. It was originally a Byzantine fort, built in the 6th century AD to guard the port in conjunction with the smaller *ksibah* (small fort) on the southern side. The structure that stands today was built by the Ottomans in the 17th century.

The walls are 10m high in places and up to 11m thick – built to withstand artillery bombardment. They enclose a small town of narrow, winding streets surrounding the kasbah mosque. The only entrance is through the gateway at the western end.

Ksibah & Oceanographic Museum

The ksibah forms the southern bastion of the harbour defences built by the Byzantines. It comprises a small round tower linked to a larger rectangular fort. The fort was modified by the Aghlabites, who added the attractive arched *skifa* (gate) and a courtyard with a set of cells – not for prisoners but for silent study of the Qur'an. The Ottomans later strengthened the walls to withstand an artillery bombardment.

The fort, also known as Fort Sidi Henni, now houses a small Oceanographic Museum

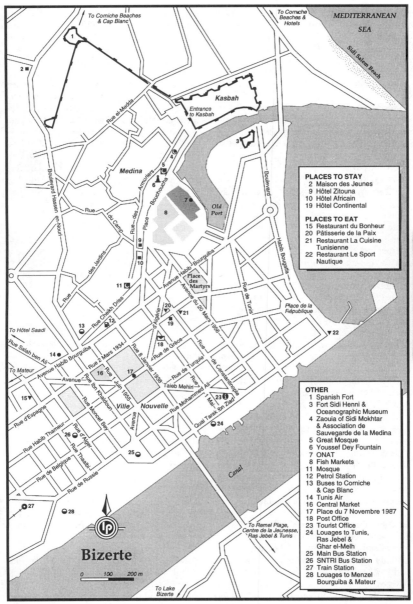

To Corniche Beaches & Cap Blanc

To Corniche Beaches & Hotels

MEDITERRANEAN
SEA

Sidi Salem Beach

Kasbah

Entrance to Kasbah

Rue el-Medja

Medina

Armuriers

Place Bouchoucha

Old Port

Rue des

Rue du Caïme

Boulevard Hassen en-Nouri

Rue des Jardins

Boulevard

Habib Bougatfa

PLACES TO STAY
2 Maison des Jeunes
9 Hôtel Zitouna
10 Hôtel Africain
19 Hôtel Continental

PLACES TO EAT
15 Restaurant du Bonheur
20 Pâtisserie de la Paix
21 Restaurant La Cuisine Tunisienne
22 Restaurant Le Sport Nautique

Avenue Habib Bourguiba

Place des Martyrs

Avenue du 20 Mars 1956

Rue de Tunis

Place de la République

Rue Cheikh Driss

Rue d'Algérie

Rue 8 Janvier 1938

Rue de Grèce

Rue de Turquie

Rue de Constantinople

Avenue Habib Bourguiba

Rue 2 Mars 1934

Rue 1 Juin 1955

Taieb Mehiri

Rue Mohammed Ali

Ville   Nouvelle

Rue Ibn Khaldoun

Rue Moncef Bey

Avenue

Quai Tarak Ibn Ziad

To Hôtel Saadi

Rue Salah ben Ali

To Mateur

Rue d'Espagne

Rue Habib Thameur

Rue d'Alger

Rue Thaalbi

Rue de Belgique

Rue de Russie

Canal

To Remel Plage, Centre de la Jeunesse, Ras Jebel & Tunis

OTHER
1 Spanish Fort
3 Fort Sidi Henni & Oceanographic Museum
4 Zaouia of Sidi Mokhtar & Association de Sauvegarde de la Medina
5 Great Mosque
6 Youssef Dey Fountain
7 ONAT
8 Fish Markets
11 Mosque
12 Petrol Station
13 Buses to Corniche & Cap Blanc
14 Tunis Air
16 Central Market
17 Place du 7 Novembre 1987
18 Post Office
23 Tourist Office
24 Louages to Tunis, Ras Jebel & Ghar el-Melh
25 Main Bus Station
26 SNTRI Bus Station
27 Train Station
28 Louages to Menzel Bourguiba & Mateur

Bizerte

0   100   200 m

To Lake Bizerte

– which is a rather grand description for a small collection of sea beasties. They include a mean-looking moray eel, a couple of lobsters and assorted fish. It's open Tuesday to Sunday from 9 am to 12.30 pm and 2.30 to 6.30 pm, and admission is 400 mills (200 mills for children).

Place Bouchoucha

This extended square lies at the heart of the old Ottoman town, flanked by the old port to the east and the medina to the west. It's more of a thoroughfare than a square, and it connects the old and new towns.

The best place to start a tour of the area is the **Zaouia of Sidi Mokhtar**, near the kasbah, which now houses the Association de Sauvegarde de la Medina, the group responsible for the preservation of the medina. You'll need to speak French or Arabic to extract much information from the staff, but they do have a fascinating map which shows how the town looked in 1881 when the French arrived.

In 1881, Place Bouchoucha was the western channel of the canal system connecting Lake Bizerte with the sea. It rejoined the eastern channel at Ave Habib Bourguiba, creating an island where the European merchants and town's elite once lived. This area now houses the lively **fish markets**.

The medina's most important buildings are close together on the edge of Place Bouchoucha and include the **Great Mosque**, built in 1652. Its striking octagonal minaret is best viewed from Rue des Armuriers, behind the mosque.

Just south of the mosque is the **Youssef Dey fountain**, built in 1642. It has a typically Andalusian inlaid arch around an inscription inviting users to avail themselves until the waters of paradise become available.

Spanish Fort

The so-called Spanish Fort overlooks the town from the hill north of the medina. It's actually Turkish and was built between 1570 and 1573 AD by Ulj Ali, the military ruler of Algiers, after he had kicked out the Spanish. It was built to reinforce the town's outer

defensive wall, which had existed in one form or another since Roman times. All that remains of the wall are the two sections either side of the fort.

Beaches

There are some good beaches north of the town, towards Cap Blanc. A strip of hotels has a monopoly on the first few kilometres of sand, a stretch known as the Corniche, but it's not too difficult for westerners to slip in and use the beaches and facilities. The best beach is **Les Grottes**, right at the foot of Cap Blanc. It's about 8km from town and hard to get to without a car. If you catch the No 2 bus from town, you will have to walk – or hitch – the last couple of kilometres.

In the other direction, towards Tunis, **Remel Plage** (3km from Bizerte) has a good strip of white sand and is a little easier to get to on your own. Buses from the main bus station heading for Raf Raf or Ras Jebel can drop you off at the turn-off, from where it's a 15 minute walk.

Places to Stay – budget

Camping The *Centre de la Jeunesse de Remel Plage* (☎ 440 819), is a good camp site and hostel 3km east of Bizerte at Remel Plage. It's signposted at the turn-off to Remel Plage. The hostel facilities are basic, but there are good shady sites beneath the pine trees and the beach is only five minutes walk away. It charges TD2 per person for camping, and TD3 for dorm beds. To get there, take a bus going to Ghar el-Melh, Ras Jebel or Raf Raf and get off at the Remel Plage turn-off. If you're here outside the summer months, phone first to check that it's open.

Hostel The *Maison des Jeunes* (☎ 431 608) is just north of the town centre, signposted off Boulevard Hassen en-Nouri near the Spanish Fort. As usual, it's more like a prison block than a hotel.

Hotels The budget hotels are all in and around the city centre. The best of the bunch is the *Hôtel Saadi* (☎ 422 528), opposite the soccer stadium on Rue Salah ben Ali, 400m from the centre of town. It has clean singles/doubles with shared bathroom for TD7/11.

The *Hôtel Africain* (☎ 434 412), on Place Bouchoucha, is another reasonable option. It has singles/doubles/triples with shared bathroom for TD6/8/10, doubles with shower for TD12 and a four bed family room for TD20. The *Hôtel Zitouna* (☎ 438 760), a few doors to the north on Place Bouchoucha, has very basic singles/doubles for TD4/6. Both hotels are not for light sleepers – the markets are right outside and the action starts early.

The crumbling *Hôtel Continental* (☎ 431 437), on Rue 2 Mars 1934, charges TD5/6 for singles/doubles, plus 500 mills for a cold shower. Don't expect much in the way of frills: the door handles fall off and the toilet door doesn't close, but at least the staff are friendly.

Places to Stay – middle & top end

The rest of the hotels are out along the Corniche beach strip to the north of the town.

The best place is the *Hôtel Le Petit Mousse* (☎ 432 185; fax 437 595), about 4km from the city centre. Rates are TD25.200/36.400 for singles/doubles with breakfast in low season, rising to TD32.600/51.200 in summer. The owner is a serious Francophile and runs one of the best restaurants in the country. Even if you don't stay here it's nice to have a drink at the bar or a meal in the garden in the evening. The only drawback is that the beach is extremely narrow and right next to the road at this point.

The best patch of beach is the preserve of the most expensive hotel, the *Hôtel Corniche* (☎ 431 844; fax 431 830), where rates are TD23/34 in low season and TD59/98 in high season. It may be three star inside, but from the street it makes the architecture of the average maison des jeunes look positively inspired. During summer you're unlikely to have the option of sampling this delight, or any of the other resort-type hotels, because they're usually all booked out with package tourists from Europe.

The cheapest of these places is the *Hôtel Nador* (☎ 431 848; fax 433 817), which has a good stretch of beach, a swimming pool, a

tennis court, pool-side restaurant and all the other trappings. Singles/doubles with breakfast are TD15/23 in low season, rising to TD39.500/60.200 in summer.

Places to Eat

The restaurants in the city centre offer nothing out of the ordinary. The *Restaurant La Cuisine Tunisienne*, just over the road from the Hôtel Continental, on the corner of Rue 2 Mars 1934 and Rue de Constantinople, does a decent three course menu for TD2.500. The *Restaurant Erriadh*, a little further along Rue 2 Mars 1934 towards Place des Martyrs, has similar fare.

The *Restaurant du Bonheur*, just off Ave Habib Bourguiba on Rue Thaalbi, is a popular spot that does the simple things well eg delicious, thick fish chorba for TD1.700. It also sells alcohol.

The best of the upmarket restaurants is *Le Petit Mousse* (☎ 432 185), out on the Corniche at the hotel of the same name. An excellent three course meal with wine will set you back about TD20. The *Restaurant Eden* (☎ 439 023), opposite the Hôtel Corniche, specialises in seafood and comes highly recommended.

The setting is the star feature at the rather overpriced *Restaurant Le Sport Nautique* (☎ 431 495), right at the entrance of the shipping canal on the edge of town. It also does seafood. Expect to pay TD30 for two, plus wine.

For coffee, cakes and ice creams, try the *Pâtisserie de la Paix*. Right opposite the Hôtel Continental, it's something of a local hang-out. It's open long hours and has good products.

Getting There & Away

Air The Tunis Air office (☎ 432 201) is at 76 Ave Habib Bourguiba. There is no airport in Bizerte; the nearest is Tunis-Carthage.

Bus The main bus station is down near the canal at the end of Ave d'Algérie, less than 10 minutes walk from the cheap hotels.

There are frequent buses to Tunis (1¾ hours, TD2.900) every half-hour from 5 am,

NORTHERN TUNISIA

and regular buses to Ras Jebel (one hour, TD1.280), the connecting point to Raf Raf. There is a 6 am departure to 'Ain Draham (4¼ hours, TD6.700) via Tabarka (3½ hours, TD6.100). Buses to Ras Jebel can drop you at the Remel Plage turn-off for the beach and camp site.

SNTRI services leave from the SNTRI depot (☎ 431 222) on Rue d'Alger. There are buses to Jerba (TD21.650) at 6 am and 6.30 pm. The morning bus goes via Kairouan and the evening bus travels via Sousse and Sfax.

Train Train is the most convenient way of travelling between Tunis and Bizerte. The train station is by the shipping canal at the south-western end of Rue de Russie. There are trains to Tunis at 5.40 and 8.10 am and at 1.50 and 6.30 pm. Services from Tunis leave at 5.50 and 11.55 am, and at 2.30, 4.05 and 6.20 pm. The journey takes one hour and 40 minutes and costs TD2.250.

Louage Louages to Tunis (TD2.800), Ras Jebel (TD1.450) and Ghar el-Melh (TD1.550) leave from near the bridge over the shipping canal. Louages to Menzel Bourguiba and Mateur depart from opposite the entrance to the train station. There are no louages to Tabarka.

Car Rental The following agencies have offices in Bizerte: ABC Rent-a-Car (☎ 434 624), 33 Ave Habib Bourguiba; Avis (☎ 433 076), 7 Rue d'Alger; Hertz (☎ 433 679), Place des Martyrs; and Europcar (☎ 431 455), 19 Rue Rejiba, Place des Martyrs.

Getting Around
Everything in the town centre is within easy walking distance. To get out to the Corniche hotels and beaches, catch either a taxi (about TD2) or a local bus (310 mills). The bus stop is at the corner of Blvd Hassen en Nouri and Ave Habib Bourguiba. The bus numbers to look out for are Nos 2 and 29. If you want to get to the beaches at Cap Blanc, the No 2 can drop you at the T-junction where the road leads off to the right to the beach. From there

it's a 2km walk to Les Grottes beach, but it's usually possible to hitch a ride.

AROUND BIZERTE
Ras Jebel
Ras Jebel is the main town on the large promontory south-east of Bizerte. It's a service town for the surrounding grape (wine and eating) and vegetable-growing district, and there's no reason to stay any longer than it takes to change bus or louage. You'll see a sign in the middle of town pointing to a beach. It's 3km north of town and not worth the trouble unless you have your own transport. The beaches at Raf Raf and Sidi Ali el-Mekki are much better.

Places to Stay & Eat It's hard to think of a reason why anyone would want to stay overnight, but there is a hotel – the tiny *Hôtel Okba* (☎ (02) 447 462). It's on the northern side of town, signposted from the bus stop. The sign does no more than point people in vaguely the right direction, but locals know the hotel and can direct you. It charges TD4/6 for very basic singles/doubles with shared bathroom, and TD15 for a reasonable double with bathroom.

There are no restaurants to speak of in town. There is a small *sandwich shop*, which sells casse-croûtes and chips, on the road out of town towards Raf Raf.

Getting There & Away The bus and louage stations are opposite each other at the main intersection in the middle of Ras Jebel.

There are regular buses to both Bizerte (TD1.280) and Raf Raf (550 mills), and louage services to Raf Raf (800 mills), Bizerte (TD1.450), Tunis (TD2.550) and Ras Jebel.

Raf Raf
Few travellers make it to Raf Raf, but it is a favourite summer spot with holidaying Tunisians, particularly at weekends. There are numerous restaurants as well as a hotel.

The attraction is the beach, which ranks among the best in the country – a long stretch of white sand fringed by pine trees. It has a beautiful setting, tucked beneath the rugged escarpment that runs east from Jebel Nadour (325m) for about 2km to Cap Farina. Unfortunately, the white sand is overlaid with more than its fair share of both garbage and people. You can escape the people by walking along the beach a bit, but there's no escape from the rubbish.

Raf Raf town itself lies about 1km inland and is of no interest. The main road from Ras Jebel bypasses the town centre and goes straight to the beach.

Places to Stay & Eat The only place to stay is the *Hôtel Dalia* (☎ (02) 441 688) to the left of the main road leading down to the sea. It has singles/doubles with bathroom for TD23/32, or TD25.500/34.500 with a sea view. There are only 10 rooms, so bookings are advisable in summer. The restaurant on the ground floor does meals, but – in keeping with the area's tourist status – at rather inflated prices.

The unbelievably kitsch *Café Restaurant Andalous*, on the main street, further down towards the sea, has better prices and does excellent fish.

There are more restaurants down by the sea, but they are expensive and aimed at day-trippers.

Getting There & Away Buses to Ras Jebel leave from the bus stop on the main street 50m before the beach. Louages to Ras Jebel leave from outside the Banque de l'Habitat in town. In summer the transport gets pretty crowded, particularly around 7 pm when everyone heads back to Tunis or Bizerte.

Ghar el-Melh

The sleepy little village of Ghar el-Melh lies on the southern side of Jebel Nadour, sandwiched between the hillside and a silted-up lagoon known as Lake Ghar el-Melh. It's

---

Pirates of the Barbary Coast

Early in the 16th century the coast of Tunisia was threatened by naval raids from the newly resurgent Spain. Khair ed-Din Barbarossa, a Turk from the island of Lesbos in the Aegean, stepped into the breach and began an age of piracy along the Barbary Coast (the Mediterranean coast of North Africa) which lasted until the 19th century.

Together with his brother Aruj, Barbarossa hoped to carve out a domain in North Africa with the help of Muslim refugees expelled from Andalusia in Spain. Fearing defeat by the Spanish, he paid homage to the Ottoman sultan and in 1518 he was granted a title and sent military reinforcements. With his increased forces Barbarossa was able to capture Algiers in 1529, and soon after became the admiral-in-chief of the Turkish navy.

In 1534 Barbarossa captured Tunis and turned it into a secure base from which to attack coastal towns in Europe and to raid merchant vessels in the Mediterranean. By the time he died in 1546 his legend was secure. Khair ed-Din's associate Dragut, who had been captured by the Spanish and ransomed by Barbarossa, continued the fight against the Spanish – after one clash on Jerba, Dragut built a pyramid of skulls on the beach which remained there until 1849.

The Barbary corsairs were mostly based in Tunis and Algiers, and commanded cruisers fitted out by wealthy backers who in turn received 10% of the loot. Galleys were replaced by sailing ships by the 17th century, an innovation brought in by a Flemish renegade, Simon Danser. The crews often had a European element – Christian sailors were said to have 'taken the turban' or converted to Islam when they entered the employ of the Barbary captains. Nevertheless, the legendary drunkenness of English pirates at their Tunis base indicates they kept some of their old customs.

The gradual decline of the Ottoman Empire after the 17th century saw the Barbary Coast become increasingly independent, and Tunis became so tolerant of piracy that it was known as a pirate state. The beys of Tunis received a considerable amount of protection money from sea-going nations wishing to ensure their security.

The pirates lived on into the 19th century, with naval conflicts between Tripolitania (now western Libya) and the USA starting in 1804, the first time the USA sent forces into the Middle East. Tunis was attacked by the US Navy in 1815, and by 1830 the French had finally rid the Mediterranean of pirates.

Richard Plunkett

only a few kilometres south of Raf Raf as the crow flies but it's almost 20km by road.

It is a place with quite a history. It was founded during the reign of Osta Murad Dey (1637-40) as the pirate base of Porto Farina, which stood on the edge of a deep lagoon at the mouth of the Oued Medjerda. Its notoriety was such that in 1654 it was attacked and temporarily knocked out of action by the celebrated English admiral Sir Francis Drake. The compact, early Ottoman-style **Borj Osta Murad Dey**, built in 1638, is the only reminder of this period. It overlooks the lagoon on the western edge of town.

After privateering was abolished at the beginning of the 19th century, the Husseinite beys attempted to turn the port into a major naval base. During his reign, Ahmed Bey (1837-55) ordered the construction of two new forts, a surrounding defensive wall and a new port flanked by armouries. His efforts were soon defeated by the silt-laden waters of the Oued Medjerda which began to fill the lagoon about this time. Attempts to dredge the lagoon failed, and the port was soon abandoned in favour of La Goulette (Tunis). Today the lagoon is more like a coastal swamp, and only tiny fishing boats can use the narrow channel connecting the port to the sea.

Places to Stay & Eat There was once talk of major tourist development for the town and the nearby beach at Sidi Ali el-Mekki, but nothing has happened and it remains a charming little backwater. There are no hotels, and there's nowhere to eat other than a couple of seasonal fish restaurants.

Getting There & Away You can get to Ghar el-Melh by public transport from Bizerte. There are two buses a day (one hour, TD1.280) and occasional louages (TD1.550). There is no public transport out to Sidi Ali el-Mekki.

Sidi Ali el-Mekki

The beach at Sidi Ali el-Mekki, 6km east of Ghar el-Melh on the southern side of Cap Farina, is every bit as good as Raf Raf – but nowhere near as crowded.

There is no accommodation, but camping out is OK. The small *cafe/restaurant* on the beach operates only in summer; at other times of the year you will have to bring your own supplies.

The problem is getting here without your own transport. There is no public transport and little transport of any kind heads this way except on summer weekends. There is nothing at Sidi Ali el-Mekki other than the beach and a small fishing port – built to replace the silted-up port at Ghar el-Melh.

Utica

At one stage, after the fall of Carthage, this port city was the capital of the Roman province of Africa. It was originally situated on the banks of the Oued Medjerda, but after the river silted up it went from being a fine city to an insignificant farming village.

The **ruins** today are unimpressive – not worth the effort unless you have your own vehicle. The site is 33km north of Tunis and is signposted to the east from the small settlement of Zana on the main Bizerte-Tunis road.

You'll come to the **museum** first, on the left 2km from the main road. It houses an extensive collection of bits and pieces found on the site. Some mosaics are displayed outside. The site itself is a further 500m along the road, at the bottom of the slope. The only significant ruin is the **House of the Cascade**, named after the fountains which used to decorate this mansion. The best mosaics, of men fishing from boats with nets and rods, are small; they're protected from the elements by wooden covers which can be lifted.

Both the museum and site are open every day from 9 am to 7 pm in summer, and from 8.30 am to 5.30 pm in winter. Admission is TD2.100, plus TD1 to take photos.

Getting There & Away The only way to get to the ruins by public transport is to catch a bus or louage travelling between Tunis and Bizerte and ask to be dropped off at the turn-off to the ruins, 2km from the site. After

Ichkeul National Park

This world heritage-listed national park, 30km south-west of Bizerte, covers Lake Ichkeul and adjoining Jebel Ichkeul (511m). It is an important bird sanctuary, particularly in winter when the waters of Lake Ichkeul and the surrounding marshes are home to more than 200,000 migratory waterfowl from all over Europe. They include large numbers of coot and wigeon and half a dozen other species of duck as well as rarer birds like the purple gallinule and the park's emblem, the greylag goose. For more information on bird-watching in Tunisia see the illustrated Flora & Fauna in Tunisia section in the Facts about the Country chapter earlier in this book.

Ichkeul is the only national park in Tunisia with facilities for visitors. As well as an information centre, on a ridge above the car park, there are picnic tables and a network of paths. The information centre at the park has a display area with details on the area's fauna and flora. Animals include mongooses, porcupines, jackals, wild boar and a herd of water buffalo – descendants of a pair given to Ahmed Bey in 1840. They live in the marshes around the lake.

There is no accommodation in the park, and camping is not permitted. The park is open from 7 am to 6 pm every day. Admission is free.

Getting There & Away There is no public transport to the park, making it very difficult to visit without your own vehicle. Access is from the south-eastern side of the lake, 10km north of Mateur. Coming from Bizerte, follow the main road south to Menzel Bourguiba for 21km to the village of Tinja and fork right onto the Mateur road. The turn-off to the park is signposted on the right after 9km. This road runs dead straight along a causeway for 7km to the base of Jebel Ichkeul and the park entrance. Officials will check you in (and out later) and wave you on your way for the last 3km to the car park and information centre.

Buses and louages between Bizerte and Mateur can drop you at the park turn-off, but you will have to walk or hitch from there. There is very little traffic, except at weekends. ■

visiting the site, you will have to walk back to the road and either hitch or wait for a bus – a lot of work for very little reward.

Menzel Bourguiba

Menzel Bourguiba, 20km south of Bizerte, is an industrial town on the south-western side of Lake Bizerte. It was here that the French developed the major naval base that they refused to leave after independence – see History in the Bizerte section earlier in this chapter for more details. Today it plays host to a large Tunisian army base, which stretches for several kilometres east of the railway line.

There is absolutely no reason to stop here, but if you get stuck, the only hotel is the *Hôtel L'Ichkeul* (☎ (02) 461 606), 3km east of town on the shores of Lake Bizerte. It has singles/doubles with breakfast for TD9/12. The hotel is also the main drinking establishment in Menzel Bourguiba and is quite pleasant in the evenings with its outdoor terrace by the water – although in summer the mosquitoes come in droves.

There is no public transport from town to the hotel, so you'll have to take a taxi.

NORTH COAST

The rugged stretch of coastline between Bizerte and Tabarka, dotted with isolated bays, is virtually uninhabited and is inaccessible for most of its length. The main road runs a fair way inland, and much of the country between the road and the sea is covered with plantation forest. There are a couple of secluded coastal settlements, but they are very hard to get to unless you have a vehicle. If you do have a vehicle, this a good area to get right off the beaten track.

Mateur

Mateur is a dull regional town 40km south of Bizerte. It is worth mentioning only because it is large enough to have useful transport links. Trains travelling on the Bizerte-Tunis line stop here, and there are regular buses and louages to Bizerte, Sejnane and Tabarka. The town is best known for its cheese.

Sejnane

The town of Sejnane, halfway between Mateur and Tabarka, is famous for as the source of a primitive, moulded style of pottery known as Sejnane ware. The style has now been copied by the sophisticated pottery workshops of Nabeul and Jerba, but this is the only area where traditional methods are still employed.

The techniques used by the potters of the Berber settlements around here date back to Neolithic times. Clay is hand-moulded into an assortment of unusual animal figurines, as well as bowls of all shapes and sizes, and pit-fired before being decorated with traditional Berber motifs in rusty reds and deep browns. You'll see it for sale at roadside stalls around town.

Sejnane is also the starting point for trips to the coastal settlements of Cap Serrat and Sidi Mechrig.

SNTRI buses travelling the northern route (via Mateur) between Tabarka and Tunis can drop you at Sejnane. There are also regular local buses and louages between Mateur and Sejnane.

Cap Serrat

Cap Serrat, 27km north of Sejnane, is one of Tunisia's undiscovered gems – a remote peninsula flanked to the east by an unspoiled sandy bay. You will probably come across a few campers in summer, but for much of the year the place is completely deserted. It's likely to stay that way for a while. There is no public transport and there are no shops, hotels, restaurants or facilities of any kind. If you plan to camp here, you will need to bring your own supplies.

The access road to Cap Serrat is signposted 11km north of Sejnane along the back road to Bizerte (which skirts around the northern edge of Lake Ichkeul). From the turn-off, the road winds down through dense pine forest and emerges at the mouth of a small valley dotted with a few farmhouses. The main track continues across the valley to a lighthouse on Cap Serrat, while a turn-off to the right leads to the beach.

A rough track (4WD only) runs south-west from Cap Serrat to Sidi Mechrig.

Sidi Mechrig

The small coastal settlement of Sidi Mechrig is signposted from the village of Tamra, 9km west of Sejnane. It's another 17km from Tamra to the coast, as the road, which is mostly sealed, twists across two ranges of low hills covered with large tracts of pine and eucalypt plantation. The road ends at a brand new fishing port.

There's not much at Sidi Mechrig other than a few houses and the basic Hôtel Sidi Mechrig (no telephone), which is on the left as you approach the settlement. It has a great location overlooking a small sandy beach and a photogenic Roman arch – the only remains of an old bathhouse.

The location makes up for the rooms, which are dingy little boxes with a couple of saggy single beds. It charges TD8 per person with breakfast during July and August, and TD6 per person during the rest of the year. The hotel is open all year because it happens to have the only bar between Tabarka and Mateur, guaranteeing a steady flow of customers. It also has a restaurant, open daily for lunch and dinner, with terrace seating overlooking the sea. It's a good spot to sit down to a large plate of grilled fish, chips and salad (TD6), washed down by a cold beer.

Getting There & Away Public transport out to Sidi Mechrig is very limited. In July and August, there are two buses (TD1) a day from Sejnane; there are no buses the rest of the year. There are also occasional camionnettes – ask at the bus station in Sejnane.

TABARKA
Pop 10, 000 ☎ *Area code 08*

The small resort town of Tabarka is the last town on the north coast before the Algerian border, 22km to the west. It has one of the prettiest settings in Tunisia, nestled below the densely forested slopes of the Kroumirie Mountains. The beautiful little bay on the northern edge of town is watched over by an impressive-looking Genoese fort on Tabarka Island (now linked by a causeway), while a long stretch of beach curves away eastwards towards Cap Nègre.

It's hard to believe that the package tourism operators stayed away for so long, but they are now trying hard to make up for lost time. There is an expanding *zone touristique* (tourist strip) 4km to the east of town, complete with its own golf course, and an international airport opened here in July 1992. In spite of this, the town remains a relaxing place to spend a few days.

History
Like so many towns along the North African coast, Tabarka began life as a Phoenician settlement. Originally called Thabraca, it remained a minor outpost until Roman times, when it was developed into a major port to handle the export of marble from the mines at Chemtou, 60km inland. It was also the exit point for many of the African big cats en route to the colosseums of Rome and elsewhere.

In the 16th and 17th centuries, Tabarka became one of a string of ports used by the Muslim corsairs (see the boxed text 'Pirates of the Barbary Coast' in the Around Bizerte section earlier). They included the notorious Khair ed-Din, who was obliged to hand over Tabarka Island to the Genoese in the 1540s as ransom for the release of his cohort Dragut. The castle the Genoese built on the island enabled them to hold out against the Ottomans until 1741, when it fell to the bey of Tunis.

The modern town was laid out by the French, who also built the causeway connecting the island to the mainland. Despite these developments, Tabarka was considered to be a backwater far enough removed from mainstream life to be a suitable place of exile for Habib Bourguiba in 1952. He spent a short time here, staying at the Hôtel Les Mimosas and the Hôtel de France.

Tourism is now the mainstay of the local economy, while the modern port is the main shipment point for the tonnes of cork harvested from the forests of the Kroumirie. The red coral which is found just offshore is still exploited for the jewellery trade.

Orientation
It's hard to get lost in Tabarka. The compact town centre is laid out on the traditional French grid, bisected by the main street, Ave Habib Bourguiba.

Ave Habib Bourguiba begins at the large roundabout at the south-eastern edge of town and ends at the old harbour. The causeway to Tabarka Island leads off from here, flanked to the west by a small beach and to the east by the marina and port facilities.

The roundabout south-east of town lies at the junction of the roads south to 'Ain Draham and east to Sejnane. The zone touristique is 4km east of town, signposted off the road to Sejnane. The airport is 14km east of town on the road to Sejnane.

Information
Tourist Office The regional tourist office (☎ 643 496) is on Rue de Bizerte, near the roundabout at the south-eastern edge of town. It hasn't got much to offer apart from an ancient brochure. The office is open Monday to Thursday from 8.30 am to 1 pm and 3 to 5.45 pm, and Friday and Saturday from 8.30 am to 1.30 pm.

Money Most of the banks are on Ave Habib Bourguiba in the centre of town.

Post & Communications The main post office is on Ave Hedi Chaker, diagonally opposite the Hôtel de France. There are plenty of Taxiphone offices around town.

Beaches
Tabarka has two beaches. The building of the causeway linking Tabarka Island to the mainland created the sheltered bay known as **Old Harbour**, providing locals with a good, safe swimming beach just a couple of minutes walk from the town centre.

Montazah Beach is a great sweep of sand stretching east from the marina. The section

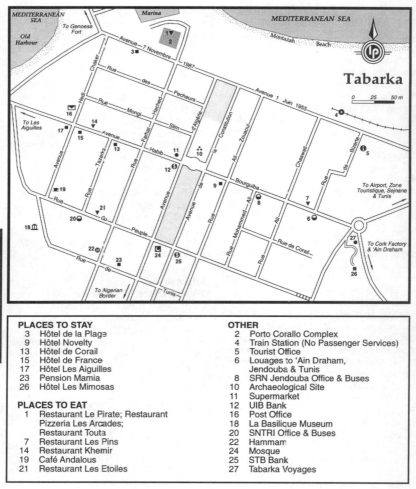

PLACES TO STAY
3	Hôtel de la Plage
9	Hôtel Novelty
13	Hôtel de Corail
15	Hôtel de France
17	Hôtel Les Aiguilles
23	Pension Mamia
26	Hôtel Les Mimosas

PLACES TO EAT
1	Restaurant Le Pirate; Restaurant Pizzeria Les Arcades; Restaurant Touta
7	Restaurant Les Pins
14	Restaurant Khemir
19	Café Andalous
21	Restaurant Les Etoiles

OTHER
2	Porto Corallo Complex
4	Train Station (No Passenger Services)
5	Tourist Office
6	Louages to 'Ain Draham, Jendouba & Tunis
8	SRN Jendouba Office & Buses
10	Archaeological Site
11	Supermarket
12	UIB Bank
16	Post Office
18	La Basilique Museum
20	SNTRI Office & Buses
22	Hammam
24	Mosque
25	STB Bank
27	Tabarka Voyages

near the marina is polluted and no good for swimming. The hotels of the zone touristique monopolise the best bit.

Genoese Fort

The magnificent-looking Genoese fort is unfortunately a military zone and out of bounds to the public. The best views are from **Les Aiguilles** (The Needles), a line of dramatic, sheer pinnacles of rock opposite the fort on the western side of Old Harbour Bay. Les Aiguilles are signposted from the beach end of Ave Habib Bourguiba and are a popular place for an evening stroll. Head out there an hour before sunset when the light is at its best.

La Basilique Museum

This small museum is housed in an old Roman cistern that was converted into a church by French missionaries at the end of the 19th century. The star exhibits are some early Christian mosaics. The museum was closed at the time of writing.

Cork Museum

The Cork Museum is at the cork factory, 2km south of town on the road to 'Ain Draham. It has an information display on the local cork industry as well as lots of tacky cork souvenirs. It's open daily from 8 am to noon and 2 to 5 pm. Admission is free.

Activities

Diving There are some good dive sites close to Tabarka. The Club de Plongée (☎ 644 478), at the marina, organises trips, rents equipment and offers courses for beginners.

Golf Golfers will find the 18 hole layout at Tabarka Golf Club (☎ 644 321) hard to resist, although the cost might help – reckon on TD50 by the time you've finished paying green fees and club and buggy hire. The course overlooks the sea out at the zone touristique.

Horse Riding Horse riding can be arranged through the Hôtel Paradise Golf (☎ 643 002), next to the golf course at the zone touristique. The hotel's stables are run by Fershishi Rahim. He charges TD10 per hour for short rides, or TD90 per day for overnight treks into the forests of the Kroumirie Mountains. These treks involve camping out and all meals are included. However, Fershishi deals only with groups and a minimum of six people is required for treks.

The reception desk at the hotel will be able to tell you if a group is going out.

Organised Tours

Tabarka Voyages (☎ 643 740; fax 643 726), just off the roundabout on the 'Ain Draham road, has a half day tour to 'Ain Draham and Bulla Regia on Tuesday for TD30, and a full day tour to 'Ain Draham, Bulla Regia and Dougga on Saturday for TD55. Carthage Tours, based at the Hôtel Les Mimosas, offers much the same but at higher prices.

Places to Stay – budget

Budget accommodation is at a premium, especially in summer when you'll be lucky to find a room after noon.

The cheapest place is the run-down *Hôtel de Corail* (☎ 643 082), on the corner of Ave Habib Bourguiba and Rue Tazerka. It's no great bargain at TD6 per person without breakfast, rising to TD7.500 in summer.

Pension Mamia (☎ 671 058), on Rue de Tunis, is a better bet. The rooms are basic but spotlessly clean, and are laid out around a small tiled courtyard. Facilities include hot showers or bath, a kitchen and a TV room. It's good value at TD8 per person with breakfast, rising to TD13.500 in peak season.

The *Hôtel de la Plage* (☎ 670039), on Ave 7 Novembre 1987, has spent a lot of money upgrading its facilities in the last couple of years. It has excellent singles/doubles with bathroom for TD23/26, and singles/doubles with shared bathroom for TD21/26, year-round. Prices include breakfast.

Places to Stay – middle

The friendly *Hôtel Les Aiguilles* (☎ 643 789; fax 643 604), at the beach end of Ave Habib Bourguiba, is highly recommended. It's an old colonial building, originally a bank, which has been converted into a comfortable, modern two star hotel. The rooms have air-conditioning, satellite TV and bathroom. Singles/doubles with breakfast are TD19/30 in low season and TD30/50 in high season.

Opposite is the *Hôtel de France* (☎ 644 577), which looks a lot better after a long overdue face-lift. Single/double rooms with bathroom are TD13/26 in low season and TD17.500/35 in summer.

The hotel's moment of glory came in 1952 when Bourguiba spent a couple of nights there, an event that is commemorated by a plaque at the head of the stairs.

Bourguiba spent most of his stint in Tabarka at the three star *Hôtel Les Mimosas* (☎ 643 018; fax 643 276), signposted at the roundabout on the way into town. It has commanding views over the town to the sea; facilities include a swimming pool, tennis court and mini golf. Singles/doubles with bath are TD23/34 (low season) or TD48/72 (high season), including breakfast.

Another choice in town is the *Hôtel Novelty* (☎ 670 178; fax 643 008), about halfway along Ave Habib Bourguiba. It's a well run, modern two star hotel with singles/doubles for TD27/44 in low season and TD31/50 in high season.

Places to Stay – top end

Tabarka's top hotel is the four star *Iberotel Mehari* (☎ 670 001; fax 643 943), which overlooks the beach at the zone touristique. Rooms are TD32/48 in low season and TD63/98 in high season. The adjoining *Residence Mehari* has self-catering studio apartments. Rates for two people are TD50 in low season and TD75 in high season. Four-person apartments are TD75, rising to TD115 in high season.

Other zone touristique hotels include the three star *Abou Nawas Montazah* (☎ 643 532; fax 643 530), the *Paradise Golf* (☎ 643 002; fax 643 918), the *Royal Golf* (☎ 643 625; fax 643 838), and the *El-Morjane* (☎ 643 411; fax 643 888). They are usually fully booked with charter tourists.

Places to Eat – budget

Fish features prominently on the menus, and not just at the smart tourist restaurants. There are lots of small places serving excellent, grilled fish for about TD2.500 – look for the telltale charcoal grills, particularly around the junction of Rue du Peuple and Ave Farhat Hached. The *Restaurant Les Etoiles*, on Rue du Peuple, has daily specials like spicy beans with chicken (TD1.400) as well as grilled fish and chicken. The *Restaurant Les Pins*, towards the roundabout on Ave Habib Bourguiba, has a wider choice than many, with most meals under TD3.

For coffee, head for the *Café Andalous*, at the southern end of Ave Hedi Chaker. It has an amazing collection of Ottoman-era bric-a-brac. Self caterers can stock up at the

supermarket by the roundabout in the middle of town.

Places to Eat – middle

There are so many good places to choose from that it's hard to know where to begin. Just for starters, there are the restaurants at the four mid-range hotels in town. The three course menu (TD7) at the *Hôtel de France* is something of an institution in Tabarka, but these days it has to compete with the more sophisticated menus offered by the *Hôtel Les Aiguilles* and the *Hôtel Novelty*. Both offer similar three-course deals for TD8. The *Hôtel Les Mimosas* charges TD9 for a three course menu – and eating there qualifies you to use the pool.

The *Restaurant Khemir*, opposite the Hôtel de France on Ave Habib Bourguiba, has a good range of seafood at prices that won't break the bank. There's a cluster of more upmarket tourist restaurants in the Porto Corallo complex by the marina. *Restaurant Pizzeria Les Arcades*, *Restaurant Le Pirate* and *Restaurant Touta* all do meals for TD15 to TD20.

Getting There & Away

Air Tabarka has a new international airport, but it has very little in the way of action apart from the occasional charter flight from Europe. There are no domestic flights to or from Tabarka.

Bus The SNTRI (☎ 644 404) office is on Rue du Peuple, one block behind the Hôtel de Corail. The company provides the only scheduled services between Tabarka and Tunis, with six buses daily via Mateur and three via Beja. For those who like to spend the shortest possible time on board, it's 15 minutes quicker via Mateur at 3¼ hours – and fractionally cheaper at TD6.370.

SNTRI also has buses to 'Ain Draham at 9.30 am (900 mills) and to Bizerte at 12.45 pm (TD6.100).

SRN Jendouba is the other major player, with an office on Ave Habib Bourguiba at the junction with Rue Mohammed Ali. It has six buses a day to Jendouba (two hours, TD2.450) via 'Ain Draham. The 6 am service to Jendouba continues to Le Kef (TD4.300).

Train There are no passenger services to or from Tabarka at present, and there's little likelihood of them resuming.

Louage Louages for 'Ain Draham (TD1), Jendouba (TD2.700) and Tunis (TD6.700) leave from the south-eastern end of Ave Habib Bourguiba, near the roundabout.

Getting Around

The town is too small to warrant local buses, leaving taxis as the main form of transport. In summer, a 'Noddy' train shuttles back and forth between the Porto Corallo complex and the zone touristique.

To/From the Airport There is no public transport to the airport, which is 14km east of town on the road to Sejnane. A taxi costs about TD5.

TABARKA TO 'AIN DRAHAM

The road south from Tabarka to 'Ain Draham, 26km inland, passes through some beautiful countryside as it climbs from the narrow coastal plain into the forests of the Kroumirie Mountains. The area is marketed by tourist authorities as 'Green Tunisia', and it's not hard to see why as you head out of Tabarka along tree-lined roads flanked by contented dairy cattle grazing in well manicured fields. Even in late summer, the fields around here are remarkably green and lush.

The climb begins a few kilometres south of Tabarka, and the early stages offer some lovely views back over the coast. The road then starts to twist and turn its way up the valley of the Oued Kebir, and the paddocks gradually give way to forest. The predominant species is the cork oak, and the deep red, tannin-stained trunks of freshly harvested trees are everywhere.

At the small village of **Babouch**, 21km from Tabarka, there is a turn-off to the Algerian border. The border is 3km to the west, and it's another 28km from there to the coastal town of El-Kala.

'AIN DRAHAM
Pop 2500 ☎ Area code 08

'Ain Draham, 26km south of Tabarka, is Tunisia's hill station. It's a pretty town of red-tiled houses that tumbles down the western flank of Jebel Biri (1014m), the highest peak of the Kroumirie Mountains. The elevation means that in summer it's a lot cooler than on the plains or the coast, and snow is quite common in winter.

The town was popular with hunters in the days of the French administration – the last of Tunisia's lions and leopards were shot in the forests around here early this century. Hunting continues to be an attraction, with wild boar now the prime target, but most visitors come to relax and escape the summer heat.

The architecture here, and at nearby Beni Metir, is quite unlike anything else in Tunisia, with steep tiled roofs designed to handle the winter snows. Locals, who obviously haven't been to Switzerland, reckon it looks just like a Swiss Alpine village.

Orientation & Information

The main road through town becomes the main street – Ave Habib Bourguiba, believe it or not. It dips into a small valley as you come into town from Tabarka, then climbs steeply through the centre of town and continues towards Jendouba.

The bus and louage stations are just west of the main street at the bottom of the hill, while everything else of importance is up the hill towards Jendouba. There is a small *syndicat d'initiative* office (☎ 647 115) halfway up the main street on the left. It has nothing apart from a couple of brochures, although the woman who runs the place is very welcoming. There are also a couple of banks, a post office and Taxiphone offices on the main street.

Trekking

The forests around 'Ain Draham have great potential as a trekking destination. It remains largely unrealised, mainly because tourist operators have been slow to wake up to the possibilities.

Les Tapis de Kroumirie

Carpets and *kilims* (woven rugs) are produced in 'Ain Draham by a small women's cooperative called Les Tapis de Kroumirie. The project was launched in the early 1980s by two French doctors working in 'Ain Draham. Run with the assistance of the 'Ain Draham Centre d'Action Sociale, its joint aims are to provide employment for local women and to revive local carpet-making traditions.

It's an interesting place to visit. The produce is sold directly from the workshop, where about a dozen looms are in operation. The appearance of a foreigner is likely to create a fair amount of interest. If you decide to buy a carpet, there's a good chance that you will get to meet the person who wove it.

The carpets are the thick-pile Berber type known as *alloucha*, produced in natural tones and decorated with simple, traditional Berber motifs. The wool is all spun by hand. Prices are fixed, but they're not high – a carpet measuring 140cm x 75cm costs TD85.

To get there, turn right at the bottom of the steps opposite the syndicat d'initiative. The cooperative is above the Ministère des Affaires Sociales, about 50m along on the right. The carpets are also sold in Tunis at Mains de Femmes, at 47 Ave Habib Bourguiba. ■

Full marks then to Nabil ben Abdallah, the owner of the Hôtel Rihana (☎ 655 391; fax 655 396), for being the first to see the potential for ecotourism in this beautiful region. The hotel has long specialised in organising wild boar hunting parties in winter, and Nabil has now hit on the bright idea of using the same guides to lead trekking groups in spring and autumn. He offers a range of guided treks for small groups for about TD40 per day.

The absence of decent maps makes it difficult to head off trekking independently, although there are some good short walks close to town. One easy option is to walk out along the Tabarka road to the Hôtel Nour el-Ain and then take the well-trodden forest track that leads back to town. The circuit takes about two hours.

Places to Stay & Eat

The *Maison des Jeunes* (☎ 647 087), at the top of the hill on the road to Jendouba, is the only budget option, at the usual TD4.

The only other place in town is the *Hôtel Beauséjour* (☎ 655 363; fax 655 527), at the top of the hill, 100m from the Maison des Jeunes. It was once popular with hunting parties and trophies line the walls. Singles/doubles cost TD19.500/28 for with breakfast, and full or half board is available at TD4 for each three course meal. There is no hot water, which makes showering a painful process in winter.

The two star *Hôtel Rihana* (☎ 655 391; fax 655 396) is about 1km south of town on the road to Jendouba. It offers magnificent views and a superior level of comfort (hot water). The hotel handles lots of hunting parties, and in winter the place is full of men in a bizarre array of paramilitary camouflage costumes. Singles/doubles are TD21.500/34 in low season and TD26.500/44 in high season. It also has a good restaurant. Wild boar pâté features on the menu in season.

Seven kilometres along the road to Jendouba is the two star *Hôtel Les Chênes* (☎ 655 211; fax 655 578), an old hunting lodge dating back to the 1920s. There are lots of hunting trophies, including an enormous stuffed boar, in the dining room. Rooms with bath and breakfast cost TD22/36 in winter and TD28.500/40 in summer. Unless you've got your own transport, you'll have to pay an extra TD5 per person for half board because there is nowhere else to eat in the area around the hotel.

'Ain Draham's smartest establishment is the three star *Hôtel Nour el-Ain*, which overlooks the town from the Col des Ruines, 2km to the north. It has single/double rooms for TD30.500/48 and TD35.500/58 in low season and high season, respectively. Facilities include a hammam, a fitness centre and an indoor pool.

There are several basic restaurants in Ave Habib Bourguiba; the *Restaurant du Grand Maghreb* is the most popular.

Getting There & Away

Bus SRN Jendouba operates frequent buses to Jendouba (one hour, TD1.550) and Tabarka (40 minutes, 900 mills), as well as services to Le Kef (TD3.400) at 8.15 and 9 am and to Bizerte (TD6.700) at 6 am. It also has two buses a day to Hammam Bourguiba (750 mills).

SNTRI has three services a day between Tunis and 'Ain Draham (TD7.100).

Louage Louages leave from outside the bus station. There are regular services to Tabarka (TD1) and Jendouba (TD1.700), and a few to Tunis (TD7.300). You'll need to be quick off the mark as demand normally exceeds supply.

AROUND 'AIN DRAHAM
Hammam Bourguiba

The resort village of Hammam Bourguiba, 15km south-west of 'Ain Draham, is tucked away in a small valley near the Algerian border. The **hot springs** here have been developed into a health farm offering a range of steam-based treatments which are popular with elderly Tunisians. It was once a favourite retreat of the country's former president, Habib Bourguiba.

Places to Stay & Eat The *resort* (☎ (08) 632 552; fax 632 497) looks decidedly tatty these days. It's hard to work out how a place with so many missing tiles and so much flaking paint can earn the three stars awarded to its hotel and bungalow accommodation. Single/double rooms are TD30/40 with breakfast, but there is no option but to take half board (TD33/46) because there is nowhere else to eat.

Getting There & Away To get there, take the road that leads to the Algerian border from Babouch and turn left after about 1km. There are two buses a day from 'Ain Draham (750 mills).

Beni Metir

The village of Beni Metir, 16km south-east of 'Ain Draham, was built by the French in the 1950s to house the workers who constructed the dam that is the reason for the place's existence. Once the work was completed, the village was handed over to the locals.

The area is a much-touted beauty spot, popular with family groups at weekends. The large lake created by the dam is surrounded by forest and overlooked by the pretty red-roofed houses of Beni Metir. It's interesting to observe the old French church and the new mosque standing almost side by side.

The turn-off to Beni Metir is about 10km south of 'Ain Draham on the road to Jendouba, just beyond the brand new sports complex custom-built to the requirements of the national soccer team. From the turn-off, the road winds down to the lake through dense forest of holm oak and myrtle.

Places to Stay & Eat The only accommodation option is the *Maison des Jeunes* in the middle of the village. It charges the usual TD4. There are no restaurants, but there are *shops* where you can stock up on food.

Getting There & Away Your own transport is the best option. That way you can enjoy the 20 minute drive from 'Ain Draham at your leisure. Public transport is restricted to occasional camionnettes – ask around at the bus station in 'Ain Draham or outside the Maison des Jeunes in Beni Metir.

BULLA REGIA

Bulla Regia, 9km north of Jendouba, is famous as the place where the Romans went underground to escape the heat – they built their villas with one storey above ground and another below.

History

The dolmens (Neolithic tombs) that dot the hills around the site are evidence that the area was inhabited long before the Romans arrived. The town of Bulla emerged in about the 5th century BC as part of Carthage's moves to develop the Medjerda Valley as a

NORTHERN TUNISIA

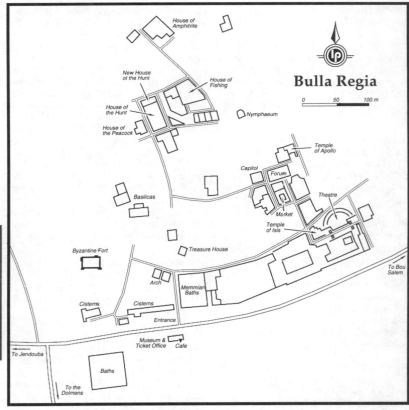

Bulla Regia

wheat-growing area. The 'Regia' was added later when it became the capital of one of the short-lived Numidian kingdoms tolerated by Rome following the destruction of Carthage.

The town flourished under subsequent Roman rule, its citizens growing rich on the income from wheat. It reached the peak of its prosperity in the 2nd and 3rd centuries AD, and most of the site's buildings belong to that era.

Bulla Regia was occupied by the Byzantines, who added their standard fort, but was abandoned after the Arab conquest in the 7th century.

Things to See

The entrance to the site is right opposite the museum and ticket office, just to the left of the Memmian Baths. Named after Julia Memmia, wife of the Emperor Septimius Severus, the **Memmian Baths** are the most extensive of the remaining above-ground buildings and are a good orientation point.

The street in front of the baths leads east to a small but beautifully preserved **theatre** with a large mosaic of a bear adorning the stage. The seating is in particularly good condition. Note that the front three tiers are extra wide and separated from the rest by the remains of a low wall – dress-circle seating for VIPs. South-west of the theatre are the remains of a small **Temple of Isis**, the Egyptian goddess who was a fashionable addition to the Roman pantheon at the time.

A path leads north from the temple past the old **market square** to the **forum**, which is surrounded by the ruins of two temples – the **capitol** to the west and the **Temple of Apollo** to the north. Excavation of the Temple of Apollo revealed a magnificent collection of statues, now housed at the Bardo Museum in Tunis.

The site's main attraction, however, are the underground villas of the city's wealthy quarter. Seven villas have been excavated so far, and several others remain unexplored. The villas vary in their level of sophistication, but are all built to the same basic plan. Above ground, they would have looked little different from any other Roman villa of the time. The surface structures were built around an excavated central courtyard, open to the sky, off which lay a second, subterranean level of rooms.

The villas are clustered together at the northern edge of the site, and are named according to the mosaics they contained. The earliest of them is the **House of Fishing**, built during the reign of the Emperor Hadrian (117-38 AD). Most of the other villas were built during the reign of Hadrian's successor, Antoninus Pius (138-61 AD), and are a good deal more sophisticated – both in construction and in decoration. The most impressive of these later villas is the **House of the Hunt**. Although the mosaics have been removed, the elegant, colonnaded courtyard and large entertaining area are enough to give the visitor an insight into the lifestyle of its former occupants.

The hunting mosaic has been left in situ next door at the **New House of the Hunt**. Large chunks are missing, but there's still plenty left to view, including the obligatory lion hunt. The best of the mosaics is to be found at the **House of Amphitrite**, just north of the main cluster. Its beautifully preserved mosaic of Venus and a cupid riding dolphins is regarded by most as the site's *pièce de*

résistance. Other villas to investigate are the **House of the Peacock**, where a peacock mosaic was found, and the **Treasure House**, so-called because a horde of Byzantine coins was found during excavation.

The **spring** that once supplied the ancient city with water lies just east of the main cluster of houses. It is now covered by a modern pump house, which delivers its cool waters to nearby Jendouba.

A visit to the small **museum** outside the site, across the road from the entrance, is included in the admission fee. There are a couple of mosaics from the site, a collection of chipped Roman busts, sundry old things and an interesting layout of the area in Numidian times.

The hill behind the museum is covered with Neolithic tombs and is worth a stroll if time permits.

The site is open Tuesday to Sunday from 8 am to 7 pm in summer and from 8.30 am to 5.30 pm in winter. Admission is TD2.100, plus TD1 to take photos.

Organised Tours All the major tour companies offer trips to Bulla Regia, normally in combination with Dougga. See Organised Tours in the main Getting Around chapter for more details. A day trip from Tunis to both sites costs about TD60, including lunch.

Getting There & Away
The turn-off to Bulla Regia is 6km north of Jendouba on the road to 'Ain Draham. Any bus or louage travelling between the two towns can drop you there. It's another 3km from the turn-off to the site. Hitching along this stretch is easy enough, but it's also a pleasant walk if it's not too hot.

Most people visit the site from Jendouba. There are occasional share taxis (500 mills) from the louage station, but the easiest option is to pay about TD3 for your own taxi.

JENDOUBA
Pop 19,000 ☎ Area code 08

It's hard to get enthusiastic about the dull regional centre of Jendouba, 153km west of Tunis. It exists to service the needs of the surrounding wheat-growing country rather than to titillate tourists, but it's hard to avoid the place if you want to visit Bulla Regia.

Orientation & Information
One thing the town does have going for it is that it's easy to negotiate. Most things of importance are around the central square, including the post office, a range of banks, a supermarket, the train station and the police station. Look out for the collection of storks' nests on the roof of the police station – arguably the most interesting feature of the town.

The bus and louage stations are at the major roundabout on the western side of town. To get there, follow the main street (Ave Hedi Chaker) west from the central square for about 500m. The roundabout is the town's major traffic distribution point, situated at the intersection of the roads going north to 'Ain Draham, north-east to Tunis (bypassing the city centre), south to Le Kef and west to Ghardimao.

Places to Stay
The best advice is to time your comings and goings to eliminate the need to stay overnight. If you do get stuck, you'll be doing yourself a favour if you stay away from the town cheapie, the grim *Pension Saha en-Noum* on Blvd Khemais el-Hajiri. It charges TD3 per person for a bed in a shared room. Blvd Khemais el-Hajiri runs north off Ave Hedi Chaker halfway between the central square and the roundabout.

The town's premier establishment is the *Hôtel Simitthu* (☎ 634 043; fax 632 595), directly opposite the SRN Jendouba bus station at the roundabout. It's on Blvd 9 April 1938, which doubles as the main road west to Ghardimao. It's a clean, modern two star hotel managed by an expatriate French woman and her husband. It charges TD29/42 for singles/doubles with breakfast. The only other possibility is the *Hôtel Atlas* (☎ 633 217), just off the central square behind the police station with all the storks' nests. It was closed, supposedly for renovations, at the

time of writing – but there was no evidence of anyone doing any renovating.

Places to Eat
There are a several small restaurants and rôtisseries around the central square. The restaurant at the *Hôtel Simitthu* does a good three course menu for TD6 – or TD3.500 if you're staying there.

If you're heading out to Bulla Regia, you can pick up the makings of a picnic at the *supermarket* on the central square.

Getting There & Away
Jendouba is an important regional transport hub with good links to all the major centres of the north.

Bus SNTRI has five buses a day to Tunis (four hours, TD5.650) from the bus station at the roundabout on the western edge of town. The last bus to Tunis leaves at 4 pm.

The bus station is the home of regional company SRN Jendouba. Its services include six buses a day to Tabarka (1¾ hours, TD2.450) via 'Ain Draham, six to Ghardimao (40 minutes, TD1.250) and five to Le Kef (1½ hours, TD1.850). To get to Bulla Regia, take any bus going to 'Ain Draham and ask to be dropped off at the turn-off.

Train If you're travelling to Tunis, the train is the way to go. There are five departures a day to Tunis, the first at 6 am and the last at 5 pm. The fare is TD5.050 in 2nd class and TD6.350 in 1st class. First class is worth the extra because there's little chance of getting a seat in 2nd class. The journey takes just over three hours.

Louage Louages leave from a range of locations around the roundabout at the western edge of town. The main destinations are 'Ain Draham (TD1.700), Ghardimao (TD1.300), Le Kef (TD2.400), Tabarka (TD2.700) and Tunis (TD6.700).

CHEMTOU
The ancient quarries at Chemtou, about 25km west of Jendouba, were once the

source of an unusual pink-veined yellow marble that was prized throughout the Roman world.

History

The site, on the north bank of the Oued Medjerda near the village of Oued Melliz, was originally the Numidian settlement of Simitthu. Little is known about the area before the Romans began to exploit the marble of the surrounding hills during the reign of Augustus (27 BC to 16 AD).

Such was the demand for its marble that Chemtou quickly developed from a work camp into an important town. The quarrying operation was said to be the most sophisticated in the Roman world. Each block carried the stamp of the emperor of the day, as well as that of the proconsul for Africa, the quarry supervisor and a reference mark. A special road was built across the Kroumirie Mountains to link the quarries with the port of Thabraca (Tabarka).

The mines were worked until Byzantine times, but were abandoned following the Arab invasion in the 7th century.

Things to See

The site sprawls over a wide area on the north bank of the Medjerda, sandwiched between the river and a band of low hills that were the source of the town's marble wealth.

Despite the town's proximity to the Medjerda, the river was not deemed to be a suitable water supply. Instead, water was brought to the town by **aqueduct** from a spring in the hills 30km to the north. If you arrive from the north, the first ruins you see are the remains of this aqueduct. The aqueduct ends at the ruins of the old **baths** on the right of the entrance road. The road continues past a somewhat better preserved Roman **theatre** and stops outside the brand new **museum** (not yet opened at the time of writing) and **archaeological institute**. Presumably the museum will house the finds unearthed by a German/Tunisian team who have been excavating the site since 1992. The museum is right at the heart of the site and is the best point to get your bearings.

Excavations to date have concentrated on the nearby **forum**, and have revealed that it was built on the foundations of a Numidian temple.

The **quarries**, three in all, are opposite the museum. They are an impressive sight – the amount of work it must have taken to carve out these mighty holes by hand is daunting.

A path leads up to the ruins of a **temple** on top of the easternmost hill. It was originally a Numidian site before being converted first into a temple to Saturn by the Romans and then a Byzantine church.

Other features that are worth checking out are the remains of a **Roman bridge** over the Medjerda just downstream from the modern ford crossing. Judging by the massive pylons, the Romans took the river more seriously than locals do today. Downstream from the bridge are the ruins of a **mill**.

The site is open Tuesday to Sunday from 8 am to 7 pm in summer and from 8.30 am to 5.30 pm in winter. Admission is TD2.100, plus TD1 to take photos. Outside the museum, you will find guides waiting to show you around. They charge TD5 for a tour, which is a good investment.

Organised Tours

There were no organised tours to the site at the time of writing, but this situation can be expected to change once the museum and archaeological institute have opened.

Getting There & Away

There is no public transport to the site, which makes visiting hard work without your own vehicle. The easiest solution is to strike a deal with a taxi driver in either Jendouba or Ghardimao. Reckon on paying about TD25 to get there and back, with a couple of hours at the site.

If your budget doesn't stretch to such luxuries as chartered taxis, another possibility is to catch any bus or louage travelling between Jendouba and Ghardimao and ask to be dropped at the Chemtou turn-off, just east of the village of Oued Melliz. That will leave you with a 3km walk to the site. The only problem is that you will have to ford the

Oued Medjerda. The flow is not much more than a trickle for most of the year, but it can become a mighty torrent after winter rains.

If you do have your own vehicle, the best approach is via the C59 loop road that runs north of the Oued Medjerda. This road begins at the Bulla Regia junction 6km north of Jendouba and emerges just west of Ghardimao. Chemtou is clearly signposted from the Bulla Regia end.

THUBERNICA

The minor Roman site of Thubernica lies about 13km north of Ghardimao in the foothills of the Kroumirie.

It's not worth going to any great effort to get there, but it makes a pleasant diversion if you have your own vehicle. It is best visited in conjunction with Chemtou – the C59 loop road from Bulla Regia to Ghardimao goes past both sites. Thubernica is about 12km west of Chemtou on the C59, signposted at the village of Sidi Ali Belgassem. The ruins are scattered around the wooded hillside above the village. They are not enclosed, and there is no admission charge.

GHARDIMAO

If anything, Ghardimao is even more deadly boring than Jendouba. It really is the end of the line, especially since the suspension of the *Al-Maghreb al-Arabi* (Trans Maghreb Express) train service that once linked Tunisia with Morocco via Algeria.

The only reason to pass through here these days is as part of the circuit that takes in the Roman sites of Chemtou and Thubernica on the C59 loop road, which starts 2km west of town along the road to the Algerian border.

Places to Stay & Eat

There's no reason to stay the night in Ghardimao, but if you do get stuck the choice is at least a straightforward one. The only place in town is the depressing *Hôtel Tibournik* (☎ (08) 660 043), opposite the railway station in the middle of town. Half the letters on the hotel sign have fallen off, giving a fair indication of what's in store inside. It charges TD9 per person for bed and breakfast, or

TD13 with an evening meal as well. The restaurant is surprisingly good given the place's general air of dereliction. The hotel also has the only bar in town.

Getting There & Away

There are five trains a day to Jendouba (25 minutes) and Tunis (3½ hours), departing between 5.30 am and 4.35 pm. Buses and louages leave from next to the railway line, about 200m towards Jendouba from the station. Jendouba is the main destination. There is one direct bus a day to Tunis (3¾ hours, TD6.500).

LE KEF

Pop 30,000 ☎ Area code 08

The ancient fortress town of Le Kef (El-Kef in Arabic, meaning 'The Rock'), 170km south-west of Tunis, is a place not to be missed. Crowned by a mighty kasbah, the town tumbles down a rocky spur reaching out from the southern flank of Jebel Dyr (1084m), a solitary peak that rises dramatically from the surrounding wheat-growing plains.

Much of the appeal of the place lies in the fact that there is no single attraction important enough to warrant an invasion of tour buses – although the narrow streets of the old medina contain more than enough points of interest to keep you occupied for a couple of days.

Foreigners remain something of a rarity, and you can expect a fair amount of polite curiosity. Locals are very proud of their town, and any conversation you strike up will soon require you to give your verdict.

One aspect of life in Le Kef that it's easy to offer an immediate opinion on is the climate. At an altitude of 800m, it's pleasantly cooler here than on the surrounding plains. Nights can be cool, even in summer, and it snows in winter.

History

Le Kef's strategic position means that it has experienced just about everything there is to experience in Tunisian history. People have lived around here since prehistoric times, drawn by the copious springs on this flank of Jebel Dyr. The first town, known as Sicca, was established in about 500 BC by Carthage to protect the western fringe of its newly won empire. It was known for the temple prostitutes who hung out at its sanctuary to the goddess Astarte, whose portfolio included love. After the fall of Carthage, it became a stronghold of the Numidian king, Jugurtha, during his rebellion against Rome. In Roman times, the sanctuary to Astarte became a temple to Venus, and the town became known as Sicca Veneria.

The Vandals came and went, followed by the Byzantines and then by the Arabs – who captured the town in 688 AD and changed its name to Shaqbanaria. Locals proved to be reluctant converts to the cause, rebelling against the central government at every opportunity before becoming autonomous after the Hilalian invasions of the 11th century. The town fell briefly to the Almohads in 1159, but soon returned to its independent ways. By the time the Ottomans arrived in the 16th century, the region had become the private fiefdom of the Beni Cherif tribe.

Le Kef prospered under the Ottomans, who put a lot of effort into rebuilding its fortifications. The town did nicely for itself under the beys, too. Hussein ben Ali, founder of the Husseinite line of beys (1705 to 1957), was born in Le Kef.

Orientation & Information

The kasbah can be seen from just about everywhere in town, which makes finding your bearings easy.

Most things of importance to travellers are to be found within a couple of minutes walk of Place de l'Indépendance, below the kasbah in the centre of town. The exceptions are the bus and louage stations, which are side by side on Ave Mongi Slim, approximately 15 minutes walk downhill from Place de l'Indépendance.

There is no tourist information centre, but the guy at the Association de Sauvegarde de la Medina, on Place de l'Indépendance, can handle most questions. The post office is nearby on Rue Hedi Chaker. There are plenty of banks around the town centre.

Kasbah

After years of neglect, the kasbah was in the middle of a major face-lift at the time of writing. It was being transformed from a crumbling ruin into a slick new tourist complex that will house a museum, shops and a restaurant. No doubt opening hours will change once the work is complete. Until that happens, it's open from Tuesday to Sunday from 7 am to 5 pm and admission is free.

A fort of some sort has existed on the site since about 500 BC, and the complex that stands today represents the end product of 2000 years of constant remodelling by a succession of owners.

It assumed its present form during the 17th century. The name kasbah is misleading. There are actually two kasbahs, linked by a drawbridge, enclosed within the huge surrounding wall. The first, which lies just inside the entrance gate at the end of Rue el-Kasbah, was constructed in Byzantine times and was strengthened by the Turks at the end of the 16th century. The second fort was built by Mohammed Bey in 1679.

There is usually someone hanging around to show you the various points of interest – the Turkish mosque, prison cells, several gates and walls of various vintages.

Museum

The town's small Museum of Art and Popular Traditions is housed in the former Zaouia of Sidi Ali ben Aissa, 400m from the kasbah on Place Ben Aissa. The emphasis is on the culture of the region's Berber nomads and the exhibits include a tent, some crude utensils, jewellery and looms used to weave *kilims* (rugs). The museum is open Tuesday to Sunday from 9 am to 1 pm and 4 to 7 pm in summer, and from 9.30 am to 4.30 pm in winter. Admission is TD1.100, plus an extra TD1 to take photos.

Medina

The principal monuments of the medina are located around Place Boumakhlouf, down

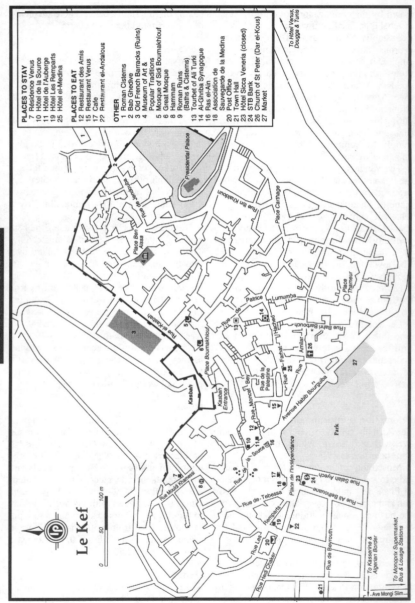

Le Kef

0   50   100 m

PLACES TO STAY
7   Résidence Venus
10 Hôtel de la Source
11 Hôtel de l'Auberge
19 Hôtel Les Remparts
25 Hôtel el-Medina

PLACES TO EAT
12 Restaurant des Amis
15 Restaurant Venus
17 Cafe
22 Restaurant el-Andalous

OTHER
1   Roman Cisterns
2   Bab Ghedive
3   Old French Barracks (Ruins)
4   Museum of Art &
    Popular Traditions
5   Mosque of Sidi Boumakhlouf
6   Great Mosque
8   Hammam
9   Roman Ruins
    (Baths & Cisterns)
13 Tourbet of Ali Turki
14 Al-Ghriba Synagogue
16 Ras el-Ain
18 Association de
    Sauvegarde de la Medina
20 Post Office
21 Town Hall
23 STB Bank
24 Hôtel Sicca Veneria (closed)
26 Church of St Peter (Dar el-Kous)
27 Market

To Hôtel Venus,
Dougga & Tunis

Presidential Palace

Rue Ibn Khaldoun

Place Carthage

Place Ben Aissa

Rue de Jendouba

Rue el-Kasbah

Place Boumakhlouf

Kasbah
Entrance

Kasbah

Rue Moyld Khames

Place Thameur

Patrice Lumumba

Rue de l'Hached
Rue Farhat

Amilar

Rue Barri Barbouch

Rue Mohd Bey
Rue de la Palestine

Rue la Source

Rue de
Fartal

Avenue Habib Bourguiba

Park

Place de l'Indépendance

Rue de-Tebessa

Remparts

Rue Ali Belhaona

Rue Salah Ayech

Rue Lea J

Rue Hed Chaker

Rue de Beyrouth

Ave Mongi Slim

To Monoprix Supermarket,
Bus & Louage Stations

To Kasserine &
Algerian Border

NORTHERN TUNISIA

the steps on the eastern side of the kasbah. The most unusual of them is the plain building that is generally referred to as the **Great Mosque**, although it ceased to operate as a mosque long ago. No-one seems to know what its original function was – or even when it was built. The cruciform design indicates that its role was connected with the church in some way. The current theory is that it was built by the Byzantines in the 6th century, and that it was either a monastery or some sort of social security centre. It was converted into a mosque in the 8th century, after the Arab invasion.

Next to the Great Mosque is the **Mosque of Sidi Boumakhlouf**, built in sharply contrasting style with gleaming white cupolas surrounding an octagonal minaret. The mosque was built at the beginning of the 17th century and named after the town's patron saint, who is buried next to the mosque along with his family.

The **Tourbet of Ali Turki**, just off Place Boumakhlouf on Rue Patrice Lumumba, houses the tomb of the father of Hussein ben Ali, founder of the Husseinite line of beys who ruled Tunisia for 250 years (from 1705 to 1957) until independence.

Al-Ghriba Synagogue This ancient synagogue is on Rue Farhat Hached at the heart of the medina's former Jewish quarter, the Harah. Virtually nothing is known about the history of the Harah. Early 19th century travellers reported finding a thriving Jewish community, and there is a sizeable Jewish cemetery east of the Presidential Palace, with graves dating back to Roman times.

Recent renovation work at the synagogue uncovered a collection of old manuscripts (as yet undated) and an ancient copy of the Torah (Jewish holy book).

Church of St Peter The remains of this 4th century church, also known as the Dar el-Kous, are on Rue Amilcar just south of the synagogue. It contains a remarkably well-preserved apse that was added in Byzantine times.

Ras el-Ain
The town owes its very existence to this spring, located right in the heart of town on Place de l'Indépendance. Its waters once supplied the huge Roman bath complex next door that was discovered during a recent archaeological dig. The site is fenced off, but the ruins are clearly visible on the southern side of Rue de la Source. The spring also supplied the Roman cisterns opposite the baths on the northern side of Rue de la Source.

Places to Stay – budget
The *Hôtel el-Medina* (☎ 220 214), 18 Rue Farhat Hached, is a safe choice, with clean doubles for TD8 but no singles. There are good views from the rooms at the back, which are also much quieter. Hot showers cost 500 mills.

The *Hôtel de la Source* (☎ 224 397), on Rue de la Source, improves once you make it past the mustard yellow lobby. It has basic singles/doubles for TD8/10, and a four bed family room for TD20. The incredibly ornate stucco ceiling of the family room is the owner's pride and joy.

The cheapest rooms in town are just down the street at the *Hôtel de l'Auberge* (☎ 220 036), but the place is an absolute dump. Don't bother with the seedy *Hôtel Les Remparts*, a run-down, one star hotel behind the post office on Rue Les Remparts.

Places to Stay – middle
The best value in town is the excellent *Résidence Venus* (☎ 224 695), nestled beneath the walls of the old kasbah on Rue Mouldi Khamessi. It's a small, family-run pension with comfortable singles/doubles for TD20/32, including breakfast. All rooms come with private bathroom and central heating – important in winter. At the time of writing, the family had just completed construction of a new three star hotel, the *Hôtel Venus*, about 2km east of town on the road to Tunis. It is the only upmarket hotel around following the closure of the *Hôtel Sicca Veneria*.

NORTHERN TUNISIA

Places to Eat

The town is not overflowing with restaurants, but there are a couple of good ones. The *Restaurant el-Andalous*, diagonally opposite the post office on Rue Hedi Chaker, is recommended as a cheap, reliable restaurant. It has a small menu of standard dishes – written out neatly in French for the benefit of tourists – plus daily specials. A bowl of spicy chorba (700 mills) is delicious at any time, but is perfect on a cold day. Nothing on the menu costs more than TD2.700. You'll find similar fare at similar prices at the *Restaurant des Amis*, up the steps next to the Hôtel de l'Auberge. Both places are popular with locals.

The *Restaurant Venus*, on Rue Farhat Hached, is operated by the owners of the Résidence Venus and is the best restaurant in town. It has a set menu for TD8 as well as an extensive à la carte selection.

Self caterers can stock up at the *Monoprix supermarket* next to the bus station.

Getting There & Away

Bus Transport is centred on the bus station, 15 minutes walk downhill from Place de l'Indépendance. SNTRI has eight daily buses to Tunis (3½ hours, TD6.200), travelling via Tebersouk (TD2.680; change here for Dougga).

There are regular local buses to Jendouba, and occasional services to Kairouan (via Makthar), Kasserine and Tabarka.

Louage The louage station is right next to the bus station. There are frequent louages to Tunis (TD6.850). Other destinations include Jendouba, Kasserine and Makthar. There are no louages to Tebersouk.

DOUGGA

The Roman ruins at Dougga, 106km southwest of Tunis, rate as the most spectacular and best preserved in the country. They occupy a commanding position on the edge of the Tebersouk Mountains, overlooking the fertile wheat-growing valley of the Oued Kalled.

History

The Romans built their town on the site of ancient Thugga, a Numidian settlement that was already well established in Carthaginian times. The unusual pre-Roman monument just below the Roman ruins (known as the Libyco-Punic Mausoleum) dates back to the 2nd century BC.

Following the destruction of Carthage, Thugga's fortunes followed the familiar pattern of Roman towns in North Africa: great prosperity in the 2nd to 4th centuries AD, followed by a steady decline during the Byzantine and Vandal occupation.

The site was occupied until the early 1950s when the inhabitants were moved to protect the ruins from further decay. They were relocated to the village of Nouvelle Dougga, below the ancient site, on the Tunis-Le Kef road. Most of the excellent mosaics from the site are on display in the Bardo Museum in Tunis.

Things to See

Dougga is one of Tunisia's most visited sites. You should aim to arrive as early as possible if you want to avoid the worst of the crowds. The site is open daily from 8.30 am to 5.30 pm in winter and from 8 am to 7 pm in summer. Admission is TD2.100, plus an extra TD1 to take photographs.

There's a lot to see at Dougga and, unless you are operating on a very tight budget, it's a good idea to engage the services of a licensed guide. You won't have any trouble finding a guide – there's always a group of them hanging out at the entrance. They speak a range of languages, including English. Rates vary according to the number of people. One person on their own can expect to pay TD8 for a tour.

There's a small cafe near the entrance, but you're better off bringing your own supplies.

Theatre The first monument you come to is the theatre, which is tucked into the hillside above the entrance. Built in 188 AD by one of the city's wealthy residents, Marcus Quadrutus, its 19 tiers could accommodate an audience of 3500.

Dougga

0   50   100 m

Circus

Temple of Minerva

Dolmens

Numidian Wali

Cisterns of Aïn Mizeb

To Tebersouk

Temple of Satum

Sanctuary of Neptune

Church & Cemetery

Ticket Office

Amphitheatre

Theatre

Aqueduct

Cisterns of Aïn el-Hammam

Arch of Alexander Severus

Temple of Mercury

Administration Office

Cafe

Temple of Caelestis

Capitol

Byzantine Tower

Temple of Augustan Piety

Square of the Winds

Temple of Concordia

Forum

Market

Temples of Liberi Patris & Frugiferi

House of the Seasons

Temple of Tellus

Licinian Baths

Temple of Pluto

Dar el-Achab

House of Dionysus & Ulysses

Cyclops Baths

Arch of Septimius Severus

Fountain

Trifolium House

Cisterns of Aïn Doura

To Libyco-Punic Mausoleum

House of the Gorgon

To Nouvelle Dougga

NORTHERN TUNISIA

It has been extensively renovated, and makes a spectacular setting for floodlit performances of classical drama during the Dougga Festival in July and August. Travel agents in Tunis and major resort areas organise special excursions during the festival.

Temple of Saturn Just past the theatre, a track up to the right leads to the Temple of Saturn, which was erected on the site of an earlier temple dedicated to the Carthaginian god Baal Hammon. The temple's surviving columns are visible for miles around on their hill-top location.

Square of the Winds Just south-west of the theatre, beyond the site administration office, an unusual winding street (the Romans were generally great ones for straight lines) leads down to the irregularly shaped Square of the Winds.

On the square's paving is an enormous inscription, not unlike a compass, which lists the names of the 12 winds. It is still possible to make out some of the names, including Africanus (the sirocco). The **Temple of Mercury** borders the square to the north, while the market and capitol lie to the south and west, respectively.

Capitol The capitol is a remarkable monument – one of the finest in Tunisia. It was a gift to the city in 166 AD from two members of the wealthy Marcia family. The inscription carved on the portico records that it was dedicated to the gods Jupiter, Juno and Minerva. Six enormous, fluted columns support the portico, which is some 8m above the ground. The frieze has an unusually unweathered carving depicting the emperor Antonius Pius being carried off in an eagle's claws. Inside the capitol was an enormous statue of Jupiter, fragments of which are now in the Bardo Museum in Tunis.

The Byzantines were responsible for the fortifications that intrude on the forum and capitol here. They filched the stones from various Roman buildings, including the forum, in order to build them.

Temple of Caelestis About 100m out to the west, among the olive trees, is the Temple of Caelestis with its unusual (for North Africa, anyway) semicircular courtyard. It was dedicated to the cult of Juno Caelestis, who was the Roman version of the Carthaginian god Tanit. The sanctuary was built early in the 3rd century and was funded by a resident who was made a flamen (a Roman priest) in 222 AD.

Licinian Baths South of the forum, a track runs through an old residential area to the Licinian Baths, built at the height of the town's prosperity in the 3rd century. The walls of this extensive complex remain largely intact, and the functions of the various rooms are labelled. Opposite the baths is the **House of Dionysus & Ulysses**. It was once a sumptuous residence, and it was here that the mosaic of Ulysses mesmerised by the sirens was found (now in the Bardo Museum in Tunis).

Trifolium House This was the town brothel, named after the clover-leaf shape of the main room.

Cyclops Baths Next door to Trifolium House are the Cyclops Baths, named after the mosaic found here (now also in the Bardo Museum in Tunis). The baths are largely in ruins, except for the horseshoe-shaped row of latrines just inside the entrance. The Romans obviously thought that using the latrine should be a communal experience!

Arch of Septimius Severus Across from the baths is the derelict Arch of Septimius Severus, which was erected in 205 AD when Thugga became a municipality.

Libyco-Punic Mausoleum From the House of Dionysus & Ulysses a track leads southeast down to the Libyco-Punic Mausoleum, which is one of the few surviving examples of pre-Roman architecture in Tunisia. According to an inscription, the mausoleum was erected in memory of a Numidian leader, Ateban, in the 3rd century BC. In 1842, the British consul removed the inscription stone and the whole thing collapsed. The stone was taken to England (where it is now the property of the British Museum) and the tower was rebuilt.

The Libyco-Punic Mausoleum at Dougga is one of the very few surviving examples of Punic architecture in Tunisia.

Getting There & Away

The site is 6km west of the small town of Tebersouk along a good bitumen road. The easiest way to get there is to catch a bus to Tebersouk, and then organise for a taxi to take you to the site and collect you again at a time of your choice. You'll have to bargain hard, but reckon on paying about TD10 for two people. It's possible to stay the night in Tebersouk and make an early start.

If the weather is not too hot, you can walk up to the ruins from the village of Nouvelle Dougga, west of Tebersouk on the main Tunis-Le Kef road. The track is signposted from the Mobil station at the western end of the village. It's a fairly gentle climb, but it still takes about an hour to cover the 3km.

TEBERSOUK

This small town sees its fair share of tourists, but no-one actually seems to stop; they are all in a hurry to get to Dougga and on to the next place. Not a bad plan really, as there is nothing to do here.

Places to Stay & Eat

The sole reason you might want to stay overnight is to give yourself a chance to get to the ruins at Dougga before the crowds arrive. The only place to stay in town is the two star *Hôtel Thugga* (☎ (08) 465 713; fax 465 800), which is popular with the many tour groups who regularly visit the site. It has singles/doubles for TD27/30 with breakfast, as well as the option of half or full board. The hotel is about 2km out of town, down by the main Tunis-Le Kef road.

Getting There & Away

Bus is by far the easiest way to travel. All SNTRI services operating between Tunis and Le Kef call in at Tebersouk, meaning that there are services in each direction roughly every hour. The fare to Le Kef is TD2.680, and the fare to Tunis is TD3.800.

THUBURBO MAJUS

The remains of the Roman city of Thuburbo Majus are about 60km south-west of Tunis, near the small town of El-Fahs.

History

The town was first settled in the 5th century BC in the early days of Carthaginian expansion into the hinterland. It prospered in Roman times when it became an important trading centre for the region's agricultural produce – oil, wheat and wine. Most of the buildings date from the 2nd century AD, when the town was declared a municipality following a visit by the Emperor Hadrian.

Things to See

The site is open Tuesday to Sunday, from 9 am to 1 pm and 4 to 7 pm in summer and from 9.30 am to 4.30 pm in winter. Admission is TD2.100.

Forum The forum was the focal point of the city, where political and economic affairs were discussed. It is colonnaded on three sides; the columns were erected in 182 BC.

Capitol On the north-western side of the forum lies the capitol. It's in the required position of dominance, built on an artificial platform raised above the level of the forum. Built in 168 AD, it is reached by a wide flight of stairs which leads to the entrance with its grooved pillars of pink limestone. The capitol was dedicated to two emperors, Marcus

Arch from the Sanctuary of Baal at Thuburbo Majus. Baal Hammon was the chief deity of the Carthaginians, identified with Saturn by the Romans.

NORTHERN TUNISIA

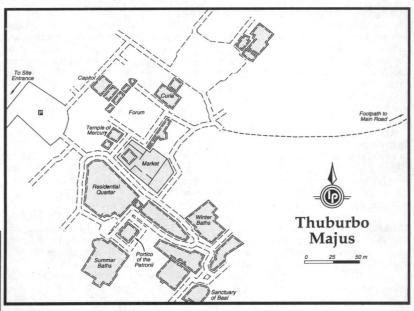

Thuburbo Majus

Aurelius and Commodus, and was under the protection of the ancient trinity of Jupiter, Juno and Minerva. Fragments of a statue of Jupiter were found here (now in the Bardo Museum in Tunis); the size of the pieces indicates that the statue stood some 7.5m high.

Temple of Mercury & Market The Temple of Mercury, on the south-western side of the forum, abuts the market, naturally enough, as Mercury was the god of trade. The stalls of the market can be discerned on three sides of the courtyard below the temple. Directly behind the market is a very un-Roman tangle of residential streets, which were obviously in existence before the Romans arrived.

Portico of the Petronii The Portico of the Petronii is named after the family of Petronius Felix, who paid for the construction of this gymnasium complex in 225 AD. The columns are unusual in that they are built of a yellow-veined grey marble.

Baths Another unusual feature of the town is the two baths within 150m of each other. The Summer Baths are on the lower level, while the Winter Baths are higher up and contain some interesting veined marble columns. The most plausible explanation that has been put forward for having two baths so close to each other is that the well supplying the Winter Baths with water dried up in summer, necessitating the construction of the other baths lower down the hill.

Both these bath complexes were full of mosaics, which are now on display in the Bardo Museum in Tunis.

Getting There & Away

Thuburbo Majus is just west of the Tunis-Kairouan road, 3km north of El-Fahs. There is no public transport to the site, but any bus operating between Tunis and Kairouan can drop you at the turn-off, leaving a short uphill walk to the site entrance and car park. There are buses and louages from El-Fahs to

Zaghouan. There are louages to El-Fahs from the southern louage station in Tunis.

ZAGHOUAN
Pop 10,000 ☎ Area code 02

This sleepy town, tucked in at the foot of the rugged Jebel Zaghouan (1295m) used to supply ancient Carthage with fresh water. In those days a 70km long aqueduct was built to carry the water, and parts of it (in remarkably good condition) can still be seen along the Tunis-Zaghouan road, about 20km from Tunis. The springs are still used today by local residents; there are a couple of gushing outlets on strategic corners in the town.

There are some fairly unremarkable Roman ruins in the form of the rather clumsily renovated Temple des Eaux, a once grand fountain surrounded by 12 niches that used to hold statues depicting each month. It's not worth the walk unless you're stuck at the Hôtel Les Nymphes with nothing else to do.

Places to Stay & Eat

The only hotel in town is the two star *Hôtel Les Nymphes* (☎ (02) 227 094), nestled at the foot of the mountain overlooking the town. Singles/doubles with breakfast are TD24/38 in summer and TD21/34 in winter. Rates are most definitely negotiable during the week, but not at weekends when the hotel fills up with people escaping from Tunis. The hotel doubles as the only bar in town, and also has its own restaurant.

The only other accommodation option is the *Maison des Jeunes*, signposted off the road leading uphill to the Hôtel Les Nymphes in the middle of town. However, it's singularly uninviting, even by the standards of the organisation.

Getting There & Away

Public transport leaves from the middle of town, near the junction with the road leading uphill to the Hôtel Les Nymphes. There are regular louages and buses to both El-Fahs and Tunis. Louages take 40 minutes to cover the 55km to Tunis and cost TD2.650. To El-Fahs, a bus costs 870 mills and a louage is TD1.050 mills. There are also daily buses to Nabeul (TD2.700) and Sousse (TD3.450).

NORTHERN TUNISIA

Central Tunisia

Central Tunisia can be divided into two main regions. The flat eastern one-third, known as the Sahel, occupies the large coastal bulge between the Gulf of Hammamet and the Gulf of Gabès and includes the booming resort towns of the east coast. The port cities of Sousse, in the north, and Sfax, in the south, are the largest in the country after Tunis; Kairouan, the fourth holiest city in Islam, lies on the plains an hour's drive west of Sousse. The western two-thirds, known as the Tell, cover the high plains of the Tunisian Dorsale, which are an extension of Algeria's Tell Atlas mountains.

The Sahel has long been one of Tunisia's most important regions, both economically and politically. Its prosperity was founded on agriculture. The Romans turned the whole area into a vast olive grove, and the wealth generated through the trade in olives and olive oil financed spectacular construction projects such as the enormous amphitheatre at Thysdrus (El-Jem). Huge areas of olive groves remain, notably around Sfax. Market gardening is also big business on the more fertile soils south of Sousse, supplying winter salad vegetables to Northern Europe as well as to local markets.

Tourism has emerged as the mainstay of the modern economy. The beautiful, sandy beaches around Sousse and Monastir are flanked by countless big hotels. A constant flow of charter flights from Northern Europe to the international airport at Monastir keeps them topped up with package tourists. Tourist development becomes steadily more low-key as you head south around the coast.

Mahdia, custom-built capital of the Fatimids (909-69 AD), is a delightful old town that remains relatively unaffected by mass tourism. Few tourists make it to Sfax – which is good news for those who do make the effort because its fascinating old medina is the least touristy around. Sfax is also the departure point for ferries to the Kerkennah

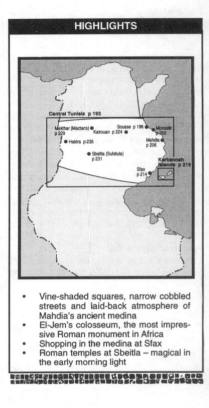

HIGHLIGHTS

Central Tunisia p 193

Makthar (Mactars) p 229
Haïdra p 235
Sbeïtla (Sufetula) p 231
Kairouan p 224
Sousse p 196
Monastir p 203
Mahdia p 206
Kerkennah Islands p 219
Sfax p 214

- Vine-shaded squares, narrow cobbled streets and laid-back atmosphere of Mahdia's ancient medina
- El-Jem's colosseum, the most impressive Roman monument in Africa
- Shopping in the medina at Sfax
- Roman temples at Sbeitla – magical in the early morning light

Islands, which offer an opportunity to escape the crowds altogether.

The Tell was also an important agricultural region in Roman times. The Roman Empire's ever-increasing demand for wheat meant that new land had to be found to grow it, and most of the region's once extensive forest cover disappeared in the process – destroying the ecology of the high plains for ever.

Wheat is still grown in some places, but much of the land is badly degraded and has now reverted to marginal grazing country.

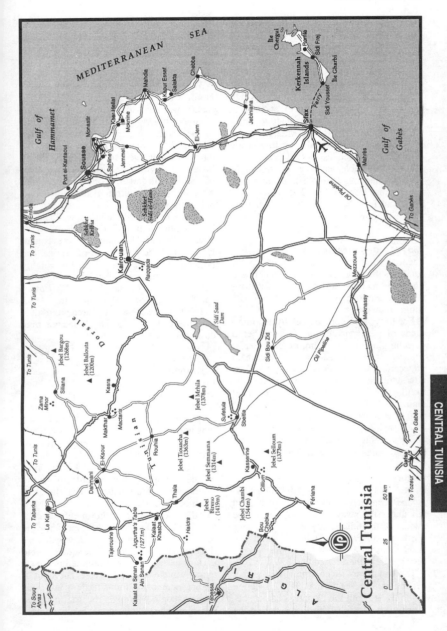

This desolate terrain comes to life briefly in spring, when there are spectacular displays of wild flowers, but for the rest of the year it's difficult to work out how even goats can survive. The summers are impossibly hot, while the winters are cold and bleak.

Roman ruins, in particular the remarkably well preserved temple complex at Sufetula (modern Sbeitla), are the main attraction of the Tell region. The Roman sites at Haidra and Makthar are harder to get to and are consequently much less visited.

Jugurtha's Table, legendary stronghold of the Numidian king Jugurtha during his rebellion against Rome in the 2nd century BC, makes an interesting side trip if you have your own transport.

SOUSSE
Pop 230,000 ☎ Area code 03

The major industrial centre of Sousse is the country's third-largest city and a major port. The huge medina and impressive fortifications are evidence of its long history as a commercial centre.

For today's visitors, especially the thousands of package tourists, the long beach stretching north to the purpose-built tourist enclave of Port el-Kantaoui is the main drawcard. The coastline is virtually one hotel after another, with more under construction to fill any gaps that remain. Each new hotel seems to boast more stars and bigger and better facilities than its neighbours. Fortunately for independent travellers, the medina and town centre offer a good range of budget and mid-range accommodation.

History

Sousse was founded in the 9th century BC as the Phoenician outpost of Hadrumète, and fell under the sway of Carthage from the middle of the 6th century BC. The famous Carthaginian general Hannibal used the town as his base against the Romans in the final stages of the Second Punic War in 202.

The town was saved from the fate that befell Carthage (see the main History section in the Facts about the Country chapter) because it allied itself with Rome during the Third and final Punic War. Hadrumètum, as it became known, prospered under Roman rule. Emperor Diocletian made it the capital of Byzacèe Province, which covered the southern half of Tunisia.

When the Vandals hacked their way across North Africa in the 5th century AD, Hadrumètum was a city of sufficient stature to be renamed Hunericopolis in honour of the son of the Vandal chief. When the Byzantines dislodged the Vandals 100 years later, the name was changed to Justinianopolis in honour of the ruling emperor. True to their obsession with fortification, the Byzantines were the first to surround the city with a defensive wall.

Justinianopolis was levelled, wall and all, by Uqba bin Nafi al-Fihri after it fell to the Arabs in the late 7th century. It was eventually rebuilt as the Arab town of Soussa, and became the main port of the 9th century Aghlabite dynasty based in Kairouan. It was captured by the Normans in the 12th century and then by the Spanish in the 16th.

The town, especially the area around the port, was badly damaged by Allied bombing during WWII.

Orientation

Life in Sousse revolves around its huge central square, Place Farhat Hached. The medina lies to the south-west of the square, the port to the east and Ave Habib Bourguiba runs north from the square to the beach and the hotels of the *zone touristique* (tourist strip). Ave Habib Bourguiba forks when it reaches the coast: Ave Hedi Chaker runs north-west along the beachfront, while Boulevard de la Corniche runs parallel to it, one block inland.

All the city's major thoroughfares converge on Place Farhat Hached, including the main Tunis-Sfax railway line, which runs right through the middle of the square. There is constant talk of rerouteing the line, but it remains in the too-hard basket. The sight of a giant locomotive, lights flashing and bells ringing, edging through the traffic in the square will be around for a while to come.

Information

Tourist Offices There is an unusually efficient branch of the national tourist office (☎ 225 157; fax 224 262) at 1 Ave Habib Bourguiba, on the north side of Place Farhat Hached. It has a notice board with all sorts of useful information, including up to date timetables for buses and trains and details of local attractions. The staff speak English, French and German. They can give you a list of hotels with all the latest prices as well as a map of the city and surrounding area.

Opening hours vary with the season. For most of the year, the office is open Monday to Thursday from 8.30 am to 1 pm and 3 to 5.45 pm, and Friday and Saturday until 1.30 pm. During July and August, it is open Monday to Saturday from 7.30 am to 7pm, and Sunday from 9 am until noon.

The local *syndicat d'initiative* (municipal tourist office; ☎ 220 431) occupies the small, white-domed building on the western side of Place Farhat Hached near the main entrance to the medina.

Money There are plenty of banks along Ave Habib Bourguiba and up by the beach.

Post & Communications The main post office is right in the thick of things, on Ave de la République just off Place Farhat Hached. There are plenty of Taxiphone offices around the city centre, including a convenient one on Rue du Caire, near the Hôtel Claridge.

Bookshops Cité de Livre, at 3 Ave Habib Bourguiba, just north of the tourist office, stocks a small range of airport-type novels in English, and a larger range of similar books in French and German.

International Newspapers Cité de Livre stocks a large selection of international newspapers and magazines. You'll also find international newspapers for sale at the train station.

Medical Services The city's main hospital is the Farhat Hached University Hospital (☎ 221 411), north-west of the medina on Ave Ibn el-Jazzar. The Clinique Les Oliviers (☎ 242 711), near the Hôtel Orient Palace on the tourist strip north of town, is more used to dealing with foreigners and insurance forms etc.

Dangers & Annoyances Petty theft seems to have become a problem on Boujaffar Beach, so don't leave valuables lying around unattended.

Medina

Most of the city's attractions are to be found within the walls of its fine old medina. The walls themselves are an impressive sight, stretching 2.25km at a height of 8m and fortified with a series of solid square turrets. They were built by the Aghlabites in 859 AD on the foundations of the city's original Byzantine wall. The north-eastern section of the wall, adjoining Place Farhat Hached, was destroyed by Allied bombing in 1943.

It's hardly surprising, given the scale of package tourism in the area, that the medina is overrun with tourists, tourist shops and over-enthusiastic shopkeepers. The situation is particularly bad around the two best known monuments, the *ribat* (fortified Islamic monastery) and the Great Mosque, which are both in the north-eastern corner of the medina. You can escape the worst of the crowds by starting early, or by wandering off on your own into the medina's quieter southern streets.

The usual point of entry to the medina is through the missing section of wall off Place Farhat Hached. It leads to Place des Martyrs, a small square on the corner of the Great Mosque.

Great Mosque The Great Mosque is a typically austere Aghlabite affair. It was built, according to a Kufic (early Arabic) inscription in the courtyard, in the year 851 AD by a freed slave called Mudam on the instructions of the Aghlabite ruler Abul Abbas. If

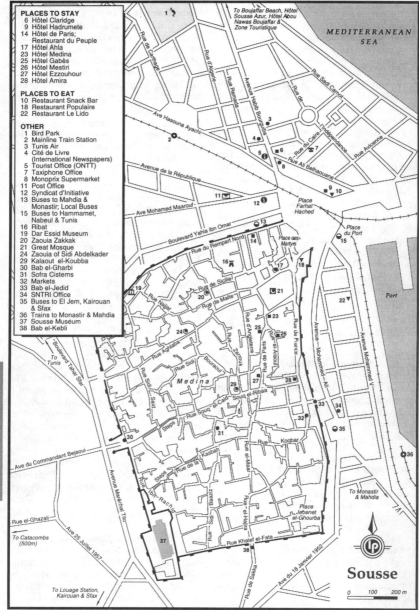

PLACES TO STAY
6 Hôtel Claridge
9 Hôtel Hadrumete
14 Hôtel de Paris;
   Restaurant du Peuple
17 Hôtel Ahla
23 Hôtel Medina
25 Hôtel Gabès
26 Hôtel Mestiri
27 Hôtel Ezzouhour
28 Hôtel Amira

PLACES TO EAT
10 Restaurant Snack Bar
18 Restaurant Populaire
22 Restaurant Le Lido

OTHER
1 Bird Park
2 Mainline Train Station
3 Tunis Air
4 Cité de Livre
   (International Newspapers)
5 Tourist Office (ONTT)
7 Taxiphone Office
8 Monoprix Supermarket
11 Post Office
12 Syndicat d'Initiative
13 Buses to Mahdia &
   Monastir; Local Buses
15 Buses to Hammamet,
   Nabeul & Tunis
16 Ribat
19 Dar Essid Museum
20 Zaouia Zakkak
21 Great Mosque
24 Zaouia of Sidi Abdelkader
29 Kalaout el-Koubba
30 Bab el-Gharbi
31 Sofra Cisterns
32 Markets
33 Bab el-Jedid
34 SNTRI Office
35 Buses to El Jem, Kairouan
   & Sfax
36 Trains to Monastir & Mahdia
37 Sousse Muséum
38 Bab el-Kebli

Sousse

0   100   200 m

CENTRAL TUNISIA

you think it looks more like a fort than a mosque with its turrets and crenellated wall, it's because Mudam adapted an earlier kasbah, built to protect the town in conjunction with the nearby ribat. The mosque has since undergone 17th century modifications and 20th century restoration.

Non-Muslims aren't allowed beyond the courtyard, so you won't get to see inside Mudam's grand barrel-vaulted prayer hall. The courtyard is open from 9 am to 1 pm every day, and entry is TD1.100. Modest dress is essential. If your garb fails to meet the required standard, you can rent a gown (400 mills) from one of the shops opposite the entrance.

Ribat The oldest monument in the medina is the ribat, built in the final years of the 8th century AD. This small square fort lies just to the north-west of the Great Mosque, and is easily identifiable thanks to the round watchtower that stands out above the surrounding rooftops. The tower, known as a *nador*, was added by the Aghlabites in 821 AD. The entrance to the ribat is through a narrow arched doorway flanked by columns. It opens out into a courtyard surrounded by porticos. Steps lead up to the roof, and it's possible to walk right around the ribat.

A narrow winding staircase leads to the top of the watchtower, from where there are excellent views over the city and into the courtyard of the Great Mosque just below.

It's open daily, except Friday, from 8 am to 7 pm in summer and from 8.30 am to 5.30 pm in winter. Admission costs TD2.100. There is an additional charge of TD1 to take photographs.

Zaouia Zakkak Located 150m south-west of the ribat at the junction of Rue Zakkak and Rue de Sicilie, the 17th century Zaouia Zakkak is the medina's leading example of Ottoman architecture. Non-Muslims can do no more than admire the splendid octagonal stone minaret and gleaming white cupola from the street. The complex comprises a mosque, a *medersa* (Qur'anic school) and a mausoleum. The original structure was built in Aghlabite times.

Kalaout el-Koubba The Koubba rates as the most unusual building in the medina. Its origins and purpose remain unclear. It is thought to have been built in the late 11th or

---

Sousse Museum

Sousse's excellent archaeological museum is one place not to be missed. It occupies the old kasbah at the south-western corner of the medina. The kasbah is impressive enough in itself. The formidable set of fortifications that stand today evolved over almost 700 years. The oldest part is the central **Khalef tower**, constructed by the Aghlabites in 859 AD at the same time as the city walls. This imposing square tower superseded the ribat as the city's watchtower. It now serves as a lighthouse, and is closed to the public. The fortress that surrounds the tower was begun in the 11th century, and was steadily expanded over the centuries.

The museum is housed in the rooms around the kasbah's courtyard and contains the best collection of mosaics (see also the boxed text on mosaics under Arts in the Facts about the Country chapter) in the country outside the Bardo Museum in Tunis. The star exhibit is the **Triumph of Bacchus** in Room 3, which depicts the Roman god of wine riding in a chariot at the head of a parade of satyrs. The triumph in question is that of wine over beer. Another mosaic to seek out is the scene of a group of gladiators preparing to dispatch an array of wild beasts in Room 11. Room 6 contains a collection of funerary objects from a Punic grave uncovered when the museum was created.

The museum is open daily, except Friday, from 8 am to noon and 3 to 7 pm in summer, and from 9 am to 12.30 pm and 2 to 6 pm in winter. Admission is TD2.100, plus TD1 to take photos. The entrance is on Ave Maréchal Tito. It's not possible to enter the museum from inside the medina – you'll need to exit the medina by either the southern gate, Bab el-Kebli, or the western gate, Bab el-Gharbi. ■

CENTRAL TUNISIA

early 12th century AD; the dimensions suggest it may have been some sort of palace reception area. The most striking feature is the cupola with its remarkable zigzag ribbing. The fluted interior is just as impressive. The Koubba is now a museum, open daily except Friday. Admission is TD2.

To get there, follow Rue de Paris south from the Great Mosque for about 300m, turn right into Souq el-Ribaa and you'll see the cupola roof from the corner of the second street on the right, Rue Zarrouk.

Catacombs

The catacombs are a huge disappointment, especially if you go along expecting to see some of the features mentioned in the brochure available at the tourist office. According to this, the network of tunnels extends for almost 5.5km and is in better condition than the catacombs of Rome. They contain the tombs of more than 15,000 local Christians, mostly from the 3rd and 4th centuries and are divided into four main areas, three of which have been excavated – the Catacombs of the Good Shepherd, the Catacombs of Hermes and the Catacombs of Severus.

Unfortunately, the only section open to the public is a very small stretch (about 40m) of the Catacombs of the Good Shepherd – and there's very little to see apart from a hasty restoration job. The site is about 1km west of the medina and is signposted off Rue el-Ghazali, but it's hardly worth the effort.

The catacombs are open daily, except Friday, from 8 am to noon and 3 to 7 pm in summer, and from 9 am to noon and 2 to 6 pm in winter. Admission is TD1.100. There's a small display of finds from the catacombs in Room 8 at the museum, which also has a map of the excavated area.

Beach

Sousse's main tourist drawcard is Boujaffar Beach (named after a local marabout or Muslim holy man), which stretches north from the northern end of Ave Habib Bourguiba, a 1km walk from the city centre. It is quite a decent strip of white sand, but it's backed by

a line of high-rise hotels and apartments and can get ridiculously crowded in summer.

You'll find all sorts of water sports equipment for hire along the beach, as well as activities like waterskiing and parasailing.

Bird Park

Bird Park is a rather grand description for this sorry little collection of caged birds. The small park lies one street to the west of the northern end of Ave Habib Bourguiba. The entrance is on the coast road, Boulevard de la Corniche. Admission is 400 mills for adults and 200 mills for children.

Places to Stay – budget

The cheapest hotels are in the medina on the streets south of the Great Mosque. The most presentable of them is the *Hôtel Gabès* (☎ 226 977) at 12 Rue de Paris. It's a friendly place that is more accustomed to westerners than most hotels of this category. It charges TD6 per person with free hot showers. Other possibilities in this price range are the *Hôtel Ezzouhour* (☎ 228 729), further south along the same street at No 48, and the *Hôtel Mestiri* (☎ 222 120), at 19 Rue el-Araoui.

You can do a lot better for a few dollars more. The best budget place is the spotless *Hôtel de Paris* (☎ 220 564), just inside the medina's north wall at 15 Rue du Rempart Nord. It has a few tiny singles for TD8, and larger singles/doubles for TD9/13 – rising to TD11/15 in summer, when you can also negotiate to sleep out on the roof. There are free hot showers and laundry facilities. The place is very popular with travellers.

Another good place is the *Hôtel Ahla* (☎ 220 570), just north of the Great Mosque on Place de la Grand Mosquée. It charges TD12 for clean doubles.

Places to Stay – middle

The *Hôtel Medina* (☎ 225 157) is a popular one star place on the southern side of the Great Mosque, on the corner of Rue de Paris, with rooms opening out onto a small courtyard. Single/double rooms with attached bathroom are TD16/24, including breakfast, in summer, falling to TD11/16 in winter.

You'll need to get in early in summer, because a lot of tour groups use the hotel as an overnight stop.

The *Hôtel Amira* (☎ 226 325), on Rue de France near Bab el-Jedid on the eastern edge of the medina, is a bit more upmarket. In summer, it charges TD20/28 for single/ double rooms with breakfast, dropping to TD13/16.500 in winter. Rooms come with bath or shower, and some have little private courtyards with a table and chairs. You can opt to have your breakfast served outside on the upstairs terrace.

There are a couple of good places around Place Farhat Hached, including the *Hôtel Hadrumete* (☎ 226 291; fax 226 863), on the northern side of the square. It's a former two star hotel that no longer cuts the mustard with the tourist authorities and is now starless, in spite of facilities that include a roof-top swimming pool. It charges TD20/ 30 in summer for singles/doubles with attached bathroom, and TD14/20 in winter, including breakfast.

As its name suggests, the one star *Hôtel Claridge* (☎ 224 759), just off Place Farhat Hached at 10 Ave Habib Bourguiba, was once the poshest place in town. Now it's a good old-style hotel with large rooms for TD18.500/27.500, including breakfast, in summer, or TD12/18 in winter. All rooms come with private bathroom. Breakfast is served in the cafe next door.

Lastly, for those who want to be close to the beach, there is the friendly and comfortable *Hôtel Sousse Azur* (☎ 227 760; fax 228 145) at 5 Rue Amilcar, opposite the town Hôtel Abou Nawas Boujaffar. Bed and breakfast here will set you back TD26/40 in summer, or TD20.500/31 in winter.

Places to Stay – top end

The beachfront north of Sousse has been transformed into a row of big hotels that stretches as far as the eye can see. They are best avoided, unless you have a desperate urge to mingle with thousands of package tourists. Most of them are booked out in summer, so they aren't an option anyway.

The line-up starts immediately north of

Ave Habib Bourguiba with a few relatively low-key three star places. The hotels get steadily bigger and smarter as you head up the beach, culminating in the five star *Hôtel Orient Palace* (☎ 242 888; fax 243 345), 4km north of town. Facilities here include no less than three swimming pools, tennis courts, fitness centre and disco. Singles/ doubles are TD88/126 in summer, dropping to TD40/60 in winter. The four star *Hôtel Abou Nawas Boujaffar* (☎ 226 030; fax 226 595), at the northern end of Ave Habib Bourguiba, is the only posh hotel in town. Rates are the same as for the Hôtel Orient Palace.

Places to Eat

Restaurants The medina is the place to go for a cheap feed. The *Restaurant Populaire*, at the entrance to the medina on Place des Martyrs, is a local favourite. There is no indication in English above the restaurant, but there is a sign pointing to it a few buildings away – just to let you know you're getting warm. It has a good choice of traditional dishes for under TD3. You pay for your meal before sitting down. Another good place is the *Restaurant du Peuple*, right next door to the Hôtel de Paris on Rue du Rempart Nord. It does a big plate of couscous with spicy chicken stew for TD2.600.

The *Restaurant Snack Bar*, facing the port next to the Hôtel Hadrumete, is a rough and ready joint specialising in grilled fish and meat. A plate of fish with chips and salad costs TD3. It also serves alcohol – in fact, the atmosphere is more like a bar than a restaurant. If you want to enjoy your fish in more refined surroundings, try the *Restaurant Le Lido*, opposite the port on Ave Mohammed V. Reckon on at least TD25 for two people, plus wine.

There are dozens of upmarket restaurants along the northern section of Ave Habib Bourguiba and on Boulevard de la Corniche. You'll find menus in three or four languages and waiters who can speak any or all of them. The *Tip Top* (☎ 226 158), 73 Boulevard de la Corniche, is one place that gets consistently good reports. Seafood is a prominent feature on the menu (as it is everywhere in

Sousse), and it's possible to eat very well for about TD20 per person.

The *Hong Kong*, on Boulevard de Rabat (off Boulevard de la Corniche opposite the El-Hana Beach Hôtel), is only for those who can't live without Chinese food. By Tunisian standards, it's expensive, and the food is nothing to get excited about.

Fast Food *King Food*, just off Ave Habib Bourguiba on Rue Amilcar, has burgers from 950 mills, pasta from TD1.800, pizzas from TD2.250 and salads.

Self Catering The *Monoprix supermarket* at the junction of Ave Habib Bourguiba and Rue Ali Belhaouane has a reasonable range of cheese and other dairy products, but not much else in the way of food. It also stocks wine and beer. The main produce *markets* are in the medina, just inside the Bab el-Jedid.

Getting There & Away

Air Sousse is served by Monastir's airport (Habib Bourguiba international, believe it or not), which is 12km south of town on the main road to Monastir. See the Monastir Getting There & Away section later in this chapter for more details of flights to and from the airport. The Tunis Air office (☎ 225 232) is at 5 Ave Habib Bourguiba.

See the following Getting Around section for information on transport to and from the airport.

Bus Sousse has a host of bus stations. The SNTRI office, which is the main departure point for buses south and inland, is on Ave Mohammed Ali, just south of Bab el-Jedid. Services from here include:

Destination	Time	Fare (TD)	Frequency
Douz	8 hours	14.910	1/day
El-Jem	1¼ hours	2.690	5/day
Gabès	5 hours	9.910	5/day
Jerba	7 hours	13.560	2/day
Kairouan	1½ hours	2.560	4/day
Matmata	7 hours	11.280	1/day
Medenine	7 hours	12.690	5/day
Sfax	2½ hours	5.310	5/day
Tataouine	9 hours	14.580	2/day

Northbound intercity services leave from the Place du Port, by the harbour. There are regular buses making the 2½ hour trip to Tunis (TD5.930), three buses to Hammamet (TD3.090) and Nabeul (TD3.590), and a daily connection to Bizerte (TD8.510) at 3 pm. Buses to Monastir (45 minutes, 890 mills) and Mahdia (1½ hours, TD2.200) leave from the local bus station just outside the medina's northern wall on Boulevard Yahia ibn Omar. They leave hourly at 15 minutes past the hour. This is also the place to catch buses to Port el-Kantaoui (450 mills), which leave every half-hour.

Train The trains are the best way to travel. The mainline station is conveniently central, 500m west of Place Farhat Hached on Ave Hasouna Ayachi.

There are eight trains a day north to Tunis (2¼ hours), and five south to Sfax (two hours). Three of these continue south from Sfax to Gabès, and one goes south-west to Gafsa and Metlaoui.

There are also frequent services on the branch line, which runs south around the coast to Monastir and Mahdia. They leave from Bab el-Jedid station, which is by the port near the south-eastern corner of the medina. There are 15 trains a day to Monastir, leaving almost hourly between 6.05 am and 7.10 pm. Seven of these continue to Mahdia. It takes 30 minutes to reach Monastir, and another hour to Mahdia.

Fares (in TD) from Sousse are as follows:

Destination	2nd Class	1st Class	Confort
El-Jem	2.800	3.700	4.900
Gabès	7.950	10.650	11.350
Gafsa	8.400	11.250	12.000
Mahdia	2.000	2.820	–
Monastir	0.780	1.150	–
Sfax	4.400	5.850	6.250
Tunis	4.850	6.500	6.900

Louage Catching a louage from Sousse has become a hassle since the louage station was moved from outside the medina to a new station at the Souq el-Ahad, about 2km south-west of the medina on the road to Kairouan and Sfax. You now have to spend

TD2 on a taxi from the town centre, or 250 mills on a local bus from Boulevard Yahia ibn Omar, just to get started. It's easier to stick to the buses and trains.

For the record, the major destinations include El-Jem (TD2.900), Kairouan (TD3), Mahdia (TD2.500), Monastir (TD1.100), Sfax (TD5.600) and Tunis (TD6.200).

Getting Around

To/From the Airport The airport is 12km south of town, TD6 by taxi from the town centre. You can also get there by train; the airport has its own station (L'Aeroport) on the branch line from Sousse to Monastir. The station is about 200m from the airport terminal. There are trains roughly every hour between 6.05 am and 7.15 pm, leaving from Sousse's Bab el-Jedid station. The trip takes 20 minutes and costs 520 mills.

Bus The city has an extensive local bus network operating from the terminal just north of the medina on Boulevard Yahia ibn Omar. You're unlikely to have much reason to use it, though, because most places of interest in Sousse are within easy walking distance.

Train There is a 'Noddy' train that runs up and down the main road of the tourist strip. It goes from the northern end of Ave Habib Bourguiba to Port el-Kantaoui, 9km to the north. It leaves Ave Habib Bourguiba hourly on the hour, returning on the half-hour. The fare is TD2 one way and TD3 return. It operates from 9 am to 11 pm in summer, and until 6 pm in winter.

Taxi Taxis are the easiest way to get around. There are lots of them, particularly in the main tourist areas, and you'll struggle to run up a fare of more than TD2 around the city.

AROUND SOUSSE
Port el-Kantaoui

Touted as 'the pleasure port of the Mediterranean', Port el-Kantaoui, 9km north of Sousse, represents the luxury end of the package tourism market. The focal point is a large marina complex surrounded by flash hotels, expensive restaurants and souvenir shops full of stuffed camels.

Many people come to Port el-Kantaoui specifically to play golf. The beautifully manicured 27-hole championship layout is spread through the olive groves opposite the marina. If you want to play, you'll need to book a tee-off time with the club (☎ (03) 241 500). The experience will set you back about TD50 by the time you've finished paying for green fees, club hire, balls etc. Hackers are not allowed on the course – you will need to show proof of your handicap before you can play.

The beach is the other big attraction, but it's monopolised by huge five star hotels which emphasise their level of luxury by tacking palace onto their names (eg El-Hana Palace and Hannibal Palace).

The best advice is to steer well clear of Port el-Kantaoui unless your wallet/purse is crying out to be bled dry.

MONASTIR
Pop 40,000 ☎ Area code 03

Situated on a headland some 20km south of Sousse, Monastir must once have been a pleasant little fishing village. Today it has been transformed into a monument to the package tourism industry, its beaches lined with giant hotel complexes and its medina filled with souvenir shops. It has also become a monument to the family of the country's first president, Habib Bourguiba, who was born here and had a lot to do with the transformation.

The Bourguiba name is everywhere, with streets named after just about every member of the household except the cat. Bourguiba lives on at his villa south-west of town. When his time comes, he will take his place in the grand Bourguiba family mausoleum, which dominates the cemetery on the northern edge of town. Place du Gouvernorate, in the middle of town, sports a bronze statue of a chechia-clad Bourguiba as a young man. There's even a mosque named in his honour, although Bourguiba spent his time in power doing battle with the country's religious

Ribat

Monastir's star attraction is its well preserved (some would say over restored) ribat. The original ribat was built in 796 AD as part of a chain of look-out posts along the Tunisian coast. The layout is very similar to that of the ribat in Sousse – a small, square fort surrounded by four round towers, one of which is the watchtower. The ribat is contained within the walls of a kasbah, begun by the Aghlabites in the 9th century and completed in the 11th century. It has been remodelled many times over the centuries, notably in the 17th century when the octagonal corner towers were added.

Virtually every stone of both the ribat and the kasbah appear to have been relaid in the course of modern renovations. It has remained extremely photogenic, however, and has been used as a film set on a number of occasions. Zeffirelli came here to shoot scenes for his *Life of Christ*, and the Monty Python team used it for *Life of Brian*.

There are excellent views of the town and the coastline all the way back to Sousse from the top of the watchtower. The ribat's prayer room houses a

DAMIEN SIMONIS

small Museum of Islamic Art – fairly uninspiring unless your hobbies include Arabic calligraphy.

The ribat complex is open daily from 8 am to 7 pm in summer, and from 8.30 am to 5.30 pm in winter. Admission is TD1.100, plus TD1 to take photographs. ■

---

authorities. The Bourguiba Mosque is at the eastern entrance to the medina on Rue de l'Indépendance.

The well developed zone touristique runs all the way from Monastir to Skanes, 8km to the west. Most independent travellers leave Monastir to the package tourists, although there's enough to see to warrant a day trip from Sousse.

Information

Tourist Offices The ONTT office is at the airport. It's open – in theory – 24 hours a day, seven days a week, which is a remarkable waste of effort since it has nothing to offer except a fairly useless map and a few hotel brochures.

More convenient, but not much more useful, is the syndicat d'initiative (☎ 461 960), opposite the Bourguiba Mosque on Rue de l'Indépendance. It's open Monday to Thursday from 8.30 am to 1 pm and 3 to 5.45 pm; Friday and Saturday until 1.30 pm; and it's closed Sunday.

Money There are two banks in Place du 3 Septembre 1934 in the middle of the medina, and others near the post office on Ave Habib Bourguiba.

Post & Communications The somewhat chaotic main post office is on Ave Habib Bourguiba, just south of the medina. The best bet for international telephone calls is the Taxiphone office at the northern end of the Habib Complex on the Corniche.

Medina

The interior of the medina was demolished after independence, along with the eastern section of the 9th century walls, in an ill-considered rush to modernise the town in keeping with its status as birthplace of the president. The bulk of the town's medieval buildings thus disappeared in one fell swoop. The only significant buildings that remain are the ribat and the Great Mosque, which stand by the coast outside the medina. They used to be part of the medina, but this section

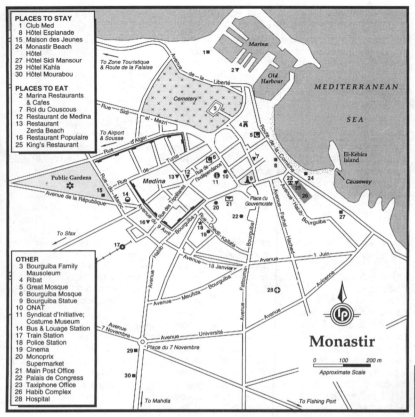

PLACES TO STAY
1 Club Med
8 Hôtel Esplanade
15 Maison des Jeunes
24 Monastir Beach
   Hôtel
27 Hôtel Sidi Mansour
29 Hôtel Kahla
30 Hôtel Mourabou

PLACES TO EAT
2 Marina Restaurants
  & Cafes
7 Roi du Couscous
12 Restaurant de Medina
13 Restaurant
   Zerda Beach
16 Restaurant Populaire
25 King's Restaurant

OTHER
3 Bourguiba Family
  Mausoleum
4 Ribat
5 Great Mosque
6 Bourguiba Mosque
9 Bourguiba Statue
10 ONAT
11 Syndicat d'Initiative;
   Costume Museum
14 Bus & Louage Station
17 Train Station
18 Police Station
19 Cinema
20 Monoprix
   Supermarket
21 Main Post Office
22 Palais de Congress
23 Taxiphone Office
26 Habib Complex
28 Hospital

Monastir

of the wall was knocked down to create Route de la Corniche.

Great Mosque The Great Mosque stands just south of the ribat. It was built in the 9th century during the same burst of activity that produced the medina walls and the beginnings of the kasbah surrounding the ribat. It's a typically severe-looking Aghlabite creation, apart from the graceful horseshoe arches at the northern end. The Roman columns that support these arches were salvaged from the ruins of ancient Ruspina, the minor Roman settlement that once stood on the site of the medina. More columns were used to support the roof of the prayer room, which is closed to non-Muslims.

Costume Museum This museum is next to the syndicat d'initiative in the medina, and is worth a quick look. Opening hours are from 9 am to 1 pm and 4 to 7 pm in summer and from 9 am to noon and 2 to 6 pm in winter; closed Sunday. Entrance is 800 mills.

Beaches
Conveniently enough, the best beach around is the main town beach just across Route de

la Corniche from the ribat and the Great Mosque. The beach curves around a small bay, protected by the marina wall at its northern end and the island of El-Kebira to the south. The island is linked to the mainland by a causeway. The beaches west of town are dominated by the resort hotels of the zone touristique.

Marina

The new marina, a short walk from the ribat at the northern end of the beach, is surrounded by a host of restaurants and cafes, and is a pleasant spot to enjoy a coffee and ponder the fortunes that have been spent on some of the luxury cruisers.

Markets

Saturday is market day in Monastir and the area around the bus station is jam-packed with stalls and people. The markets are surprisingly untouristy, selling mainly bric-a-brac, second-hand clothes and cheap plastic goods.

Places to Stay – budget

Monastir is not a budget destination. The only cheap accommodation is at the *Maison des Jeunes*, which is opposite the bus station – set in the corner of the public gardens off Ave de la République. As usual, it offers all the comforts of an army barracks. A bed costs TD4. Platoons of 10 or more can apply for breakfast at 800 mills per person.

Places to Stay – middle

The situation improves a lot if you're willing to spend a bit more. The choice includes one of the most unusual hotels in the country, the *Monastir Beach Hôtel* (☎ 464 766; fax 463 594). It runs virtually the length of the main town beach, set beneath the massive sidewalk of the Route de la Corniche. It's invisible from the street – the entrance is via a tunnel on the landward side of Route de la Corniche, in front of the Habib Complex. The rooms are basic but clean, and come with toilet and hot shower. Every room has huge French doors opening onto the beach. The views are great, although opening the

doors doesn't do much for your privacy. Single/double rooms, including breakfast, cost TD22/32 in summer, falling to TD12/17 in winter. That's good value for this part of the world.

Another good choice is the one star *Hôtel Yasmine* (☎ 462 511), 2km west of town on the Route de la Falaise – the coast road west of Ave de la Liberté. It's a small family-run pension with singles/doubles, with breakfast, for TD23.500/33, dropping to TD19/26 in winter.

The other two options are out on the road to Mahdia – a fair hike from both the town and the beach. The better of the two is the *Hôtel Kahla* (☎ 464 570) on Place du 7 Novembre. It has very comfortable singles/doubles for TD19/26, including breakfast, in July and August, or TD15/20 for the rest of the year. A further 100m out of town is the drab *Hôtel Mourabou* (☎ 461 585), which charges TD16.500/25, including breakfast, in summer, dropping to TD10/14 in winter. To get to these hotels, follow Ave Habib Bourguiba south from the medina.

Places to Stay – top end

Most of the three and four star resort hotels are located along the beaches of the zone touristique, which runs all the way from Monastir to Skanes, 8km to the west. These places are geared towards charter groups, not casual drop-ins.

There are a few upmarket places by the beach in town. The three star *Hôtel Esplanade* (☎ 460 148; fax 460 050), south of the Great Mosque on Route de la Corniche, has singles/doubles for TD50/70, including breakfast, in summer, or TD28/36 in winter. You'll find very similar rates at the three star *Hôtel Sidi Mansour* (☎ 460 215; fax 460 980), beyond the beach at the southern end of the Corniche.

Club Med (☎ 460 033) is here in a big way, with a complex next to the marina.

Places to Eat

Monastir is not the best place in the country to go looking for a cheap meal. Places like the *Restaurant de Medina*, in the centre of the medina, lead the way in charging over the odds for some ordinary offerings. You're better off walking around the corner to the *Restaurant Zerda Beach*, which has similar stuff for a couple of TD less.

Better still, try the *Roi du Couscous* on the beach side of Place du Gouvernorate. It has couscous of the day for TD2.600 and a good general selection. The small *Restaurant Populaire*, south-west of the medina on Ave du 9 Avril, is a tiny place with a daily selection of three or four local dishes, all for under TD2.500.

There's no shortage of tourist restaurants. The *King's Restaurant* (☎ 463 394), in the Habib Complex, has a good blackboard menu, with dishes for TD11. The best restaurant in town is *Le Grill* (☎ 642 136) out at the marina.

Self caterers can head for the well stocked *Monoprix supermarket*, next to the post office just south of the medina.

Getting There & Away

Air Monastir's airport handles a lot of international traffic, but no domestic flights (although the Tunis Air brochure persists in listing weekly flights to Jerba and Tozeur, which don't exist). Most of the international flights are charters from Europe. Tunis Air also has weekly flights to a dozen European cities, including Amsterdam, Frankfurt, Marseilles, Munich, Paris and Rome. See the main Getting There & Away chapter at the beginning of this book for more information on international flights to and from Monastir.

The Tunis Air office (☎ 468 189) in Monastir is in the Habib Complex on Route de la Corniche.

Bus The bus station is at the western edge of the medina. There are hourly departures for Sousse (890 mills).

Train Train is the most popular way to travel. The station is about 150m south of the bus station on the western edge of the medina. There are at least 15 departures a day to Sousse (30 minutes), stopping at all stations, including L'Aeroport for the airport, from

6.50 am to 8 pm, and eight a day to Mahdia (one hour) between 6.40 am and 7.45 pm. The fares in 2nd/1st class are 780 mills/TD1.150 to Sousse, and TD1.470/2.040 to Mahdia.

There are also two trains a day to Tunis (three hours, TD5.650), leaving at 12.35 and 5.38 pm. These trains do not stop between Monastir and Sousse.

Louage Louages leave from the bus station. Mahdia (TD2) and Sousse (TD1.100) are the main destinations. Demand often exceeds supply, so it is a matter of making a dive for a door handle to secure a place.

Car Rental Avis (☎ 463 031), Europcar (460 300) and Hertz (☎ 461 314) are all based at Monastir's airport.

Getting Around

Monastir town is not big enough to warrant a local bus network, so taxis are the only option apart from walking.

To/From the Airport Monastir's airport is actually at Skanes, 8km west of town on the road to Sousse. The trip costs about TD4.500 by taxi from the town centre. You can also get to the airport on any of the trains between Monastir and Sousse. The trip takes 10 minutes and costs 350 mills in 2nd class. L'Aeroport station is 200m from the airport terminal.

MAHDIA
Pop 30,000 ☎ Area code 03

Mahdia is one of the few towns on this section of coast that has managed to escape being turned into a tourist trap. It's a beautifully relaxed place, set on a small peninsula 60km south-east of Sousse.

History

The town was founded in 916 AD by the first Fatimid caliph, Obeid Allah, known as El-Mahdi, the Saviour of the World. Fresh from his conquest of the Maghreb, Obeid Allah wanted a coastal base from which to plan his attack on his ultimate goal, Cairo. He also

CENTRAL TUNISIA

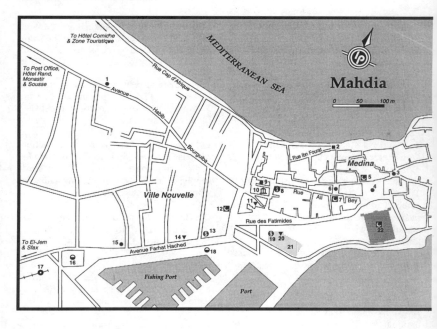

needed an easily defensible position to act as a safe refuge for his minority Shiite followers against the possibility of attack by the Sunni majority (see under Religion in the Facts about the Country chapter). The narrow, rugged peninsula at Mahdia fitted the bill perfectly on both counts.

The original Fatimid city was protected by a massive wall, up to 10m thick, that cut across the peninsula at its narrowest point. Entry was through a single gate, the imposing Skifa el-Kahla. A smaller wall encircled the remainder of the peninsula, creating an enormous kasbah. The area within these walls was a royal compound, reserved for the Mahdi and his entourage. It contained a couple of palaces and their outbuildings, a mosque and a port. The Mahdi's subjects lived outside the walls in the suburb of Zawila.

The Fatimids abandoned Mahdia in 947 for a new palace compound at Sabra Mansouriya, near Kairouan, and the inhabitants

of Zawila moved inside the walls. The population grew rapidly during the 11th century as Mahdia became a place of refuge for people fleeing the Hilalian invasions. In 1052, the Zirid ruler El-Moez retreated briefly to Mahdia.

The present medina was well established by the time the famous historian Ibn Khaldoun visited in the 14th century and reported that Mahdia had become the wealthiest city on the Barbary Coast.

Its fortunes took a dive during the struggle between the Spanish and the Turks for control of the Tunisian coast in the 16th century. It was captured by Spanish troops in 1550, who blew up the walls when they abandoned the city to the Turks four years later – destroying the original Fatimid mosque in the process.

In the 19th century, Mahdia emerged as the major port for the agricultural produce, in particular olive oil, of the Sahel. It was superseded by the ports of Sfax and Sousse

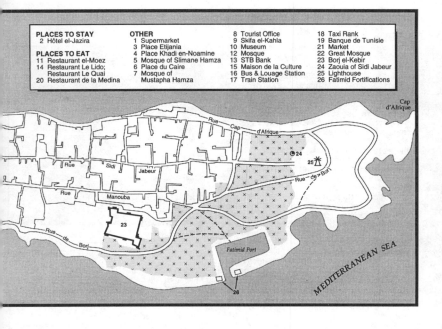

PLACES TO STAY	OTHER	8 Tourist Office	18 Taxi Rank
2 Hôtel el-Jazira	1 Supermarket	9 Skifa el-Kahla	19 Banque de Tunisie
	3 Place Etijania	10 Museum	21 Market
PLACES TO EAT	4 Place Khadi en-Noamine	12 Mosque	22 Great Mosque
11 Restaurant el-Moez	5 Mosque of Slimane Hamza	13 STB Bank	23 Borj el-Kebir
14 Restaurant Le Lido;	6 Place du Caire	15 Maison de la Culture	24 Zaouia of Sidi Jabeur
Restaurant Le Quai	7 Mosque of	16 Bus & Louage Station	25 Lighthouse
20 Restaurant de la Medina	Mustapha Hamza	17 Train Station	26 Fatimid Fortifications

after WWI. Fishing, mainly for sardines, and tourism are now the town's main income earners. There's a growing band of big hotels along the beach to the north-west of town.

The medina remains alive and well as a residential area, but the majority of the town's 30,000 inhabitants live in the modern suburbs that spread west from Skifa el-Kahla.

Information

There is a small tourist office (☎ 681 098) just inside the medina, through the Skifa el-Kahla. As usual, there's not much information available apart from an ancient brochure with a useless map. If pushed, staff can come up with some bus times.

All other services are to be found in the *ville nouvelle* (new town). The post office is about 650m west of the medina along Ave Habib Bourguiba, while most of the banks are on the southern side of the peninsula. They include a branch of the Banque de Tunisie by the markets, and the STB on Ave Farhat Hached.

Ave Farhat Hached runs west alongside the port to the bus and louage stations and the train station.

Medina

Mahdia's main attraction is its fascinating old medina, which stretches out along the peninsula from the Skifa el-Kahla to the lighthouse on Cap d'Afrique 1.5km to the east. A good way to see the major points of interest in the medina is on a walking tour – see the boxed text on the following page.

Beaches

Mahdia's main beach is north-west of town and is monopolised by the big hotels of the zone touristique; you can use the beach even if you're not staying at one of the hotels. Local kids make do with swimming off the rocks along Rue Cap d'Afrique.

Medina Walking Tour

This walking tour should take about two hours, depending on how much time you spend exploring – or sitting at cafes.

The tour starts at the **Skifa el-Kahla**, the massive fortified gate which is all that survives of the original Fatimid city. 'Gate' is a bit of a misnomer; entry is through a narrow, vaulted passageway, almost 50m long, that was once protected by a series of gates – one of them a suitably oversized iron portcullis. Once inside the medina, there are steps leading up to the top of the gate, from where there are great views over the town.

The Skifa el-Kahla opens onto the medina's narrow, cobbled main street, **Rue Ali Bey**. It was once the souq, and is now occupied by a growing band of souvenir shops. Follow Rue Ali Bey east to **Place du Caire**, which is a delightful small square, complete with shady trees, vines and cafes. The ornate arched doorway and octagonal minaret on the southern side of the square belong to the **Mosque of Mustapha Hamza**, built in 1772 when the square was the centre of the town's wealthy Turkish quarter.

DAVID WILLETT

The Skifa el-Kahla dominates the medina entrance.

Continuing east, Rue Ali Bey emerges after a short distance at **Place Khadi en-Noamine**, on the northern side of the **Great Mosque**. The mosque that stands today is a modern replica of the original Fatimid mosque, built by Obeid Allah in 921 AD and destroyed when retreating Spanish troops blew up the city walls in 1554. The replica was completed in 1965, and involved razing another mosque that had been built in the interim. The houses surrounding the mosque were pulled down at the same time, which is why the modern version stands in unusual isolation. Non-Muslims are allowed into the courtyard outside prayer times.

The small minaret at the north-western side of Place Khadi en-Noamine marks the **Mosque of Slimane Hamza**, built by another member of the well-to-do Hamza family. A road, which provides vehicle access to the inner reaches of the medina, leads north-east from here to tiny Place Etijania and then forks to form the two main residential streets, Rue Sidi Jabeur and Rue Manouba. They run parallel, about 50m apart, and eventually emerge at the large cemetery on the eastern side of the medina. Both streets are lined with dozens of short, zigzagging cul-de-sacs, each of which represents a small neighbourhood of five or six houses.

Take the southern fork, Rue Manouba, and follow it east for about 500m until you come to a side street leading up to the **Borj el-Kebir**, a large fortress standing on the highest point of the peninsula. It was built in the 16th century on the ruins of an earlier Fatimid structure. There is not much to see inside, but the views from the ramparts are worth the TD1 entry fee. It's open every day, except Friday, from 9 am to noon and 2 to 6 pm in summer, and from 9.30 am to 4.30 pm in winter.

From the fort, walk down to the coast road, Rue de Borj, and follow it as it winds through the cemetery towards the lighthouse. On the right are the remains of the **Fatimid port**, now largely silted up. The crumbling pillars flanking the entrance are all that remain of the harbour defences.

Keep following Rue de Borj as it loops around the lighthouse. The small, white-domed building west of the lighthouse is the **Zaouia of Sidi Jabeur**. Head back to town along Rue Cap d'Afrique, which hugs the coastline all the way. The water along here is amazingly clear and blue. ■

Port

Film buffs will doubtless be interested to learn that Mahdia's otherwise uninspiring modern port was used as the setting for the German invasion of Benghazi in the film *The English Patient*.

Places to Stay – budget

Budget accommodation is in very short supply. The small, family-run *Hôtel el-Jazira* (☎ 681 629) at 36 Rue Ibn Fourat is the only hotel inside the medina. It's on the seafront on the northern side of the peninsula. To get

DAMIEN SIMONIS

FRANCES LINZEE GORDON

Top: Bizerte's old quarter around the harbour is just one reason for visiting this refreshingly untouristy north coastal town.
Bottom: Just one more ... *Makhroud*, a date-filled semolina cake soaked in honey, is one of Kairouan's many delicious sweet specialities.

HUGH FINLAY

A visit to the Ksour district in the south should be on every traveller's agenda. Ksour, like this one at Medenine, were originally built by the Berbers to store grain, but after the Arab invasion of the 7th century, they were expanded and turned into fortresses. A night in one of the ksour hotels is an unforgettable experience.

there, turn left as soon as you enter the medina through the Skifa el-Kahla and aim for the seafront. Rue Ibn Fourat is a small alleyway on the right just before you reach the sea. Some of the rooms look out over the water. It's good value at TD10/16 for singles/doubles in summer and TD8/12 in winter, including breakfast and hot showers. There's a table and chairs on the roof, where you can sit and enjoy the view.

The *Hôtel Rand* (☎ 680 525) is a reasonable place, but it's a long way from anything else of interest at 20 Ave Taieb Mehiri, in the middle of the new town. For the grimly determined, follow Ave Habib Bourguiba (the Sousse road) away from the medina and fork left at the post office, then turn left after another 500m at the first major intersection; the hotel is on the right. It charges TD13.500/24 in summer and TD9/16 in winter, including breakfast.

The friendly *Hôtel Corniche* (☎ 694 201) is a stone's throw from the beach on Route de la Corniche, about 2km north-west of town. It charges TD15/24 in summer and TD10.500/15 in winter, including breakfast and hot shower. Route de la Corniche is the north-west extension of Rue Cap d'Afrique.

Places to Stay – middle & top end
Most of Mahdia's hotels are spread along the beaches to the north-west of town and are aimed at the package tourist market. As usual, they are packed in summer and dead in winter. All prices in this section include breakfast. The line-up starts with relatively low-key places like the one star *Hôtel Sables d'Or* (☎ 681 137; fax 681 431), which charges TD29/44 for singles/doubles in summer and TD21.500/34 in winter. It has nothing to offer, apart from the beach.

The three star *Hôtel el-Mehdi* (☎ 681 300; fax 680 309) boasts facilities that include indoor and outdoor swimming pools, tennis courts and a disco. Rates range from a steep TD52/80 in summer to a budget TD18/30 in winter.

Mahdia's top hotel is the brand new five star *Mahdia Palace* (☎ 696 339; fax 696

337), which charges TD115/170 in summer and TD70/100 in winter.

Places to Eat
Beware of thin chefs, or so the saying goes. Well, there's nothing to be afraid of at the excellent *Restaurant el-Moez*, tucked away on a small side street between the Skifa el-Kahla and the markets. It's run by a big man who obviously enjoys his food. He specialises in traditional dishes like mloukhia (lamb in thick sauce made from ground herbs) and kammounia (a spicy stew made with lots of cumin). The choice is limited to three or four daily specials, one of which will be fish. Most meals are priced under TD2. Lunch is the best time to visit as the choice of dishes shrinks by the evening.

Another good place is the *Restaurant de la Medina*, situated at the rear of the market building by the port. It's right next to the fish markets, and fish features prominently on the menu. A plate of rouget (red mullet), chips and salad costs TD3.500.

Most tourists head for the restaurants facing the port along Ave Farhat Hached, where you can enjoy a glass of wine with your meal. The *Restaurant Le Lido* and the nearby *Restaurant Le Quai* both offer three course menus for TD9, not including drinks.

The produce section of the *market* building is the best bet for self caterers. The only *supermarket* is about 400m west of the Skifa el-Kahla on Ave Habib Bourguiba.

Getting There & Away
Mahdia's bus, train and louage stations are conveniently located within 100m of each other, just west of the port on Ave Farhat Hached.

Bus There are hourly departures to Sousse (1½ hours, TD2.200) and five a day to El-Jem (one hour, TD1.750). There are no direct services to Sfax or Tunis; change at El-Jem for Sfax and at Sousse for Tunis.

Train Train is the recommended way to travel. There are at least eight trains a day to Monastir (one hour). They depart between

CENTRAL TUNISIA

5.50 am and 6.30 pm. Seven of these continue to Sousse. Fares in 2nd/1st class to Monastir are TD1.470/2.040 and to Sousse TD2/2.820.

There is also a daily service to Tunis (four hours) at 4.35 pm. The fare is TD6.700 in 2nd class or TD8.900 in 1st class.

Louage Sousse (TD2.500) is the most popular destination. Other regular services are to El-Jem (TD2.700), Monastir (TD2), Sfax (TD4.150) and Tunis (TD7.600).

EL-JEM
Pop 10,000 ☎ Area code 03

There can be few more remarkable sights in Tunisia than the first glimpse of El-Jem, the ancient colosseum dwarfing the matchbox buildings of the modern town. Built on a low plateau halfway between Sousse and Sfax, the colosseum can be seen from miles around across the flat surrounding plains. It rates as one of the most impressive Roman monuments in Africa.

The colosseum was once the crowning glory of ancient Thysdrus, a thriving market town that grew up at the junction of the Sahel's main trade routes during the 1st century AD. They must have been valuable trade routes, because the site didn't have much else going for it. In the absence of suitable local building material, stone for construction had to be hauled all the way from the quarries at Sullectum (modern Salakta), 30km away on the coast, and water had to be brought 15km by underground aqueduct from the hills north-west of town.

The town continued to flourish in spite of these logistical problems, and reached the peak of its prosperity in the 2nd and 3rd centuries AD. By this time it had become the hub of a network of Roman roads that distributed goods between the interior and the cities on the coast.

In contrast to the drab buildings of modern El-Jem, Thysdrus was a town of sumptuous villas. The mosaics uncovered here include some of the finest in Tunisia – they're now distributed between the Bardo Museum in Tunis and the town's own museum.

El-Jem lies almost exactly halfway between Sousse and Sfax on the main road between the two towns.

Orientation & Information

It's hard to get lost in a place as small as El-Jem, especially when there's a landmark as big as the colosseum standing right in the middle of town.

The main street is Ave Habib Bourguiba, which runs from the colosseum to the train station on the southern edge of town. The post office and only bank are south-west of here on Ave Fahdel ben Achour, signposted as the road to Sfax. There is a left luggage office at the train station.

Museum

El-Jem's museum, about 1km south of the amphitheatre on the road to Sfax, houses some beautiful mosaics. All were found in the site behind the museum building, which was an area of particularly luxurious villas. Some of the mosaics have been left *in situ* while the best have been moved into the museum. Particularly impressive is the huge and intricate depiction of the nine Muses.

Admission is included in the price of the ticket to the colosseum. Opening times are the same as for the colosseum.

Other Sites

The colosseum was not the first amphitheatre to be built at Thysdrus. Opposite the museum are the ruins of an earlier **amphitheatre**, dug into a low hill just east of the railway line. The site is not enclosed and is worth a look if you've got time to burn. There is also a second area of **Roman villas** to the north of the colosseum, signposted off Ave Farhat Hached, the road to Sousse.

Other sites are still to be uncovered. Aerial photographs have indicated the remains of another, even larger amphitheatre, barely visible from the ground.

Special Events

In late July and early August, the colosseum is transformed into a splendid floodlit venue for the El-Jem International Symphonic

Colosseum

El-Jem's well preserved colosseum is almost as big as its counterpart in Rome. It rises spectacularly from the flat surrounding plains and completely dominates the town.

Its vital statistics are impressive – 138m long by 114m wide, with three tiers of seating 30m high. Its seating capacity has been estimated at 30,000, which is considerably more than the population of the town itself – indicating that people came from far and wide to watch events here.

The structure is believed to have been built between 230 and 238 AD, and is generally attributed to the African pro-consul Gordian, a local landowner and patron. In 238 AD, at the age of 80, Gordian was declared emperor of Rome here during an ill-fated rebellion against oppressive taxes imposed by Emperor Maximus. Gordian reportedly committed suicide in the colosseum when it became obvious that the rebellion was doomed.

The colosseum has been used as a defensive position many times in its history. Byzantine troops regrouped here after their defeat at Sbeitla in 647 AD, and the Berber princess Al-Kahina was besieged here by Arab forces 50 years later (see the boxed text 'A Berber Boadicea' under History in the Facts about the Country chapter).

It suffered badly in the 17th century when the troops of Mohammed Bey blasted a hole in the western wall to flush out local tribesmen who had rebelled against taxation demands. The breach was further widened during another rebellion in 1850. The emphasis is now on preservation, and the site has been added to the UN's World Heritage List.

You can still climb up to the top tiers of seating and gaze down on the arena; it's also possible to explore the two long underground passageways that were used to hold the animals, gladiators and other unfortunates before they were thrust into the arena to provide entertainment for the masses.

The colosseum is open daily from 7 am to 7 pm in summer and from 8 am to 5 pm in winter. Admission is TD4.200, plus TD1 to take photographs. ■

Music Festival. You'll find a program of events at the tourist office in Sousse.

Places to Stay & Eat

Although it's easy to visit El-Jem on a day trip, it's well worth considering staying the night so that you can get up early and visit the colosseum before the tour groups arrive.

The only accommodation is at the one star *Hôtel Julius* (☎ 690 044), next to the train station. Rooms, arranged around a pleasant courtyard, cost TD8.500/15 for singles/doubles. The rooms fill up fast in summer, so it's a good idea to book first if you're planning on arriving late in the day. The hotel also has the only bar in town, and a *restaurant* with a set menu for TD5, or TD4 for hotel guests.

Getting There & Away

El-Jem lies on the main road and rail route between Sousse and Sfax and is very well served for public transport. Everything happens at the train station, 500m south of the colosseum at the end of the main street, Ave Habib Bourguiba.

Bus Local buses leave from outside the train station. There are five buses a day to Mahdia (one hour, TD1.750), Sousse (1¼ hours, TD2.690) and Sfax (1¼ hours, TD2.720). A lot of SNTRI buses pass through town on their way north and south, but they are often already full and you can't rely on getting a seat. These buses stop at the train station as well as at the SNTRI office on the road to Sfax, on the right just before the museum. The train is a better bet.

Train Train is by far the best way to travel, and it's a good idea to organise your visit around the train timetables. Don't mock the precision of the times given in this entry – Tunisian trains usually run on time.

Heading south, there are trains to Sfax (one hour, TD3.700 in 1st class) at midnight and 10.07 am, and at 3.58, 5.02 and 8.26 pm. The morning train continues to Gabès (4¼ hours), while the midnight train goes to Gafsa and Metlaoui. Heading north, there are departures to Sousse (one hour, TD3.700 in 1st class) and Tunis (three hours, TD8.900 in 1st class) at 2.54 and 7 am, and at 1.18, 2.23 and 7.08 pm.

Louage Louages leave from opposite the train station. There are frequent departures to Mahdia (TD2.700) and occasional services to Sousse and Sfax (both TD3.250).

SFAX
Pop 275,000   ☎ Area code 04
Sfax, 266km south of Tunis, is the second largest city in the country. This rather unglamorous place is largely bypassed by Tunisia's otherwise all-pervasive package tourism industry. Sfaxiens are famous for their business acumen, a fact that makes them the butt of jokes told by Tunisians from other areas, jealous of this reputation. You'll probably be mocked, too, if you announce that you're going to Sfax.

All the more reason for going there, reckoned writer Paul Theroux, who records his impressions of Sfax in *The Pillars of Hercules*. Like others before him, Theroux came away pleasantly surprised by the laid-back city he found. The only attraction is the unspoiled old medina, used as a location in the film *The English Patient*, but the general absence of hype makes it a pleasant place to spend a couple of days. Sfax is also the departure point for ferries to the nearby Kerkennah Islands.

History
The coast around Sfax has been settled since Phoenician times, but none of the towns amounted to very much until Sfax was established by the Arabs at the beginning of the 8th century AD. It is thought to occupy the site of the minor Roman town of Taparura, no trace of which remains. The closest Roman town of any consequence was Thaenae, the meagre remains of which lie on the coast 12km to the south-west.

The city's ramparts were built by the Aghlabites in the middle of 9th century AD. They proved effective enough for the city to hold out against the Hilalian invasions in the 11th century, and Sfax survived the invasions as the major city in the south of Tunisia. In the 14th century, it controlled a stretch of coastline reaching as far as Tripoli, in Libya. It remained largely independent of the central government in Tunis until the beginning of the 17th century.

The modern city was shaped by the French in the 1920s. They built their customary ville nouvelle on reclaimed land to the south of the medina, and developed the port to handle the export of phosphates from the mines at Gafsa.

Two of the heroes of the country's independence movement, trade union leaders Hedi Chaker and Farhat Hached, were from Sfax. Their names feature on streets signs throughout the country.

Orientation
While the modern city of Sfax fans out over a wide area, the city centre is compact and

easy to negotiate. Most services of importance to travellers are located around the streets of the ville nouvelle, which is laid out in the traditional French grid pattern between the medina and the port. The main street is Ave Habib Bourguiba (just for a change), which runs east through the town centre from the train station.

Information
Tourist Office The tourist office (☎ 211 040) is out by the port on Ave Mohammed Hedi Khefecha. There is more information here than is first apparent, including bus, train and ferry timetables, all kept in the folder on the desk. It's open Monday to Thursday from 9 am to 1 pm and 3 to 5.30 pm, and Friday and Saturday until 1.30 pm; it's closed Sunday.

Consulates France, Italy and Libya have consulates in Sfax, all in the new town.

The French Consulate (☎ 220 788), at the northern end of Rue Alexandre Dumas, is open for visa business Monday to Friday between 8.30 and 11.30 am. The Italian Consulate (☎ 298 973) is on the 3rd floor of the new office building on the corner of Rue Salem Harzallah and Rue Habib Thameur. It's open Monday to Friday from 9 am until noon.

The Libyan Consulate (☎ 223 332), 35 Rue Alexandre Dumas, is open Monday to Friday from 9 am to 2 pm. There's no sign in English – look for the eagle motif.

Money There are plenty of banks for changing money along Ave Habib Bourguiba and Ave Hedi Chaker. The post office has a separate foreign exchange counter, but it won't change travellers cheques.

Post & Communications The post office is the enormous edifice on Ave Habib Bourguiba which occupies the entire block just west of the train station. It is open Monday to Saturday from 8 am to 6 pm and Sunday from 9 to 11 am.

International Newspapers Foreign newspapers are sold at the kiosk on the northern side of Place Hedi Chaker.

Hammam The Hammam Sultan is near the Dar Jellouli Museum on Rue de la Driba in the heart of the medina. It costs TD1 and is open for women from noon to 4 pm, and for men from 4 pm to midnight.

Medina
Most of the city's attractions are found within the massive stone walls of the medina. These ramparts were built by the Aghlabites in the 9th century, replacing an earlier 8th century earthen wall. They have been remodelled many times since, but they retain some of the original features. They include the delightful arched Bab Jebli, the medina's northern gate. The main access to the medina from the ville nouvelle is through the 14th century Bab Diwan in the middle of the southern wall. The main street through the medina is Rue Mongi Slim, which runs between Bab Diwan and Bab Jebli. Like all the streets, it's little more than a footpath and is incredibly narrow.

Apart from the small cluster of souvenir shops around Bab Diwan, the medina is remarkably untouched by tourism and remains a good example of a working medina. However, the population has declined dramatically over the last decade because residents can't match the rents that merchants are prepared to pay.

Dar Jellouli Museum of Popular Arts & Traditions This museum occupies a fine 17th century mansion, Dar Jellouli, in the heart of the medina at the junction of Rue de la Driba and Rue Sidi Ali Ennouri. It's signposted off Rue Mongi Slim, just south of the Hôtel Medina. The house alone is worth a visit, with its beautiful carved wood and stuccowork. The exhibits portray the everyday life of the bourgeoisie in the times of the beys, and include costumes, jewellery and household implements. The museum is open daily, except Monday, from 9.30 am to 4.30 pm. Admission is TD1.100, plus TD1 to take photos.

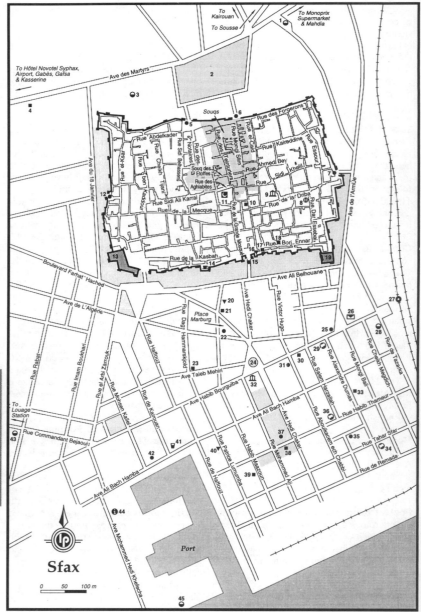

To Kairouan
To Sousse

To Monoprix
Supermarket
& Mahdia

1

To Hôtel Novotel Syphax,
Airport, Gabès, Gafsa
& Kasserine

Ave des Martyrs

2

3

4

Souqs

6

Rue des Forgerons

5

Rue el-Caïd

Rue Mong Slim

Rue Abdelkader

Rue Cheikh Tijani

Rue Ben Kacbour

Rue Sidi Behassen

Rue des
Notaires

Rue des
Teinturiers

Rue Kaireddine

Rue Essouq

Ave du 18 Janvier

Rue el-Kasr

Souq des
El Etoffes

Rue des
Aghlabites

Ahmed Bey

Rue

Sidi Khelil

Ave de l'Armée

12

Rue Sidi Ali Karral

Rue de la Mecque

11

10

9

Rue de la Driba

8

Rue Darf Essebaa

Rue de la Grande Mosquée

17

18
Rue Borj Ennar

16

15

13

Rue de la Kasbah

14

19

Boulevard Farhat Hached

Ave Ali Belhouane

Ave de L'Algérie

20

21

Place
Marburg

Ave Hedi Chaker

Rue Victor Hugo

27

26

Rue Dag Hammarskjold

22

25

28

Rue Hafftouz

23

Ave Taieb Mehiri

24

31

30

29

32

Rue Salem Harzallah

Rue Alexandre Dumas

Rue Mong Bali

Rue Cheikh Meghdich

Rue de Tazarka

Rue Habib Thameur

33

Rue Rabat

Rue Imam Bouchari

Rue el Arbi Zarrouk

Rue Mohsen Kallel

Rue de Kairouan

Ave Habib Bourguiba

36

Ave Ali Bach Hamba

Rue Abdoulncan edt Chabbi

To
Louage
Station

Rue Commandant Bejaoui

43

41

42

40

Rue Patrice Lumumba

Rue Habib Mazhoun

Ave Hedi Chaker

Ave Mohammed Ali

37

38

35

Rue Tahar Star

34

39

Rue de Remada

Ave Ali Bach Hamba

Ave Mohammed Hedi Khefacha

44

Sfax

0   50   100 m

Port

45

PLACES TO STAY
4   Hôtel el-Andalous
10 Hôtel Medina
17 Hôtel Maghreb
18 Hôtel el-Habib;
    Hôtel Essaada
21 Hôtel Thyna
23 Hôtel La Colisée
30 Hôtel Abou Nawas Sfax Centre
33 Hôtel Alexander;
    Hôtel de la Paix
38 Hôtel Les Oliviers
39 Hôtel Mondial

PLACES TO EAT
14 Café Diwan
16 Restaurant Tunisienne
20 Restaurant Le Corail
40 Restaurant Chez Nous

OTHER
1   Northern Bus Station
2   Market
3   Local Buses
5   Bab Jedid
6   Bab Jebli
7   Bab el-Chergui

8   Hammam
9   Dar Jellouli Museum
11 Great Mosque
12 Bab el-Gharbi
13 Kasbah
15 Bab Diwan
19 Borj Ennar
22 International Newspapers
24 Place Hedi Chaker
25 Tunis Air
26 Post Office
27 Train Station
28 SNTRI Buses; Restaurant
    Colombia
29 French Consulate
31 Monoprix Supermarket
32 Town Hall & Archaeological
    Museum
34 Libyan Consulate
35 ONAT
36 Italian Consulate
37 Children's Playground
41 Bar
42 Fish Market
43 Southern Bus Station
44 Tourist Office
45 Ferries to Kerkennah

Great Mosque The Great Mosque in Sfax was founded by the Aghlabites in the middle of the 9th century AD, around the same time that the medina walls were constructed. The mosque is closed to non-Muslims, which means that many tourists won't get to see much more than a small section of the ornate northern wall, visible along Rue des Aghlabites. The minaret, a smaller replica of the three tiered square minaret at Kairouan, was added by the Fatimids in 988 AD.

Souqs The most interesting part of the medina is the souq district stretching north from the Great Mosque, particularly the covered area around Souq des Etoffes. This is the part of the medina that was used as the setting for the Cairo markets in the film *The English Patient*.

Kasbah The kasbah is at the south-western corner of the medina. It began life as a lookout tower, built by the Aghlabites as part of the ramparts, and was steadily expanded into a kasbah over the centuries. It now houses a museum of Islamic architecture, but the main reason to pay the TD1.100 admission fee is to gain access to the views from the roof and surrounding walls. The kasbah is open daily, except Monday, from 9.30 am to 4.30 pm.

Borj Ennar This fort was added in the 17th century to protect the south-eastern corner of the medina. It is now the headquarters of the Association de Sauvegarde de la Medina, the group responsible for preserving the medina. It has a good map of the medina, showing all 69 mosques, as well as the souqs and other points of historical interest.

Ville Nouvelle
The places of interest in the ville nouvelle are few and far between. The focal point is the very formal main square, **Place Hedi Chaker**, at the junction of Ave Hedi Chaker and Ave Habib Bourguiba.

The grand colonial building with the dome and clock tower on the southern side of the square is the **town hall**. It houses the city's small **archaeological museum**, open daily, except Monday, from 9.30 am to 4.30 pm. Admission is TD1.100.

Parents travelling with children can check out the **children's playground** in the park north of the Hôtel Les Oliviers, between Ave Hedi Chaker and Rue Mohammed Ali.

Places to Stay – budget

As is the case in all the major cities, the cheapest places are to be found in the medina. You'd need to be desperate to consider staying at any of the rock-bottom places on Rue Borj Ennar, just inside the medina walls east of the Bab Diwan. Places like the *Hôtel Maghreb*, the *El-Habib* and the *Essaada* are worth noting only as places to avoid.

The *Hôtel Medina* (☎ 220 354), on Rue Mongi Slim, is the only hotel in the medina worth considering. It's a spotless place, with rooms for TD4 per person.

Most travellers prefer to head for the relative comforts of the ville nouvelle. The best value in town is the excellent *Hôtel Alexander* (☎ 221 911), an old-style one star place on Rue Alexandre Dumas. It has large, comfortable singles/doubles with bathroom for a bargain TD15/20, including breakfast. The baths are enormous, and there's plenty of hot water. The only catch here is that on Saturday night a folk band plays in the restaurant. The action doesn't quieten down until 2 am, making sleep all but impossible.

The alternative is the *Hôtel de la Paix* (☎ 296 437), a few doors north of the Alexander, which has rooms with shower for TD10/12. There's hot water, but the shower only delivers water when held at knee height, which makes washing your hair a challenge. Breakfast is an extra TD1.

Places to Stay – middle

The first place to check out is the splendid old *Hôtel Les Oliviers* (☎ 225 188; fax 223 623), which occupies a whole block of Rue Habib Thameur between Ave Hedi Chaker and Rue Mohammed Ali. It was the smartest place in town when it opened in 1923, and it retains an air of elegance with its ornate façade, balconies and shuttered windows. It

could use a coat of paint and some new carpets, and the plumbing is a bit erratic, but it's still good enough to merit its three stars. Large singles/doubles with bathroom cost TD25/40, which includes a generous buffet breakfast. Air-conditioning is available for an extra TD3. The hotel has a good bar and a swimming pool.

The *Hôtel Thyna* (☎ 225 266; fax 225 773), on the corner of Rue Habib Maazoun and Place Marburg, is a small two star hotel that is also popular with travellers. It has rooms with breakfast for TD15/24. Other options include the two star *Hôtel La Colisée* (☎ 227 800; fax 299 350), on Ave Taieb Mehiri, and the *Hôtel Mondial* (☎ 226 620), at the harbour end of Rue Habib Maazoun. Both have rooms for around TD20/30, including breakfast. The Mondial is an outstandingly dull example of functional concrete architecture.

Places to Stay – top end

The city's top hotels are priced with business people in mind, not travellers. The top hotel in town is the four star *Hôtel Abou Nawas Sfax Centre* (☎ 225 700; fax 225 521) on Ave Habib Bourguiba. Single/double rooms are TD150/170 with air-conditioning; there's a swimming pool and all the other frills. The *Hôtel Novotel Syphax* (☎ 243 333; fax 245 226), west of the city centre on the way to the airport, charges TD139/148.

After these two, the *Hôtel el-Andalous* (☎ 299 100; fax 299 425) is a relative bargain at TD91/106. The hotel is north-west of the medina on Ave des Martyrs.

Places to Eat

The *Restaurant Tunisienne*, on the right just inside the medina's Bab Diwan, is a very popular place that is always full of locals tucking into dishes like beans in spicy sauce with chicken (TD2.200) or couscous with lamb (TD2.500).

The *Restaurant Colombia*, next to the SNTRI bus station on Rue de Tazarka, is a good spot to grab a bite while you wait for your bus. You have to pay first – the owners got fed up with people running for their buses without paying!

The *Hôtel Alexander* has one of the better restaurants around. A huge plate of spaghetti with seafood (aux fruits de mer) will set you back TD4.200 – and the place serves alcohol, so you can wash it down with a cold beer (TD1.600). The stylish *Restaurant Chez Nous*, on Rue Patrice Lumumba, does a set menu for TD9, or you can choose from an extensive à la carte menu featuring loads of seafood for about TD15 per person, plus wine. The best seafood restaurant in town is reputed to be *Restaurant Le Corail* at 39 Rue Habib Maazoun, near the Hôtel Thyna.

An essential stop during a tour of the medina is coffee at the *Café Diwan*, built into the medina's southern wall off Rue de la Kasbah.

There is a *Monoprix supermarket* on Rue Aboulkacem ech Chabbi, near Ave Habib Bourguiba. It's open daily from 8.30 am to 7 pm. There's another branch of the Monoprix supermarket on Ave des Martyrs, west of the Mahdia louage station.

The city's main *markets* are in the Souq el-Omrane building just north of the medina. The meat section is not for the squeamish. As elsewhere, the butchers hang up the heads of the day's victims to show what they've got. The *fish markets* are opposite the port on Ave Ali Bach Hamba, and there's a small *fruit and vegetable market* next door.

Entertainment

If you're after a cold beer, the nicest surroundings are at the *Hôtel Les Oliviers*. It'll set you back TD2.300 though. If you're after several cold beers, the spit-and-sawdust-style small *bar* opposite the harbour on Ave Ali Bach Hamba is perfectly adequate and charges TD1.450 for a beer.

The restaurant at the *Hôtel Alexander* has a folk band on Saturday night. This is the real thing, not a stunt laid on for tourists. The music starts at about 8 pm and continues until the small hours. Proceedings get increasingly raucous as the night wears on.

Things to Buy

The medina is a good place to go souvenir shopping, provided you stay away from the

shops inside the Bab Diwan. The shops in the Souq des Etoffes stock a good range of Berber rugs, blankets and other handicrafts from the villages of the Gafsa region. The shop owners here seem to take the view that they're more likely to secure a sale if they don't scare tourists away with absurdly high first prices – and it works! ONAT has a crafts shop on the southern part of Rue Salem Harzallah, which is open Monday to Saturday from 9.30 am to noon and 3 to 7 pm.

Getting There & Away

Air Tuninter operates four flights a week between Tunis and Sfax (45 minutes). One-way/return fares are TD42.500/82.800. They run to a strange timetable, with daily flights Monday to Thursday, and none Friday to Sunday.

There are also two flights a week between Sfax and Paris – a Thursday flight with Tunis Air, and a Saturday flight with Air France. The Tunis Air office (☎ 228 028) is at 4 Ave de l'Armée; Air France (☎ 224 847) has an office at 15 Ave Taieb Mehiri.

Bus Sfax has three main long-distance bus stations. Fortunately, you're unlikely to need to look beyond the services operated by the national line, SNTRI, which leave from opposite the train station on Rue de Tazarka. Departures from here include the following:

Destination	Time	Fare (TD)	Frequency
Douz	5 hours	10.910	1/day
El-Jem	1¼ hours	2.720	5/day
Gabès	2 hours	5.510	5/day
Jerba	5 hours	9.280	3/day
Kairouan	2 hours	5.280	5/day
Medenine	3 hours	7.690	5/day
Sousse	2½ hours	5.310	5/day
Tataouine	4 hours	10.300	2/day
Tunis	4 hours	10.260	5/day

SNTRI also operates a daily international bus service to Tripoli, in Libya (seven hours, TD17.350). It leaves at 8.30 pm Monday to Friday and at 5 pm Saturday and Sunday.

There are two stations for buses run by the local transport authority, Soretras. Services to the north, including Sousse, Kairouan and Mahdia, leave from the station north of the medina on Ave des Martyrs, while services to Gafsa, Gabès, Jerba, Medenine and other points south leave from the bus station on Rue Rabat, at the western end of Ave Habib Bourguiba.

Train The train station is a grand colonial affair at the eastern end of Ave Habib Bourguiba, just east of the post office.

Heading south, there are trains to Gabès (three hours) at 2.30 and 11.25 am and 4.50 pm, and a night train to Gafsa (3½ hours) and Metlaoui (4¼ hours) leaving at 1.30 am.

Heading north, there are five trains a day to El-Jem (one hour), Sousse (two hours) and Tunis (four hours). They leave Sfax at 2 and 6.05 am, and 12.25, 1.30 and 6.15 pm.

Fares (in TD) are as follows:

Destination	2nd Class	1st Class	Confort
El-Jem	2.800	3.700	4.900
Gabès	4.700	7.150	7.900
Gafsa	5.650	7.800	8.650
Sousse	4.400	5.850	6.250
Tunis	7.950	10.650	11.350

Louage Most louages now leave from the station 100m west of the southern Soretras bus station on Rue Commandant Bejaoui. There are frequent departures to Gabès, Sousse and Tunis. Other destinations from here are Jerba, Medenine, Tataouine, Gafsa and Sbeitla. There are also regular louages to Tripoli, leaving from just east of the medina's Bab Diwan on Ave Ali Belhouane. These vehicles are a distinctive yellow and white, and often have Libyan markings.

Mahrès (on the coast 33km south of Sfax) and Mahdia used to be served by separate louage stations, at the western end of Ave Ali Belhouane and north of the medina on Ave des Martyrs, opposite the northern Soretras bus station, respectively. However, at the time of research, these appeared to have been relocated to the main louage station.

Car Rental The following agencies have offices in Sfax: Avis (☎ 224 605), Rue Tahar Sfar; Europcar (☎ 226 680), 16 Rue Tahar Sfar; and Hertz (☎ 228 626), 47 Ave Habib Bourguiba.

Boat Ferries for the Kerkennah Islands leave from the south-western corner of the port off Ave Mohammed Hedi Khefecha. Timetables change seasonally, the frequency ranging from eight crossings a day in summer to four a day in winter. Current timetables are displayed at the port and at the tourist office. The trip costs 570 mills for passengers and TD4 for a car. The crossing takes about 1¼ hours in good weather. There can be long queues to take a vehicle across in summer. There is no reservation system, so you'll need to join the queue early to get a place.

Getting Around
To/From the Airport The airport (☎ 278 000) is 6km from town on the Gafsa road at Thyna – about TD3 by taxi. There's no public transport out to the airport.

Bus Travellers are unlikely to have much need for the city's local bus network. They operate from the vacant lot to the north of the medina near the junction of Ave des Martyrs and Ave du 18 Janvier.

KERKENNAH ISLANDS
Pop 16,000 ☎ Area code 04
There are few quieter places in Tunisia than the Kerkennah Islands, a cluster of nine islands 25km off the coast from Sfax. If you're looking for a place to hang out and do nothing for a few days, this could well be the place for you.

However, if you're after a tropical island with palm-fringed beaches, this definitely isn't it. Once used as a place of exile, the islands have a rather desolate air about them. They are flat and featureless – the highest point is only 13m above sea level – and nothing appears to relish growing in the arid conditions. Even the palm trees are turning up their toes.

Fishing is the islanders' main activity. They still use traditional fish traps made from palm fronds. Lines of fronds are stuck in the sea bed in a 'V' shape, and the fish are then driven into this large funnel and into a small trap at the end.

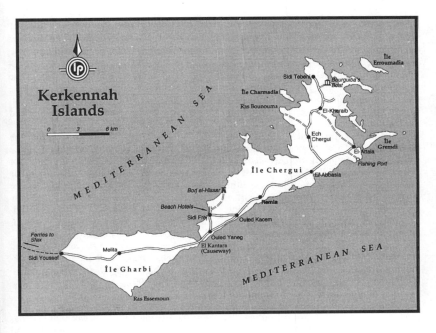

Orientation

The two main islands, **Île Gharbi** and **Île Chergui**, are connected by a small causeway dating back to Roman times. Île Gharbi has little more than the ferry port at Sidi Youssef, from where it's a 16km drive to the causeway.

Most of the population lives on Chergui. The only place of any consequence is the small town of **Remla** on the south coast, which is the administrative and service 'capital' of the islands. Tourist development is restricted to a few very low-key resort hotels on the north coast around the small village of **Sidi Frej**.

Information

There is a branch of the UIB bank in Remla, on the road leading down to the sea next to the Hôtel el-Jazira. It's open Monday to Thursday from 8 to 11.30 am and 2 to 5 pm, and Friday from 8 to 11 am and 1.30 to 4 pm. In July and August, it's open Monday to Friday from 7.30 am till noon.

It's much easier to change money at one of the hotels. The Cercina, Farhat and Grand all offer facilities, but only at certain times. Check at reception.

Borj el-Hissar

The Borj el-Hissar is an old fort on the coast about 3km north of the hotels at Sidi Frej. It is well worth the 40 minute walk; it's clearly signposted from near the Hôtel Le Grand. The small fort itself was built by the Spanish in the 16th century, but the most interesting aspect of the site is the Roman ruins that surround the fort. You get the feeling that you are stumbling across something previously undiscovered, with mosaics covered by sand and ruins disappearing into the sea. The guardian is very happy to talk about the site – for a small consideration.

Beaches

The beaches are not good enough to promote as an attraction. The sea is very shallow around here and no good for swimming – you can walk out 100m before your knees get wet. The best beach is supposedly at Ras Bounouma, north-east of Sidi Frej on the large bay that cuts into the north coast of Chergui, but it's a long, hot haul to get there and there is no public transport.

Bourguiba's Boat

Tunisian independence leader Habib Bourguiba was exiled to all the remotest places in the country, including the Kerkennahs, in the course of his long campaign to oust the French. He was sent here in 1945, and this small, privately run museum commemorates his escape from the islands by boat to Tripoli. The museum is at the north-eastern tip of Chergui. There's no public transport, and it's not worth a special trip.

Fishing Trips

The Farhat and Le Grand hotels both offer half-day outings for TD20 complete with fish lunch, half-bottle of wine and all the gear. If you want a less formal outing, it's normally possible to arrange a short trip with one of the fishermen who moor their boats near the Hôtel Cercina.

Places to Stay & Eat

Remla The only hotel in Remla is the very basic *Hôtel el-Jazira* (☎ 481 057), opposite the bus station on the main street through town. It charges TD7 per person, with breakfast. The hotel also has the only public bar on the islands (TD1.450 for a beer).

The friendly *Restaurant Wafa*, on the main street, can fix a plate of grilled fish, chips and salad for TD4. The *Restaurant La Sirène* has a prime location on the waterfront at the end of the road next to the Hôtel el-Jazira. It has a shady terrace overlooking the sea and does meals for around TD10, plus wine.

Sidi Frej Most tourists stick to the beach hotels at Sidi Frej, 8km from Remla. There's nothing else at Sidi Frej, so if you decide to stay in one of these hotels you're pretty much committed to eating there as well – unless you have transport.

The *Hôtel Cercina* (☎ 259 453; fax 281 262) is both the cheapest and by far the most convenient place to stay if you are on foot; it's just 200m from the bus stop at the junction of the road to Remla. For most of the year, you'll find a room for a very reasonable TD7.500 per person, including breakfast. The rates shoot up ridiculously in July and August, to TD20/ 30 for singles/doubles.

The alternative is to head for either the *Hôtel Farhat* (☎ 281 236; fax 281 237) or *Le Grand* (☎ 281 265; fax 281 485), a couple of two star hotels about 800m east of the bus stop. Both tend to be fully booked by the charter trade in summer, but in the low season you can enjoy their facilities (including tennis courts and a swimming pool) for TD30 a double with breakfast.

The best restaurant in the resort strip is at the *Hôtel Cercina*. Ask for the local speciality, a thick, spicy octopus soup called tchich (TD1.600).

Getting There & Away

See the Getting There & Away section under Sfax for details of ferries between Sfax and Sidi Youssef.

Getting Around

Bus There is a small network of buses which connect the villages of the islands. There are always at least two or three to meet each ferry. All the buses go to Remla. One has a 'hotel' sign in the window and goes via Sidi Frej (900 mills), from where it's about a 1km walk to the Farhat and Le Grand hotels. There are buses from Remla and the Sidi Frej junction to Sidi Youssef about an hour before the ferry. Times are posted in the bus station window in Remla.

The Remla bus station is opposite the Hôtel el-Jazira. There are a couple of buses daily to El-Attaia (650 mills), a small fishing village at the eastern end of Chergui. Be careful that you don't get stranded there, because the last bus returns about 3 pm and there's not much local traffic.

Bicycle The lack of hills makes cycling the ideal way of getting around. All the resort hotels rent out bikes. Rates start at TD1.500 per hour, or TD8 per day.

KAIROUAN
Pop 110,000 ☎ Area code 07

Kairouan, 68km west of Sousse, is Tunisia's holy city. It was here that Islam gained its first foothold in the Maghreb, and the city ranks behind only Mecca, Medina and Jerusalem among Islam's holy places.

The main attraction is the Great Mosque, but it is just one of many fine buildings lining the streets of the old medina. Kairouan is well known for its carpet-making; it also lies at the centre of a major fruit-growing region.

History

Although legend indicates otherwise (see the boxed text 'The Founding of Kairouan'), Kairouan was most likely founded on the site of an earlier Roman settlement. The first Arab settlement lasted a few years only before it was destroyed by a Berber rebellion. It was refounded in 694 AD by Hassan ibn Nooman.

The city's golden age began when it became the capital of the Aghlabite dynasty at the beginning of the 9th century. Although they preferred to rule from their palace at Raqqada, 9km south of Kairouan, it was the Aghlabites who endowed the city with its most important historic buildings.

Kairouan fell to the Fatimids in 909 AD, and the city fell into decline after the capital

---

The Founding of Kairouan

Kairouan was founded in 670 AD by the Arab general Uqba bin Nafi al-Fihri and takes its name from the Arabic word *qayrawan*, meaning 'military camp'. According to legend, the site for the city was chosen after Uqba's horse stumbled on a golden goblet that lay buried in the sands. The goblet turned out to be one that had mysteriously disappeared from Mecca some years previously. When it was picked up, water sprang from the ground – supplied, it was concluded, by the same source that supplied the holy well of Zem-Zem in Mecca. ∎

---

was moved to Mahdia. Its fortunes hit rock bottom when it was sacked in 1057 during the Hilalian invasions. Although Kairouan was rebuilt in the 13th century, it was never again to regain its position of political pre-eminence. It remains, however, the most important religious centre in the country.

Orientation

Life in Kairouan revolves around the medina, which is in the centre of town. The French built their customarily well-ordered ville nouvelle to the south. The two meet at the large open space outside the medina's main southern gate, the Bab ech Chouhada, where the tour buses gather. The medina's principal street, Ave Ali Belhouane, runs north-west from here to the main northern gate, the Bab Tunis. Rue des Aghlabites continues north from the Bab Tunis past the large regional hospital to link up with the main road to Tunis at the tourist office.

The biggest problem for travellers is negotiating the way to the medina from the bus and louage stations, which are about 2km to the north-west on the road to Sbeitla. The streets of the outer suburbs can be very confusing – it's a good idea to start off by catching a taxi into town.

Street Names Street names seem to change so often in Kairouan that the street signs can't keep up. It's hard to find two people who agree on a name. The names of the monuments and hotels don't change, however, so ask for them rather than for the street they're in.

Information

Tourist Offices The ONTT office (☎ 221 797) is next to the Aghlabite Basins on the northern edge of town, at the junction of Rue des Aghlabites and Ave Zama el-Belaoui. Don't expect to come away from here much the wiser. The only offerings are a glossy brochure (available anywhere) and a list of hotels (out of date). The staff don't appear to know a whole lot about the town.

They do, however, know the way to the local syndicat d'initiative, which is just

Want to Buy a Carpet?

Kairouan is plagued by carpet touts posing as tour guides. Everywhere you go, you will be pestered by people wanting to show you around. You will be told constantly that the place you're heading for has closed, has moved, no longer exists etc. Their sole purpose in telling you this is to redirect you into the clutches of one of the medina's smooth-talking carpet sellers. The persistence of these blokes starts to get on your nerves after a while, and it can be quite an effort to remain polite.

If you want a genuine guide, they can be hired from outside the tourist office. The TD10 that they charge for a tour is much less than anything the touts have in mind! ∎

across the corridor. This is useful, because it's the only place where tickets to the attractions can be bought. The multiple entry ticket costs TD4.200 and covers the six major attractions in town – the Great Mosque, the Aghlabite Basins, the Zaouia of Sidi Sahab, the Zaouia of Sidi Amor Abbada, the Bir Barouta and the Zaouia of Sidi Abid el-Ghariani as well as the Islamic Art Museum at Raqqada, on the road to Sfax. The ticket is valid for two days, which gives you time to explore at your leisure.

The syndicat d'initiative is open daily from 8 am to 6 pm in summer and to 5.30 pm in winter.

If you want a guide to show you around, you'll usually find several hanging around outside the tourist office looking for business. These guys carry accreditation, with photos, and they know their stuff. They charge TD10 for a tour of all the major sites. They all speak Arabic and French; some also speak English and/or German.

Money There are plenty of banks for changing money, including one just inside Bab ech Chouhada and a couple more opposite on Blvd Habib Bourguiba.

Post & Communications The main post office is about 600m south-west of Bab ech Chouhada at the large roundabout on the

southern edge of town, between Ave de la République and Rue Étienne. It is open Monday to Saturday from 8 am to 6 pm in winter and from 7.30 am to 12.30 pm in summer.

Taxiphone offices are everywhere – just look for the signs. A couple of the more convenient ones are the office on Ave de la République near the Tunisia Hôtel, and the office on the pedestrian precinct section of Blvd Habib Bourguiba, opposite the Bab ech Chouhada.

Hammam There's a hammam for men next to the Hôtel Sabra which is open daily until 3 pm. A bath costs TD1, or TD2.500 with massage.

Medina

Most of the attractions are found within the walls of the medina. The first walls were built towards the end of the 8th century, but they have been razed and rebuilt many times since then. The walls that stand today mainly date from the 18th century.

Kairouan gets an enormous number of tourists, mostly day-trippers from the resorts of Sousse and Monastir. You can set your clock by the wave of tourist buses that rolls up outside the medina at 9 am every day, so you'll have to set out early if you want to avoid the worst of the crowds. Don't forget to go to the syndicat d'initiative first to buy your multiple entry ticket to the six major monuments.

Great Mosque The Great Mosque occupies a large portion of the north-eastern corner of the medina. It is also known as the Sidi Oqba Mosque, after the founder of Kairouan who built the first mosque to stand on this site back in 670 AD. The original version was completely destroyed, and most of what stands today was built by the Aghlabites in the 9th century.

The outside has a typically austere Aghlabite design, lacking in decoration of any kind. With its buttressed walls, it looks more like a fort than the country's most hallowed mosque. Entry is through the main gate on

Blvd Brahim ben Lagheb. The other eight gates are closed to non-Muslims.

Impressions change once you step into the huge marble-paved courtyard, surrounded by an arched colonnade made up of columns salvaged from various Roman and Byzantine sites. The courtyard was designed for water catchment, and the paving slopes towards an intricately decorated central drainage hole which delivers the collected rainwater into the 9th century cisterns below. The decorations were designed to filter dust from the water. The marble rims of the two wells in the courtyard both have deep rope grooves worn by centuries of hauling water up from the depths.

The northern end of the courtyard is dominated by a square three tiered minaret. The lowest level was built in 728 AD, making it the oldest standing minaret in the world.

The prayer hall is at the southern end of the courtyard. The enormous, studded wooden doors date from 1829 AD; the carved panel above the doors is particularly fine. Non-Muslims are not allowed inside the prayer hall, but the doors are normally open enough to allow a glimpse of the interior. The 400 or so pillars that hold up the roof were filched from various Roman sites throughout the country, including Carthage and Sousse. At the far end of the hall, it's just possible to make out the precious 9th century tiles behind the *mihrab* (prayer niche in the mosque wall which indicates the direction of Mecca), which were imported from Baghdad along with the wood for the *minbar* (pulpit) next to it.

The mosque is open every day. It closes at noon on Friday, otherwise it's open from 7.30 am to 2 pm in summer and from 8 am to 2.30 pm in winter. Visitors must be appropriately dressed; robes are available at the entrance for those whose dress is deemed inappropriate. Admission is covered by the multiple entry ticket available only at the syndicat d'initiative. Several travellers have noted that it is easy enough to get in on the tails of a tour group if you happen to turn up at the mosque without a ticket.

Bab el-Khoukha Blvd Brahim ben Lagheb runs south-east through the medina from the Great Mosque and emerges at a small square just inside the Bab el-Khoukha, the oldest of the medina's many gates. Featuring a horseshoe arch supported by columns, it was built by Hussein ben Ali in 1706 AD.

Zaouia of Sidi Abid el-Ghariani Just inside the Bab ech Chouhada, on Rue Sidi el-Ghariani, this *zaouia* (shrine) is another of the monuments featured on the multiple entry ticket. Recently restored, the building dates from the 14th century and contains some fine woodcarving and stuccowork. The custodian here is a very willing talker and will guide you around pointing out the finer points (in French). The zaouia also houses the tomb of the Hafsid sultan Moulay Hassan who ruled from 1525 to 1543.

Bir Barouta The biggest tourist trap in the whole city is the building known as the Bir Barouta, just north of Ave Ali Belhouane and recognisable by its single white cupola. It was built by the Ottoman ruler Mohammed Bey in 1676 to surround the well that features in the city's foundation legend. This means that its waters are supposedly linked to those of the well of Zem-Zem in Mecca.

The main attraction is a poor, blindfolded camel that trudges around all day, drawing water from the well for people to taste, while a long line of tourists files through, taking the obligatory photo and leaving the obligatory tip. Architecturally, the main point of interest is the fancy open brickwork on the inside of the cupola roof. Admission is covered by the multiple entry ticket.

Mosque of the Three Doors This small mosque was founded in 866 AD by Mohammed bin Kairoun el-Maafri, a holy man from the Spanish city of Cordoba. The interior is closed to non-Muslims, but that's not a problem because the main feature is the elaborate façade. The mosque's three arched doorways are topped by three friezes of Kufic (early Arabic) script interspersed with floral reliefs and finally crowned with a carved cornice.

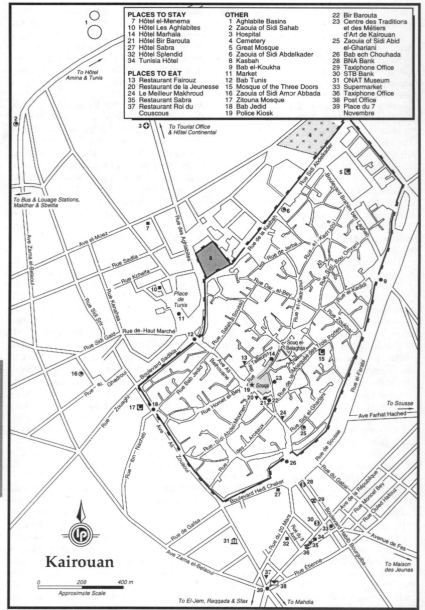

PLACES TO STAY
7 Hôtel el-Menema
10 Hôtel Les Aghlabites
14 Hôtel Marhala
21 Hôtel Bir Barouta
27 Hôtel Sabra
32 Hôtel Splendid
34 Tunisia Hôtel

PLACES TO EAT
13 Restaurant Fairouz
20 Restaurant de la Jeunesse
24 Le Meilleur Makhroud
35 Restaurant Sabra
37 Restaurant Roi du Couscous

OTHER
1 Aghlabite Basins
2 Zaouia of Sidi Sahab
3 Hospital
4 Cemetery
5 Great Mosque
6 Zaouia of Sidi Abdelkader
8 Kasbah
9 Bab el-Koukha
11 Market
12 Bab Tunis
15 Mosque of the Three Doors
16 Zaouia of Sidi Amor Abbada
17 Zitouna Mosque
18 Bab Jedid
19 Police Kiosk

22 Bir Barouta
23 Centre des Traditions et des Métiers d'Art de Kairouan
25 Zaouia of Sidi Abid el-Ghariani
26 Bab ech Chouhada
28 BNA Bank
29 Taxiphone Office
30 STB Bank
31 ONAT Museum
33 Supermarket
36 Taxiphone Office
38 Post Office
39 Place du 7 Novembre

Kairouan

CENTRAL TUNISIA

FRANCES LINZEE GORDON

The striking cupola of the Zaouia of Sidi Sahab.

The mosque is about 400m north-east of the Bir Barouta along Rue de la Mosquée des Trois Portes.

Aghlabite Basins
These two cisterns were built by the Aghlabites in the 9th century to hold the city's water supply. Water was delivered by aqueduct from the hills 36km west of Kairouan and flowed first into the smaller settling basin. From there it flowed on into the main holding basin, which was 5m deep and 128m in diameter. In the centre of the main pool are the remains of pillars which once supported a pavilion where the rulers could come to relax on summer evenings.

The basins were heavily restored about 20 years ago and are now mostly concrete, but they are still worth a look – especially since they are right next to the tourist office. The site is open daily from 7.30 am to 6.30 pm in summer and from 8.30 to 6 pm in winter.

Admission is covered by the multiple entry ticket covering Kairouan's major attractions.

Zaouia of Sidi Sahab
This extensive zaouia is about 1.5km northwest of the medina on Ave Zama el-Belaoui, just north of the road leading to the bus and louage stations.

It houses the tomb of Abu Zama el-Belaoui, a companion (*sahab*) of the Prophet Mohammed. He was known as the barber because he always carried three hairs from the Prophet's beard around with him, and the zaouia is sometimes referred to as the Mosque of the Barber. While the original mausoleum dates back to the 7th century AD, most of what stands today was added at the end of the 17th century. The additions include a *funduq* (caravanserai or inn) to house pilgrims, a medersa and a mosque.

The entrance to the zaouia is along an unusually decorative marble passageway that leads to a stunning white central courtyard. Sidi Sahab's mausoleum is to the right, topped by a cupola added in 1629. The small room on the opposite side of the courtyard contains the tomb of the architect of the Great Mosque. Non-Muslims are not allowed beyond this courtyard. It's open daily from 7.30 am to 6 pm year-round, and admission is covered by the multiple entry ticket.

As at the Great Mosque, robes are available at the entrance for those who are not suitably dressed.

Zaouia of Sidi Amor Abbada
This zaouia was built in 1860 around the tomb of Sidi Amor Abbada, a local blacksmith with a gift for prophecy. He specialised in the production of oversized things, like a set of giant anchors that were supposed to secure Kairouan to the earth.

The zaouia is just to the west of the medina off Rue Sidi Gaid and is easily identified by its seven gleaming white cupolas. It was closed for repairs at the time of research. When open, admission is covered by the multiple entry ticket.

Raqqada Islamic Art Museum

The museum occupies a former presidential palace at Raqqada, 9km south of Kairouan on the road to Sfax. Exhibits include a model of the Great Mosque of Kairouan, a faithfully reproduced plaster copy of the mihrab and lots and lots of calligraphy.

Unless you have your own transport and happen to be driving past, it's not worth the effort involved in getting there. It can be reached by taking a bus from Ave Haffouz (the main street leading south to Sfax) to the university, and then walking the remaining couple of kilometres. There are buses at 8, 9, 10 and 11 am, and at noon. The museum is open daily, except Monday, from 9.30 am to 4.30 pm.

ONAT Museum

People thinking of investing in a carpet should call in first at the ONAT Museum (free admission) on Ave Ali Zouaoui for a look at its collection of old rugs. They will discover that the local rugs don't last very long. The oldest of the ancient-looking threadbare things on the wall turns out to be only 50-odd years old – and it's been hanging on a wall for a while.

Places to Stay – budget

Hostel The city's *Maison des Jeunes* (☎ 228 239) is about 1km south-east of the medina on Ave de Fes. It's particularly uninviting, even by the organisation's low standards. It charges the standard TD4 per person.

Hotels Most travellers head for the *Hôtel Sabra* (☎ 230 263), conveniently located right opposite the Bab ech Chouhada on the southern side of the medina. The staff are used to dealing with budget travellers, and the rooms are good value at TD10/16 for singles/doubles with breakfast and free hot showers. It has very few singles, so individuals often end up enjoying a double to themselves for the price of a single.

An interesting alternative is the friendly *Hôtel Les Aghlabites* (☎ 220 880), a converted funduq off Place de Tunis to the north of the medina. The rooms here open out onto a splendid tiled courtyard. It charges TD6/12 for clean singles/doubles with hot showers. The hotel is right next to the fruit and vegetable markets, so ask for a quiet room away from the street.

Another possibility is the *Hôtel Marhala* (☎ 220 736) at 35 Souq el-Belaghija, one of the covered souqs off Ave Ali Belhouane right in the heart of the medina. It was closed at the time of research, but it's worth checking out because it occupies an old medersa and offers something a little different from the average medina hotel. It can be hard to find: the entrance to Souq el-Belaghija is through the big arch with the crenellated top on the northern side of Ave Ali Belhouane. It's easy to miss during business hours because it is obscured by all sorts of offerings from the souvenir shops. The hotel is about 150m along on the left.

One place to avoid like the plague is the squalid *Hôtel Bir Barouta*, just around the corner from the Bir Barouta.

Places to Stay – middle

The place to head for is the two star *Tunisia Hôtel* (☎ 231 775; fax 231 597), a good older-style hotel about 400m south of the medina on Ave de la République. It has large single/double rooms with bathroom for TD18/30, including breakfast. The rooms are centrally heated in winter.

The *Hôtel el-Menema* (☎ 220 182) is a small modern hotel north of the medina on Ave el-Moez. Rooms are arranged around a covered courtyard, and cost TD14/22 for singles/doubles with bathroom, including and breakfast.

Places to Stay – top end

There's not much call for upmarket accommodation in Kairouan. Most tourists come on day trips, and disappear back to the resort hotels on the coast in the evenings.

The best rooms are to be found at the *Hôtel Amina* (☎ 225 466; fax 225 411), about 400m east of the tourist office on the road to Tunis. The hotel is set back from the main road just beyond the Hôtel Continental. It's a comfortable, modern three star place, with singles/doubles for TD37/54 plus breakfast. Facilities include a swimming pool.

The *Hôtel Continental* (☎ 221 135; fax 229 900) has been recently renovated and now deserves its three-star rating. Rates are TD33/47.600 for single/double rooms, and facilities include a swimming pool.

If the Amina is full, the only real alternative is the *Hôtel Splendid* (☎ 227 522; fax 220 229), near the Tunisia Hôtel on Rue du 9 Avril. It also qualifies for three stars and single/double rooms cost TD30/60, including breakfast. Rue du 9 Avril is the small street running between Ave de la République and Rue du 20 Mars.

Places to Eat
The *Restaurant de la Jeunesse*, opposite the main souq area on Ave Ali Belhouane, specialises in couscous. It's the only dish on the menu, and comes with a choice of accompanying spicy stews. There's couscous with lamb for TD2.600, couscous with chicken for TD2.800 or couscous with vegetables for TD2.200.

You'll find a much wider choice of dishes at the *Restaurant Fairouz*, on Rue des Tailleurs, signposted off Ave Ali Belhouane just north of the souqs. It's quite expensive by the standards of local restaurants, with main courses priced from TD4, but it does serve cold beer – unofficially, judging by the waiter's conspiratorial wink.

Much better value is the friendly *Restaurant Sabra*, next to the Tunisia Hôtel on Ave de la République. It has a choice of set menus priced from TD2.700.

If you want a glass of wine with your meal, head for the *Roi du Couscous*, near the post office on Place du 7 Novembre. It does a three course meal for TD6, or just couscous and dessert for TD4.

Kairouan is famous for its sticky sweets, especially a date-filled semolina cake soaked in honey called makhroud which can be found everywhere. A good place to sample this and other specialities is *Le Meilleur Makhroud*, in the middle of the medina on Ave Ali Belhouane.

For a breakfast with a difference, the small *gargotte* right next to the Hôtel Sabra serves dragh, a kind of porridge made from sorghum, until 10 am. Dragh starts life as a rather disconcerting looking grey slop, into which sugar, halva and various other powders are piled. It's not as bad as it looks or sounds, and costs 500 mills a bowl.

Self caterers can head for the *supermarket* on Blvd Habib Bourguiba. Lots of fruit is grown around Kairouan, especially cherries and other stone fruit. You'll find whatever's in season at the *stalls* around Place de Tunis, just north of the medina.

Things to Buy
Kairouan is one of the country's major carpet centres, producing classical knotted carpets as well as the woven *mergoum*. If you are in the market for a carpet, this is as good a place as any to do your shopping.

It is important, however, to do your homework first. Initial prices can be ridiculously high, often as much as three times the true price. Remember that all carpets which have been inspected and classified by ONAT carry a label and seal on the back.

A good place to go looking for souvenirs is the Centre des Traditions et des Métiers d'Art de Kairouan, just to the north of the Bir Barouta on a side street leading to the souqs. It was set up by ONAT to promote local handicrafts. The ground floor acts as a sales outlet, while the rooms upstairs are set up to demonstrate traditional techniques for weaving, embroidery and carpet making etc.

Getting There & Away
The bus and louage stations are right next to each other about 2km north-west of the medina on the road to Sbeitla, signposted off Ave Zama el-Belaoui near the Zaouia of Sidi Sahab. It's too far to walk in summer, especially if you're staying at one of the hotels to the south of the medina. A taxi from the medina to the bus or louage station costs about TD2.500.

Note that there is no direct public transport from Kairouan to El-Jem; you'll have to go via Sousse.

Bus The bus station is one of the busiest in the country. Kairouan lies on the shortest route between Tunis and the cities of the south and south-west, and there is a constant stream of long-distance traffic 24 hours a day. There are separate ticket offices for SNTRI services and for regional services; each has destinations and departure times clearly indicated in English.

The following table lists the journey times, fares and frequency of services to the main destinations.

Destination	Duration	Fare (TD)	Frequency
Douz	7 hours	14.600	1/day
El-Jem	3 hours	8.150	5/day
Gabès	4¼ hours	8.700	6/day
Gafsa	3¼ hours	8.130	4/day
Jerba	5 hours	12.440	4/day
Kasserine	2½ hours	6.650	4/day
Makthar	1¾ hours	3.980	5/day
Medenine	5¼ hours	10.600	6/day
Nabeul	2¼ hours	4.280	3/day
Nefta	7½ hours	11.980	2/day
Sbeitla	1¾ hours	4.200	3/day
Sfax	2 hours	5.280	5/day
Sousse	1½ hours	2.560	4/day
Tozeur	4½ hours	11.230	2/day
Tunis	2¼ hours	6.500	hourly

Louage There are frequent departures to Sousse, Sfax and Tunis, and occasional services to Makthar and Sbeitla.

MAKTHAR
Pop 8000 ☎ Area code 08
The bleak little town of Makthar lies on the high plains of the Tunisian Dorsale range 114km west of Kairouan on the road to Le Kef. The only reason to stop here is to visit the ruins of ancient Mactaris, which are spread over a wide area on the south-eastern edge of town. The modern town has nothing going for it, but it's easy enough to visit the ruins en route from Kairouan to Le Kef, a further 69km to the north-west.

History
Mactaris is thought to have been founded by the Carthaginians at the end of the 5th century BC as part of Carthage's push to settle the hinterland. It was captured by the Numidian king Massinissa, an ally of the Romans,

before the Third and final Punic War, and remained in Numidian hands until the beginning of the 1st century AD, when Rome began to take the settlement of Africa seriously. The Roman town reached the peak of its prosperity in the 2nd century, and most of the buildings at the site date from this time. The Vandals and the Byzantines both left their mark at the site in subsequent centuries, and the town continued to be occupied until the 11th century, when it was destroyed during the Hilalian invasions.

Things to See
The site is on the south-eastern edge of town at the junction of the main roads running south-east to Kairouan and north to Tunis and Le Kef. It is opposite a large triumphal arch that once marked the entrance to the town. It's open every day, except Monday, from 8 am to 6 pm in summer and from 8.30 am to 5.30 pm in winter. Admission to the site, including the museum, is TD2.100, plus TD1 if you want to take photographs.

If you're visiting the site in winter, come suitably dressed. At an altitude of more than 1000m, the winds that blow off the surrounding hills can be bitterly cold.

Museum The entrance to the site is through the museum. It houses some interesting old gravestones found at the site as well as the obligatory collection of chipped Roman busts, lamps and old coins.

Amphitheatre Immediately south of the museum are the remains of the town's small amphitheatre, built in the 2nd century AD and looking in remarkably good condition after recent restoration.

Trajan's Arch The site's main path runs south from the amphitheatre towards the crumbling remains of an enormous triumphal arch, built in 116 AD and dedicated to the emperor Trajan. The arch overlooks the Roman forum, built at the same time. The four columns at the north-eastern corner of the forum mark the location of the town's

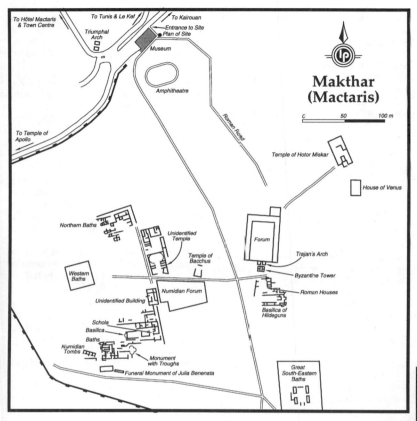

Makthar (Mactaris)

To Hôtel Mactaris & Town Centre

To Tunis & Le Kef

To Kairouan

Entrance to Site
Plan of Site

Triumphal Arch

Museum

Amphitheatre

Roman Road

To Temple of Apollo

Temple of Hotor Miskar

House of Venus

Northern Baths

Unidentified Temple

Forum

Temple of Bacchus

Trajan's Arch

Byzantine Tower

Western Baths

Numidian Forum

Roman Houses

Unidentified Building

Basilica of Hildeguns

Schola
Basilica
Baths

Numidian Tombs

Monument with Troughs

Funeral Monument of Julia Benenata

Great South-Eastern Baths

market. The foundations south of the arch are of a Byzantine tower built in the 6th century.

Temple of Hotor Miskar A path leads north-east from the forum to the scanty remains of an early temple dedicated to the Carthaginian god Hotor Miskar. Nearby are the remains of a Roman villa known as the House of Venus after the mosaic of Venus found there, now in the museum.

Basilica of Hildeguns The group of columns south of Trajan's Arch belong to a small Vandal church, built in the 5th century

AD and named after the fellow who lies buried beneath the mosaic-covered grave by the entrance on the western side. Look out for the ornate baptistry font, hidden behind the apse at the eastern end.

Schola The jumble of arches and columns at the south-western corner of the site was once the home of the town's *schola juvenum*, a sort of youth club where local boys learned how to be good Romans. It was converted into a church in the 3rd century AD. It's a pleasant shady spot to sit and contemplate.

The area just south of the schola was the

town's cemetery and is dotted with graves and funeral monuments dating back to Numidian times.

Great South-Eastern Baths The massive walls of this enormous bath complex dominate the southern part of the site. Built at the peak of the town's prosperity in the 2nd century AD, it was converted into a fortress by the Byzantines in the 6th century. In spite of this, the baths are among the best preserved in Tunisia and the layout is still quite easy to follow. The star feature is the blue and green mosaic floor of the central room.

Temple of Apollo If you have time, it's an interesting walk out to the ruins of the Temple of Apollo, about 800m south-west of town and signposted from the museum. It was the town's principal temple in Roman times and was built on the site of an earlier Carthaginian temple to the god Baal Hammon. Adjoining the site are the crumbling remains of the Roman aqueduct that once supplied water to the town.

Places to Stay & Eat
You'd need to be desperate to consider spending a night at Makthar's only hotel, the tiny *Hôtel Mactaris* (☎ 876 465), near the ancient site on the road into town. Location is about all it has going for it. The three very basic rooms are above the only bar in town, and you'd need to drink a skinful before you even considered lying down on one of the saggy old iron beds. For the record, the rooms cost TD10 and can sleep up to three people.

If you are desperate, the hotel is on the left, 150m beyond the National Guard building as you head into town from the ancient site. It also has a cheap *restaurant* serving grilled food and salads. There's no sign, but everybody knows the place. It's a much better idea to hop on a bus and keep going to either Le Kef or Kairouan.

Getting There & Away
Bus Buses leave from the T-junction 100m

north of the Hôtel Mactaris. There are five buses a day to Le Kef (1¼ hours, TD2.440) and to Kairouan (1¾ hours, TD3.980), and a daily bus to Tunis (three hours, TD6.670).

Louage You can also get to Tunis, Le Kef and Kairouan by louage. They leave from the main street in the middle of town. To get there, follow the signs to El Ksour and Dahmani from the bus stop.

SBEITLA
Pop 6000 ☎ *Area code 07*
Stuck right out in the middle of nowhere on the plains 117km south-west of Kairouan, Sbeitla merits a mention only because it is the site of the ancient town of Sufetula, famous for its remarkably well preserved Roman temples.

The modern town has very little going for it, although it does at least have a couple of decent hotels to cater for the steady flow of tourists lured here by the ruins.

History
Given the importance of Roman Sufetula, surprisingly little is known about its early history. It is assumed that it followed a similar evolutionary path to other Roman towns in the region, such as Ammaedara and Mactaris, and was established at the beginning of the 1st century AD on the site of an early Numidian settlement.

The surrounding countryside proved ideal for olive growing, and Sufetula quickly developed into a wealthy town. The temples were built when Sufetula was at the height of its prosperity in the 2nd century. Its olive groves ensured that the town continued to prosper long after other Roman towns slipped into decline, and it became an important centre of Christianity in the 4th century.

The Byzantines made Sufetula their regional capital, transforming it into a military stronghold from which to tackle the area's rebellious local tribes. It was here in 647 that the Prefect Gregory declared himself independent of Constantinople. His moment of glory lasted only a few months before he was

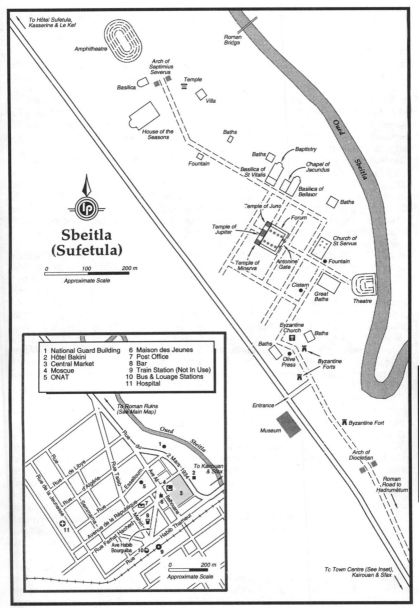

To Hôtel Sufetula,
Kasserine & Le Kef

Amphitheatre

Arch of
Septimius
Severus

Basilica

Temple

Villa

House of the
Seasons

Roman
Bridge

Baths

Baptistry

Baths

Chapel of
Jucundus

Fountain

Basilica of
St Vitalis

Basilica of
Bellaior

Baths

Temple of Juno

Forum

Temple of
Jupiter

Oued Sbeitla

Church of
St Servus

Temple of
Minerva

Antonine
Gate

Fountain

Cistern

Great
Baths

Theatre

Byzantine
/ Church

Baths

Baths

Olive
Press

Byzantine
Forts

Entrance

Museum

Byzantine Fort

Arch of
Diocletian

Roman
Road to
Hadrumétum

Sbeitla (Sufetula)

0   100   200 m
Approximate Scale

CENTRAL TUNISIA

1 National Guard Building
2 Hôtel Bakini
3 Central Market
4 Mosque
5 ONAT
6 Maison des Jeunes
7 Post Office
8 Bar
9 Train Station (Not In Use)
10 Bus & Louage Stations
11 Hospital

To Roman Ruins
(See Main Map)

Oued Sbeitla

Rue du 2 Mars 1934

To Kairouan
& Sfax

Rue Taieb Esselloumi

Rue d'Algérie

Rue de Libye

Rue de la Jeunesse

Rue Semmari

Avenue de le République

Rue Farhat Hached

Ave Ali

Mellili

Bahouani

Rue Habib Thameur

Ave Habib
Bourguiba

Habib Thameur

To Town Centre (See Inset),
Kairouan & Sfax

0   200 m
Approximate Scale

defeated and killed by the Arabs, who also destroyed much of the town.

Things to See

The site is about 1km north of the modern town centre, on the road to Kasserine. The first sign that you are approaching the site is the massive **Arch of Diocletian.** This arch once stood at the southern entrance to the ancient town. The site entrance is 200m further north, opposite the museum. The site and museum are both open every day from 7 am to 7 pm in summer, and from 8.30 am to 5.30 pm in winter. The admission fee of TD2.100 covers entry to the site and the museum. There is an additional charge of TD1 to take photographs.

The best time to visit the site is very early in the morning, which means spending the night at one of the nearby hotels. It's well worth it, though, for the spectacular sight of the temples glowing orange in the morning sun.

Temples The celebrated temples hold centre stage; built on a low mound in the middle of town, they tower over the surrounding ruins.

The wall that surrounds the temples was not part of the original scheme. It was built by the Byzantines in the 6th century AD, who used the temples as one wall of a fortress surrounding the old forum.

The entrance is on the south-eastern side of the complex through the magnificent triple-arched Antonine Gate, built in 139 AD and dedicated to the Emperor Antoninus Pius and his adopted sons Marcus Aurelius and Lucius Verus. It opens onto a large paved forum flanked by two rows of columns which lead up to the temples. There are three temples, each dedicated to one of the three main gods of the Roman pantheon. The Temple of Jupiter, in the centre, is flanked by slightly smaller temples to his sister deities Juno and Minerva.

Great Baths The ruins of these extensive baths lie to the south-east of the temples, on the road leading down towards the Oued Sbeitla. They are remarkable mainly for the

complex under-floor heating system used in the hot rooms, easily distinguishable now that the floors themselves have collapsed.

Theatre The ancient theatre, just east of the Great Baths, has a prime position overlooking the Oued Sbeitla. Built in the 3rd century AD, not much remains except for the orchestra pit and a few scattered columns, but it's worth visiting for the views along the Oued Sbeitla – especially pretty in spring.

Church of St Servus The four precarious-looking pillars of stone on the left as you walk between the temples and the Great Baths mark the site of the Church of St Servus, built in the 4th century AD on the foundations of an unidentified pre-Roman temple.

Basilica of Bellator The Basilica of Bellator is the first of a row of ruined churches about 100m east of the temples on the main path leading north-west towards the Arch of Septimius Severus. Built at the beginning of the 4th century AD, its unusual name derives from an inscription found at the site. Like the Church of St Servus, it was built on the foundations of an unidentified pre-Roman temple. The tiny adjoining chapel was the basilica's baptistry until the 5th century, when it was converted into a chapel in honour of the Catholic bishop Jucundus, who is thought to have been martyred by the Vandals.

Basilica of St Vitalis The nearby Basilica of St Vitalis was built in the 6th century AD as a bigger and grander replacement for the Basilica of Bellator. The basilica itself doesn't amount to much now, but hidden away in the baptistry at the back is a beautiful baptismal basin that has been left *in situ* in the ground. The rim is decorated with an intricate floral mosaic in brilliant reds and greens.

Other Sites The path running north-west from the churches crosses a neat grid of unexcavated streets before arriving at the remains of Sufetula's second monumental gate, the **Arch of Septimius Severus**. To the west before you reach the arch are the meagre remains of the **House of the Seasons**, named for the mosaic discovered here, which is now in the Bardo Museum in Tunis.

A rough path continues north from the arch, past the ruins of a small **basilica**, to the site of the town's **amphitheatre**, which has yet to be excavated and is so overgrown that you have to look hard to find the outline. Another path leads east from the arch down to a restored **Roman bridge** over the Oued Sbeitla.

Museum You start to wonder about the value of a museum when the guy at the door tells you it's not worth visiting! He's not far wrong. The only exhibits worth seeking out are the statue of Bacchus reclining on a panther, which was discovered at the site's theatre, and the mosaics.

Places to Stay & Eat

The only budget accommodation option is the unbelievably grim *Maison des Jeunes* (no telephone), signposted off Ave Habib Bourguiba in the middle of town. It's not worth considering, even at TD6 for a double room.

The best place to head for is the two star *Hôtel Sufetula* (☎ 465 074; fax 465 582), which overlooks the ancient site from its hill-top location 1.5km north of town on the road to Kasserine. It's a comfortable modern hotel charging TD27.400/38.800 for large singles/doubles with breakfast. If you're staying here, you're pretty much obliged to eat here as well. The restaurant does a perfectly adequate three course menu for an extra TD5.300 per person. The hotel also has a swimming pool.

The alternative is the uninspiring *Hôtel Bakini* (☎ 465 244), at the eastern edge of town on Rue du 2 Mars 1934. It has rooms with breakfast for TD23.500/34.

The *bar/restaurant* on Ave Habib Bourguiba is more bar than restaurant, but it does serve basic grilled food like brochettes (kebabs), salad and chips for TD2.800.

Getting There & Away

Buses and louages leave from a dusty vacant lot on the southern edge of town off Rue Habib Thameur. The old train station is nearby, but the trains stopped running long ago.

There are frequent buses to Kasserine (45 minutes, TD1.050), and three buses a day to Kairouan (1¾ hours, TD4.200). There's a direct bus to Le Kef (three hours, TD6.100) every morning at 8 am, otherwise change at Kasserine. SNTRI has three services a day to Tunis (3¾ hours, TD9.350).

There are regular louages to Kasserine and Kairouan.

KASSERINE
Pop 30,000 ☎ *Area code 07*

The town of Kasserine, 38km south-west of Sbeitla, would be a strong contender in any poll to nominate the dullest town in Tunisia. It is, however, an important regional centre with useful transport connections and it makes a useful base for a trip to the remote Roman town of Haidra (see the following section). Most travellers attempt to stick around long enough only to catch the next bus or louage.

The only attraction of any note is the minor Roman site of **Cillium**, 5km south-west of town on the road to Gafsa. It's not worth the effort involved in getting there unless you happen to be driving past. It's next to the Hôtel Cillium.

Places to Stay & Eat

If you wind up getting stuck, the place to head for is the friendly *Hôtel de la Paix* (☎ 471 465), just east of the central square on Ave Habib Bourguiba, which is the road to Sbeitla. It has singles/doubles with breakfast for TD7/13, or TD9/16 with dinner as well at the hotel's bar/restaurant. A step up from this is the *Hôtel Pinus* (☎ 470 164), a small one star place about 300m further out towards Sbeitla on Ave Habib Bourguiba. It has rooms with bathroom for TD13/16 with breakfast, or TD18/26 with dinner as well.

The upmarket option is the three star *Hôtel Cillium* (☎ 470 682), right next to the ancient site, 5km from town on the road to Gafsa. It has rooms for TD27/40. In winter there's a chance that you'll end up sitting at the bar with a bunch of elderly European men dressed up in paramilitary costumes; they're hunters who come here to go pig-hunting in the forests east of Kasserine.

Getting There & Away
The bus and louage stations are side by side about 1km east of the town centre on the road to Sbeitla.

Bus Useful services include frequent buses to Sbeitla (45 minutes, TD1.050), six buses a day to Gafsa (1¾ hours, TD3.900) and five buses a day north to Le Kef (3½ hours, TD6.820) via Kalaat Khasba (two hours, TD3.600). SNTRI has three services a day to Tunis (4½ hours, TD10.300).

Louage Travelling by louage around here involves lots of short journeys and frequent changes of louage. There are frequent services to Sbeitla, but travelling south to Gafsa involves changing louages at Fériana; travelling north to Kalaat Khasba or Le Kef involves a change at Thala.

HAIDRA
The remote border village of Haidra, 18km south-west of Kalaat Khasba, is the site of ancient Ammaedara, one of the oldest Roman towns in Africa. It's a wonderfully evocative site, spread along the northern bank of the Oued Haidra. The problem is that it's a hard place to get to without your own transport, especially if you want to stick around for the fabulous sunsets. The sun sets slowly behind the mountains of Algeria to the west, bathing the site in a rich orange light.

Modern Haidra is no more than a customs post on the road to the Algerian town of Tébessa, just 41km south-west of here. There are no shops, no restaurants and no hotels, so you will need to bring your own supplies, especially water. The closest accommodation is 78km away in Kasserine. The Algerian border is 10km west of Haidra.

History
Ammaedara is a Berber name, which indicates that the Romans weren't the first to occupy the site. The only evidence of pre-Roman occupation are the foundations of a Carthaginian temple to the god Baal Hammon, overlooking the Oued Haidra to the south-east of the site.

The first Roman settlement here was established by the troops of the Augustine Third Legion at the beginning of the 1st century AD as a base during their campaign to suppress a rebellion by the Numidian chief Tacfinares. Nothing from this period survives apart from a cemetery near the Arch of Septimius Severus. After Tacfinares was defeated, the legion moved its camp west to Theveste (Tébessa), and Ammaedara was repopulated with retired soldiers.

Ammaedara developed into a prosperous trading town at the junction of the Roman roads west to Theveste, north-east to Carthage, and south to Thelepte and Gafsa. The disproportionate number of churches – Roman, Vandal and Byzantine – indicate that it continued to be an important town until the arrival of the Arabs in the 7th century AD.

Things to See
The road from Kalaat Khasba passes through the middle of site, which is not enclosed and can be visited at any time. Admission is free, but the amiable custodian appreciates a tip. Few tourists pass this way and he appears to enjoy having the opportunity to point out the highlights.

The site is dominated by the walls of an enormous **Byzantine fort**, built in 550 AD. It straddles the old Roman road and runs down to the banks of the oued. Look out for the small **Chapel of the Citadel** at the south-western corner.

Very little of the Roman town remains standing. The modern road passes over the old **forum**, while a single giant column marks the site of the great temple that once stood at the **capitol**. The rest of the columns lie scattered around. Around the capitol are the meagre remains of the old **baths** and the **market**.

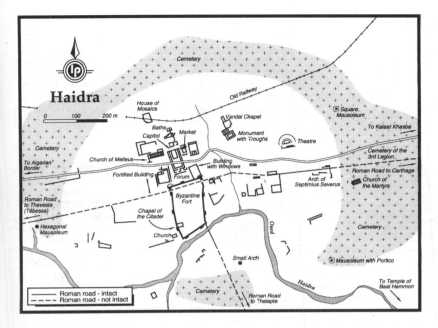

Haidra

Roman road - intact
Roman road - not intact

Haidra's principal Roman monument is the extremely well preserved **Arch of Septimius Severus**, which stands on the Roman road at the eastern edge of the site. It was built in 195 AD, and remains in good condition because it was protected for centuries by a surrounding Byzantine wall. About 300m south of here, the **mausoleum with portico** stands silhouetted on a small rise overlooking the oued.

While the site is dotted with the ruins of numerous small churches, the only one that warrants serious inspection is the **Church of Melleus**, just west of the forum. Originally built in the 4th century, it was later expanded by the Byzantines and is named after a bishop who was buried here. The church was partly reconstructed in the 1960s.

Getting There & Away
Visiting Haidra without your own transport is a challenge, but can be achieved with a bit of determination. Access is via the small

market town of Kalaat Khasba, 18km to the north-east. You can get to Kalaat Khasba on any bus travelling between Kasserine and Le Kef, or by louage from Kasserine via Thala. There are also two trains a day from Tunis (five hours, TD9.800), which depart at 6.10 am and 2.15 pm, and return from Kalaat Khasba at 5.50 am and 12.45 pm.

Buses and louages will deposit you on the main street of Kalaat Khasba, where you will find occasional louages out to Haidra (15 minutes, 800 mills). The alternative is to hitch from the roundabout on the main road at the southern side of town. Whatever you do, you will need to set out early, because public transport dries up by mid-afternoon.

JUGURTHA'S TABLE
Jugurtha's Table (1271m) is a spectacular flat-topped mountain that rises sheer from the surrounding plains close to the Algerian border. It's near the small town of Kalaat es Senan, 73km south-west of Le Kef.

CENTRAL TUNISIA

The mountain is named after the Numidian king Jugurtha, who used it as a base during his seven year campaign against the Romans from 112 to 105 BC. Its sheer, impregnable walls make it a superb natural fortress. The only access to the summit is by a twisting set of steps hewn into the escarpment at the eastern end. The Byzantines added the small gate at the base of the steps, but there is no other indication that they used the site.

The walk to the steps starts from the western side of the mountain at the small village of Ain Senan, 3km east of Kalaat es Senan. If you haven't got your own vehicle, you can save yourself a hot uphill walk by forking out TD1.500 for a taxi.

Follow the road to the highest point of the village, and then take the rough track that leads off uphill around the northern side of the mountain. There's only one path, and locals are used to pointing it out if you need reassurance. Keep following the path around the base of the escarpment until you get to the eastern side of the mountain, when you will see the steps that provide access to the summit.

The reward for those who climb to the top is a spectacular view over the surrounding countryside. The hills you can see to the west lie across the border in Algeria. There's little to see apart from a small *marabout* (shrine) and a network of low stone walls.

The return walk from Ain Senan takes about two hours. You'll need a decent pair of walking shoes to handle the rough terrain, and take sufficient water because there's none to be found along on the way. Tourists are supposed to register at the National Guard office on the main street of Kalaat es Senan before they set out, and check back afterwards to announce their safe return.

Places to Stay & Eat

There's very basic accommodation at the *Hôtel Kalaat Senan* (☎ (08) 286 356), next to the National Guard building on the main street of town. It charges TD2.500 per person for a bed in a triple room, or TD7.500 if you want the room to yourself. The hotel also doubles as the only bar in town, and has a small restaurant where you can get a plate of grilled chicken, chips and salad for TD2.500. The closest decent rooms are in Le Kef.

Getting There & Away

There are occasional direct louages to Kalaat es Senan from Le Kef (TD3.150), and more frequent services from the small town of Tajerouine, 35km south of Le Kef on the main road to Kasserine. There are louages to Tajerouine from Le Kef, and all buses travelling between Le Kef and Kasserine stop there.

Southern Tunisia

Tourism has boomed in the south in recent years. The resort island of Jerba has long been a popular spot, luring holiday-makers with its claim to be the legendary land of the Lotus Eaters. These days, more and more people are heading inland. Here you will find some of the country's most dramatic landscapes: the desert dunes of the Great Eastern Erg near Douz, shimmering chotts (salt lakes), the spectacular hill-top fortifications of the Ksour district around Tataouine and the bizarre lunar landscapes surrounding the troglodyte village of Matmata.

Winter is the best time to visit. While Northern Europe shivers, the mercury rarely falls below 15°C in Southern Tunisia. Summer can be so hot, especially inland, that it can be a real effort to move. If you are here at this time of year, it makes a lot of sense to adopt the local habit of disappearing indoors during the heat of the day.

Gafsa Region

The Gafsa region occupies the transitional area between the wheat-growing and grazing lands of the Tell to the north and the Saharan regions to the south. It is one of the least visited areas of Tunisia, mainly because it has steadily been turned into one giant mine since the French discovered that the hills west of Gafsa were made almost entirely of phosphate. The mines are the source of a large slice of the nation's export earnings – as well as being the source of the layer of fine, grey dust that coats everything in the region.

People have been living around here for 150,000-odd years. These early residents would have enjoyed a much wetter climate than today. Conditions were still ideal when the Capsian people arrived around 8000 BC.

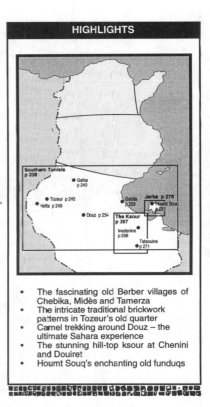

HIGHLIGHTS

Southern Tunisia p 238
Gafsa p 240
Tozeur p 245
Nefta p 249
Douz p 254
Gabès p 259
Jerba p 278
Houmt Souq p 281
The Ksour p 267
Medenine p 268
Tataouine p 271

- The fascinating old Berber villages of Chebika, Midès and Tamerza
- The intricate traditional brickwork patterns in Tozeur's old quarter
- Camel trekking around Douz – the ultimate Sahara experience
- The stunning hill-top ksour at Chenini and Douiret
- Houmt Souq's enchanting old funduqs

As the climate became steadily drier, settlement began to concentrate around the oases of the region, particularly at Gafsa and at nearby El-Ksar and Lella. These oases are quite different from those of the Jerid (the strip of land between the two salt lakes, the Chott el-Jerid and the Chott el-Gharsa – see the Jerid section later in this chapter) as it is too cold in winter for the date palms to fruit. The palms you see are grown solely for the shade they provide for other crops, mainly beans and wheat.

SOUTHERN TUNISIA

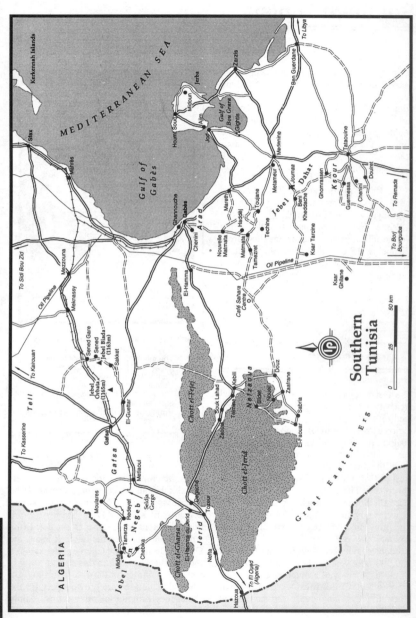

GAFSA
Pop 60,000 ☎ Area code 06

Despite its long history, modern Gafsa is one of the least inspiring towns in Tunisia. The town is, however, the hub of the region's transport network so there's a fair chance you'll pass through here sooner or later.

History

The oasis at Gafsa first grew to prominence as a staging post on the caravan route between the Sahara and the Tunisian coast. In Numidian times it became the town of Capsa, which was captured and destroyed by the Roman consul Marius in 107 BC as part of the campaign against Jugurtha, the Numidian king (see the main history section in the Facts about the Country chapter for more details). It went on to become an important Roman town – although a couple of pools and a few mosaics are the only surviving evidence.

Information

There is a small tourist office (☎ 221 644) in the small, dusty square by the Roman Pools. It opens standard government hours.

There are branches of all the major banks in and around the centre, and the post office is on Ave Habib Bourguiba, 300m north of the kasbah (citadel or fort). For international phone calls, try the Taxiphone offices next to the Mosque of Sidi Bou Yacoub and on Rue Houcine Bouzaiane, off Ave Taieb Mehiri. The offices are open every day from 7 am to 10 pm.

Things to See & Do

The twin **Roman Pools** (Piscines Romaine) are easily located at the southern end of Ave Habib Bourguiba – turn left through the arch and then take the steps down to the right. There is little to see, but there is a pleasant cafe next to one of the pools, and it's easy to while away an hour or so watching the young boys jumping off the nearby roofs into the water.

Right by the entrance to the pools is a small **museum** which houses, among other things, a couple of large mosaics from an-

cient Capsa. It is worth a quick look; it's open Tuesday to Sunday from 8 am to noon and 2 to 5 pm. Admission is TD1.100.

Places to Stay – budget

The cheap accommodation is concentrated in the area around the bus station. The pick of the bunch is the *Hôtel de la République* (☎ 221 807), on Rue Ali Belhaouane around the corner from the bus station. The place is clean and friendly and asks TD6/10 for singles/doubles with breakfast. Hot showers are 500 mills.

The *Hôtel el-Bechir* (☎ 223 239), right next door, is cheaper and has free hot showers, but the toilets are seriously on the nose. Other budget possibilities include the spartan *Hôtel Tunis* (☎ 221 660), off Ave 2 Mars, at TD3 per person with free cold shower. The *Hôtel Khalfallah* (☎ 221 468), off Ave Taieb Mehiri, charges TD6 per person with breakfast. It used to be quite a reasonable joint, but these days it's heading for skid row. It claims to have hot water; maybe it does sometimes.

The gloomy *Hôtel Moussa* (☎ 223 333), about 1km from the town centre on Ave de la Liberté (the Tozeur road), charges TD7/12 for singles/doubles with breakfast.

Places to Stay – middle

The best hotel in town is the three star *Hôtel Maamoun* (☎ 222 740; fax 226 440), just south of the main market square on Ave Jamel Abdelnasser. Large, comfortable rooms with en suite bathroom cost TD37/54 for singles/doubles. Full board, available for TD45/70, is not a bad idea given the lack of reasonable restaurants in town. The hotel also has a swimming pool.

It's hard to miss the *Hôtel Gafsa* (☎ 224 000; fax 224 747), the only multistorey building in the middle of town. It charges TD35/55 for singles/doubles with breakfast. A third option is the *Hôtel Lune* (☎ 222 212), a good one star place about 200m south of the Maamoun on Rue Jamel Abdelnasser. Singles/doubles with breakfast are good value at TD18.500/27.

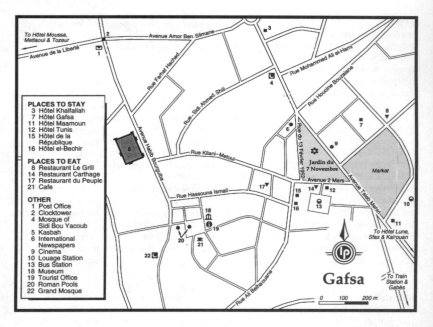

Gafsa

PLACES TO STAY
3 Hôtel Khalfallah
7 Hôtel Gafsa
11 Hôtel Maamoun
12 Hôtel Tunis
15 Hôtel de la
     République
16 Hôtel el-Bechir

PLACES TO EAT
8 Restaurant Le Grill
14 Restaurant Carthage
17 Restaurant du Peuple
21 Cafe

OTHER
1 Post Office
2 Clocktower
4 Mosque of
    Sidi Bou Yacoub
5 Kasbah
6 International
    Newspapers
9 Cinema
10 Louage Station
13 Bus Station
18 Museum
19 Tourist Office
20 Roman Pools
22 Grand Mosque

Places to Eat

Gafsa is not a place to visit for its restaurants, and if you're here on a Friday the pickings are especially thin. There are a few basic places around the central square outside the bus station; the best of these is the *Restaurant Carthage* (closed Friday).

The *Restaurant du Peuple* is one of three gargottes in the first street on the left through the arch opposite the Hôtel Alaya Pacha.

For something a bit better, the basement restaurant in the *Hôtel Gafsa* is very popular, probably because it serves alcohol, although the food is also pretty good. The *Restaurant Le Grill* behind the market also looks promising, but it too is closed on Friday.

The *Hôtel Maamoun* does a three course menu for TD9.

Getting There & Away

Bus The bus station is right in the centre of town, next to the Hôtel Tunis. There are ticket windows for booking, and even boarding announcements.

SNTRI runs eight buses a day to Tunis (six hours, TD13.450). There are four between 9.30 am and 2.30 pm, then four more between 11.30 pm and 1.30 am.

The buses run by the local company, Sotregafsa, are an amazing collection of wrecks that somehow are kept running – minus the odd panel etc. Eight buses a day attempt the run to Tozeur (two hours, TD3.850) and Nefta (2½ hours, TD4.600), with departures from 7.15 am to 6.15 pm. There are also six buses a day to Kasserine (1¾ hours, TD3.900), four to Kairouan (3¼ hours, TD8.130) and four to Sfax (3½ hours, TD7.900). There are regular buses to Metlaoui; some of these services continue to Redeyef and Tamerza.

Train Train services from Gafsa are of little more than academic interest. The station is

FRANCES LINZEE GORDON

JON DAVISON

JON DAVISON

There's more to southern Tunisia than sand and desert landscapes. Check out the weird optical effects created by the Chott el-Jerid, Tunisia's largest salt lake (top left); witness traditional Berber culture (top right); and spend the night in a nomad's tent (bottom).

DAMIEN SIMONIS

JON DAVISON

JON DAVISON

Tunisia's architectural diversity reflects its cultural heritage. Islamic traditions are epitomised by this minaret in the medina at Kairouan; the Berber influence is shown by the traditional brickwork of Nefta and Tozeur; and the European influence is evident in the Mediterranean-type whitewashed houses of the coastal suburb of Sidi Bou Saïd.

3km to the south of town, about 800 mills by taxi. There is just one train a day to Metlaoui, at 5.53 am, and a train to Sfax at 8.38 pm. It's much more convenient to take a bus or louage.

Louage The louage station is near the Hôtel Maamoun. There are regular departures for Metlaoui (TD1.400) and Tozeur (TD3.500) and other departures to Tunis (TD14), Sfax (TD8.100), Kasserine and Gabès.

AROUND GAFSA
Metlaoui & the Seldja Gorge
Metlaoui is a drab, dusty town 42km south-west of Gafsa that exists almost entirely because of phosphate mining. The only reason to come here is because it's the starting point for rides through the spectacular Seldja Gorge on the *Lezard Rouge* (Red Lizard), the train originally used by the bey of Tunis.

Both are attractions in their own right. Train enthusiasts will love the *Lezard Rouge*, built in 1910, which the bey of Tunis once used for journeys between Tunis and his summer palace at Hammam Lif. Everything, from the fine timber panelling to the light fittings, was restored to mint condition during a major refit by the national railway company, SNCFT, in 1995.

The gorge features some weird and wonderful rock formations as it follows the path carved out by the Oued Seldja. The oued is dry most of the time, but there is enough moisture around to support small pockets of greenery.

The journey through the gorge uses the line built in 1906 by the Gafsa Phosphate and Railway Company to connect Metlaoui and Redeyef, 46km to the west. In theory, the *Lezard Rouge* leaves Metlaoui every day at 11 am and returns from Redeyef at 12.45 pm the same day; the return fare is TD20. In practice, it's often chartered by tour companies for special outings, so you should contact the operators at the Hôtel Tamerza Palace (☎ (06) 453 844; fax 453 845) before you head out to Metlaoui.

Places to Stay Metlaoui has just one hotel, the incredibly shabby *Hôtel Ennacim* (☎ (06) 240 271), 1km or so from the centre of town on the road to Tozeur. You'd have to be desperate to fork out TD9/13 for a single/double. The place survives because it has the only bar in town – also somewhere to steer clear of.

Getting There & Away All buses between Gafsa and Tozeur pass through Metlaoui. There are also occasional buses from Metlaoui to Redeyef and Tamerza and there are regular louages to Gafsa and Tozeur.

Train services to Metlaoui are of little more than academic interest. There's one train a day from Tunis (8½ hours), which departs Tunis at 9.20 pm and deposits you on the streets of Metlaoui at 5.40 am. The only departure from Metlaoui is at 8 pm.

Mountain Oases
The beautiful old Berber villages of Tamerza, Midès and Chebika lie close to the Algerian border in the rugged Jebel en-Negeb ranges, about 120km west of Gafsa. The three have existed since Numidian times and were part of the Limes Tripolitanus defensive line developed by the Romans to keep out marauding Saharan tribes.

All three villages were abandoned after the region was hit by 22 days of torrential rain in 1969. The freak rains turned the earthen houses into mud, and the villagers moved to new settlements that were hastily constructed nearby. The original villages are now 'ghost villages', and they are fascinating places to explore.

Tamerza Nestled in a small valley right in the heart of the mountains, Tamerza is the largest of the villages and the only one accessible by public transport. The shell of the old walled town is about 1km east of new Tamerza, on the southern bank of the Oued Horchane. Tamerza's water comes not from the oued but from a spring that rises in the hills south of old Tamerza. The spring supplies water to the old town and then to an extensive *palmeraie* (palm grove), which

JON DAVISON

The ruins of Tamerza, abandoned after a storm destroyed the village in 1969.

locals claim produces the finest dates in Tunisia. From this main palmeraie, the water flows on to a smaller palmeraie at new Tamerza. There are a couple of small waterfalls along the way. The new town is a characterless modern sprawl. There's a bank and a few small shops.

Midès The setting at Midès is little short of spectacular, with the site cut in half by a deep gorge that was previously employed strategically as the town's southern fortification. Midès is a few kilometres north-west of Tamerza as the crow flies, but it's 11km by road. The town is only 1km from the Algerian border.

Chebika This village, 16km south of Tamerza, lies on the southern edge of the mountain range and overlooks the Chott el-Gharsa. The palmeraie is visible for miles – a great blob of green set against the barren mountains. Old Chebika is up the hill behind the palmeraie, next to a small spring-fed stream. You can trace the waters back upstream through a pretty little gorge.

Organised Tours There are plenty of tour companies in Tozeur offering day trips that

call at all three villages, as well as pausing at a small waterfall between Chebika and Tamerza. These include Abdelmoula Voyages (☎ (06) 451 130), Route de Degache, and Tunisie Voyages (☎ (06) 452 404), Route de Nefta. They charge about TD35 per person. There are no tours from Gafsa.

Places to Stay & Eat Tamerza has two hotels. The *Hôtel Les Cascades* (☎ (06) 448 520) has a great setting, at the edge of the palmeraie, next to a small waterfall. However, rooms are uninviting palm-thatched boxes with bare concrete floors, costing over the odds at TD13/18 for singles/doubles with breakfast. The place is signposted in the middle of new Tamerza.

The well-heeled will probably prefer the four star luxury of the *Hôtel Tamerza Palace* (☎ (06) 453 844; fax 453 845), an unusual example of a big hotel attempting to blend in with its surroundings. Bed and breakfast here will set you back TD58/78. It's worth visiting the hotel to take in the views of old Tamerza from the swimming pool terrace.

Tamerza has several restaurants, most of which cater to tour groups. The tiny *Restaurant de Tamerza*, on the right on the road leading down to the Hôtel Les Cascades, turns out a filling bowl of couscous with vegetables for TD2.800. The *Hôtel Tamerza Palace* has a good restaurant, and does a three course set menu for TD9.

There are two places at Midès calling themselves camping grounds. Neither have any set fees or facilities – just a patch of ground on which to pitch a tent. You need to take your own food, or you can buy meals from local families.

Getting There & Away The three villages are on the loop road that heads north off the Gafsa-Tozeur road at Metlaoui and rejoins it about 10km north of Tozeur. There's not much traffic along this way other than 4WDs loaded up with tourists, so you could be in for a long wait if you're hitching.

Tamerza is the only place with public transport. There are two SNTRI buses a day from Tunis (eight hours, TD18.360), and three buses a day from Gafsa (2½ hours) and Metlaoui (two hours). There are no direct services from Tozeur – take a bus to Redeyef and pick up another to Tamerza from there. These buses can drop you at the Midès turn-off, 7km north of Tamerza, leaving a walk of 4km to the village.

East of Gafsa

There are half a dozen traditional Berber villages east of Gafsa. They are spread along the mountain range that runs south of the Gafsa-Sfax road. Most of them are very difficult to get to unless you have a 4WD.

The most accessible of them is **Sened**. A reasonable dirt road leads up to it from the modern village of **Sened Gare**, an expanded railway station 46km east of Gafsa on the road to Sfax. Old Sened is 10km to the south, spread along the banks of a river in the hills below Jebel Biada (1163m). Unlike the mud structures of the villages west of Gafsa, the houses at Sened are built of stone and are still in pretty good condition. People have lived around here for thousands of years – the escarpment behind the village is dotted with caves.

Depending on road conditions (check at Sened Gare), it may be possible to continue

---

Compensation Dams

For centuries, the inhabitants of the mountain villages around Gafsa have scraped together a living from the arid landscape through a traditional dry-land farming technique known as compensation dams (*jesseur* in Arabic). The dams are rough stone walls which are built across watercourses and backfilled with soil, producing a pocket of land that gets the maximum benefit from any flow of water from seasonal rains. The water is held up by the wall of the dam, and soaks down through the soil before flowing on to the next dam further downstream.

The dams vary in size from tiny pockets of soil growing a patch of wheat to half-hectare plots with fruit trees and vegetable gardens. These dams are also a feature of the landscape in the hills around Matmata and in the Ksour District further south. ■

---

from Sened to **Sakket**, a smaller village 10km further south. The road improves again beyond Sakket and you can keep going south-west for another 24km to **El-Guettar**, a busy little oasis town 18km south-east of Gafsa on the road to Gabès.

The Jerid

The Jerid occupies the narrow strip of land between the region's two major salt lakes, the Chott el-Jerid and the Chott el-Gharsa. It has long been one of the most important agricultural districts in Tunisia. The oases at Degache, El-Hamma du Jerid, Nefta and Tozeur are famous for their high quality dates. The harvest is in November, which makes it a good time to visit the area; the weather is cooling down and there's lots of activity. Many villagers work in other parts of the country but return home every year for the date harvest.

TOZEUR

Pop 22,000 ☎ Area code 06

Tozeur is one of the most popular travellers' places in Tunisia. It's an interesting old town with a great setting overlooking an enormous palmeraie on the northern edge of the Chott el-Jerid. Just getting there is half the attraction – the road from Kebili crosses the chott by causeway. Tozeur's main attractions are its enormous palmeraie; the labyrinthine old quarter, the Ouled el-Hadef; and the excellent Dar Charait Museum.

History

The oasis at Tozeur has been inhabited since Capsian times (from 8000 BC). It was the site of the Numidian town of Thuzuros, and it later became part of the Roman Limes Tripolitanus defensive system. This ancient town lay within the palmeraie, around the area now occupied by the district of Bled el-Hader. Tozeur's prosperity peaked during the age of the great trans-Saharan camel caravans in the 14th to 19th centuries.

Chott el-Jerid

The Chott el-Jerid is an immense salt lake covering an area of almost 5000 sq km, the bulk of it stretching away to the horizon south of the Kebili-Tozeur road. It's part of a system of salt lakes that stretches from the Gulf of Gabès to near the Algerian city of Biskra, 400km inland. The Chott el-Jerid is dry for the greater part of the year, when the surface becomes blistered and shimmers in the heat. The Kebili-Tozeur road crosses the northern reaches of the chott on a 2m high causeway – it's a trip not to be missed. It's weird driving across and seeing the colour of the water that has collected on either side of the road – because of the chemicals present, it may be pink on one side and green on the other. Mirages are a common occurrence, and if you've picked a sunny day to cross you're bound to see some stunning optical effects. ■

Orientation

Tozeur is fairly easy to find your way around because there are only three main streets: Ave Abdulkacem Chebbi, which runs along the edge of the palmeraie on the southern side of town; Ave Farhat Hached, which skirts the northern edge of town before becoming the Route de Nefta; and Ave Habib Bourguiba, which links the two.

Ave Habib Bourguiba qualifies as the main street. It is certainly the most attractive, with its carpet shops draped with brightly coloured Berber rugs. Ave Abdulkacem Chebbi has most of the accommodation. Its western extension is known as the Route Touristique, which is where you'll find the Dar Charait Museum and the hotels where tour groups stay.

Most people's first glimpse of town will be Ave Farhat Hached. The roads into town from Gafsa and Kebili merge into Ave Farhat Hached at a roundabout at the north-eastern edge of town. The bus and louage stations are on the other side of town, opposite each other in a couple of dusty lots north of the Route de Nefta. If you're arriving by louage, you can save yourself the 600m walk back to town by asking to be dropped off on the way through.

Information

Tourist Offices There is an ONTT office (☎ 454 088) at the western end of Ave Abdulkacem Chebbi, which is open standard government hours. The staff are helpful and a couple of them speak English. There is also a *syndicat d'initiative* (municipal tourist office; ☎ 462 034) on Place Ibn Chabbat, near the corner of Ave Farhat Hached and Ave Habib Bourguiba.

Money You'll find all the major Tunisian banks around the town centre, including the STB on Ave Habib Bourguiba.

Post & Communications The post office is on the main square by the market. There is a small Taxiphone office nearby, and others around town.

International Newspapers The kiosk near the Hôtel Khalifa on Ave Habib Bourguiba stocks English-language and other international newspapers, usually two or three days after publication.

Dar Charait Museum

Apart from the Bardo in Tunis, this is the only museum in the country that's worth going out of your way to see. It's expensive by museum standards at TD3.200, plus TD1.500 to take photos, but it's a class act.

It has an extensive collection of pottery and antiques, as well as an art gallery, but the star features are the rooms set up as replicas of scenes from Tunisian life, past and present. They include the bedroom of the last bey, a palace scene, a typical kitchen, a hammam, wedding scenes and a Bedouin tent. The museum attendants, dressed as servants of the bey, set the tone. The museum is open from 8 am until midnight every day.

The latest addition to the Dar Charait complex is a sound and light show called '1001 Nights', open every night from 6 to 11 pm for TD5.

There's also a bookshop selling a good range of the Editions Alif publications, including their pop-up Tunis medina and oasis books, jigsaws and other books that are hard

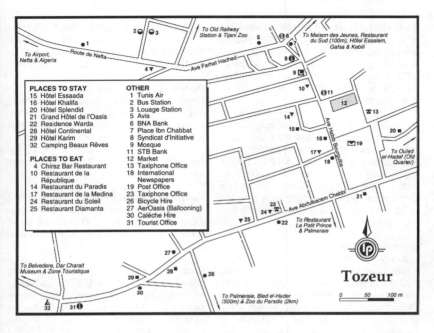

Tozeur

PLACES TO STAY
15 Hôtel Essaada
16 Hôtel Khalifa
20 Hôtel Splendid
21 Grand Hôtel de l'Oasis
22 Residence Warda
28 Hôtel Continental
29 Hôtel Karim
32 Camping Beaux Rêves

PLACES TO EAT
4 Chiraz Bar Restaurant
10 Restaurant de la République
14 Restaurant du Paradis
17 Restaurant de la Medina
24 Restaurant du Soleil
25 Restaurant Diamanta

OTHER
1 Tunis Air
2 Bus Station
3 Louage Station
5 Avis
6 BNA Bank
7 Place Ibn Chabbat
8 Syndicat d'Initiative
9 Mosque
11 STB Bank
12 Market
13 Taxiphone Office
18 International Newspapers
19 Post Office
23 Taxiphone Office
26 Bicycle Hire
27 AerOasis (Ballooning)
30 Calèche Hire
31 Tourist Office

to find elsewhere. (For more details, see under Children in the Books section of the Facts about the Country chapter.)

Palmeraie
Tozeur's palmeraie is the second largest in the country with around 200,000 palm trees spread over an area of more than 10 sq km. It is a classic example of tiered oasis agriculture. The system is watered by more than 200 springs that produce almost 60 million litres of water a day. It is distributed around the various holdings under a complex system devised by the mathematician Ibn Chabbat in the 13th century AD.

The best way to explore the palmeraie is on foot. Take the road which runs south off Ave Abdulkacem Chebbi next to the Hôtel Continental and follow the signs to the Zoo du Paradis. After about 500m the road passes the old quarter of Bled el-Hader, thought to be the site of ancient Thuzuros. The main square has a minaret built on a Roman base

as well as an 11th century mosque. Further on is the village of Abbes, where the *marabout* (shrine) of Sidi Bou Lifa stands in the shade of an enormous jubube (Chinese date) tree. There are lots of paths leading off into the palmeraie along the irrigation canals. It's delightfully cool among all the vegetation – it must be 5°C cooler than in town.

If you want to see more of the oasis, the bicycle hire place on the road leading into the palmeraie has bikes for TD2 per hour or TD6 for half a day. Equipped with a bike, you can complete a loop through the palmeraie that emerges further west on Ave Abdulkacem Chebbi near the Grand Hôtel de l'Oasis. If that sounds too energetic, *calèches* (horse-drawn carriages) can be hired from opposite the Hôtel Karim for TD5 per hour.

Ouled el-Hadef
The town's delightful old quarter was built in the 14th century AD to house the El-Hadef

clan, which had grown rich on the proceeds of the caravan trade. The area is a maze of narrow, covered alleys and small squares. It's famous for its amazing traditional brickwork, which uses protruding bricks to create intricate relief patterns. The style is found only here and in nearby Nefta.

The entrance to the Ouled el-Hadef is along the small road that runs east beyond the Hôtel Splendid. Follow the signs pointing to the small **Museum Archéologique et Traditionnel**, which occupies the old Kobba of Sidi Bou Aissa. It houses a small collection of local finds as well as costumes and displays on local culture. It's open Monday to Saturday from 8.30 am to noon and 3 to 5 pm; admission is TD1.100.

Belvedere Rocks

A sandy track running south off the Route Touristique near the Dar Charait Museum leads to a group of rocks known as the Belvedere. Steps have been cut into the highest rock, giving access to a spectacular view over the oasis and the chott. It's a pleasant 20 minute walk; the best views are in the early morning.

Zoos

For some reason, Tozeur has two zoos. The owners of the **Zoo du Paradis**, which is on the southern side of the palmeraie, must have a strange vision of paradise if the depressingly small cages are anything to go by. The star turn is a Coca-Cola-drinking camel. Admission is TD1.

It looks good, however, when set against the **Tijani Zoo**, also known as the Zoo du Desert, which is north of town near the old train station. This place is worth a mention only as somewhere to avoid like the plague. It's a disgrace, complete with live scorpions housed in cigarette packets – 'just the thing for the mother-in-law' touts the attendant.

Ballooning

AerOasis (☎ 452 361), opposite the Hôtel Continental on Ave Abdulkacem Chebbi, is a small French-run company that organises balloon rides at a range of locations around Tozeur. Flights are timed to catch either the sunrise or sunset and cost TD80 for an hour. They will travel as far as Douz in search of the right conditions.

Places to Stay – budget

Camping *Camping Beaux Rêves* (☎ 453 331), near the tourist office on Ave Abdulkacem Chebbi, is a good, shady site that backs onto the palmeraie. It charges TD4 per person to camp or to sleep in one of the communal nomad-style tents. Hot showers are TD1.

Hostel Tozeur's *Maison des Jeunes* (☎ 452 335) is only for the dedicated. It's opposite the police station on the Gafsa road, about 800m from the town centre. A bed in a dorm costs TD4.

Hotels The cheapest hotel in town is the grim *Hôtel Essaada* (☎ 450 097), which is on a small street that runs behind the carpet shops on Ave Habib Bourguiba. It charges TD3.500 per person, plus an extra 500 mills for a cold shower. The nearby *Hôtel Khalifa* (☎ 454 858), which is on the western side of the square at the middle of Ave Habib Bourguiba, isn't much better at TD7 per person, including breakfast. Hot showers are TD1. The only rooms with windows overlook busy Ave Habib Bourguiba.

Inconvenient, but much better than either of these, is the *Hôtel Essalem* (☎ 452 981), 150m past the roundabout at the western end of Ave Farhat Hached. It's quiet and friendly and has singles/doubles for TD7/14 with breakfast and hot showers or bath.

Places to Stay – middle

The *Residence Warda* (☎ 452 597) is an excellent place on Ave Abdulkacem Chebbi. The owners have just completed a major renovation/extension that has doubled the number of rooms and created a choice of rooms with private bathrooms. The changes haven't affected the plumbing: the Warda still boasts the hottest hot water around and showers that deliver it at a great rate – a welcome change from the usual dribble. The rates are very reasonable for the standard of the facilities. Singles/doubles are TD11/16 with shared bathroom, or TD12/18 with private bathroom. Prices include breakfast.

Another good choice is the *Hôtel Karim* (☎ 454 574), opposite the calèche waiting area further west along Ave Abdulkacem Chebbi. It's a friendly, well run place offering a similar deal to the Warda – large, clean singles/doubles with bathroom for TD12/18, including breakfast.

The *Hôtel Splendid* (☎ 450 053), behind the post office on the edge of the old town, probably was splendid – once. These days it's a sad old colonial relic that is asking over the odds at TD15/22 for singles/doubles with breakfast. The owner does, however, have a splendid collection of notes and coins from all over the world. The noisy bar is another reason not to stay here.

Places to Stay – top end
Three and four star hotels are popping up like mushrooms in the new *zone touristique* (tourist strip) beyond the Dar Charait Museum. They are used almost exclusively by tour groups, and they aren't much fun for individuals. They are also expensive compared with what you can find elsewhere. The cheapest hotel is the *Basma* (☎ 452 340; fax 452 294), where single/double rooms are TD43/66.

You'll find much better value at the *Hôtel Continental* (☎ 450 526; fax 452 109), an older three star place on Ave Abdulkacem Chebbi. It's set back from the road among the palm trees and has a shaded swimming pool right next to the palmeraie. It charges TD27/40 for comfortable rooms with breakfast. Full board costs only TD3.800 extra per person.

The *Grand Hôtel de l'Oasis* (☎ 452 699; fax 452 153), on Ave Abdulkacem Chebbi at the junction with Ave Habib Bourguiba, looks quite a sight at night with its illuminated, traditional-style brick façade. Most of the customers are small tour groups, who are probably getting a better deal than the listed rates of TD47/68 for singles/doubles with breakfast.

If money is no object, you can lash out around TD250 a night for a double room at the new *Palm Beach Palace* (☎ 453 211; fax 453 911) or the *Dar Charait* (☎ 454 888; fax 452 399), which adjoins the museum. Both offer the full five star treatment.

Places to Eat
Tozeur is better served for cheap restaurants than most places. For cheap food and friendly service, you can't beat the *Restaurant du Paradis*, just a couple of doors along from the Hôtel Essaada. They have good soups and salads, and the tables outside are a pleasant place to sit on a warm evening.

The *Restaurant de la Medina*, just around the corner from the Hôtel Khalifa, doesn't have a lot to choose from but the food is good. A generous serving of couscous and turkey costs TD2.600.

The two places opposite the Residence Warda, the *Restaurant du Soleil* and *Restaurant Diamanta*, are both good. The *Restaurant du Soleil* is a bit smarter than the others and seems to get the lion's share of the business. It serves a generous escalope de dinde (turkey schnitzel) with chips and salad for TD3.500.

The inconspicuous *Restaurant du Sud*, north-east of the city centre on Ave Farhat Hached, has a good choice of meals for under TD3. The remaining budget option is the *Restaurant de la République*, in an arcade off Ave Habib Bourguiba near the mosque. It has similar fare but is more expensive.

If you want a drink with your meal, the options start with the *Chiraz Bar Restaurant* at the western end of Ave Farhat Hached. It's a lively no-nonsense bar with beers for TD1.100 and wine by the bottle. It also offers basic grilled meals like chicken and chips with salad for TD2.

Many notches up from the Chiraz are the restaurants at the bigger hotels. The *Hôtel Continental* is the place to head for. It does a three course menu for TD9 and has a reasonable wine list. The *Restaurant Le Petit Prince* is popular with tour groups but not particularly good value. The Dar Charait's *Restaurant Shehrezad* is a good place for a splurge. It has a TD20 menu and the setting is positively palatial. The museum's cafe (separate from the restaurant), with its divan seating and elaborate tilework, has performances by local musicians in the evening. The cafe overlooks the palmeraie, which is illuminated at night.

There are plenty of cafes and a couple of patisseries along Ave Habib Bourguiba.

Getting There & Away

Air The airport is 4km from town, TD2 by taxi. Tuninter runs five flights a week to Tunis (TD40.100/79.400 one way/return), as well as flights to Jerba (TD27.800 one way). The airport handles a growing number of international flights, mainly charters from Europe. Tunis Air also operates scheduled services from Tozeur to Brussels, Milan, Paris and Zurich.

The Tunis Air (☎ 450 038) office is out towards the airport along the Nefta road. It's the unmarked white building opposite the Hertz car rental agency.

Bus There are two air-conditioned SNTRI buses a day to Tunis, leaving at 11 am and 11 pm. The trip takes seven hours and costs TD16.550. It's advisable to buy tickets the day before from the SNTRI office at the bus station.

Regional buses operate to Gafsa (six daily, TD3.850) and Nefta (six daily, 950 mills), as well as to Redeyef (three daily, TD4), Douz (2.30 pm, TD4.620) and Gabès (3 pm, TD6.970). The 9.30 am bus to Nefta goes all the way to Hazoua on the Algerian border.

Train Tozeur has a train station to the north of town but passenger services have been discontinued. Trains from Sfax now run only as far as Metlaoui, 50km to the north (see Getting There & Away under Metlaoui in the Around Gafsa section).

Louage The louage station has regular departures to Nefta (TD1), Gafsa (TD3.500) and Kebili (TD3.750). There are also occasional louages to Tunis (TD15.850) and Redeyef (TD4.050).

Car Rental There is an Avis (☎ 450 547) office on Ave Farhat Hached, and the Hertz (☎ 450 214) office is on the Nefta road.

NEFTA
Pop 18,000 ☎ Area code 06

The oasis of Nefta, 23km west of Tozeur, is the last town before the Algerian border at Hazoua. In many ways, it is a smaller version of Tozeur. The architecture is similar, with some very good examples of the highly distinctive ornamental brickwork in the old sections of town. The oasis is of equal size and importance.

Nefta is also the home of Sufism in Tunisia (see the boxed text 'Sufism' in the Religion section of the Facts about the Country chapter) and there are a couple of important religious sites here, including the Zaouia of Sidi Brahim and the Mosque of Sidi M'Khareg.

Orientation

Nefta's main street, Ave Habib Bourguiba (just for a change!), is also the main Tozeur-Algeria road. The main feature of the town is the *corbeille* (literally 'basket'), a huge gully north of Ave Habib Bourguiba that cuts the town in two and runs into the palmeraie proper on the southern side of town. The Route de la Corbeille does a loop around the corbeille off Ave Habib Bourguiba, providing access to a couple of flash hotels that overlook the corbeille from the north.

Most of the tourist hotels are on the edge of the palmeraie at the western (Algerian) end of Ave Habib Bourguiba.

Information

The small syndicat d'initiative office (☎ 430 236) is on the right as you come into town from Tozeur, just before the ring-road junction. The guys who staff the office are quite helpful but are there primarily to promote their services as guides. One of them speaks English.

The bus station is opposite the syndicat d'initiative, while louages hang around outside the restaurants about 100m further west on Ave Habib Bourguiba. The post office is

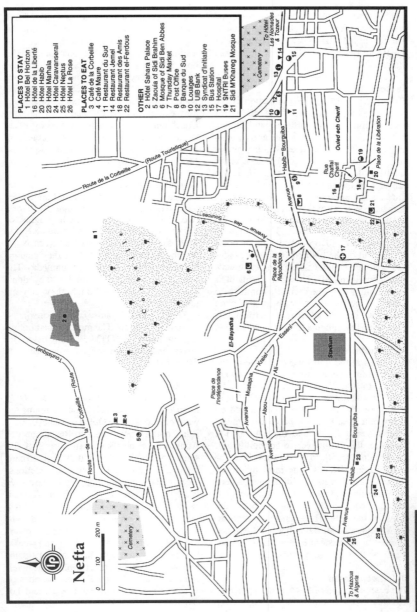

Nefta

0   100   200 m

PLACES TO STAY
1 Hôtel Bel Horizon
16 Hôtel de la Liberté
20 Hôtel Habib
23 Hôtel Marhala
24 Hôtel Caravanserail
25 Hôtel Neptus
26 Hôtel La Rose

PLACES TO EAT
3 Café de la Corbeille
4 Café Maure
11 Restaurant du Sud
14 Restaurant Jemel
18 Restaurant des Amis
22 Restaurant el-Ferdous

OTHER
2 Hôtel Sahara Palace
5 Zaouia of Sidi Brahim
6 Mosque of Sidi Ben Abbes
7 Thursday Market
8 Post Office
9 Banque du Sud
10 Louages
12 UIB Bank
13 Syndicat d'Initiative
15 Bus Station
17 Hospital
19 SNTRI Buses
21 Sidi M'Khareg Mosque

another 250m along on the left, where the road descends to cross the corbeille. There is a branch of the UIB bank at the beginning of the Route de la Corbeille, near the tourist office.

La Corbeille

The town's most obvious attraction is the corbeille, the deep palm-filled gully that takes up much of the northern part of town. It measures almost 1km across at its widest point and is about 40m deep, which makes it an impressively large hole. The best views are from the north-western side. Here you can take in the setting over a coffee at the Café de la Corbeille or Café Maure, which both have terraces overlooking the corbeille.

Unfortunately the area was looking a bit sad at the time of research. The hot spring which used to feed a couple of bathing pools at the head of the corbeille below the cafes had dried up, with locals blaming the town's hotels for using all the water to fill their swimming pools. The corbeille contracts to a narrow gorge which leads to the main **palmeraie** on the southern side of town. It is every bit as fascinating as the one at Tozeur.

El-Bayadha

The cafes at the north-western edge of the corbeille are a good starting point for a walk through the old El-Bayadha neighbourhood, which lies south-west of the corbeille. Many of the houses here were badly damaged by heavy rain in early 1990, which also caused several landslides around the edge of the corbeille. Just about every other building in El-Bayadha seems to have some level of religious significance. The most important of them is the **Zaouia of Sidi Brahim**, where the Sufi saint and some of his followers are buried. The zaouia is 100m south of the cafes, on the right. The open space opposite the Mosque of Sidi Ben Abbes, off Ave des Sources at the eastern edge of El-Bayadha, stages Nefta's Thursday market.

Ouled ech Cherif

The best preserved of Nefta's old districts is the Ouled ech Cherif, which occupies the south-eastern quarter of town south of Ave Habib Bourguiba. To get there, follow the signs to the Hôtel Habib on the main road leading south next to the bus station. The hotel is on Place de la Libération, at the heart of the Ouled ech Cherif. The layout is very similar to the Ouled el-Hadef in Tozeur, with winding vaulted alleyways and some stunning examples of traditional brick designs. Check out the street that runs west off Place de la Libération to the palmeraie, emerging next to the quarter's principal mosque, the Mosque of Sidi M'Khareg.

Organised Tours

The guides at the syndicat d' initiative offer a range of services. They charge TD15 for a two hour tour of the town's highlights, or TD40 for a full day in and around Nefta. They say they know a spot between Nefta and the Algerian border where they guarantee you will see a mirage on a sunny day. The fees are only for their time – they don't provide transport, although they can organise it for you.

They can also organise **camel rides** in the surrounding desert. The most popular outing is a four hour ride (TD24), leaving in the late afternoon so that you are out in the desert for the sunset.

Places to Stay

Nefta's cheapest hotel is the *Hôtel de la Liberté*, off Place de la Libération among the winding alleys of the Ouled ech Cherif. Take Rue Chaffai Cherif, next to Restaurant des Amis on the north-western corner of the square, and look for the sign. It's not too hard to find, but if you need to ask directions, locals call it the Hôtel Mahmoud – the owner is a bit of a character. What awaits you is a basic but friendly old hotel built around a vine-filled central courtyard. Beds are TD3.500 per person, with free cold shower.

The *Hôtel Habib* (☎ 430 497), on Place de la Libération, seems to have spent its paint budget on signs directing people to the hotel. Still, the staff are friendly and the rates of TD7 per person include breakfast and hot showers.

An interesting option is the *Hôtel Les Nomades* (☎ 430 052), just through the arch on the edge of town as you arrive from Tozeur. It's right next to the Chott el-Jerid, although the place seems to have been laid out with the intention of minimising the views. The best views are from the bar/restaurant. The rooms are clean but basic. Singles/doubles are TD12/18.

The *Hôtel Marhala* (☎ 430 027; fax 430 511) is one of the four excellent places run by the Touring Club de Tunisie (the others are at Gammarth, Matmata and Jerba). It occupies a converted brick factory next to the palmeraie on the western side of town, about 20 minutes walk from the bus station. The rooms are small but they are spotless and comfortable. Singles/doubles, with breakfast are TD9.500/16 with breakfast, or TD11/18 for rooms with shower. It's worth considering half or full board at TD2.500 per meal because the town isn't exactly brimming with good restaurants.

By now, the Marhala should also be operating a second, rather more upmarket, hotel right next door, charging TD18/36 with breakfast. The new version has a large swimming pool, open to residents of both hotels.

The Marhala is surrounded by a growing band of three star hotels built right on the edge of the palmeraie. The *Hôtel Caravanserail* (☎ 430 355; fax 430 344) leads the way on the price scale with singles/doubles for TD68/92 with breakfast. The nearby *Hôtel Neptus* (☎ 430 321; fax 430 647) and *Hôtel La Rose* (☎ 430 696/7; fax 430 385) aren't far behind. All have swimming pools.

The *Hôtel Bel Horizon* (☎ 430 328; fax 430 500) has a great location on the north-eastern side of the corbeille. Singles/doubles cost TD46/62. The *Hôtel Sahara Palace*, on the north-western side of the corbeille, has failed to reopen its doors after closing for renovations in 1994.

Places to Eat

The sum total of Nefta's eateries is a few basic restaurants on Ave Habib Bourguiba near the bus station and around Place de la Libération, plus the hotel restaurants. The best of the cheapies is the *Restaurant Jemel*, next to the tourist office, which has a blackboard menu listing meals for TD2. The range isn't exactly riveting. Opposite the louage station, the *Restaurant du Sud* has a choice of couscous – take it or leave it – for TD2.

The *El-Ferdous* is a popular small bar/restaurant in the palmeraie. It's a quiet spot to have lunch, but it gets quite rowdy in the evenings.

Getting There & Away

Bus The bus station is on the southern side of Ave Habib Bourguiba on the way into town from Tozeur. There are hourly buses to Tozeur (30 minutes, 810 mills) and six a day to Gafsa (2½ hours, TD4.500). There is also one bus to the Algerian border at Hazoua (one hour, TD1.250), 36km south-west of Nefta. Before the troubles in Algeria, this was a popular crossing – just 80km from the fascinating desert town of El-Oued by good bitumen road. There is 4km of neutral territory between the Tunisian and Algerian border posts.

SNTRI has buses to Tunis (7½ hours, TD17.250) at 10.30 am and midnight. The SNTRI office is on Place de la Libération, opposite the Hôtel Habib – which is where the drivers stay.

Louage Louages leave from outside the restaurants on Ave Habib Bourguiba. You won't have to wait long for a ride to Tozeur (TD1), and there are also occasional departures for Hazoua (TD1.500).

The Nefzaoua

The Nefzaoua covers the area stretching east from the Chott el-Jerid to the edge of the Jebel Dahar ranges. It's bounded by the Chott el Fejej in the north and the sands of the Great Eastern Erg to the south.

Like the Jerid, the Nefzaoua is an important date-growing area, with a string of oases running south from Kebili around the edge of the Chott el-Jerid. The palmeraie at Douz is the largest in Tunisia with around 400,000 date palms. The settlements of the Nefzaoua, like those of the Jerid, formed part of the Roman defensive system, the Limes Tripolitanus. The main Roman settlement was Turris Tamelleni (modern Telmine), a few kilometres west of Kebili.

Located right at the edge of the Roman world, it became one of the first regions to be reclaimed by Berber nomads when the empire began to wane. Tribes began to move in from the south at the end of the 4th century AD, bringing with them the first camels to be seen in Tunisia. By the end of the 5th century, the area was under the control of the Nefzaoua confederation – a loose grouping of half a dozen Berber tribes. The descendants of these tribes continue to live a semi-nomadic existence in the south around Douz.

KEBILI
Pop 10,000 ☎ Area code 05

This small town at the eastern edge of the Chott el-Jerid has very little to commend it, but it's a regional transport hub and there is a good chance that you will pass through here on the way between Douz and Gabès or Tozeur. Facilities include a post office and bank (open for changing money from 9 am to noon only). Both are located in the centre of town around the junction of the Gabès-Tozeur road and Ave Habib Bourguiba, which becomes the road south to Douz.

If you've got time to kill between buses, you can check out the only attraction: the hot-spring baths on the road to Douz. The baths are about a kilometre from the centre of town. The men's pool is right by the roadside and has a couple of cafes around it. The pool for women is about 150m upstream and is screened by palm fronds stuck in the ground. The slightly sulphurous water gushes out of the ground at a high temperature, a couple of hundred metres from the women's pool.

Places to Stay

There is no reason to stay overnight in Kebili. If you do get stuck, the *Hôtel Ben*

Said (☎ 491 573) is a good little hotel, 150m south of the town centre on Ave Habib Bourguiba. Clean singles/doubles with shared bathroom are TD5/8. The budget alternative is the *Maison des Jeunes* (☎ 490 635), behind the Total station on the road out to Tozeur.

The *Hôtel Kitam* (☎ 491 338) is a reasonable, modern two star hotel on the road into town from Gabès. It has singles/doubles for TD24/35. A more interesting option is the *Hôtel Fort des Autruches* (☎ 490 233; fax 490 933), the veteran of the resort hotels in the palmeraie. Follow the signs to Fort des Autruches, off to the left near the military base on the Douz road and about 30 minutes walk – or a short taxi ride – from the bus station. It's a pleasant spot with a swimming pool and terrace. Rooms are TD37.500/42 for singles/doubles with breakfast.

You'll see signs in town directing people to the *Hôtel Les Dunes de Nefzaoua* (☎ 499 211; fax 499 153), 22km west of town near the village of Bechri – which means that it's only really an option if you have your own transport. The turn-off south to Bechri is clearly signposted in the small village of Zaouia, which is the last village before the causeway on the Kebili-Tozeur road. You'll come to the hotel after about 2km. It has a fantastic setting on the edge of the Chott el-Jerid and an inviting swimming pool, but the calm is shattered at dusk when 4WD safari groups descend. At least you get to enjoy the displays of folk music and dancing that are put on for their benefit. Rooms are TD45/64, with breakfast.

Places to Eat

There are several restaurants, but nothing to get excited about. The *Restaurant Les Palmiers*, right in the centre by the bus station, is as good as any. There used to be a restaurant opposite the louage station, but it is now just a cafe.

Getting There & Away
Bus The bus station is no more than an office on the main street, near the junction with the Gabès-Tozeur road.

There are frequent buses and minibuses to Douz, as well as regular departures for Tozeur and Gabès.

The SNTRI office, usually closed, is 100m away on the opposite side of the dusty square. There is one bus a day to Tunis, leaving at 11 am.

Louage It's only a short walk from the bus station to the louages, which leave throughout the day for Gabès (TD4.750), Douz (TD1.450) and Tozeur (TD4.200). You can relax over a coffee at the cafe opposite while you wait for your louage to fill up.

DOUZ
Pop 12,000 ☎ Area code 05
The small town of Douz, 28km south of Kebili, lies at the north-eastern edge of the Great Eastern Erg and touts itself as the gateway to the Sahara. You certainly get the feeling that you're driving out into the desert as you head south from Kebili. A long dune flanks the road, held back by a fence of palm fronds.

Douz remains fairly laid-back in spite of the huge numbers of 4WDs that pass through town. Most of them head straight for the hotels of the small *zone touristique* (tourist strip), which faces the desert on the southern edge of the enormous palmeraie. The peak season is during the Sahara Festival in December and January. In spite of the crush, it is generally possible to find a place to sleep – even if it's only on a mattress in a corridor.

The town's main attraction is the colourful Thursday market in the old souq. Douz also makes a good base from which to organise camel trekking (see under Camel Trekking later in this section).

Orientation & Information
Douz isn't big enough to get lost in. The town centre is laid out in a rough grid around the souq. Ave des Martyrs leads west from the town centre to Place des Martyrs, which is where you'll find the small syndicat d'initiative (☎ 470 341). Halfway between the town and Place des Martyrs, a road leads south through the palmeraie to Place du Festival and the zone touristique.

Buses and louages will drop you at the north-western edge of the town centre on Ave Taieb Mehiri, which skirts the town centre and heads south-west to link up with Ave des Martyrs. You can change money at the bank by the roundabout on the way into town from Kebili. Opposite the bank is a wall map showing a rough outline of the town. The post office is on Ave Taieb Mehiri, just west of the town centre.

Souq
For most of the week, the souq is little more than a sleepy square with a scattering of souvenir shops selling local rugs. It springs to life on Thursday when it becomes the setting for the famous Douz market. It is still an authentic market, although the huge numbers of tourists have led to a rise in the number of souvenir stalls. Villagers from the surrounding oases also come in large numbers to buy and sell produce. It's a great place for people watching.

Don't miss the livestock markets, nearby off the southern end of Rue des Affections, where the last of Tunisia's nomadic camel herdsmen come to trade.

Palmeraie
The palmeraie is deceptively large – it is the largest of all the Tunisian desert oases, with more than 400,000 palm trees. The best way to explore it is to walk out along the road to the Place du Festival and zone touristique and strike off on one of the many paths leading into the palmeraie.

A second road leads south through the palmeraie from Place des Martyrs, passing the Hôtel Roses des Sable and emerging about 1km west of the zone touristique at a small concrete-block settlement. The government built these basic houses in an effort to encourage the area's Marazig tribespeople to stop their wanderings – which it hasn't.

The road to the Hôtel Roses des Sable goes past a hammam fed by its own hot spring. It costs 500 mills to bathe.

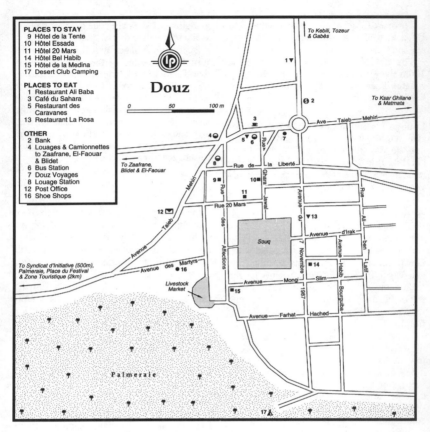

Douz

PLACES TO STAY
9 Hôtel de la Tente
10 Hôtel Essada
11 Hôtel 20 Mars
14 Hôtel Bel Habib
15 Hôtel de la Medina
17 Desert Club Camping

PLACES TO EAT
1 Restaurant Ali Baba
3 Café du Sahara
5 Restaurant des
   Caravanes
13 Restaurant La Rosa

OTHER
2 Bank
4 Louages & Camionnettes
   to Zaafrane, El-Faouar
   & Blidet
6 Bus Station
7 Douz Voyages
8 Louage Station
12 Post Office
16 Shoe Shops

To Kebili, Tozeur & Gabès

To Ksar Ghilane & Matmata

Ave – Taieb – Mehiri

To Zaafrane, Blidet & El-Faouar

Rue de – la Liberté

Rue 20 Mars

Souq

Avenue – d'Irak

Avenue – Mong – Slim

Avenue – Farhat – Hached

To Syndicat d'Initiative (500m), Palmeraie, Place du Festival & Zone Touristique (2km)

Avenue – des – Martyrs

Livestock Market

Palmeraie

0   50   100 m

Great Dune

The much-touted Great Dune lies on the fringe of the desert just beyond the Place du Festival. The convenient location opposite the tourist hotels, combined with the absence of any other dunes, has led some to suggest that this phenomenon might not be entirely natural. It is, however, a good spot for those all-important 'been there, done that' Sahara photos.

There are plenty of real sand dunes around, but you need to travel a bit further south to see them. The Great Eastern Erg is one of the Sahara's two great sand seas, extending almost 500km south-west into neighbouring Algeria.

Camel Trekking

Most people come to Douz to go camel trekking, which isn't difficult to organise. Trekking touts can now be found as far afield as the bus station in Gabès, and the offers are flying thick and fast by the time you reach Douz. Most of the time, they are touting for a couple of big operators at Zaafrane – which is the place to go to get the best deals. Zaafrane is covered in the following Around Douz section.

SOUTHERN TUNISIA

If you don't feel like heading out to Zaafrane (there's not much else there), there are several small-time operators in Douz, charging around TD25 for an overnight trip. It's a good idea to seek out someone who's been on a trek before taking up an offer. If you just want to know what it feels like to sit on a camel, the place to go looking is the cafe beside the syndicat d'initiative. Expect to pay about TD5 per hour – quite long enough for the average backside.

The two travel agencies in town, Douz Voyages (☎ 495 315) on Ave Taieb Mehiri, and Abdelmoula Voyages (☎ 470 282), at the Hôtel Roses des Sable, both offer a range of desert excursions for up to eight days. They involve a combination of camel trekking and 4WD touring.

Special Events
The Sahara Festival is held in December and January, when the place is packed with tourists coming to watch activities like camel racing and hunting with the famous Saluki desert dog, an animal constructed along the same lines as the greyhound.

Places to Stay – budget
Camping The *Desert Club* (☎ 470 575) camping ground is set among the palm trees to the right at the end of Ave du 7 Novembre 1987. It's a friendly place with plenty of shade. Rates are TD4 per person in tents or TD10 per person with breakfast staying in their nomad-style tents. There's hot water and the site has its own restaurant and bar.

Hotels All the cheapies are in the town centre, around the souq and the bus station.

Management doesn't come any friendlier than at the *Hôtel 20 Mars* (☎ 470 269) on the street of the same name, just north of the souq. Rooms are set around a small courtyard and cost TD6 per person; breakfast is TD1.500. Just around the corner on Rue Ghara Jawal, the *Hôtel Essada* (☎ 470 824) charges TD5 per person; breakfast is TD1.

Other budget possibilities include the *Hôtel Bel Habib* (☎ 495 115), at the southern end of Ave du 7 Novembre, and the *Hôtel de*

la Tente (☎ 495 468), right by the louage station on Rue des Affections.

Places to Stay – middle
The *Hôtel de la Medina* is a new hotel at the southern end of Rue des Affections, which was nearing completion at the time of research. Expect to pay about TD10 per person with breakfast.

There are a couple of reasonable mid-range places in the palmeraie, off Ave des Martyrs, about 20 minutes walk from the centre of town. Offering similar facilities are the huge *Hôtel Saharien* (☎ 471 337; fax 470 339) – turn left at the Maison de Culture – and the *Hôtel Roses des Sable* (☎ 470 597; fax 471 484), to the left opposite the tourist office. Both have swimming pools and restaurants. Rates at the Roses des Sables are TD13/20 for singles/ doubles, including breakfast. The Hôtel Saharien is considerably more expensive at TD22/34.

Places to Stay – top end
All the upmarket hotels are in the zone touristique on the southern side of the palmeraie, facing the sand hills of the desert. They include the *Hôtel Touareg* (☎ 470 057; fax 470 313), which is built in the image of an old-style kasbah, complete with crenellations. There's a palm- covered island in the middle of the swimming pool. Singles/ doubles are TD54/78 with breakfast. Prices are very similar at the neighbouring *Hôtel Sahara Douz* (☎ 470 865; fax 470 566) and the *Mehari* (☎ 495 088; fax 495 589). The Mehari allows visitors to use its pool for TD2.500 per day.

Places to Eat
Douz has plenty of budget restaurants, including the excellent *Restaurant La Rosa*, near the souq on Ave du 7 Novembre 1987. It's well set up for travellers and has a good range of dishes for under TD3. *Restaurant Ali Baba*, 100m north of the roundabout on the Kebili road, gets mixed reports. Some people rave about the warm welcome and the spicy couscous (TD2.400); others despair about the standards of hygiene.

The *Restaurant des Caravanes*, next to the bus station on Ave Taieb Mehiri, does a generous turkey schnitzel, chips and salad for TD3. Opposite here is the *Café du Sahara*, a favourite meeting place for the men of Douz.

Things to Buy

There are three shops along Ave des Martyrs, just west of the souq, selling Saharan sandals (slip-on shoes made from camel skin). The tourist versions normally come decorated with palm motifs etc. The prices vary from TD12 to TD18, depending on the level of decoration and quality.

Getting There & Away

Bus Buses leave from the intersection of Ave Taieb Mehiri and Rue Ghara Jawal on the northern side of town, which is where you'll find the office of the regional bus company, Sotregames.

There are regular buses to Kebili (30 minutes, TD1.250), as well as buses south to Tozeur (2½ hours, TD4.620) at 8 am and to Gabès (three hours, TD5.110) at 6.45 am and 9 pm. There are buses to Zaafrane at 7, 9 and 11 am and 1 and 2.30 pm.

SNTRI has air-conditioned services to Tunis (nine hours, TD19.240) via Tozeur, Gafsa and Kairouan (seven hours, TD14.600) at 6 am. Services to Tunis via Gabès, Sfax (five hours, TD10.910) and Sousse (seven hours, TD14.910) leave at 9 pm.

Louage The louage station, the only covered one in the country, is a block west of the bus station on Ave Taieb Mehiri. There are regular departures to Kebili (TD1. 450) and Gabès (TD5.950), but none to Tozeur – change at Kebili.

Camionnette Camionnettes to Zaafrane (500 mills) and the other oases south of Douz leave regularly from the corner of the Zaafrane road, opposite the louage station.

AROUND DOUZ

A good sealed road runs south-west from Douz to a string of smaller oases, which are bases for the region's semi-nomadic tribes who continue to prefer life in the desert to the concrete-block settlements provided by the government.

Zaafrane

The small oasis town of Zaafrane, about 12km south-west of Douz, has emerged as the camel trekking capital of Tunisia in the past few years. The town is home to the Adhara tribe, who have found tourism to be a good way of turning their desert skills into an income.

The town itself is not particularly attractive – a collection of utilitarian block houses, but it's right on the edge of some impressive dune country.

Camel Trekking Zaafrane's two biggest trekking operators are not too hard to find – just keep an eye out for about 200 camels sitting about on the edge of town, on the left as you approach from Douz. Among the camels are two small palm-thatch huts, bases for two rival organisations. The bulk of their business comes from taking tour groups out on one hour rides, but they also specialise in longer treks.

Before you get too ambitious, it's a good idea to go for a one hour ride (TD3.500) first. The circuit they lead you around takes in some good-sized dunes. If you want to dress up, you can hire the necessary scarves and cloaks that will transform you into something resembling a semi-nomad.

The pick of the longer treks is an eight day, oasis-hopping journey across the desert to Ksar Ghilane and back, travelling via Ksar Tarcine. Meals are cooked by camp fire and you sleep in basic nomad-style tents. This eastern edge of the Nefzaoua region is the traditional grazing land of the Adhara tribe, so you are in good hands. You'll pay TD30 a day for an experience like this.

You'll need to be properly equipped. Essential items include a sensible hat which you can secure to your head, sunscreen and sunglasses (preferably wraparound). Sunglasses keep the sand as well as the sun out of your eyes. Long trousers are a good idea

The Sands of Time

An overnight trip is enough to get an idea of desert life. The trips start in the late afternoon after the heat of the day has gone and you ride out into the desert for about three hours before pitching camp. Your guides prepare a fire and food, including a delicious damper-style bread cooked in the ashes. After dinner, they entertain you with desert songs before you bed down under the stars. Fire and food are repeated in the morning before the ride home. My trip was made more memorable by waking up in the middle of a fierce sandstorm. By morning I had become a sand dune – and the fine sand had penetrated everything, including the alarm clock inside my bag! ∎

JON DAVISON

to prevent your legs getting chafed. Cameras and watches should be kept wrapped in a plastic bag to protect them from the very fine Saharan sand that gets into everything.

Places to Stay & Eat The only hotel, the *Hôtel Zaafrane* (☎ (05) 495 074), is not worth considering. It's far too basic to be charging TD17/28 for singles/doubles with breakfast. It serves a simple evening meal for an extra TD3 per person. There are no restaurants in Zaafrane.

Getting There & Away There are buses from Douz at 7, 9 and 11 am and 1 and 2.30 pm, as well as frequent camionnettes. They all charge 500 mills. Most people just stand at the corner of the road to Zaafrane, opposite

the louage station in Douz, and flag down whatever goes past. The flow of traffic dries up around 4 pm and there is never anything much on Friday afternoons.

The place to wait for lifts in Zaafrane is by the well in the middle of the village.

Beyond Zaafrane

The road continues from Zaafrane to **El-Faouar**, 30km south-west of Douz. It's a smaller version of Zaafrane and home to the Gherib tribe. The large hotel in the desert on the edge of town is not a mirage, however surreal it might look. It's the three star *Hôtel Faouar* (☎ (05) 491 531; fax 491 295), which comes complete with swimming pool and restaurant. The hotel looks out over some classic dunes; activities include **camel rides** and **dune skiing**. Rates are TD40/60 for singles/doubles with breakfast, or TD50/80 with all meals.

A turning about 5km before El-Faouar leads to the smaller settlement of **Sabria**, occupied by the tribe of the same name. There are some large dunes around here too. Buses from Douz to Zaafrane continue to both El-Faouar and Sabria, and there are regular camionnettes.

There is a back road that loops north from Zaafrane to Kebili via the small oasis villages of **Noueil** and **Blidet**. The turn-off is just west of Zaafrane on the road to El-Faouar. Noueil is nothing much, but Blidet has a great setting on the edge of the Chott el-Jerid. Blidet can be reached by bus and camionnette from Kebili.

KSAR GHILANE

The once remote oasis settlement of Ksar Ghilane, 126km south-east of Douz, has been transformed into the desert headquarters of the 4WD brigade in the last few years. Three huge camp sites around the oasis cater for tour groups who use the place as an overnight stop on desert safari tours of the south.

In spite of the number of people passing through, Ksar Ghilane is still an amazing spot and well worth the effort involved in getting there. The oasis is surrounded by some dramatic desert country. The ruins of the Roman fort of Tisavar, a desert outpost on the Limes Tripolitanus defensive line, lie 3km north-west of the oasis. You can visit them on camel tours (TD15) organised from the camping grounds.

Places to Stay
Camping Rhilane is the best of the three camping grounds, offering plenty of shade beneath tamarisk trees and palms. It has sites for TD3 per person, or beds in large nomad-style tents for TD5 per person with breakfast or TD8 with an evening meal as well. The site has a licensed restaurant where you can relax with a cold beer.

Camping L'Erg has sites at TD4 for two people, or beds in nomad-style tents for TD10 with breakfast and dinner. It also has a swimming pool and licensed restaurant. The third option is *Camping Le Paradis*.

You will need to bring your own bedding to stay at any of these sites.

Getting There & Away
Don't be put off by all the talk of 4WDs. You can get to Ksar Ghilane by conventional vehicle from Douz – just don't tell the car hire company where you're going! A lot of money has been spent on upgrading the Douz-Matmata road in the last few years, starting at the Douz end. There is no public transport to Ksar Ghilane.

The road is clearly signposted off the large roundabout at the northern edge of Douz. From here, follow the main road for 51km to the Café Sahara Centre, where the road forks. The left fork is the road to Matmata, while the right fork veers south towards Ksar Ghilane, linking up with the main pipeline road south after 25km. Turn right onto this road and keep going south for another 50km until you reach a turn-off on the right for the final 13km to Ksar Ghilane.

You can also get to Ksar Ghilane from Matmata by conventional vehicle, although it's slow-going on the bumpy 18km stretch between Tamezret and the pipeline road. If you have a 4WD, there are several other possibilities, including the two roads from

Douiret and Guermessa (see the entries on these two towns in The Ksour section later in this chapter).

If you break down on any of these roads, stay with your vehicle. There's plenty of passing traffic. Carry plenty of water with you just in case.

Gabès

Pop 90,000 ☎ Area code 05

Gabès is a sprawling modern industrial city on the coast 137km south-west of Sfax. It's not a particularly glamorous place, but its oasis is well worth a visit and there are enough things to see to warrant an overnight stop.

HISTORY
Gabès is the largest of a cluster of oases occupying the narrow strip of land between the Chott el-Fejej and the Gulf of Gabès. The oases have been inhabited since prehistoric times, and the settlement at Gabès grew into the Roman town of Tacapae.

The town grew rich in the 14th century AD as the principal Tunisian destination for the great camel caravans that brought gold from West Africa and slaves from Sudan. After the French invasion of the Sahara in the 19th century killed off the caravans, Gabès slipped back into a humbler role as the main town of the Arad, the coastal plain that flanks the Gulf of Gabès. It boomed again following the discovery of offshore oil in the gulf and the subsequent construction of a huge petrochemical complex on the coast just north of town.

ORIENTATION
Although Gabès is a coastal city, the coast barely features in the layout of the town. The town centre lies a couple of kilometres inland, skirted by the Oued Gabès to the north and the disgustingly polluted Gabès Canal to the south.

If you arrive in Gabès by bus or louage, you will be dropped at the terminal next to a

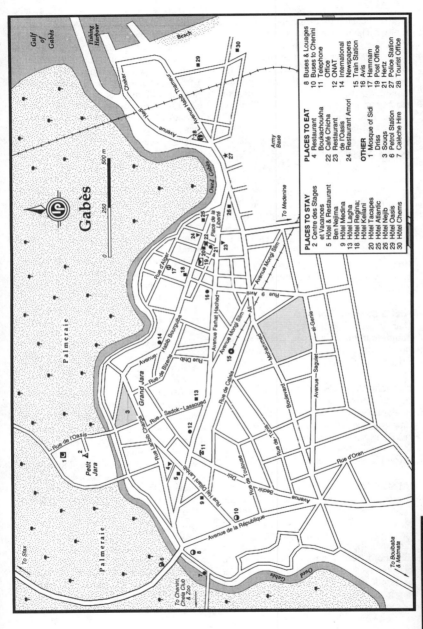

Gabès

Gulf of Gabès

Fishing Harbour

Beach

Palmeraie

Palmeraie

Grand Jara

Petit Jara

Army Base

Oued Gabès

Oued Gabès

To Sfax

To Chenni, Chela Club & Zoo

To Medenine

To Boubaba & Matmata

0   250   500 m

PLACES TO STAY
2   Centre des Stages
     et Vacances
5   Hôtel & Restaurant
     Ben Nejima
9   Hôtel Medina
13   Hôtel Lagha
18   Hôtel Regina;
     Hôtel Keilani
20   Hôtel Tacapes
25   Hôtel Atlantic
26   Hôtel Nejib
29   Hôtel Oasis
30   Hôtel Chems

PLACES TO EAT
4   Restaurant
     Boukachoukha
22   Café Chicha
23   Restaurant
     de l'Oasis
24   Restaurant Amori

OTHER
1   Mosque of Sidi
     Driss
3   Souqs
6   Petrol Station
7   Calèche Hire
8   Buses & Louages
10   Buses to Chenini
11   Telephone
     Office
12   ONAT
14   International
     Newspapers
15   Train Station
16   Avis
17   Hammam
19   Post Office
21   Hertz
27   Police Station
28   Tourist Office

large roundabout on the north-western edge of town. The main road to Sfax heads north from here, across a bridge over the Oued Gabès, while Ave de la République leads south across the canal to Medenine and Matmata. Ave Farhat Hached runs south-east through the modern town centre to the port and beach, becoming Ave Habib Thameur for the final stretch.

INFORMATION
Tourist Office
The tourist office (☎ 270 254) occupies the small building in the middle of the intersection of Ave Habib Thameur and Ave Hedi Chaker, down towards the waterfront. They don't see many tourists and are keen to offer whatever help they can. There is a complete list of bus departures posted on the door.

Money
There are a couple of banks along Ave Habib Bourguiba.

Post & Communications
There is an enormous new post office on Ave Habib Bourguiba. There are telephones here too, or you can use one of the Taxiphone offices around town.

International Newspapers
English, German and French newspapers are available year-round from the Librairie Jemai on Ave Habib Bourguiba, opposite Rue Bonté. In summer, the kiosk at the junction of Ave Habib Bourguiba and Ave Farhat Hached is another option.

PALMERAIE
The palmeraie stretches inland along the Oued Gabès, mostly on the north bank. It begins on the coast at **Ghannouche**, now the site of a giant petrochemical plant, and ends more than 4km west of Gabès beyond the village of **Chenini** (not to be confused with the more well known village of Chenini in the Ksour district – see The Ksour section later in this chapter). This western section is the most interesting (and least polluted) part

of the palmeraie, but it's also where all the tour groups head.

There are numerous ways of getting there. The turn-off to Chenini is signposted off the road to Sfax, about 300m north of the oued. You can get there on the No 7 bus from Rue Haj Djilani Lahbib or pay around TD2.500 for a taxi. Most people opt for a tour (TD10) on one of the calèches that lie in wait for the tour buses behind the bus station.

If the weather's not too hot, there's no reason not to walk. You can follow the shortcut used by the calèches, crossing the oued by the bridge behind the bus station and turning left onto the Chenini road. The road then twists and turns through the palmeraie to El-Aouadid, where a left turn leads down to Chenini. It's a pleasant walk of about an hour. The palmeraie looks its best during the pomegranate season in November and December, when the many trees are weighed down with huge ruby-red fruit.

Chenini itself has not much more to offer than a depressing crocodile farm and zoo and a small, partly reconstructed Roman dam on the Oued Gabès. It also has lots of souvenir stalls selling all sorts of junk at inflated prices – this is where the tour buses come to pick up their passengers after their calèche ride through the palmeraie. Don't waste your money on the zoo.

A path (negotiable by bicycle) heads off around the back of the dam and winds around through the palmeraie to the Chela Club, a rather run-down resort hotel tucked away in the palms (see also Places to Stay in this section). It's about a 20 minute walk and you can continue on along the oued to the end of the valley. Climb up the small escarpment for a view of the surrounding area. From the Chela Club, the road leads back to Chenini.

BEACH
It's hard to work out why anyone would come to Gabès for a beach holiday. Some people do – there are a couple of resort-type hotels by the beach at the end of Ave Habib Thameur. It's not that the beach is that bad. The problem is the petrochemical complex

in the background and the filthy water that emerges from the Oued Gabès.

JARA

The Jara is the old district that straddles the oued on the northern edge of town. The **Petit Jara**, amid the palm trees north of the oued, is the oldest part of town. The **Mosque of Sidi Driss**, at the far end of Rue de l'Oasis, dates back to the 11th century. The old market, where the slaves once were sold, is in **Grand Jara**, south of the oued.

The best way to approach the Jara district is along Rue Sadok Lassoued, which runs north from Ave Farhat Hached in the middle of town. It leads to Rue de l'Oasis, which continues across the oued to Petit Jara.

ZAOUIA OF SIDI BOULBABA

The city's most important religious monument, the Zaouia of Sidi Boulbaba, lies about 2km south of town in the district of Boulbaba. It houses the 7th century tomb of the man said to have been both the Prophet's barber and the founder of Gabès. The zaouia, with its ornate arched colonnades, is a modern copy; the original was destroyed by shelling in WWII. It is on the left off Rue 6 Octobre, which is the road to Matmata. There are buses out to Boulbaba, but you're better off forking out TD1.500 for a taxi.

MUSEUM

The small Museum of Art and Popular Traditions is housed in a former medersa next to the Zaouia of Sidi Boulbaba. It's open every day, except Monday, from 8 am to noon and 4 to 7 pm in summer, and from 9.30 am to 4.30 pm in winter. Admission is TD1.100.

PLACES TO STAY – BUDGET
Camping & Hostels

Gabès has a *Centre des Stages et Vacances* (☎ 271 863) in the palmeraie in the old district of Petit Jara. It's clearly signposted north of the oued off Rue de l'Oasis. It's a holiday camp version of a maison des jeunes. It has the usual spartan dorms for TD4, but it also has good shady camp sites for TD2,

plus 500 mills per person. Power and hot showers cost extra.

Hotels

Most of the budget places are at the western end of Ave Farhat Hached, not far from the bus and louage stations. The best of them is the *Hôtel Ben Nejima* (☎ 271 591), at the junction with Rue Haj Djilani Lahbib. It's very clean and charges TD7 per person, with free hot showers.

The *Hôtel Medina* (☎ 274 271), 150m south of the Hôtel Ben Nejima on Rue Haj Djilani Lahbib, charges TD7/10 for dingy singles/doubles, plus 500 mills for a shower.

The *Hôtel Lagha*, 50m from Ave Farhat Hached on Rue Sadok Lassoued, is basic but friendly and charges TD4 per person, plus 800 mills for a shower. Rooms are built around a small courtyard.

PLACES TO STAY – MIDDLE

There are two hotels virtually side by side near the post office on Ave Habib Bourguiba. The *Hôtel Regina* (☎ 272 095) is the better – and cheaper – of the two; the rooms are arranged around a pleasant courtyard and cost TD8/13 for singles/doubles with shower and toilet. Breakfast is served at the tables around the courtyard. Two doors along is the *Hôtel Keilani* (☎ 270 320). The large rooms cost TD9.500 per person.

The one star *Hôtel Atlantic* (☎ 220 234), with its fine, old French façade, is a touch better than either of these, with single or double rooms with breakfast for TD14.500 or TD23. It's at the beach end of Ave Habib Bourguiba.

The next step up from here is the *Hôtel Nejib* (☎ 271 686; fax 271 587), a big, modern two star place on the corner of Ave Farhat Hached and Blvd Mohammed Ali. At TD30/43 for single/double rooms with breakfast (dropping to TD25.500/36 in winter), the Nejib is better value than its slightly cheaper two star rival, the tatty *Hôtel Tacapes* (☎ 270 700) on Ave Habib Bourguiba. The two stars must have been awarded long ago, and it's not worth the TD25.500/38 it charges for singles/doubles with breakfast.

Out at Chenini, the *Chela Club* (☎ 227 442) charges TD23/33 for singles/doubles with breakfast, falling to TD15.500/21 in winter.

PLACES TO STAY – TOP END

The *Hôtel Chems* (☎ 270 547; fax 274 485) and the *Hôtel Oasis* (☎ 270 381; fax 271 749) are a couple of three star resort hotels overlooking the beach at the end of Ave Habib Thameur. The Chems is an enormous bungalow complex with singles/doubles for TD42/60. The Oasis is slightly cheaper and slightly more discreet.

PLACES TO EAT

There are a couple of good little restaurants just uphill from the bus and louage stations at the junction of Ave Farhat Hached and Rue Haj Djilani Lahbib. The *Restaurant Ben Nejima*, beneath the hotel of the same name, is a traveller-friendly place with nothing over TD2.600 on the menu. You can get a beer at the bar next door. Across the street from the Ben Nejima is the very similar *Restaurant Boukachoukha*.

The *Restaurant Amori*, opposite the Hôtel Tacapes, is another popular travellers' place with set meals priced from TD2.500.

The top place in town is the *Restaurant de l'Oasis* (☎ 270 098), at the beach end of Ave Farhat Hached. A meal here will set you back TD15 or more, plus wine.

For a coffee, try the *Café Chicha* on Place de la Liberté, which is at the junction of Ave Habib Bourguiba and Ave Farhat Hached. It's up the stairs next to the Hertz office. The setting, with its intricate tiling, is a cut above the rest – but so are the prices.

THINGS TO BUY

There is a large government-run ONAT showroom on Ave Farhat Hached. It has the usual range of quality carpets and other handicrafts.

Gabès is a major centre for the production of straw goods – baskets, hats, fans and mats – and the souqs here are a good place to buy things.

Henna

Gabès is well known for its high-quality henna, which is made by grinding the dried leaves of the henna tree, a small evergreen native to the region. Gabès henna produces a deep red-brown dye. Berber women use it to decorate their hands and feet, as well as to colour and condition their hair. You'll see henna powder for sale in the souqs and in the shops at the western end of Ave Farhat Hached, piled up in colourful green pyramids. Henna costs about TD1.500 for 100g. ■

GETTING THERE & AWAY
Air

Tunis Air (☎ 271 250) has an office at the beach end of Ave Habib Bourguiba. The nearest airport is on Jerba.

Bus

The bus station is next to the louage station at the western end of Ave Farhat Hached, a solid 15 minutes walk from the hotels on Ave Habib Bourguiba. All three bus companies operating from Gabès are based here. The various booking counters are upstairs in the building behind the louages. If you can't find the service you want at one counter, keep asking. They never know each other's schedules. You have to pay 50 mills for a platform ticket to get to the buses downstairs, even if you've got a bus ticket.

The most popular destination is Matmata (one hour, TD1.420), with nine buses a day between 6.15 am and 6.30 pm. There are also frequent buses to Jerba (three hours, TD4.580). Make sure that you catch one of the services that takes the shortcut via the Jorf-Ajim ferry. Some services go via Medenine and Zarzis, adding 80km and more than an hour to the journey. There are three direct buses a day to Tataouine (2½ hours, TD5), otherwise you will have to take one of the many buses to Medenine (1½ hours, TD2.820) and change there.

Heading north, SNTRI has at least five buses a day to Tunis (six hours, TD14.700). They travel via Sfax (two hours, TD5.510) and either Kairouan or Sousse. Most of these buses originate from points further south and in summer they are often full by the time they reach Gabès. Heading west, there are three buses a day to Kebili (2½ hours, TD4.050), all leaving in the morning. The 9 am service continues to Tozeur (four hours, TD6.970) and Nefta, while the noon service continues to Douz (three hours, TD5.110).

Train
The train station is just off Ave Mongi Slim, about five minutes walk from Ave Habib Bourguiba. There are two trains daily to Tunis (seven hours, TD15.200) at 3.42 and 11 pm. Gabès is the southernmost point that can be reached by rail.

Die-hard rail fans can get from Gabès to Metlaoui by train by catching the 11 pm train north, changing at Mahrès and waiting 1¼ hours for the Metlaoui service!

Louage
The louage station adjoins the bus station, with departures for Kebili, Jerba, Medenine, Sfax and Tunis. Things quieten down considerably as the afternoon wears on.

Car Rental
The major car rental agencies here are Avis (☎ 270 210), on Rue 9 Avril, and Hertz (☎ 270 525), at 30 Rue Ibn el-Jazzar.

GETTING AROUND
The small bicycle and moped shop a couple of doors along from the Hôtel de la Poste towards the souq will usually rent out bikes for TD8 for half a day. It's the best way to see the palmeraie, but make sure you aren't given an old, broken-down clunker with minor defects such as no brakes and a swivelling seat!

Matmata

Pop 1000   ☎ Area code 05
Nowhere else in Tunisia is package tourism so totally over the top as it is in the small village of Matmata, 43km south-west of Gabès. The pit houses of this troglodyte settlement have proved irresistible fare for the tour buses. They hit Matmata every morning at 9 am like a tidal wave that doesn't recede until the late afternoon. They are soon replaced by dozens of 4WD groups, who use Matmata as an overnight stop on their desert safaris.

It's hard not to feel sorry for the long-suffering residents of the village. The barbed wire that rings some of the craters is an indication that many of the residents are tired of being peered at like goldfish every day of the year. The 1000-odd locals are not all that friendly, which is understandable. Some of the children are very upfront about suggesting where tourists should go. They have picked up some very colourful language!

It's also not too hard to understand why the tourists keep on coming. There is something almost surreal about the place. The landscape is like something from the moon – no doubt the reason it was selected as a location for the movie *Star Wars*. Because there are only a few buildings above ground, there doesn't appear to be much to the town. The TV aerials and parked cars, however, are a giveaway that there is more here than first meets the eye.

ORIENTATION & INFORMATION
The road from Gabès descends into Matmata from the north and continues through town to the east as the back road to Medenine. Buses and louages stop at the square in the centre of town. The small syndicat d'initiative (☎ 230 114) is just uphill from the bus station, opposite the turn-off to Tamezret. The guy who runs the place is very enthusiastic and can help with information on getting to surrounding villages.

There is a post office up on the hill to the left as you come into Matmata from Gabès, but no bank.

THINGS TO SEE & DO
If you want to see Matmata for yourself, a good approach is to arrive late in the afternoon after the tour buses have gone. It will

Matmata Houses

The Berbers of the Matmata area went underground more than a thousand years ago to escape the extreme heat of summer. Their homes are all built along the same lines: a central (usually circular) courtyard is dug about 6m deep into the very irregular terrain, and the rooms are then tunnelled out from the sides. The main entrance is usually through a narrow tunnel leading from the courtyard to ground level. The larger houses have two or three connected courtyards.

The best examples to check out in Matmata are three troglodyte hotels, the Marhala, the Sidi Driss and Les Berbères. Some of the rooms at Les Berbères were built by the more modern method of excavating with a hoe and backfilling over the roof at the end. ■

DAMIEN SIMONIS

then be cool enough to go for a walk out beyond the Hôtel Ksar Amazigh (formerly Les Troglodytes) on the road to Tamezret. There are good views back over Matmata and north to the valley of the Oued Barrak, especially around sunset. You can then walk

back to town and slake your thirst with a cold drink at the Hôtel Sidi Driss, used as a setting for Star Wars, and you will have seen everything worth seeing in Matmata. In the morning, you can head off to one of the surrounding villages (see the Around Matmata section, following), which are far less visited.

You'll see signs along the Tamezret road indicating houses that are open for inspection, and you will frequently be asked if you want to visit homes. Before you enter, be aware that these places all double as souvenir shops, and you will find yourself feeling obliged to buy junk at ludicrously inflated prices.

ORGANISED TOURS

There are licensed guides who charge TD7 for a guided tour of the village or TD13 for tours of both Matmata and Tamezret. You will have to provide the transport to Tamezret. The six guides speak a range of languages between them, including English, French, German and Italian. You'll normally find them at the syndicat d'initiative, or hanging out around the hotels.

PLACES TO STAY

The accommodation is the best feature of Matmata. Three of the town's hotels are traditional troglodyte dwellings. They're all well signposted and within a few minutes walk of the bus stop.

The best of them is the *Hôtel Sidi Driss* (☎ 230 005), along the road opposite the bus station. It was in the bar here that the disco scene from *Star Wars* was filmed, and the movie artwork still adorns the roof and walls. It charges TD6.800 per person with breakfast and hot shower. The only real problem is that there are only a couple of double rooms – some rooms have as many as eight beds. The place once won a mention in a list of the world's loopiest hotels compiled by an airline in-flight magazine.

The *Hôtel Marhala* (☎ 230 015) is one in a chain run by the Touring Club de Tunisie. The rooms are clean and pleasant, but the 'friendly' service is way short of normal

Marhala standards. Singles/doubles with breakfast are TD9.100/14.600.

The final troglodyte option is the *Hôtel Les Berbères* (☎ 230 024). The sleeping quarters here are recent additions and are not of traditional construction; the walls are so thin that you can hear a mosquito buzzing next door. It charges TD8.800/13.600 for singles/doubles with breakfast.

There's not much to recommend at the modern *Hôtel Matmata* (☎ 230 066) except for a swimming pool. Singles/doubles cost TD23/36 with breakfast. Regular folk nights are laid on for the tour groups that use the hotel.

The *Hôtel Kouseila* (☎ 230 265) is a comfortable new three star place in the middle of town opposite the bus station. Large singles/doubles with breakfast cost TD32/44. You'll pay a fraction more at the *Hôtel Ksar Amazigh* (☎ 230 088; fax 230 173), 1km out of town on the Tamezret road, but it has a great position looking north over the Oued Barrak. The hotel was previously known as *Les Troglodytes*, and the signposts in town had yet to catch up with the name change at the time of research.

PLACES TO EAT

The nameless *restaurant* next to the Café de la Victoire by the bus station does a perfectly adequate omelette, chips and salad for TD2. The only other choice is the *restaurant* adjoining the Café Ouled Azaiz, opposite the syndicat d'initiative, which does three courses for TD5.

Otherwise, visitors are better off taking a room with full or half board, which are available at all the hotels.

GETTING THERE & AWAY

The bus station is in the centre of town next to the market. The syndicat d'initiative has a list of departures posted in the window.

There are eight buses a day to Gabès (TD1.420) between 5.30 am and 5.30 pm, as well as buses to Tamezret (800 mills) at 1.30 and 5 pm and to Techine (800 mills) at 12.30 and 5 pm. There is one SNTRI bus a day to Tunis at 8.30 pm (5½ hours, TD15.210). At

the time of writing, SRT Medenine was about to launch a new daily service linking Matmata and Jerba, leaving Matmata at 10 am and Houmt Souq at 4.30 pm.

When coming from Gabès, make sure the bus you catch is actually going all the way to Matmata – some terminate at Nouvelle Matmata, on the plains 15km north of Matmata. There are louages (600 mills) between the two Matmatas, if you get stuck.

AROUND MATMATA
Haddèj

This is a small village 3km north-east of Matmata, off the Matmata-Gabès road. It is much less developed than Matmata (with no electricity or restaurants) and the most substantial building in town is the school.

The people here are more friendly than in Matmata. Ask for someone to show you the underground olive press, where big millstones are turned by a camel in an impossibly small space. There is also a press operated by weights and levers which is used to extract the oil from the olives once they have been crushed. The guy who runs the small shop and post office can arrange for someone to take you there.

Getting There & Away There are occasional buses and louages between Nouvelle Matmata and Haddèj. Check with the Matmata tourist office for bus times. Otherwise, the only way to get to Haddèj is to catch a Gabès bus from Matmata for the 4km to Tijma, which is nothing more than the turn-off to Haddèj. From there it's a 3km walk to Haddèj; there is the occasional vehicle.

If the weather is favourable, there is an excellent walk back to Matmata along the mule track which cuts directly through the hills. It'll take you about 1¼ hours at a steady pace. Just ask the locals in Haddèj to point it out to you, as it's not obvious where it starts. Once you are on it, it's well trodden and easy to follow.

Tamezret

Very few tourists make it out to the quiet little village of Tamezret, which overlooks the

Nefzaoua plains from its commanding hill-top position 10km west of Matmata.

The houses here are built above ground, using the abundant local rock. The old quarter, above the bus stop, is a maze of little alleyways that wind around the hillside. It's an interesting place, but the bus schedule makes it difficult to spend more than a couple of hours there unless you can get a lift. There are buses from Matmata at 1.30 and 5 pm, returning an hour later.

It's probably best to have a 4WD if you want to travel the desert roads that lead west from Tamezret to Douz and Kebili.

Techine

Techine is a smaller version of Matmata, minus the tour buses. It lies 12km to the south-east of Matmata off the back road to Medenine. There are buses to Techine from Matmata at 12.30 and 5 pm, returning an hour later.

Toujane

You'll need your own transport if you want to continue east along the back road to Medenine. The only village along the way is Toujane, 23km south-east of Matmata. The road is of more interest than the village itself, as it runs through some pretty wild country, much of it covered by esparto grass which the locals gather and use for making all sorts of things, from mats to mule harnesses. Although it is an isolated place, Toujane sees its fair share of 'safari' tourists, rumbling through in 4WDs on their way to Matmata. Don't be put off by the 4WDs – the road is negotiable with care by even the smallest of rented cars, although the rental companies would no doubt have a fit if you told them where you intended to go.

The road improves considerably east of Toujane. After 22km, you come to a junction where you can turn right to Beni Kheddache (27km) or continue straight ahead to Metameur (10km). See the Around Medenine section for more information about these places.

The Ksour

Medenine and Tataouine are both fairly dull, modern administrative centres, but they're the centre of the fascinating *ksour* area of the south.

The best of the ksour are around Tataouine – a bit out of the way but well worth the effort. Some of the best sites take quite a bit of effort to get to. Having your own transport is the best solution. With your own vehicle you can make an interesting loop from Medenine to Tataouine via Beni Kheddache, Ksar Haddada, Ghomrassen, Guermessa, Chenini and Douiret, stopping for the night at Ksar Haddada where a ksar has been turned into a hotel.

The roads around here are usually not in fantastic condition and are often poorly signposted. It's easy to get lost but there are small villages and houses dotted around where you can ask directions. It doesn't rain

---

Ksour

A *ksar* (plural ksour) is a fortified Berber stronghold consisting of many *ghorfas* (rooms). Ghorfas were built to store grain and have a characteristic arched structure. They're sometimes three or more storeys high.

The Berbers originally built the ghorfas just for grain storage – the very low humidity of this arid region, combined with the cool conditions inside the ksar, meant that grain could be kept for years without deteriorating. When the Arabs invaded, however, the structures were expanded to form formidable defensive positions. As they were usually strategically sited, they occupy some spectacular hill-top sites.

Today, most of the ksour are falling into ruin, but some have been put to good use – the one at Medenine has been restored and is now a tourist market, while at Metameur part of the three storey ghorfa has been converted into a hotel and the old souq is used to stage traditional music. Some of the best ghorfas are at Ksar Ouled Soltane, 22km east of Tataouine. The upper levels are four storeys high and are reached by a network of precarious, external steps. During the Festival of the Ksour, the courtyards are used for performances of traditional dance and music. ■

The Ksour

To Gabès & Nouvelle Matmata
Mareth
To Gabès
To Jorf
Haddèj
Matmata
Bou Grara
Gightis
Tamezret
Ain Tounine
To Douz
To Zarzis
Techine
Toujane
Metameur
Medenine
To Ben Guerdane
El Hallouf
Joumaa
Beni Kheddache
Kerachfa
To Ksar Tarcine
To Ben Guerdane
Ksar Haddada
Ghomrassen
Rass el-Ain
Guermessa
Tataouine
Nouvelle Chenini
Jelidat
Chenini
Tounkett
Beni Barka
Maztouria
Debbab
Douire'
Tamelest
Ksar Ezzahra
Ksar Ouled Debbab
Remtha
Mghit
To Ksar Ghilane
Ksar Ouled Soltane
To Borj Bourguiba
To Remada
To Remada

0   10   20 km

very often, but when it does the roads become impassable.

The villages around here are among the last places where the local Berber language, Chelha, can be heard. The language is dying out, along with its elderly speakers.

MEDENINE
Pop 20,000 ☎ Area code 05

Medenine, 73km south-east of Gabès, is unexciting in the extreme. There is nothing that cannot be seen while waiting for a bus. If you get stuck overnight, there is a choice of hotels – all equally unappealing.

The skyline is dominated by the gigantic regional hospital, which seems totally out of proportion to the rest of the town. In the days when the Libyan border was closed it was a real backwater, but these days it is much busier, and seemingly every second car has Libyan numberplates.

Orientation & Information

The main street is Ave Habib Bourguiba, which runs north-south through the centre of town. It dips in the middle of town to cross the rubbish-filled Oued Medenine. About 50m south of the oued is the town's major

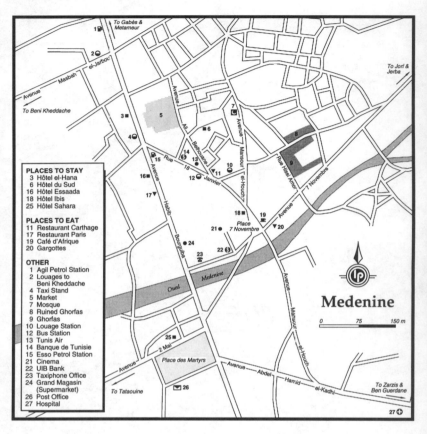

Medenine

PLACES TO STAY
3 Hôtel el-Hana
6 Hôtel du Sud
16 Hôtel Essaada
18 Hôtel Ibis
25 Hôtel Sahara

PLACES TO EAT
11 Restaurant Carthage
17 Restaurant Paris
19 Café d'Afrique
20 Gargottes

OTHER
1 Agil Petrol Station
2 Louages to
   Beni Kheddache
4 Taxi Stand
5 Market
7 Mosque
8 Ruined Ghorfas
9 Ghorfas
10 Louage Station
12 Bus Station
13 Tunis Air
14 Banque de Tunisie
15 Esso Petrol Station
21 Cinema
22 UIB Bank
23 Taxiphone Office
24 Grand Magasin
   (Supermarket)
26 Post Office
27 Hospital

0   75   150 m

intersection, adjoining Place des Martyrs.
Ave 2 Mai runs south-west from here, becoming the road to Tataouine.

The post office is on Place des Martyrs.
Most other things of importance are north of
the oued, including the bus station. This is
on Rue 18 Janvier, which forks left off Ave
Habib Bourguiba by the large petrol station
as you come into town from the north and
runs down to a huge roundabout at Place 7
Novembre. The louage station is opposite
the bus station, on a small side street.

There's a branch of the Banque de Tunisie
just uphill from the bus station, and a UIB

branch just off Place 7 Novembre. There is
no tourist office.

Ghorfas

Medenine's only tourist attraction is the
small collection of ghorfas on Ave 7 Novembre, about five minutes walk from the bus
and louage stations. To get there, follow Rue
18 Janvier down to Place 7 Novembre and
turn left onto Ave 7 Novembre, which runs
north-east, parallel to the oued. The ghorfas
are on the left after 200m.

The ghorfas are built around a small
square and are a remnant of the town's once

substantial ksar. The scene is very colourful, with the ghorfas draped in bright Berber rugs, but it's hard to classify the place as anything other than a tourist trap.

There are more ghorfas behind here, reached by taking the first turning left (Rue Hissi Amor) off Ave 7 Novembre. Some of these ghorfas rise three storeys, but they are in very poor condition.

Places to Stay – budget

The absence of decent budget accommodation is another reason not to stick around in Medenine. If you do get stuck, the best bet is the *Hôtel Essaada* (☎ 640 300), opposite the Esso station on Ave Habib Bourguiba – just a couple of minutes walk uphill from the bus station. The rooms are around a courtyard set back from the street. Single/double rooms cost TD3.500/6.

A bit further up the hill on Ave Habib Bourguiba is the *Hôtel el-Hana* (☎ 646 190), which charges TD3.500 per person for basic rooms, or TD8 for doubles with shower. If these prices are too steep, you'll pay marginally less at the old *Hotel du Sud*, in a small square behind the markets. To get to the hotel, follow Rue 18 Janvier uphill from the bus station and make a right turn after the Banque de Tunisie into a small (unnamed) street, which crosses Ave Ali Belhouane and leads to the square.

Places to Stay – middle

The poshest place in town is the *Hôtel Ibis* (☎ 643 878; fax 640 550), a smart new two star hotel on Place 7 Novembre. It looks a bit out of place in the middle of Medenine. Presumably it earns its keep as a halfway point for business people travelling between Tunis and Tripoli. It charges TD35.500/57 for singles/doubles with breakfast.

The *Hôtel Sahara* (☎ 640 007) is a characterless concrete dump on the Tataouine road – don't bother with it.

Places to Eat

The food is OK at *Restaurant Carthage*, opposite the bus station, although the level of friendliness is about what you'd expect from a place that knows that its customers will be leaving town in 10 minutes. A better bet is the *Restaurant Paris*, just downhill from the Hôtel Essaada on Ave Habib Bourguiba. It has a small selection of daily specials and most dishes go for around TD2.

The *Café d'Afrique*, on Place 7 Novembre, is a good place for a coffee. It also has delicious fresh orange juice (400 mills) in season. There are several very cheap gargottes opposite the cafe on Ave 7 Novembre. The *Hôtel Ibis* has the only upmarket restaurant in town – and the only cold beer.

If none of these eateries appeals, you can stock up on supplies at the *supermarket* just north of the oued on Ave Habib Bourguiba. You'll find fresh fruit and vegetables in the *market* building opposite the Hôtel el-Hana on Ave Habib Bourguiba.

Getting There & Away

Bus Both regional and SNTRI buses leave from the bus station on Rue 18 Janvier, halfway up the hill.

There are frequent services to Jerba, and a choice of routes. The services via the ferries at Jorf are faster and cheaper (1½ hours, TD2.700) than those via Zarzis and the causeway. There are also six buses a day to Tataouine between 7.30 am and 4.30 pm (one hour, TD1.850), and regular buses to Gabès (1¼ hours, TD2.930).

Useful local services include regular buses to Metameur (15 minutes, 380 mills) and buses to Beni Kheddache (45 minutes, TD1.300) at 10 am and 3 pm.

SNTRI has six air-conditioned services a day between Medenine and Tunis. The buses that travel inland via Kairouan are much quicker and cheaper (7½ hours, TD17.300) than those that go via Sfax, El-Jem and Sousse. Getting a seat can be a problem in summer because only the 9.15 pm service originates in Medenine, and the others are sometimes full by the time they reach here.

Louage Most louages leave from the small side street directly opposite the bus station. Destinations and fares include the following: Ben Guerdane, TD3.250; Gabès, TD3.150;

Tataouine, TD1.900; Jerba, TD2.850; and Zarzis, TD2.700.

Louages for Beni Kheddache (TD1.450) leave from the Beni Kheddache turn-off on the northern edge of town.

AROUND MEDENINE
Metameur

The attraction at the small village of Metameur, 6km west of Medenine, is the opportunity to stay overnight in the 13th century ksar. The ksar is clearly visible from the Gabès-Medenine road, 1km to the east, standing on a low hill above the modern village.

Places to Stay & Eat The *Hôtel Les Ghorfas* (☎ (05) 640 294/128) is a great little budget hotel that occupies a cluster of renovated ghorfas at the far end of the enormous main courtyard. Quite a few tour groups come through here in the day, stopping for lunch at the ghorfa restaurant. At night, hotel guests have the place pretty much to themselves – and there are only half a dozen rooms. Rates are TD12 per person for dinner, bed and breakfast. The showers are a bit erratic (the water sprays up and bounces back off the ceiling), but who cares when you can wake up in surroundings like this. The owner has plans to convert other ghorfas into more upmarket accommodation.

The place goes into a sort of hibernation when tourist numbers drop away in winter, so it's a good idea to phone first if you're going to arrive after dark.

Getting There & Away The easiest way to get to Metameur is on one of the regular buses from Medenine. If you face a wait, hitching the 6km from Medenine to the turn-off to Metameur on the Gabès road is pretty simple. The turn-off is well signposted off to the left and you can see the village, about 1km from the main road. A taxi from Medenine costs about TD3.

The back road to Matmata through Toujane runs through here, so it may be possible to hitch. Practically the only people

using this road, however, are other tourists in rented cars.

Joumaa

This is a magnificent hill-top site, 36km south-west of Medenine. The ksar, visible from the modern settlement where the bus stops, is built on a spur and appears to be just a blank wall. Inside, however, there are a couple of streets, a mosque, a courtyard and some water tanks.

Buses between Medenine (TD1.350) and Beni Kheddache stop at Joumaa on the way.

Beni Kheddache

From Joumaa you can continue on to Beni Kheddache, a market and administrative village in the hills, which has a low-lying ksar. Most of it has been demolished; the run-down remnants are signposted on the way into the village. There is no accommodation here but there are a couple of basic restaurants. There are two buses a day to Medenine (45 minutes, TD1.300) and more frequent louages (TD1.450).

TATAOUINE
Pop 8000 ☎ Area code 05

Tataouine, 49km south of Medenine, is the best base for visiting the ksour. It's a modern administrative town with few attractions of its own, but it is well set up for travellers, with hotels, restaurants and useful transport connections to outlying ksour.

Orientation & Information

Everything of importance is within a couple of minutes walk of the clock tower in the centre of town. The post office is at the southern end of the main street, Ave Habib Bourguiba, tucked in beneath the jebel – just look for the radio tower. There are a couple of banks in the streets nearby. There is no tourist office, but the hotels can help with information on getting around the area.

Ksar Megabla

The ksar is a couple of kilometres from the town centre, signposted to the right off the Remada road. It takes about an hour to walk

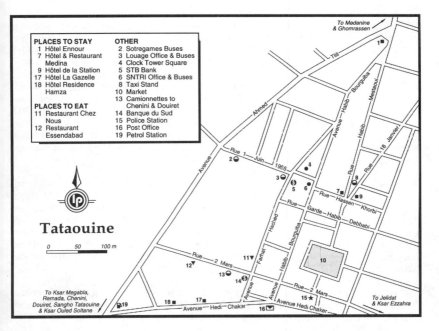

PLACES TO STAY
1 Hôtel Ennour
7 Hôtel & Restaurant Medina
9 Hôtel de la Station
17 Hôtel La Gazelle
18 Hôtel Residence Hamza

PLACES TO EAT
11 Restaurant Chez Nous
12 Restaurant Essendabad

OTHER
2 Sotregames Buses
3 Louage Office & Buses
4 Clock Tower Square
5 STB Bank
6 SNTRI Office & Buses
8 Taxi Stand
10 Market
13 Camionnettes to Chenini & Douiret
14 Banque du Sud
15 Police Station
16 Post Office
19 Petrol Station

Tataouine

0   50   100 m

To Ksar Megabla,
Remada, Chenini,
Douiret, Sangho Tataouine
& Ksar Ouled Soltane

To Medenine
& Ghomrassen

To Jelidat
& Ksar Ezzahra

up to it, and there are good views of the town and surrounding area. The ksar itself is not in the best condition – in fact you need to be a bit careful when poking about in the courtyard. The villagers still keep their livestock in the cells.

Markets
If you're in town on Monday or Thursday, don't miss the lively markets held in the souq at the southern end of Ave Habib Mestaoui.

Places to Stay
The best budget place is the *Hôtel Medina* (☎ 860 999), very close to the centre of town on Rue Habib Mestaoui. It charges TD5 a night, plus TD1.500 for breakfast. Hot showers or baths (bring a plug) are free.

Right opposite, on Rue 18 Janvier, is the basic, but very friendly, *Hôtel de la Station* (☎ 860 104), with its colourful cartoon mural. The owners seem to delight in name

changes, with three in the last four years. It was previously known as the Hôtel Nour, and before that it was the Belmeharem. The place itself hasn't changed. It has beds for TD4, or TD6 with hot shower and breakfast. The uninspiring *Hôtel Ennour*, at the junction of Ave Habib Bourguiba and Ave Ahmed Tlili, also has beds for TD4.

The *Hôtel Residence Hamza* (☎ 863 506), just along from the Hôtel La Gazelle on Ave Hedi Chaker, is more of a residence than a hotel, with just four rooms. It charges TD7 per person for bed and breakfast. There is a small kitchen but no cooking utensils.

The two star *Hôtel La Gazelle* (☎ 860 009), 150m from the post office on Ave Hedi Chaker, is the only upmarket choice in town. It has been feeling the pinch since the opening of the flash Sangho resort south-east of town, and is quick to offers discounts on its advertised rates of TD19/26 for singles/doubles with private bath, hot water and breakfast.

The three star *Sangho Tataouine* (☎ 860 102; fax 862 177) is 3km from town on the road to Chenini. It occupies a large, walled compound spreading up the hill south of the road, its name emblazoned in white on the rocky slope behind. This is where the tour groups stay before heading off to explore Chenini and Douiret. Singles/doubles with breakfast are TD46.300/76.600.

Places to Eat
The restaurant at the *Hôtel Medina* is a touch smarter than its budget rivals with its smart red tablecloths and neat table settings. The service is equally cheery, and the prices are much the same as you'll find elsewhere – 800 mills for a salad, and TD2.600 for a large turkey cutlet and chips.

The *Restaurant Essendabad*, on Rue 2 Mars, has a range of daily specials that normally includes a delicious, thick chorba (soup) for 700 mills.

The tiny *Restaurant Chez Nous*, on Ave Farhat Hached, with its cheery window painting of a chef giving a thumbs-up sign, does basic stuff such as tajine (omelette), chips and salad.

The restaurant at the *Hôtel La Gazelle* does a three course meal for TD5.500. The hotel also has the only bar in town, with cold beers for TD1.600.

All Tataouine's many patisseries sell the local speciality, corne de gazelle (250 mills) – a pastry case, shaped like a gazelle's horn, filled with chopped nuts and soaked in honey.

Getting There & Away
Bus The bus station is 200m from the clock tower on Rue 1 Juin 1955. There are buses to Medenine (45 minutes, TD1.850) at 6.30, 8 and 10 am and 2.30 pm. The 10 am bus continues to Zarzis and Houmt Souq (2½ hours, TD4.450).

Remada, the southernmost point in the country served by the bus network, can be reached by a daily bus at 3 pm (TD3.050). There are six buses a day to Ghomrassen (30 minutes, 700 mills) between 8.30 am and 5.30 pm. The last bus back from Ghomrassen

leaves at 4.30 pm. Another bus route runs south-east to Beni Barka, Maztouria and Ksar Ouled Soltane (45 minutes, 750 mills). The only useful departure is at 11.30 am.

SNTRI runs air-conditioned buses to Tunis (8½ hours, TD19.380) at 7.30 am and 7.45 pm. These buses travel via Gabès (two hours, TD5.420), Sfax (four hours, TD10.300) and Sousse (six hours, TD14.580). They leave from the SNTRI office on Ave Habib Bourguiba, just around the corner from the clock tower.

Louage Louages leave from the clock tower square, around the junction of Ave Farhat Hached and Rue 1 Juin 1955. Things are much busier in the mornings. There are departures for Ghomrassen, Medenine, Remada, Zarzis and Tunis. Seats to Tunis can be reserved at the small louage office on Rue 1 Juin 1955.

Camionnette Camionnettes leave from near the Banque du Sud on Rue 2 Mars. There are fairly regular departures for Chenini (700 mills), Douiret (TD1) and Maztouria (700 mills), while some continue to Ksar Ouled Soltane (TD1). The earlier you set off the better. The system starts to slow down around noon and is virtually non-existent after 3 pm.

Getting Around
While you can get to most of the larger ksour by public transport, there are lots of other places that you can't get to without your own transport. However, there are no hire cars to be found in town. The nearest car rental agencies are on Jerba – see the Jerba section at the end of this chapter for more details.

You can charter taxis to take you out to the ksour from the taxi stand opposite the Hôtel Medina on Rue Habib Mestaoui. Typical rates include TD20 to Chenini and TD25 to Douiret.

AROUND TATAOUINE
Chenini
The hill-top village of Chenini, 18km west of Tataouine, is the best known of the ksour.

It's also the most visited and you will need to arrive early to appreciate the setting before the tour buses descend. There is nowhere to stay overnight in Chenini.

The ruins of the original ksar, which was built in the 12th century AD, stand at the junction of two ridges. The settlement extends down and out from here, built into the rock along a series of small terraces that lead around the steep hillside. The houses themselves consist of a cave room, which has a fenced front courtyard containing one or two more rooms. Some of the doorways here are so small that you'd need to go on a diet to squeeze through.

The ksar is still used to store grain. The village still has a few occupants, but most have moved to the modern settlement of Nouvelle Chenini, several kilometres before old Chenini on the road to Tataouine.

A path leads up to a beautiful white mosque lying in a saddle between the two ridges. Just around from the mosque and below the ksar, one of the locals has turned his house into an informal museum – which he will show you around for a small fee.

Beyond here, a 20 minute walk leads to a mosque and the graves of the **Seven Sleepers**. A local legend has evolved to explain the existence of these strange 5m-long grave mounds. The legend has it that seven Christians (and a dog) went into hiding in a cave to escape persecution by the Romans. When they awoke 400 years later, they found that their bodies had continued to grow until they were 4m tall – whereupon they all promptly died. The cave in question has been closed off and can be viewed only on postcards.

There are many other extended graves in adjoining parts of the cemetery. There is a marabout's cave next to the cemetery.

Places to Eat The *Relais Restaurant* is at the bottom of the hill by the car park. It specialises in set-menu lunches for tour groups. It also sells coffee and cold drinks, including beer.

Getting There & Away There are camionnettes between Tataouine and Chenini, but you will need to set out early in the day to make use of them. Later in the day, you may need to walk to Nouvelle Chenini to get a ride back to Tataouine. Hitching is OK but it can be slow, as most of the vehicles coming out this way are tour group 4WDs which already have up to 11 people crammed in!

It shouldn't cost more than TD20 to charter a taxi for the round trip from Tataouine, and it's possible that the driver will act as a guide when you get there. An hour is the minimum time necessary for a leisurely scramble around, two hours if you want to visit the graves of the Seven Sleepers as well, so make sure the driver knows that you want to stay at least that long.

If you're driving, you can keep going south from Chenini and loop around to Douiret. The dirt road north from Chenini to Guermessa is very rough in places, but negotiable with care.

Douiret

This place is really something, with its crumbling ksar perched high on the spur of a hill above a dazzling whitewashed mosque. As at Chenini, the houses are built into the rock along terraces that follow the contour lines around the hill. The main terrace leads south for 1km to more houses, some of which are still occupied. The rest of old Douiret is abandoned, and you can explore the ruins at your leisure. Look out for some of the ornate carved doorways and Berber designs painted on the walls. There are several camel-powered olive presses – just look for the telltale black streaks down the hillsides. You can get a coffee or an expensive cave-temperature soft drink from the small *buvette* (refreshment stall) below the mosque.

For some reason, Douiret doesn't suffer from tour group overkill in the way that Chenini does. Most of the time you'll have the place to yourself.

Places to Stay There is a new *Centre de Camping et de Vacances* at the end of the road, nestled in the valley below the ksar. Expect to pay the standard TD4 for a dorm bed, and TD2.500 to camp.

Getting There & Away Douiret is 22km south-west of Tataouine, turning off the Remada road 9km south of town. As usual in this neck of the woods, transport is a bit of a hit-and-miss affair. Early morning is the best time to catch a camionnette out from Tataouine, but they normally go only as far as Nouvelle Douiret, 1.5km before old Douiret. You may be able to persuade the driver to take you the rest of the way, but you will certainly have to walk back afterwards to find a ride to Tataouine. You may be in for a long wait, as there is very little traffic along this road, but you will get there in the end.

The easy solution is to spend TD25 to get a taxi to take you out and wait while you look around. Allow at least two hours.

If you have your own vehicle, you can drive around to Chenini on the recently sealed road that leads off to the south-west between Nouvelle Douiret and old Douiret. Don't be put off by the initial direction – the road loops back to the north after a few kilometres. Another road keeps going east to Ksar Ghilane, but you need a 4WD.

Ksar Ouled Debbab

This huge ksar stands on a low hill just east of the modern village of Debbab, 9km south of Tataouine on the Remada road. It was occupied until quite recently, if the electric cables are anything to go by. Most of the buildings are still in good condition. There's a sealed road leading up to the entrance gate from Debbab. The walk takes about 20 minutes.

Ksar Ouled Soltane

Ksar Ouled Soltane, 22km east of Tataouine, has the best set of ghorfas in the south, rising a dizzying four storeys around two small courtyards. The upper levels are reached by a network of precarious, narrow, external steps. The lower courtyard is used as a stage for traditional dance and other performances during the Festival of the Ksour in late November, and the ghorfas here have been given the full renovation treatment.

You can get out to Ksar Ouled Soltane by public transport, but there are several inter-esting places along the way that you can stop and explore if you have your own vehicle. The turn-off to Ksar Ouled Soltane is sign-posted off the Remada road about 1km south of Tataouine – which is the last time you'll see the place mentioned for a long time, but don't lose faith. The road runs south through the low hills of the Jebel Abiodh range, passing through the villages of Beni Barka, Maztouria and Tamelest. The ridge is dotted with the remains of countless small ksour, the most impressive being those above Beni Barka and Tamelest.

Finally, beyond Tamelest, there is another sign to Ksar Ouled Soltane, now visible on a low hill to the left.

Getting There & Away From Tataouine, there are three buses a day to Ksar Ouled Soltane (40 minutes, 750 mills), as well as occasional camionnettes. There are more frequent camionnettes to Maztouria. There's quite a lot of traffic along this road, so hitching should not be a problem.

Ghomrassen

Located 24km north-west of Tataouine, Ghomrassen is the largest of the southern Berber villages and unofficial capital of the central Jebel Dahar – the range that runs west of the Medenine-Tataouine road. It boasts a bank, a high school, shops and a couple of restaurants.

The village is surrounded by rocky cliffs on all sides and there are cave dwellings dotted all over the place, all long since abandoned for the comforts of the 20th century.

Places to Stay There is nowhere to stay in town, but there is good budget accommodation at nearby Ksar Haddada (see under Ksar Haddada, following). The *Hotel Dakyanus* (☎ (05) 863 499; fax 862 932) is a small three star resort hotel south of Ghomrassen near the ruins of Ksar el-Farich.

Getting There & Away Ghomrassen is something of a regional transport centre. There are six buses a day to Tataouine (30 minutes, 700 mills), and five to Medenine (one hour, TD1.670), as well as services to Guermessa (15 minutes, 300 mills) and Ksar Haddada.

Ksar Haddada

The small hill-top settlement of Ksar Haddada, 5km north of Ghomrassen, deserves a place on every itinerary.

The old ksar here has been converted into the amazing *Hôtel Ksar Haddada* (☎ (05) 869 005), where you'll find singles/doubles for TD12/16 with breakfast or TD15.500/23 with an evening meal as well. You'll have to turn a blind eye to the toilet facilities, which are about as primitive as you'll encounter in Tunisia. Concentrate instead on the delightful features that have been retained, such as the old palm doors. The place is a maze of small alleyways and courtyards and a memorable place to spend the night.

Getting There & Away There are occasional buses from Ghomrassen, but it's quicker to stand by the road and flag down whatever comes your way. If you're driving, you can keep going north from Ksar Haddada on the back road to Beni Kheddache (see the Around Medenine section). The road was being upgraded at the time of writing and is fine for conventional vehicles.

Guermessa

Guermessa, 8km south-west of Ghomrassen, is another spectacular Berber site in the same league as Chenini and Douiret. Like its southern neighbours, the old hill-top village has now been largely abandoned in favour of a modern village on the plains. Unlike them, however, Guermessa remains almost undiscovered by the mass tourist trade.

You can use the school buses that operate between Ghomrassen and Guermessa, but the timetable was not devised with tourists in mind. Alternatively, it costs about TD20 to charter a taxi there and back from Tataouine. A very rough road (4WD only) runs west from Guermessa and then turns south to link up with the road from Douiret to Ksar Ghilane.

FRANCES LINZEE GORDON

Treat yourself to a night in the fabulous old ksar, now a hotel, at Ksar Haddada.

South-East Coast

The flat coastal plain on the mainland south of Jerba has few points of interest other than the minor Roman site of Gightis and some reasonable beaches on the coast around Zarzis. Tourism is very low-key, although there are a few resorts on the coast just north of Zarzis. Fishing and olive-growing are the main income earners.

GIGHTIS

The Roman port of Gightis, 20km south of Jorf on the back road to Medenine, ranks among the country's least visited ancient sites.

Established by the Phoenicians, Gightis became a busy port in Roman times – exporting gold, ivory and slaves delivered by the trans-Saharan caravan route. Most of the buildings date from the 2nd century AD and are spread around the ancient capitol and forum. The site lay buried until the early 20th century and remains relatively undeveloped.

SOUTHERN TUNISIA

It's a lovely spot for a stroll, with clumps of palms and acacia trees dotting the coast above the gleaming waters of the Gulf of Bou Grara.

The site is open every day from 8 am to noon and 3 to 7 pm in summer; from 8.30 am to 5.30 pm in winter. Don't worry if the site appears closed – the guardian lives opposite and will emerge. Admission is TD1.100, plus TD1 to take photos.

Getting There & Away
Buses and louages between Houmt Souq and Medenine can drop you at the site, which is just south of the tiny modern village of Bou Grara. You will have to pay the full fare for Houmt Souq to Medenine if you catch a louage. Getting away is more difficult; you may have a long wait for a bus, and the louages are likely to be full. The local practice is to flag down whatever comes by.

ZARZIS
Pop 15,000 ☎ Area code 05
Zarzis is one of the least exciting towns in the country. It's worth a mention only because the coast to the north of town is home to Tunisia's newest tourist strip, an area that tourism authorities are promoting with glossy brochures filled with photos of golden beaches backed by olive groves.

In reality, Zarzis is a dull, dusty, modern, single storey concrete town with nothing to see or do. The nearby beach that features in the brochures is OK but is dominated by half a dozen huge resort hotels like Club Sangho and Club Oamarit.

Places to Stay & Eat
There is not much reason to stay the night in town but, if you do, the best of a fairly motley bunch is the *Hôtel Afif* (☎ (05) 681 639) on Ave Mohammed V (the Jerba road). The place is clean and charges TD7.500/12 for singles/doubles with hot showers. Breakfast is 800 mills.

Another option is the *Hôtel de la Station* (☎ (05) 680 661) on Rue Abdulkacem Echabbi. It charges TD5 per person for a bed; this includes a hot shower. Rue Abdulkacem

Echabbi runs off Ave Farhat Hached (the road to Medenine) opposite the Sotregames bus station.

The imaginatively named *Restaurant Zarzis*, opposite the Sotregames bus station on Ave Farhat Hached, is very popular with locals, particularly at lunch time. It packs them in with dishes like thick fish chorba (800 mills) and couscous with spicy chicken stew (TD2).

Getting There & Away
Bus Local buses leave from the bus station on Ave Farhat Hached, near the junction with Ave du 20 Mars. There are regular buses to Ben Guerdane (one hour, TD2.100), Jerba (one hour, TD2) and Medenine (1½ hours, TD2.570), as well as services to Tataouine at 3.30 pm and to Gabès at 6 and 9.30 am.

SNTRI has an air-conditioned service to Tunis every evening at 9 pm; it costs TD17.990 for the 8½ hour journey. The office is a couple of doors from the Hôtel de la Station, just off Rue Abdulkacem Echabbi.

Louage The louage station is 150m past the bus station towards Medenine on Ave Farhat Hached. Destinations include Gabès (TD5.650), Jerba (TD2.250) and Medenine (TD2.700).

BEN GUERDANE
Pop 3000 ☎ Area code 05
The small town of Ben Guerdane, 33km west of the Libyan border, was once pretty much the end of the road in Tunisia. The international air embargo imposed on Libya in 1992 (for refusing to hand over suspects in the Lockerbie jumbo jet bombing) has transformed it into a boom town on Libya's road lifeline to the outside world. All land traffic between the two countries passes through here.

The main drag has become a huge market. It's a colourful scene, but there's nothing to buy unless you're looking for cheap plastic goods or cheap Libyan dinar – TD1 buys at least three Libyan dinar.

Getting There & Away

There are frequent buses and louages to Medenine, as well as services to Zarzis. There is a daily bus to Tunis (nine hours, TD19.900) at 10.30 pm.

If you're heading for Libya, the border formalities are conducted at the Ras Ajdir crossing point. Almost everybody needs a visa to enter Libya. They cannot be issued on the spot, and are notoriously difficult for individuals to obtain.

Land of the Lotus-Eaters

According to legend, Jerba is the Land of the Lotus-Eaters, where Ulysses paused in the course of his *Odyssey* and had a lot of trouble persuading his crew to get back on board. Today's islanders are said to be descendants of these people, who lived 'in indolent forgetfulness, drugged by the legendary honeyed fruit'. It makes a good story for the tourists, and it is capitalised upon by hotels with names like the Lotos (sic) and Ulysses. ■

Jerba

The island of Jerba has long been one of Tunisia's most popular tourist destinations. Its southerly location gives it a climate that is the envy of Northern Europe. Even in the middle of winter, temperatures seldom fail to reach 15°C, guaranteeing that the tourist dinars keep flowing all year.

Jerba lies about 50km north of Medenine, perched between the Jorf and Zarzis peninsulas to create the virtually landlocked Gulf of Bou Grara. Jerba has been linked to the mainland since Roman times, when a causeway was built between the south-eastern corner of the island and the Zarzis Peninsula.

The island covers an area of approximately 500 sq km. The highest point is less than 30m above sea level, which makes it ideal for exploration by bicycle or, better still, by motorbike. Both can be hired in the main town of Houmt Souq.

The tourist season peaks in July and August, although it's too hot then to do much more than stagger to the beach. Winter and spring are the best times to visit – accommodation is cheaper, facilities are less in demand and the weather is ideal for getting out and exploring.

HISTORY

Local Berber tribes were well established when the Phoenicians arrived on the scene about 2700 years ago. Among them were the Gerbitani, whose settlement of Gerba (near modern Houmt Souq) provided the island with its name. The Phoenicians were attracted by the safe anchorage provided by the Gulf of Bou Grara, and they established settlements at Meninx (modern El-Kantara) on Jerba and at Gightis on the mainland. Both grew in importance in Carthaginian times and continued to prosper after the Roman conquest. During Roman times, Meninx was a town of sufficient stature to warrant the building of 7km of causeway to link it with the mainland.

Jerba was one of the first places to fall to the Arabs on their march into Tunisia, but it later became a stronghold of the Kharijites in the wake of the Kharijite rebellion that erupted across North Africa in 740 AD. Known for their fanaticism, the Kharijites broke away from the mainstream Sunnis in 657 after the Caliph Ali was forced to concede the caliphate to the Umayyad rulers of Damascus. The Kharijites believed the decision violated the will of God. Their puritan views struck a chord with the Berbers of North Africa, and Kharijism became a vehicle for opposition to Arab rule. While the rebellion was suppressed elsewhere, the Kharijites held on in Jerba.

Their numbers were reinforced in 911 after the Fatimids overran the Kharijite Rustamid state based at Tahart in Algeria. Many refugees from Tahart wound up in Jerba. They belonged to the Ibadite sect of Kharijism, a faith still practised in the villages of southern Jerba. The Ibadites are found only here and in the villages of the M'Zab Valley in central Algeria. It is the Kharijites who are

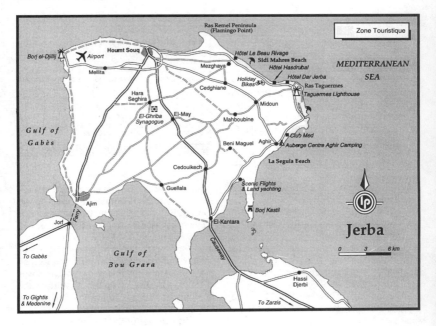

largely responsible for the huge number of mosques on the island – 213 in all.

Jerba spent most of the following 500 years outside the control of the central government, but it remained at the heart of the intrigues that affected the region. It was conquered by the Normans under Roger II of Sicily in 1135, briefly captured by the Almohads in 1159 and then occupied by the Aragonese.

In the early 16th century, the island became a battleground between the Spanish and the Muslim corsairs, whose activities paved the way for Ottoman rule in North Africa. It was used as a base by the Barbarossa brothers, and then by their offsider Dragut – later to become Dargouth Pasha, ruler of Tripoli.

Dragut's renown was enhanced by his famous escape from the Spanish in 1551 when his fleet was trapped east of the causeway, only to slip away at night by hauling the ships across a breach in the causeway.

He returned in 1560 and massacred the Spanish forces sent to dislodge him the following year – resulting in the grim Tower of Skulls that stood on the coast north of Houmt Souq for the next 300 years. (See also the boxed text 'Pirates of the Barbary Coast' in the Northern Tunisia chapter.)

Jerba did well under the Ottomans, and earned a reputation for stability that saw it develop into an important trading post. The French left the Jerbans largely to their own devices.

The tourist boom, which began in the late 1960s, has brought a lot of money to the island, but has done more damage to traditional society than all the other invaders put together. Traditional ways survive in the Berber-speaking Ibadite villages of the south like Guellala and Cedouikech, but they are dying out as young people are drawn away to jobs in the tourist business.

Jerba once had a large Jewish community but, following the formation of the state of

Israel, this has now shrunk to about 700. The Ghriba synagogue, one of 14 on the island, is the oldest in North Africa.

See the boxed text 'The Jews of Jerba' in the Around Jerba section later in this chapter.

GETTING THERE & AWAY
Air
Jerba's airport, near the village of Mellita in the north-west of the island, handles a busy schedule of international flights. There's a constant flow of charter flights from Europe. Tunis Air operates four scheduled flights a week to Paris and weekly flights to Brussels, Frankfurt, Geneva, Istanbul, Lyon, Marseille, Munich, Rome, Vienna and Zurich.

There are seven flights a day to Tunis (one hour, TD50.500 one way). The first flight leaves at 6 am and the last at 8.15 pm. There are two flights a week to Tozeur (50 minutes, TD27.800), leaving at 8.10 am on Tuesday and 3.50 pm on Saturday. The Tunis Air schedule lists flights from Jerba to Sfax and Monastir although airline staff say these services don't exist.

Bus & Louage
See under Getting There & Away in the Houmt Souq section, following, for more information on bus and louage services to/from Jerba.

Car & Motorcycle
The main road from Houmt Souq to Zarzis travels along the old Roman causeway linking El-Kantara and the mainland. This route is only worth taking if you are heading south to Zarzis or Ben Guerdane. If you're heading for Medenine or Gabès, it's much quicker to use the car ferries between Ajim and Jorf.

Boat
Car ferries operate 24 hours a day between the Jerban port of Ajim and Jorf on the mainland. They leave every 30 minutes from 6.30 am to 9.30 pm; hourly from 9.30 to 11.30 pm; two hourly from 11.30 pm to 4.30 am and hourly again from 4.30 to 6.30 am. The trip takes 15 minutes and the fare is 600 mills for a car. Passengers travel free.

HOUMT SOUQ
Pop 6500 ☎ Area code 05
The island's main town, Houmt Souq, lies at the centre of the north coast. Its 6500 residents depend fairly heavily on tourism for their livelihood; the other, more traditional, source of income is the fishing industry.

Orientation
The town centre is about 800m inland. The main streets are Ave Habib Bourguiba and Ave Abdelhamid el-Cadhi. Ave Habib Bourguiba runs north through the town centre from the bus and louage stations and finishes near the port, while Ave Abdelhamid el-Cadhi runs into town from the north-east, joining Ave Habib Bourguiba at a major intersection 150m north of the bus and louage stations. The souqs and most of the town's hotels and restaurants are found within the large V formed by these streets. This is the old part of town, a maze of narrow, winding streets dotted with small squares.

Information
Tourist Offices The local syndicat d'initiative (☎ 650 915) is set back from the main street (Ave Habib Bourguiba, would you believe?), behind the two large maps of the island opposite Place Mongi Bali. The staff have a free map of the island. The office is open Monday to Saturday from 9 am to 1 pm and 3.30 to 6 pm.

The ONTT tourist office (☎ 650 016) is out on the beach road, Rue Ulysse, about 15 minutes walk from the centre. It's not really worth the effort. Opening hours are Monday to Thursday from 8.30 am to 1 pm and 3 to 5.45 pm, and Friday and Saturday from 8.30 am to 1.30 pm.

Money There are a number of banks on Ave Habib Bourguiba and around the squares just off it. There is always one bank rostered to be open on Saturday and Sunday. The syndicat d'initiative can tell you where to look.

Post & Communications The main post office is on Ave Habib Bourguiba. There are plenty of Taxiphone offices, including one opposite the post office on Place Mongi Bali. The office just north of the Mosque of the Strangers on Ave Abdelhamid el-Cadhi is much quieter and has more phones. It's open every day from 7.30 am to 10 pm or later.

Bookshops The bookshop just north of the post office on Ave Habib Bourguiba stocks a wide range of international newspapers. It also has a small collection of novels in French.

Medical Services The large regional hospital (☎ 650 018) is about 500m south-east of the town centre on the road to Midoun. There's also the private Clinique Dar ech-Chifa (☎ 650 441; fax 652 215), which is north-east of town, off Ave Abdelhamid el-Cadhi.

Emergency The main police station is on Ave Habib Bourguiba, just south of the junction with Ave Abdelhamid el-Cadhi.

Souq

Houmt Souq is compact enough to be explored easily on foot. The old souq is the centre of things and consists of a tangle of narrow alleys and a few open squares with cafes. The place is full of souvenir shops. The owners are used to dealing with package tourists who don't bargain too hard, so prices are high.

A feature of the old town are the **funduqs** (caravanserais), former lodging houses for the travelling merchants of the camel caravans that called here in Ottoman times. They were built on two floors surrounding a central courtyard; the top floor had rooms for the merchants, while their animals were housed below. Some of these funduqs have been turned into excellent cheap hotels (see Places to Stay later in this section).

Islamic Monuments

There are some interesting Islamic monuments around the town. Just on the edge of the souq is the **Zaouia of Sidi Brahim**, which contains the tomb of the 17th century saint. On the other side of the road is the multi-domed **Mosque of the Strangers**. The 18th century **Mosque of the Turks** is north of the souq; it has a distinctly Turkish minaret. Note that these monuments are all closed to non-Muslims.

Museum of Popular Arts & Traditions

This fine little museum occupies the Zaouia of Sidi Zitouni, about 200m from the town centre along the eastern arm of Ave Abdelhamid el-Cadhi. It houses a good range of local costumes as well as other bits and pieces. One room still has the original terracotta tile ceiling. The museum is open Saturday to Thursday from 9.30 am to 4.30 pm; admission is TD2.100, plus an extra TD1 if you want to take photos. The ticket office is the small traditional weaver's hut near the entrance.

Borj Ghazi Mustapha

The town's old fort lies on the coast 500m north of the Mosque of the Turks at the end of the shady, tree-lined Rue Taieb Mehiri. Known as the Borj Ghazi Mustapha (and occasionally as the Borj el-Kebir), the fort was built by the Aragonese in the 13th century, and extended early in the 16th century by the Spanish.

The fort was the scene of a famous massacre in 1560 when a Turkish fleet under Dragut (see also under History earlier in the Jerba section) captured the fort and put the Spanish garrison to the sword. The skulls of the victims were stacked up on the shoreline 200m west of the fort (opposite the Hôtel Lotos) as a grim reminder to others not to try any funny business. This macabre Tower of Skulls stood for almost 300 years until it was dismantled on the order of the bey of Tunis in 1848. A simple monument now stands in its place.

The fort itself is worth a wander around and there are good views along the coast. Look for the mounds of cannonballs, both stone and rusting iron, that have been found in the course of recent renovations. The fort has the same opening hours as the museum. Entry is TD1.100, plus TD1 to take photos.

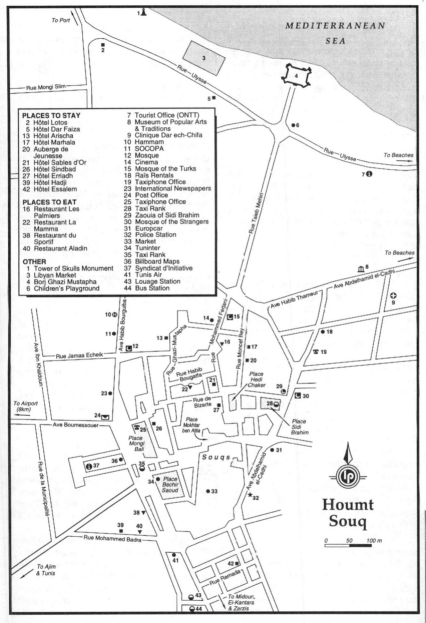

MEDITERRANEAN SEA

To Port

Rue Ulysse

Rue Mongi Slim

Rue Ulysse

To Beaches

PLACES TO STAY
2 Hôtel Lotos
5 Hôtel Dar Faiza
13 Hôtel Arischa
17 Hôtel Marhala
20 Auberge de Jeunesse
21 Hôtel Sables d'Or
26 Hôtel Sindbad
27 Hôtel Erriadh
39 Hôtel Hadji
42 Hôtel Essalem

PLACES TO EAT
16 Restaurant Les Palmiers
22 Restaurant La Mamma
38 Restaurant du Sportif
40 Restaurant Aladin

OTHER
1 Tower of Skulls Monument
3 Libyan Market
4 Borj Ghazi Mustapha
6 Children's Playground
7 Tourist Office (ONTT)
8 Museum of Popular Arts & Traditions
9 Clinique Dar ech-Chifa
10 Hammam
11 SOCOPA
12 Mosque
14 Cinema
15 Mosque of the Turks
18 Raïs Rentals
19 Taxiphone Office
23 International Newspapers
24 Post Office
25 Taxiphone Office
28 Taxi Rank
29 Zaouia of Sidi Brahim
30 Mosque of the Strangers
31 Europcar
32 Police Station
33 Market
34 Tuninter
35 Taxi Rank
36 Billboard Maps
37 Syndicat d'Initiative
41 Tunis Air
43 Louage Station
44 Bus Station

Rue Taïeb Mehiri

To Beaches

Ave Abdelhamid el-Cadhi

Ave Habib Thameur

Rue Jamaa Echeik

Ave Ben Khaldoun

Ave Habib Bourguiba

Rue Ghazi-Mustapha

Rue Habib Bougatfa

Rue Mohammed Ferjani

Rue Moncef Bey

To Airport (8km)

Ave Boumessouer

Rue de la Municipalité

Rue de Bizerte

Place Hedi Chaker

Place Mokhtar ben Attia

Place Mongi Bali

Place Bechir Saoud

Place Sidi Brahim

Souqs

Ave Abdelhamid-el-Cadhi

Rue Mohammed Badra

To Ajim & Tunis

To Midoun, El-Kantara & Zarzis

Rue Remada

Houmt Souq

0   50   100 m

SOUTHERN TUNISIA

Fishing Port

Houmt Souq's busy fishing port is just west of the Tower of Skulls monument. Check out the huge stacks of terracotta pots that are used by local octopus fishermen in a traditional technique known as *gargoulette*. The pots are tied together and thrown out on long lines; they sink to the bottom and are left there for the octopus to discover. Octopus like to hide in rocky nooks and crannies, and they obligingly crawl in.

Libyan Market

The large, walled enclosure between the fort and the port is the home of the Libyan market, held on Monday and Thursday. It was once a major event, with an interesting range of goods from across the border. These days, most Libyan traders prefer the markets at Ben Guerdane.

Beaches

The beach north of Houmt Souq isn't worth checking out. The shoreline is rocky and covered in rubbish, and the sea is too shallow for swimming. The best beaches are in the north-eastern corner of the island. The most popular is **Sidi Mahres** beach, which starts about 10km east of Houmt Souq and extends all the way to Ras Taguermes. It's normally packed with guests from the line-up of giant resort hotels. Between them, the hotels offer every conceivable form of water sports.

Things are much quieter at **La Seguia** beach, north-east of Aghir on the east coast. You can get to both beaches by local bus from Houmt Souq. The buses to the zone touristique travel along the north coast and terminate at Ras Taguermes, while buses to Club Med go to La Seguia via Midoun and Aghir. They also terminate at Ras Taguermes. (See also the Around Jerba section later in this chapter.)

Scenic Flights

Air Tropic (☎ (09) 723 344) charges TD30 for a 30 minute ride in one of its tiny Petrel hydroplanes. They operate from the sand flats 5km south of Aghir on the east coast.

Land Yachting

Air Tropic (see Scenic Flights earlier) also rents out land yachts (TD10 per hour). The sand flats south of Aghir stretch for miles and are a perfect location.

Special Events

The Ulysses Festival is held in August. This is strictly for tourists and includes events like a Miss Ulysses beauty contest.

Places to Stay – budget

Camping The island's only camp site is on the beach at Aghir, about 28km from Houmt Souq. The *Auberge Centre Aghir* (☎ 657 366), at the junction of the Midoun road, is run by the Centre des Stages et Vacances organisation – the resort version of the maison des jeunes. It charges TD2.500 per person, plus 500 mills for each tent. It also has dormitory accommodation for TD4.500. To get there from Houmt Souq, catch the bus (40 minutes, 900 mills) to Club Med via Midoun.

Youth Hostel Houmt Souq's excellent *Auberge de Jeunesse* (☎ 650 619) occupies an old funduq right next to the Hôtel Marhala on Rue Moncef Bey. It's as good as hostels get. The staff are friendly, and the hostel is open throughout the day. Beds (in dorms only) cost TD3.500. Breakfast is available for TD1, and lunch and dinner for TD3. There is a three day limit on stays in high season.

Hotels The most interesting places to stay are the old funduqs. The pick of them is the *Hôtel Arischa* (☎ 650 384), just north of the souq on Rue Ghazi Mustapha. It's a place to explore as well as a place to stay. The courtyard is filled with flowers and the large singles/doubles are good value at TD9/14 with breakfast.

Another good choice is the *Hôtel Marhala* (☎ 650 146; fax 653 317), on Rue Moncef Bey, one of the small chain of budget hotels run by the Touring Club de Tunisie. As usual, the standard is excellent, although some people find the authentic, barrel-vaulted rooms claustrophobic. Singles/doubles cost TD10.500/16 with breakfast, and additional meals are available for TD5 each.

The *Hôtel Sindbad* (☎ 650 047), off Place Mongi Bali, looks a bit tatty after the Arischa and the Marhala. Single/double rooms with breakfast are TD8/12.

An alternative to the funduqs is the *Hôtel Sables d'Or* (☎ 650 423), an old house on Rue Mohammed Ferjani that has been converted into a stylish little hotel. The two brothers who run it keep the 12 rooms absolutely spotless. They charge TD11/20 for singles/doubles with breakfast.

The modern *Hôtel Essalem* (☎ 651 029) close to the bus station on Rue Remada, looks a bit gloomy, but the staff are cheerful enough. It charges TD12.400/16.800 for large singles/doubles with breakfast. For a few dinars more you could stay in air-con comfort at the one star *Hôtel Hadji* (☎ 650 630; fax 652 221) at 44 Rue Mohammed Badra. It has standard rooms with private bathroom for TD13.500/22 or TD15.500/24 with air-con.

Places to Stay – middle
The *Hôtel Erriadh* (☎ 650 756; fax 650 487), just north of the souq on Rue Mohammed Ferjani, is the most upmarket of the old funduqs. It's a beautiful place with large air-conditioned double rooms with private bathroom around a cool vine-covered courtyard. It charges TD18/27 for singles/doubles with breakfast. This falls to TD14/20 in winter.

There are two good places facing the beach on Rue Ulysse to the west of the fort, both run by the same family. The *Hôtel Dar Faiza* (☎ 650 083; fax 651 763) is much better than the average one star hotel – and a fair bit more expensive. It's very private, with accommodation in bungalows spread through gardens at the rear of the hotel. It also has a small pool, heated in winter, and a tennis court. It charges TD28.500/47 for singles/doubles with breakfast, dropping to TD16/24 in winter. The hotel has one of the best restaurants on the island, so it's worth considering half or full board.

Its stable-mate, the *Hôtel Lotos* (☎ 650 026), represents better value with singles/doubles for TD22.500/35. This is the original tourist hotel on the island. The rooms are huge, with correspondingly large balconies, and most offer excellent views of the coast. Guests here can use the facilities at the Dar Faiza free of charge. In winter, the Lotos is a bargain at TD13.500/19. The hotel is 200m west of the Dar Faiza, opposite the Tower of Skulls monument.

Places to Stay – top end
The island's top hotels are all located out on the beaches of the zone touristique (see the following Around Jerba section for more details).

Places to Eat
The streets of Houmt Souq are filled with cafes and restaurants to suit every budget.

The *Restaurant Les Palmiers* is a great little place in the middle of Rue Mohammed Ferjani. The extensive menu is printed in English, French and German, and there's nothing over TD3. It includes briqs (filled pastry triangles) for 500 mills, salade tunisienne for 800 mills and a large plate of couscous with lamb for TD2.200. You'll find a similar range at the *Restaurant du Sportif*, centrally located on Ave Habib Bourguiba.

The tiny *Restaurant La Mamma* on Rue Habib Bougatfa is another place worth checking out. It does a roaring trade at lunch time, with local workers tucking into such staples as lablabi (chickpea broth) and chorba (soup; both 800 mills). It also has beans for TD1 and spicy, Tunisian-style macaroni for TD1.300.

The *Restaurant Aladin* is a cheery little place on Ave Mohammed Badra that specialises in fish. Prices are much lower here than at the tourist restaurants. The menu includes some interesting seafood dishes such as octopus cooked in its own ink for TD3.500.

Most of the tourist restaurants are grouped around Place Sidi Brahim. The menus are posted outside, usually in four languages, and there is not a great deal between them.

SOUTHERN TUNISIA

Beware of owners who try to persuade you to have a 'special meal', as the price will be pretty bloody special as well unless you clarify beforehand just how much you are prepared to pay.

The tourist menu at the *Hôtel Dar Faiza* is good value at TD6 for three courses. It also has a good selection of local wines. The restaurant is open every day; bookings are advisable in high season.

Getting There & Away
Air The airport is 8km west of Houmt Souq near the village of Mellita. It handles international and domestic flights. See Air under the main Jerba Getting There & Away section earlier for more details.

Bus The uncharacteristically well organised bus station is at the southern end of Ave Habib Bourguiba. All the scheduled departures are listed on a board above the ticket windows.

SNTRI runs four air-conditioned services a day to Tunis (TD17.760). The 8.30 am and 8 pm services travel via Kairouan (five hours, TD12.440) and take 7 hours, while the 6 am and 7 pm services go via Sfax (four hours, TD9.280) and Sousse (six hours, TD13.660) and take an hour longer.

The regional company, Sotregames, has five buses a day to Medenine (1½ hours, TD2.700), three to Gabès (three hours, TD4.580) and two to Tataouine (2½ hours, TD4.440). A couple of the buses to Medenine travel via Zarzis (one hour, TD2), which adds an hour to the trip. Sotregames also has a bus to Sfax at 12.45 pm. At the time of writing, SRT Medenine was about to launch a new daily service to Matmata, leaving Houmt Souq at 4.30 pm.

Louage Louages leave from opposite the entrance to the bus station. There are frequent departures for Gabès (TD4.650), Medenine (TD2.900) and Zarzis (TD2.250). Louages to Tunis (TD17.800) leave at 6 am and 6 pm and can be booked at the small office (☎ 650 475) at the side of the bus

station. Ask at the office about occasional services to Sfax and Sousse.

Car Rental Houmt Souq is a popular place to hire cars for trips around the island and to sights around the south of the country. All the companies have offices both in town and out at the airport, where the phone number for them all is ☎ 650 233.

The offices in town include: Avis (☎ 650 151) on Ave Mohammed Badra; Europcar (☎ 650 357) on Ave Abdelhamid el-Cadhi; Hertz (☎ 650 196) on Place Mongi Slim; Mattei (☎ 651 367) on Ave Habib Bourguiba; and Topcar (☎ 650 536) on Rue 2 Mars 1934.

Getting Around
To/From the Airport The airport is 8km west of Houmt Souq, past the village of Mellita. There are buses (370 mills) from the central bus station at 7.15 am and 12.30, 5.15 and 6.15 pm.

If the buses don't suit, you'll have to catch a taxi. It'll cost about TD3 from Houmt Souq, or TD7.500 from the Hôtel Dar Jerba in the zone touristique.

Bus There is a fairly comprehensive local bus network connecting the larger towns of the island.

There is a timetable and a colour-coded route map of the services around the island above the ticket windows in the bus station in Houmt Souq.

Taxi There are two taxi ranks in Houmt Souq – on Ave Habib Bourguiba in the centre of town and at Place Sidi Brahim. Sample fares include Houmt Souq to Midoun for TD4.500 and Houmt Souq to Aghir for TD6. Fares are 50% higher after 10 pm.

The taxis are forever cruising the hotel strip for fares into Houmt Souq. The big hotels, such as the Dar Jerba, have their own ranks.

In summer, demand for taxis far exceeds supply and it can be difficult to get hold of one in Houmt Souq, especially in the early afternoon when things close up for a couple of hours.

The taxis can also be hired for the day for trips around the island. A daily charter costs between TD40 and TD50, depending on your bargaining skills.

Bicycle & Moped Bicycles are available for hire from any of the hotels in Houmt Souq. In fact they just act as agents and take a small cut. Some of the bikes are in pretty poor shape, so make sure you get a decent one.

The amount you can see by bicycle in a day is very limited, as the island is too large to see the lot. If there were places to stay in other parts of the island you could make a great three or four day circuit, but this is not possible at the moment. Another factor conspiring against cyclists is the strong winds which often prevail; trying to ride into them is no joke.

Typical rates are TD1 per hour, TD5 per half day and TD8 for a full day.

Mopeds are a much better bet for seeing the whole island. Raïs Rentals (☎ 650 303), north of the Mosque of the Strangers on Ave Abdelhamid el-Cadhi in Houmt Souq, rents them for TD24 per day. It also has bicycles for TD8 per day or the five day rate for a week's rental.

Out on the tourist strip, Holiday Bikes (☎ 657 169) has 80cc scooters for TD45 per day and 125cc Yamaha trail bikes for TD65.

When riding a moped you are not covered by any insurance. Be extremely careful, especially out in the smaller inland villages where young children, wayward cyclists and suicidal dogs can be a real hazard. No licence is needed for machines under 50cc.

AROUND JERBA
Zone Touristique
The island's tourist strip covers the entire north-eastern corner of the island – 20km of uninterrupted hotels that monopolise the only decent beaches, Sidi Mahres on the north coast and La Seguia on the east coast.

· **Sidi Mahres** beach begins east of the low-lying Ras Remel Peninsula, which protrudes from the middle of the north coast 10km east of Houmt Souq. The peninsula is known as **Flamingo Point** because of the large num-

bers of the birds that gather there in winter. Sidi Mahres beach then continues east all the way to Ras Taguermes, the cape at Jerba's north-eastern tip. It's marked by a bold red and black lighthouse by the roadside. A long sand spit extends south from the cape, enclosing a large lagoon.

South of here on the east coast is **La Seguia**, the island's best swimming beach. The water is deeper here than along the north coast.

Things to Do Most of the tourists who use the resort hotels do little more than cook themselves on the beach. Many of the hotels have water sports equipment for hire.

The small **go-kart track** opposite the Ras Taguermes lighthouse charges TD12 for six laps.

Places to Stay & Eat Accommodation options along the beach are dominated by a string of massive resort hotels. They include such monsters as the *Dar Jerba*, a conglomeration of four hotels catering mainly for German tourists. More than 2700 sun seekers can enjoy the umpteen restaurants, bars, Bavarian folk nights, disco etc.

One place that's a little bit different is the *Hôtel Le Beau Rivage* (☎ (05) 757 130; fax 758 123), 10km east of Houmt Souq at the beginning of Sidi Mahres Beach. It's a small pension-style place with singles/doubles for TD30/40, including breakfast. The rates fall to TD15/24 in winter.

The smartest place around is the five star *Hôtel Hasdrubal* (☎ (05) 657 650; fax 657 730), which is 16km east of Houmt Souq on Sidi Mahres Beach. It has singles/doubles with breakfast for TD115/170, and facilities that include two swimming pools and a disco.

Getting There & Away See the Getting Around section under Houmt Souq earlier for details of transport options around the zone touristique.

Midoun
This is the island's second major town and is best known for its busy Friday market. Most

of the items on sale are really just tourist rubbish, with only a few stalls set up to sell fruit and vegetables.

Places to Stay & Eat The *Hôtel Jawhara* (☎ 600 467) is on Rue Echabi, a small street off the main market square. It's clean but basic, with singles/doubles for TD10/16. It does have hot showers.

The *Restaurant el-Guestile*, on Rue Marsa Ettefah, has a pleasant outdoor setting and meals for about TD10 plus wine. The *Restaurant Khalife*, on Ave Salah ben Youssef, specialises in fish dishes at similar prices.

For local food, try the *Restaurant de l'Orient*, which has couscous for TD2. It's next to the post office on the southern edge of town.

Getting There & Away There are eight bus services a day between Midoun and Houmt Souq (750 mills).

Cedghiane

The oasis of Cedghiane lies halfway between Houmt Souq and Midoun. It's in the most fertile part of the island, with an ample supply of sweet artesian water which has allowed the development of traditional, tiered desert oasis agriculture with tall palms providing shade for citrus and pomegranate trees, which in turn protect vegetable crops. The huge *menzels* (Jerban dwellings) of the area are evidence that this was once an important settlement, but most are in ruins and the landowners live elsewhere.

Hara Seghira

Once exclusively a Jewish settlement, Hara Seghira (or Erriadh) lies just off the main Houmt Souq-Zarzis road. With the mass migration of Jews to Israel, the population is now predominantly Muslim, but a number of synagogues still remain.

The most important Jewish synagogue is El-Ghriba (the Stranger), signposted 1km south of the town. It is a major place of pilgrimage during the Passover Festival, when Jews come to pay tribute to the grand master of the Talmud, Shimon Bar Yashai, who died more than 400 years ago.

The Jews of Jerba

The Jewish community dates its arrival in Jerba either from 586 BC, following Nebuchadnezzar's conquest of Jerusalem, or from the Roman sacking of the same city in 71 AD; either way this makes it one of the oldest Jewish communities in the world. Some historians, however, argue that many Jerban Jews are descended from Berbers who converted to Judaism. Over the centuries the community also received several influxes of Jews fleeing from persecution in Spain, Italy and Palestine. In the times of the beys in the 19th century, Jews in Jerba were required to wear distinctive clothes: black pantaloons, black skull cap and sleeveless blue shirts. Discrimination ended with the arrival of the French in 1881. The community was known for being staunchly traditional, like their neighbours the Kharijite Muslims, and it rejected financial and educational aid from the rest of the Jewish world. Communities of Jerban Jews settled all over southern Tunisia, usually working as blacksmiths or shopkeepers, but returned to the island for the summer and for religious festivals.

Most Jerban Jews emigrated to Israel after the 1956 and 1967 wars; after centuries of relative peace the clash between Arab and Israeli nationalism made their position untenable. The community also suffered during WWII, when the Germans extorted 50kg of gold as a communal fine.

The two main Jewish settlements on Jerba were Hara Kebira (Big Ghetto), just south of Houmt Souq, and Hara Seghira (Little Ghetto), in the centre of the island. While Hara Kebira has a dozen or so synagogues and a kosher restaurant, Hara Seghira features the main Jewish site on the island, the El-Ghriba synagogue. This synagogue was thought to have been founded in about 600 AD, after a holy stone fell from heaven at the site and a mysterious woman appeared to direct the construction of the synagogue. Although the present brightly decorated building dates only from the 1920s, it is home to one of the oldest Torahs in the world and numerous silver plaques from pilgrims can be seen. Today the synagogue remains an important pilgrimage site, although the Jewish community on Jerba numbers only a few hundred.

Richard Plunkett

The site dates back to 586 BC, although the present building was constructed early in the 20th century. The inner sanctuary is said to contain one of the oldest Torahs (Jewish holy book) in the world.

The site was apparently chosen after a stone fell from heaven; it is also said that an unknown woman turned up and performed a miracle or two to assist the builders.

It is open to the public but you need to be modestly dressed, and men have to don yarmulkes (skullcaps) on entering. Donations are compulsory but you don't have to leave much.

Buses from Houmt Souq to Guellala go right past the synagogue (500 mills).

Guellala

This tiny village on the south coast is known for its pottery. In the past the pottery was sold on the mainland but these days almost all of it is sold on site. A dozen or so workshops and galleries line the main road, all selling much the same stuff.

From Guellala there is a dirt track which skirts around a bay, where the local fishing people paddle around in waist-deep water.

The track continues to the village of Ajim, where the ferries connect with the mainland.

There are seven buses a day between Guellala and Houmt Souq (30 minutes, 750 mills).

Ajim

Ajim is a busy fishing port and the departure point for car ferries to Jorf on the mainland. There's nothing much to do other than watch the fishers. If you have to wait a while for a ferry, there are a few restaurants on the main street. For details of the ferry service to the mainland, see Boat under Getting There & Away at the beginning of the Jerba section.

West Coast

There is very little along the whole western coastline. There's just one dirt track, which hugs the coast all the way, and a few scattered houses.

The lighthouse at the north-western corner of the island occupies an 18th century Turkish fort, the Borj el-Djillij. It's closed to the public and there's no reason to come here other than curiosity.

Language

Tunisia is virtually bilingual. Arabic is the language of government, but almost everybody speaks some French. French was the language of education in the early Bourguiba years, and is still taught in schools from the age of six. English and German are also taught in schools, but it's rare to encounter either language outside the main tourist areas. The Berber language Chelha is heard only in isolated villages.

ARABIC

Tunisian Arabic belongs to a dialect known as Western Colloquial Arabic. There is no dictionary or phrasebook specifically for Tunisian Arabic, but the following vocabulary section includes some of the most common words and phrases. For a more comprehensive guide to Arabic, get hold of Lonely Planet's *Egyptian Arabic phrasebook*.

More specialised or educated language tends to be much the same across the Arab world, although pronunciation varies considerably. The spread of radio and television have increased all Arabs' exposure to and understanding of what is commonly known as Modern Standard Arabic (MSA). MSA, which has grown from the classical language of the Qur'an and poetry, is the written and spoken lingua franca of the Arab world. It's the language of radio, television and the press, and also the majority of modern Arabic literature.

Foreign students of the language constantly face the dilemma of whether to learn MSA first (which could mean waiting a while before being able to talk with the locals) and then a chosen dialect, or simply to acquire spoken competence in the latter. Dialects supposedly have no written form (the argument goes it would be like writing in Cockney or Strine), although there's no reason why they could not avail themselves of the same script used for the standard language. If this leaves you with a headache, you'll have some idea of why so few non-

Arabs or non-Muslims embark on the study of this complex tongue!

Pronunciation

Pronunciation of Arabic can be tongue-tying for someone unfamiliar with the intonation and combination of sounds. Pronounce the transliterated words and phrases slowly and clearly.

The following guide should help, but it isn't complete because the rules governing pronunciation and vowel use are too extensive to be covered here.

Vowels

In spoken Arabic, at least five basic vowel sounds can be distinguished:

a	as in 'had' (sometimes very short)
e	as in 'bet' (sometimes very short)
i	as in 'hit'
o	as in 'hot'
u	as in 'book'

These also have long variants, indicated here by a dash (macron) above the vowel :

ā	as in 'father'
ē	as in 'ten', but lengthened
ī	like the 'e' in 'ear', only softer
ō	as in 'for'
ū	as in 'rude'

You may also see long vowels transliterated as double vowels, eg 'aa' (ā), 'ee' (ī), 'oo' (ū).

Combinations

Certain vowels can also combine to form other vowel sounds (diphthongs):

aw	as the 'ow' in 'how'
ai	as the 'i' in 'high'
ei, ay	as the 'a' in 'cake'

These last two are tricky, as one can slide into the other in certain words. Remember that these rules are an outline and not exhaustive.

Consonants

Most of the consonants used in this section are the same as in English. However, a few of the consonant sounds need to be explained in greater detail.

Three of the most difficult sounds for a non-native speaker are the glottal stop ('), the 'ayn' ('), and the 'rayn' (**gh**). Don't be discouraged if you aren't being understood, just keep trying.

The glottal stop is the sound you hear between the vowels in the expression 'oh oh!', or the Cockney pronunciation of 'water' (wa'er). It's actually a closing of the glottis at the back of the throat so that the passage of air is momentarily halted. It can occur anywhere in a word.

The ('), or 'ayn', and the (**gh**), or 'rayn', are two of the most difficult sounds in Arabic. Both can be produced by tightening your throat and sort of growling, but the ('gh') requires a slight 'r' sound at the beginning – it's like the French 'r'. When the (') occurs before a vowel, the vowel is 'growled' from the back of the throat. If it's before a consonant or at the end of a word, it sounds like a glottal stop. The best way to learn these sounds is to listen to a native speaker pronounce their written equivalents.

Other common consonant sounds include the following:

j	more or less as in 'John'
H	a strongly whispered 'h', almost like a sigh of relief
q	a strong guttural 'k' sound. Often transcribed as 'k', although there is already a letter in the Arabic alphabet which *is* the equivalent of 'k'
kh	a slightly gurgling sound, like the 'ch' in Scottish 'loch'
r	a rolled 'r', as in the Spanish 'para'
s	pronounced as in English 'sit', never as in 'wisdom'
sh	as in 'shelf'
ẑ	as the 's' in pleasure

Double Consonants

In the Arabic language, double consonants are both pronounced. For example the word *istanna*, which means 'wait', is pronounced 'istan-na'.

Transliteration

What you read and hear will as often as not be two or three entirely different things. No really satisfactory system of transcribing the 'squiggles' of Arabic into Latin script has ever been devised, not for lack of trying.

Most modern maps, guidebooks and other books dealing with Tunisia tend to reflect French (rather than English) usage. This guidebook generally conforms with these conventions.

There is only one word for 'the' in Arabic – *al*, and it modifies before certain consonants. For example, in Arabic the name Saladin is 'Salah ad-Din' (lit: 'righteousness of the faith') – the 'al' has been modified to 'ad' before the 'd' of Din. In Tunisia *el* is more commonly used, and in practice the pronunciation is such that the initial 'a' or 'e' is hardly heard at all.

It may be useful, especially to travellers who have been elsewhere in the Arab world (and become accustomed to other transliteration systems) to consult the following list of alternatives and their 'standardised' equivalents:

ou	as in oued; it's the French equivalent of **w** in 'wadi' (a usually dry, seasonal river bed). The name 'Daoud' can also be written 'Dawud'.
dj	as in 'djebel'; the French equivalent of simple **j** in 'jebel' (mountain).
k	often corresponds to the Arabic letter 'qaf', or the English **q**; 'kasr' versus 'qasr' (castle) is an example.
e	often appears where some feel an **a** would better represent its pronunciation. Note, however, that vowels in Arabic are not as important as in other languages. Vowel and consonant order are sometimes at variance. For example the common word for school, which also refers to older religious learning institutions, is 'madrassa', but it most commonly appears as 'medersa'.

FRENCH

Almost everybody in Tunisia speaks French, so if the thought of getting your mind around Arabic is too much, it'd be a good investment to learn a little French instead.

In French, an important distinction is made between *tu* and *vous*, which both mean 'you', although in general younger people insist less on this distinction. *Tu* is only used when addressing people you know well, or children. When addressing an adult who is not a personal friend, *vous* should be used unless the person invites you to use *tu*.

Useful Words & Phrases

The following words and phrases should help you communicate on a basic level in either Arabic or French. For a more detailed list of food terms, see the Glossary in the illustrated Tunisian Cuisine section at the end of the Facts for the Visitor chapter.

Pronouns

I	*ana*	je
you (singular)	*inta/inti* (m/f)	tu (informal)/ vous
he/she	*huwa/hīya*	il/elle
we	*eHna*	nous
you (pl)	*intum*	vous
they	*huma*	ils/elles (m/f)

Greetings & Civilities

Hello.
as-salām 'alaykum (literally: 'peace be upon you')
Bonjour.
Hello. (in response – 'and upon you be peace')
wa 'alaykum as-salām
Goodbye. ('go in safety')
ma' as-salāma
Au revoir/Salut.
Good morning.
sabaH al-khēr
Bonjour.
Good morning. (in response)
sabaH an-nūr
Good evening.
masa' al-khēr
Bonsoir.

Good evening. (in response)
masa' an-nūr
Welcome.
marhaba
How are you?
kayf Hālek?
Comment allez-vous/ça va?
Fine, thank you.
bikhēr al-Hamdu lillah (thanks be to God)
Bien, merci.

Basics

Yes.	*īyeh/na'am*	Oui.
No.	*la*	Non.
No, thank you.	*la, shukran*	Non, merci.
Please.	*men fadhlek*	S'il vous plaît.

Thank you (very much).
shukran (jazilan)
Merci (beaucoup).
You're welcome. (it was nothing)
la shukran 'ala wajib
De rien/Je vous en prie.
Excuse me.
sa'mahni
Excusez-moi/Pardon.
Why?
laysh?
Pourquoi?
Is there ...?
hal hou ...?
Il y a ...?
Who is that?
mīn hadha?
C'est qui, celui/celle? (m/f)
Go ahead/move it/come on!
hay bina!
allons-y

Language Difficulties

Do you speak ...?
tatakallem ...?
Parlez-vous ...?

English	*inglīz*	anglais
French	*farans*	français
German	*almāni*	allemand

I understand.
fhemt
Je comprend.

I don't understand.
ma fhemtesh
Je ne comprend pas.

Small Talk

What's your name?
ma'howa ismok?
Comment vous appelez-vous?
My name is ...
ismī howa ...
Je m'appelle ...
How old are you?
ma' howa 'amrak?
Quel âge avez-vous?
I'm 25.
'āndī khamsa wa 'ashrīn
J'ai vingt-cinq ans.
Where are you from?
min īn inta/inti/intum? (m/f/pl)
D'où êtes-vous?
I/We are from ...
ana/eHna min ...
Je viens/Nous venons ...

America	*amrīka*	de l'Amérique
Australia	*ustralya*	de l'Australie
Canada	*kanada*	du Canada
England	*inglaterra*	de l'Angleterre
France	*firansa*	de la France
Germany	*almanya*	de l'Allemagne
Italy	*itāliyya*	de l'Italie
Japan	*al-yaban*	du Japon
Netherlands	*holanda*	des Pays Bas
Spain	*isbanya*	de l'Espagne
Sweden	*as-swīd*	du Suède

Getting Around

I want to go to ...
urīd an adhaba ila ...
Je veux aller à ...
What is the fare to ...?
mahowa assir ila ...?
Combien coûte le billet pour ...?
When does the ... leave/arrive?
emta qiyam/wusūl ...?
À quelle heure part/arrive ...?

bus	*al-otobīs*	l'autobus
train	*al-qitar*	le train
boat	*as-safīna*	le bateau

Where is (the) ...?
fein ...?
Où est ...?
bus station for ...
maHattat al-otobīs li ...
la gare routière pour ...
bus stop
mawqif al-otobīs
l'arrêt d'autobus
train station
maHattat al-qitar
la gare
ticket office
maktab at-tazkara
la billeterie/le guichet

street	*az-zanqa*	la rue
city	*al-medīna*	la ville
village	*al-qarya*	le village

Which bus goes to ...?
ey kar yamshī ila ...?
Quel autobus part pour ...?
Does this bus go to ...?
yamshī had al-kar ila ...?
Cet autobus-là va-t-il à ...?
How many buses per day go to ...?
kam kar kul yūmchi ila ...?
Il y a combien d'autobus chaque
   jour pour ...?
Please tell me when we arrive.
emta nassil men fadhlek
Dîtes-moi quand on arrive, s'il vous
   plaît.
Stop here, please.
qif honamen fadhlek
Arrêtez ici, s'il vous plaît.
Please wait for me.
intadhirnē men fadhlek
Attendez-moi, s'il vous plaît.
May I/we sit here?
(wash) yimkin ajlis/najlis hona?
Puis-je m'asseoir ici?
Where can I rent a bicycle?
fein yimkin ana akri beshklīta?
Où est-ce que je peux louer une bicyclette?

address	*'anwān*	adresse
airport	*matār*	aéroport
camel	*jamal*	chameau

LANGUAGE

car	*sayara*	voiture
crowded	*zHam*	plein
daily	*kull yūm*	chaque jour
donkey	*Humār*	âne
horse	*Husān*	cheval
number	*raqm*	numéro
ticket	*tazkara*	billet
Wait!	*intadhirnī!*	Attendez!

Directions

How far is …?
   kam kilo li …?
   Combien de kilomètres à …?
Which direction?
   aya ittijah?
   Quelle direction?

Where?	*fein?*	Où?
left/right	*yasar/yamīn*	gauche/ droite
here/there	*huna/hunak*	ici/là
next to	*bi-janib*	à côté de
opposite	*muqabbal*	en face de
north	*shamal*	nord
south	*janūb*	sud
east	*sharq*	est
west	*gharb*	ouest

Around Town

Where is (the) …?
   fein …?
   Où est …?

bank	*al-banka*	la banque
barber	*al-Hallaq*	le coiffeur
beach	*ash-shātta'*	la plage
embassy	*as-sifāra*	l'ambassade
market	*as-sūq*	le marché
mosque	*al-jām*	la mosqué
museum	*al-matHaf*	le musée
old city	*al-medīna*	la médina
palace/castle	*al-qasr*	le palais/ château
pharmacy	*farmasyan*	la pharmacie
police station	*al-bolīs*	la police
post office	*al-bōsta/ maktab al-barīd*	la poste
restaurant	*al-mat'am*	le restaurant
university	*al-jami'a*	l'université

I want to change …
   urīd/an asrif …
   Je voudrais changer …
money
   fulūs
   de l'argent
travellers cheques
   shīkāt siyaHiyya
   des chèques de voyage

Accommodation

Where is the hotel?
   fein (mawjoud) al-otēl?
   Où est l'hôtel?
Can I see the room?
   (wash) yimkin lī nshūf al-ghorfa?
   Peux-je voir la chambre?
How much is this room per night?
   kamel ghorfa ellaylar?
   Combien est cette chambre pour une nuit?
That's too expensive.
   ghālī khatiran
   C'est trop cher.
Do you have any cheaper rooms?
   hal indakum ghorfa arkhas?
   Avez-vous des chambres moins chères?
This is fine.
   hada bahi
   Ça va bien.

air-con	*klīmafīzasīyon*	climatisation
bed	*firash*	lit
blanket	*batanīya*	couverture
camp site	*mukhaym*	camping
full	*malyen*	complet
hot water	*ma skhūn*	eau chaude
key	*meftaH*	clef (or clé)
roof	*stāh*	terasse
room	*ghorfa*	chambre
shower	*dūsh*	douche
toilet	*bayt al-ma; mirHad*	les toilettes
youth hostel	*oberẑ;dar shabbab*	auberge de jeunesse

Shopping

Where can I buy …?
   fein yimkin ashterī …?
   Où est-ce que je peux acheter …?

How much?	*bi-kam?*	Combien?
too much	*ghalī awī*	trop cher
cheap	*rakhīs*	bon marché
expensive	*ghalī*	cher
big	*kbīr*	grand
small	*sghīr*	petit
open	*meHlool*	ouvert

Do you have...?
wash 'andkum ...?
Avez-vous ...?

stamps	*tawāba*	des timbres
newspaper	*al-jarida*	un journal

Time

When?	*emta?*	Quand?
now	*allān/nak*	maintenant
today	*al-yūm*	aujourd'hui
tomorrow	*ghaddan*	demain
yesterday	*al-bareh*	hier
morning	*fis-sabaH*	matin
afternoon	*fil-ashīya*	après-midi
evening	*masa'*	soir
day/night	*nahar/layl*	jour/nuit
week	*usbu'*	semaine
month	*shahr*	mois
year	*'am*	an

What time is it?
sa'a kam?
Quelle heure est-il?
At what time?
fi sa'a kam?
À quelle heure?

after	*min ba'd*	après
on time	*fil-waqt*	à l'heure
early	*bakrī*	tôt
late	*mu'attāguiz*	tard
quickly	*bisorī*	vite
slowly	*bishwayya*	lentement

Days of the Week

Monday	*(nhar) al-itnēn*	lundi
Tuesday	*(nhar) at-talata*	mardi
Wednesday	*(nhar) al-arba*	mercredi
Thursday	*(nhar) al-khamīs*	jeudi
Friday	*(nhar) al-juma*	vendredi
Saturday	*(nhar) as-sabt*	samedi
Sunday	*(nhar) al-ahad*	dimanche

Months of the Year

The Islamic year has 12 lunar months and is 11 days shorter than the Gregorian calendar, so important Muslim dates fall about 10 days earlier each (western) year. It's impossible to predict exactly when they will fall, as this depends on when the new moon is sighted.

The Islamic, or Hijra (referring to the year of Mohammed's flight from Mecca in 622 AD), calendar months are:

1st	*Moharram*
2nd	*Safar*
3rd	*Rabi' al-Awal*
4th	*Rabi' al-Akhir* or *Rabi' at-Tani*
5th	*Jumada al-Awal*
6th	*Jumada al-Akhir* or *Jumada at-Taniyya*
7th	*Rajab*
8th	*Sha'aban*
9th	*Ramadan*
10th	*Shawwal*
11th	*Zūl Qe'da*
12th	*Zūl Hijja*

In Tunisia, the names for the months of the Gregorian calendar are virtually the same as in English and are easily recognisable:

January	*yanāyir*	janvier
February	*fibrāyir*	février
March	*māris*	mars
April	*abrīl*	avril
May	*māyu*	mai
June	*yunyu*	juin
July	*yulyu*	juillet
August	*aghustus/ghusht*	août
September	*sibtimbir/ shebtenber*	septembre
October	*uktoobir*	octobre
November	*nufimbir/nu'enbir*	novembre
December	*disimbir/dijenbir*	décembre

Arabic Numbers

Arabic numerals are simple enough to learn and, unlike the written language, run from left to right across the page. An added bonus is that you you won't have to worry about learning Arabic numerals because Tunisia uses the European ones.

LANGUAGE

0	*sifr*	zéro
1	*wāHid*	un
2	*itnīn*	deux
3	*talata*	trois
4	*arba'a*	quatre
5	*khamsa*	cinq
6	*sitta*	six
7	*saba'a*	sept
8	*tamanya*	huit
9	*tissa'*	neuf
10	*'ashara*	dix
11	*wāHidash*	onze
12	*itna'ash*	douze
13	*talattash*	treize
14	*arba'atash*	quatorze
15	*khamastash*	quinze
16	*sitt'ash*	seize
17	*saba'atash*	dix-sept
18	*tamantash*	dix-huit
19	*tissa'atash*	dix-neuf
20	*'ashrīn*	vingt
21	*wāHid wa 'ashrīn*	vingt-et-un
22	*itnīn wa 'ashrīn*	vingt-deux
30	*talatīn*	trente
40	*arba'īn*	quarante
50	*khamsīn*	cinquante
60	*sittīn*	soixante
70	*saba'īn*	soixante-dix
80	*tamanīn*	quatre-vingts
90	*tissa'īn*	quatre-vingt-dix
100	*miyya*	cent

101	*miyya wa wāHid*	cent-un
200	*miyyatīn*	deux cents
300	*talata mia*	trois cents
400	*arba'a mia*	quatre cents
1000	*alf*	mille
2000	*alfīn*	deux milles
3000	*talat alāf*	trois milles
4000	*arba'at alāf*	quatre milles

Ordinal Numbers

first	*'awwal*	premier
second	*tānï*	deuxième
third	*tālit*	troisième
fourth	*rābi'*	quatrième
fifth	*khāmis*	cinquième

Emergencies

Call the police!
'eyyet al-bolis!
Appelez la police!
Call a doctor!
'eyyet at-tabīb!
Appelez un médecin!
Help me please!
saisnī men fadhlek!
Au secours/Aidez-moi!
Thief!
sarek!
(Au) voleur!
They robbed me!
lakad sourikto!
On m'a volé!

Glossary

This glossary includes terms and abbreviations you may come across during your travels in Tunisia. Where appropriate, the capital letter in brackets indicates whether the terms are French (F) or Arabic (A). See also the illustrated Tunisian Cuisine section in the Facts for the Visitor chapter at the beginning of this book for a more detailed list of common food and drink terms.

Abbasids – Baghdad-based ruling dynasty (749-1258 AD) of the Arab/Islamic Empire
Africa Proconsularis – Roman province of Africa
agha – a military commander or a title of respect (in the Ottoman Empire)
Aghlabites – Arab dynasty based in Kairouan who ruled Tunisia from 749 to 909 AD
'ain (A) – water source or spring
Allah (A) – God
ASM – Association de Sauvegarde de la Medina; group charged with preserving the medinas of a number of Tunisian towns
auberge de jeunesse (F) – youth hostel affiliated to Hostelling International

bab (A) – city gate
Barbary Coast – European term for the Mediterranean coast of North Africa in the 16th to 19th centuries
basilica – Roman building used for public administration; early Christian church
Berbers – indigenous (non-Arab) people of North Africa
bey – provincial governor in the Ottoman Empire; rulers of Tunisia from the 17th century until independence in 1957
boissons gazeuses (F) – carbonated drinks
borj (A) – fort (literally 'tower')
boukha (A) – local spirit made from figs
brochette (F) – kebab
buvette (F) – refreshment room or stall

calèche (F) – horse-drawn carriage
caliph – Islamic ruler, especially the sultans

of Turkey; originally referred to the successors of the Prophet Mohammed
camionnette (F) – small pick-up used as a taxi
capitol – main temple of a Roman town, usually situated in the forum
caravanserai – see *funduq*
casse-croûte (F) – Tunisian fast food; a sandwich made from half a French loaf stuffed with a variety of fillings
centre des stages et des vacances (F) – holiday camps that combine hostel and camp site
chechia (A) – red felt hat
chicha (A) – water pipe used to smoke tobacco
chorba (A) – soup
chott (A) – salt lake or marsh
confort (F) – class above 1st class on passenger trains
corniche (F) – coastal road
corsairs – pirates, especially those who operated on the North African coast during the 16th to 19th centuries
couscous – semolina granules, the staple food of Tunisia

dar (A) – town house or palace
deglat ennour (A) – a type of date; literally, 'finger of light'
dey – the Ottoman army's equivalent of a sergeant; rulers of Tunisia in the 16th century
diwan – assembly (in the Ottoman Empire)

'eid (A) – feast
'Eid al-Fitr (A) – the Feast of the Breaking of the Fast, which is celebrated at the end of Ramadan
emir – military commander or governor
erg – sand sea; desert

Fatimids – Muslim dynasty (909-1171 AD) who defeated the *Aghlabite* dynasty and ruled Tunisia from Mahdia in 909-69
forum – open space at the centre of Roman towns

fouta (A) – cotton bath towel provided in a *hammam*

funduq (A) – former lodging houses or inns for the travelling merchants of the camel caravans, also known as caravanserai; Arab word for hotel

gargotte (F) – cheap restaurant that serves basic food

gare routière (F) – bus station

ghar (A) – cave

ghorfa (A) – literally, room; also refers to the cells built to store grain which make up a *ksar*

guetiffa – a type of Berber knotted carpet

Hafsids – rulers of *Ifriqiyya* from the 13th to the 16th centuries

hajj (A) – the pilgrimage to the holy sites in and around Mecca, the pinnacle of a devout Muslim's life

hammam (A) – public bathhouse

harissa (A) – spicy chilli sauce

hedeyed (A) – finely engraved wide bracelets made of gold or silver

hijab (A) – woman's veil or headscarf

hijra (A) – Mohammed's flight from Mecca in 622 AD; also the name of the Muslim calendar

Hilalian tribes – tribes of Upper Egypt who invaded the Maghreb in the 11th century, causing great destruction

Hizb al-Nahda – Renaissance Party, the main Islamic opposition party

Husseinites – dynasty of *beys* who ruled Tunisia from 1705 to 1957

Ibadites – a *Kharajite* sect found only on Jerba and in the villages of the M'Zab valley in Algeria

ibn (A) – son of

Ifriqiyya – Arab province of North Africa, including Tunisia and parts of Libya

iftar (A) – (also spelt 'ftur') the breaking of the day's fast during *Ramadan*

imam (A) – Islamic equivalent of a priest; a learned man schooled in Islam and Islamic law

jami' (A) – the main district mosque

janissary – infantryman in the Ottoman army

jebel (A) – hill or mountain

jihad (A) – holy war

kasbah (A) – fort or citadel

kassa (A) – a coarse mitten used to remove the grime and dead skin after a session in the steam room of a hammam

Kharijites – puritanical Islamic sect who broke away from the mainstream *Sunnis* in 657 AD and inspired Berber rebellions in the 8th century; they made Jerba their base in Tunisia

kholkal (A) – gold or silver anklets

khutba (A) – weekly sermon in the mosque

kilim (A) – woven rug decorated with typical Berber motifs

koubba (A) – domed roof

kouttab (A) – Qur'anic primary school

ksar (A) – (plural ksour) a fortified Berber stronghold consisting of many *ghorfas*

ksibah (A) – small fort

Limes Tripolitanus – defensive line developed by the Romans in southern Tunisia to keep out marauding Saharan tribes

louage (F) – shared taxi

Maghreb – term used to describe north-west Africa, including Morocco, Algeria and Tunisia

maison des jeunes (F) – government-run youth hostel

malouf (A) – traditional Tunisian music

marabout (A) – Muslim holy man or saint; also used for the shrine of one of these holy men

masjid (A) – small local mosque

medersa (A) – Qur'anic school

medina (A) – city; the old quarter of Tunisian towns and cities

menzel (A) – square whitewashed dwelling found on Jerba

mergoum (A) – woven carpet with geometric designs

mihrab (A) – vaulted niche in a mosque which indicates the direction of Mecca

minaret – tower at the corner of a mosque

from which the *muezzin* calls the faithful to prayer

minbar (A) – the pulpit in a mosque

mouloud (A) – *Maghreb* term for the Mawlid an-Nabi, the feast celebrating the birth of the Prophet Mohammed

moussem (A) – pilgrimage to a *marabout* or shrine

muezzin (A) – mosque official who calls the faithful to prayer

ONAT – Office National de l'Artisanat Tunisien; government-run fixed price craft shops

ONTT – Office National du Tourisme Tunisien; government-run national tourist office

Ottoman Empire – former Turkish Empire, of which Tunisia was part, based in Constantinople from the late 13th century to the end of WWI

oued (A) – river; also dry riverbed

palmeraie (F) – palm grove; the area around an oasis where date palms, vegetables and fruit are grown

PSD – Parti Socialiste Destourien (called the Neo-Destour Party before 1964); the first nationalist party in Tunisia

pasha – provincial governor or high official in the Ottoman Empire

patisserie (F) – cake and pastry shop

pension (F) – guest house

Phoenicians – a great sea-faring nation, based in modern Lebanon, who dominated trade in the Mediterranean in the 1st millennium BC; founders of Carthage

place (F) – square

Punic – of or relating to ancient Carthage

Punic Wars – three wars waged between Rome and Carthage in the 3rd and 2nd centuries BC, resulting in the destruction of Carthage by the Romans in 146 BC

qibla (A) – the direction of Mecca in a mosque, indicated by the *mihrab*

Qur'an (A) – the holy book of Islam

Ramadan – ninth month of the Muslim year, a time of fasting

razzegoui (A) – a large white grape that ripens to a pink blush

RCD – Rassemblement Constitutionel Democratique; President Ben Ali's ruling party

ribat (A) – fortified Islamic monastery

rôtisserie (F) – basic restaurant serving roast chicken

sebkha (A) – salt flat

shari'a (F) – Qur'anic law

Shiites – one of two main islamic sects (see also *Sunnis*); followers believe that the true imams are descended from Ali

sidi (A) – saint

skifa (A) – gate

SNCFT – Société Nationale des Chemins de Fer Tunisiens; the national railway company

SNTRI – Société Nationale du Transport Interurbain; the national bus company

souq (A) – market

stele – grave stone

Sufi – follower of any of the Islamic mystical orders which emphasise dancing, chanting and trances to attain unity with God

Sunnis – the main Islamic sect (see also *Shiites*) derived from followers of the *Ummayyad* caliphate

syndicat d'initiative (F) – municipal tourist office

Taxiphone – public telephone

thibarine – a local spirit from the village of Thibar near Dougga

tophet – sacrificial site

tourbet (A) – mausoleum

Ummayyads – first great dynasty of Arab Muslim rulers (661-750 AD), based in Damascus

ville nouvelle (F) – literally 'new town'; the parts of town built by the French, usually alongside the existing towns and cities in Tunisia

zaouia (A) – a complex surrounding the tomb of a saint; usually includes a prayer room for pilgrims and sometimes accommodation as well

zone touristique (F) – tourist strip

Index

MAPS

TEXT

Map references are in **bold** type.

LONELY PLANET PRODUCTS

Lonely Planet is known worldwide for publishing practical, reliable and no-nonsense travel information in our guides and on our web site. The Lonely Planet list covers just about every accessible part of the world. Currently there are nine series: *travel guides, shoestring guides, walking guides, city guides, phrasebooks, audio packs, travel atlases, Journeys – a unique collection of travel writing and Pisces Books - diving and snorkeling guides.*

EUROPE

Amsterdam • Austria • Baltic States phrasebook • Britain • Central Europe on a shoestring • Central Europe phrasebook • Czech & Slovak Republics • Denmark • Dublin • Eastern Europe on a shoestring • Eastern Europe phrasebook • Estonia, Latvia & Lithuania • Finland • France • French phrasebook • Germany • German phrasebook • Greece • Greek phrasebook • Hungary • Iceland, Greenland & the Faroe Islands • Ireland • Italian phrasebook • Italy • Lisbon • London • Mediterranean Europe on a shoestring • Mediterranean Europe phrasebook • Paris • Poland • Portugal • Portugal travel atlas • Prague • Romania & Moldova • Russia, Ukraine & Belarus • Russian phrasebook • Scandinavian & Baltic Europe on a shoestring • Scandinavian Europe phrasebook • Slovenia • Spain • Spanish phrasebook • St Petersburg • Switzerland •Trekking in Spain • Ukrainian phrasebook • Vienna • Walking in Britain • Walking in Italy • Walking in Switzerland • Western Europe on a shoestring • Western Europe phrasebook

Travel Literature: The Olive Grove: Travels in Greece

NORTH AMERICA

Alaska • Backpacking in Alaska • Baja California • California & Nevada • Canada • Chicago • Deep South• Florida • Hawaii • Honolulu • Los Angeles • Mexico • Mexico City • Miami • New England • New Orleans • New York City • New York, New Jersey & Pennsylvania • Pacific Northwest USA • Rocky Mountain States • San Francisco • Southwest USA • USA phrasebook • Washington, DC & the Capital Region

Travel Literature: Drive thru America

CENTRAL AMERICA & THE CARIBBEAN

•Bahamas and Turks & Caicos •Bermuda •Central America on a shoestring • Costa Rica • Cuba •Eastern Caribbean •Guatemala, Belize & Yucatán: La Ruta Maya • Jamaica

SOUTH AMERICA

Argentina, Uruguay & Paraguay • Bolivia • Brazil • Brazilian phrasebook • Buenos Aires • Chile & Easter Island • Chile & Easter Island travel atlas • Colombia Ecuador & the Galápagos Islands • Latin American Spanish phrasebook • Peru • Quechua phrasebook • Rio de Janeiro • South America on a shoestring • Trekking in the Patagonian Andes • Venezuela

Travel Literature: Full Circle: A South American Journey

ISLANDS OF THE INDIAN OCEAN

Madagascar & Comoros • Maldives• Mauritius, Réunion & Seychelles

AFRICA

Africa - the South • Africa on a shoestring • Arabic (Moroccan) phrasebook • Cairo • Cape Town • Central Africa • East Africa • Egypt • Egypt travel atlas• Ethiopian (Amharic) phrasebook • Kenya • Kenya travel atlas • Malawi, Mozambique & Zambia • Morocco • North Africa • South Africa, Lesotho & Swaziland • South Africa, Lesotho & Swaziland travel atlas • Swahili phrasebook • Tunisia Trekking in East Africa • West Africa • Zimbabwe, Botswana & Namibia • Zimbabwe, Botswana & Namibia travel atlas

Travel Literature: The Rainbird: A Central African Journey • Songs to an African Sunset: A Zimbabwean Story

MAIL ORDER

Lonely Planet products are distributed worldwide. They are also available by mail order from Lonely Planet, so if you have difficulty finding a title please write to us. North American and South American residents should write to 150 Linden St, Oakland CA 94607, USA; European and African residents should write to 10a Spring Place, London NW5 3BH; and residents of other countries to PO Box 617, Hawthorn, Victoria 3122, Australia.

NORTH-EAST ASIA

Beijing • Cantonese phrasebook • China • Hong Kong • Hong Kong, Macau & Guangzhou • Japan • Japanese phrasebook • Japanese audio pack • Korea • Korean phrasebook • Mandarin phrasebook • Mongolia • Mongolian phrasebook • North-East Asia on a shoestring • Seoul • Taiwan • Tibet • Tibet phrasebook • Tokyo

Travel Literature: Lost Japan

MIDDLE EAST & CENTRAL ASIA

Arab Gulf States • Arabic (Egyptian) phrasebook • Central Asia • Central Asia phrasebook • Iran • Israel & the Palestinian Territories • Israel & the Palestinian Territories travel atlas • Istanbul • Jerusalem • Jordan & Syria • Jordan, Syria & Lebanon travel atlas • Lebanon • Middle East • Turkey • Turkish phrasebook • Turkey travel atlas • Yemen

Travel Literature: The Gates of Damascus • Kingdom of the Film Stars: Journey into Jordan

ALSO AVAILABLE:

Brief Encounters • Travel with Children • Traveller's Tales

INDIAN SUBCONTINENT

Bangladesh • Bengali phrasebook • Delhi • Goa • Hindi/Urdu phrasebook • India • India & Bangladesh travel atlas • Indian Himalaya • Karakoram Highway • Nepal • Nepali phrasebook • Pakistan • Rajasthan • Sri Lanka • Sri Lanka phrasebook • Trekking in the Indian Himalaya • Trekking in the Karakoram & Hindukush • Trekking in the Nepal Himalaya

Travel Literature: In Rajasthan • Shopping for Buddhas

SOUTH-EAST ASIA

Bali & Lombok • Bangkok • Burmese phrasebook • Cambodia • Ho Chi Minh City • Indonesia • Indonesian phrasebook • Indonesian audio pack • Jakarta • Java • Laos • Lao phrasebook • Laos travel atlas • Malay phrasebook • Malaysia, Singapore & Brunei • Myanmar (Burma) • Philippines • Pilipino phrasebook • Singapore • South-East Asia on a shoestring • South-East Asia phrasebook • Thailand • Thailand's Islands & Beaches • Thailand travel atlas • Thai phrasebook • Thai audio pack • Thai Hill Tribes phrasebook • Vietnam • Vietnamese phrasebook • Vietnam travel atlas

AUSTRALIA & THE PACIFIC

Australia • Australian phrasebook • Bushwalking in Australia • Bushwalking in Papua New Guinea • Fiji • Fijian phrasebook • Islands of Australia's Great Barrier Reef • Melbourne • Micronesia • New Caledonia • New South Wales • New Zealand • Northern Territory • Outback Australia • Papua New Guinea • Papua New Guinea phrasebook • Queensland • Rarotonga & the Cook Islands • Samoa • Solomon Islands • South Australia • Sydney • Tahiti & French Polynesia • Tasmania • Tonga • Tramping in New Zealand • Vanuatu • Victoria • Western Australia

Travel Literature: Islands in the Clouds • Sean & David's Long Drive

ANTARCTICA

Antarctica

THE LONELY PLANET STORY

Lonely Planet published its first book in 1973 in response to the numerous 'How did you do it?' questions Maureen and Tony Wheeler were asked after driving, bussing, hitching, sailing and railing their way from England to Australia.

Written at a kitchen table and hand collated, trimmed and stapled, *Across Asia on the Cheap* became an instant local bestseller, inspiring thoughts of another book.

Eighteen months in South-East Asia resulted in their second guide, *South-East Asia on a shoestring*, which they put together in a backstreet Chinese hotel in Singapore in 1975. The 'yellow bible', as it quickly became known to backpackers around the world, soon became *the* guide to the region. It has sold well over half a million copies and is now in its 9th edition, still retaining its familiar yellow cover.

Today there are over 240 titles, including travel guides, walking guides, language kits & phrasebooks, travel atlases and travel literature. The company is the largest independent travel publisher in the world. Although Lonely Planet initially specialised in guides to Asia, today there are few corners of the globe that have not been covered.

The emphasis continues to be on travel for independent travellers. Tony and Maureen still travel for several months of each year and play an active part in the writing, updating and quality control of Lonely Planet's guides.

They have been joined by over 70 authors and 170 staff at our offices in Melbourne (Australia), Oakland (USA), London (UK) and Paris (France). Travellers themselves also make a valuable contribution to the guides through the feedback we receive in thousands of letters each year and on our web site.

The people at Lonely Planet strongly believe that travellers can make a positive contribution to the countries they visit, both through their appreciation of the countries' culture, wildlife and natural features, and through the money they spend. In addition, the company makes a direct contribution to the countries and regions it covers. Since 1986 a percentage of the income from each book has been donated to ventures such as famine relief in Africa; aid projects in India; agricultural projects in Central America; Greenpeace's efforts to halt French nuclear testing in the Pacific; and Amnesty International.

'I hope we send people out with the right attitude about travel. You realise when you travel that there are so many different perspectives about the world, so we hope these books will make people more interested in what they see. Guidebooks can't really guide people. All you can do is point them in the right direction.'

– Tony Wheeler

LONELY PLANET PUBLICATIONS

Australia
PO Box 617, Hawthorn 3122, Victoria
tel: (03) 9819 1877 fax: (03) 9819 6459
e-mail: talk2us@lonelyplanet.com.au

USA
150 Linden St
Oakland, CA 94607
tel: (510) 893 8555 TOLL FREE: 800 275-8555
fax: (510) 893 8563
e-mail: info@lonelyplanet.com

UK
10a Spring Place,
London NW5 3BH
tel: (0171) 428 4800 fax: (0171) 428 4828
e-mail: go@lonelyplanet.co.uk

France:
71 bis rue du Cardinal Lemoine, 75005 Paris
tel: 01 44 32 06 20 fax: 01 46 34 72 55
e-mail: bip@lonelyplanet.fr

World Wide Web: http://www.lonelyplanet.com
or *AOL keyword: lp*